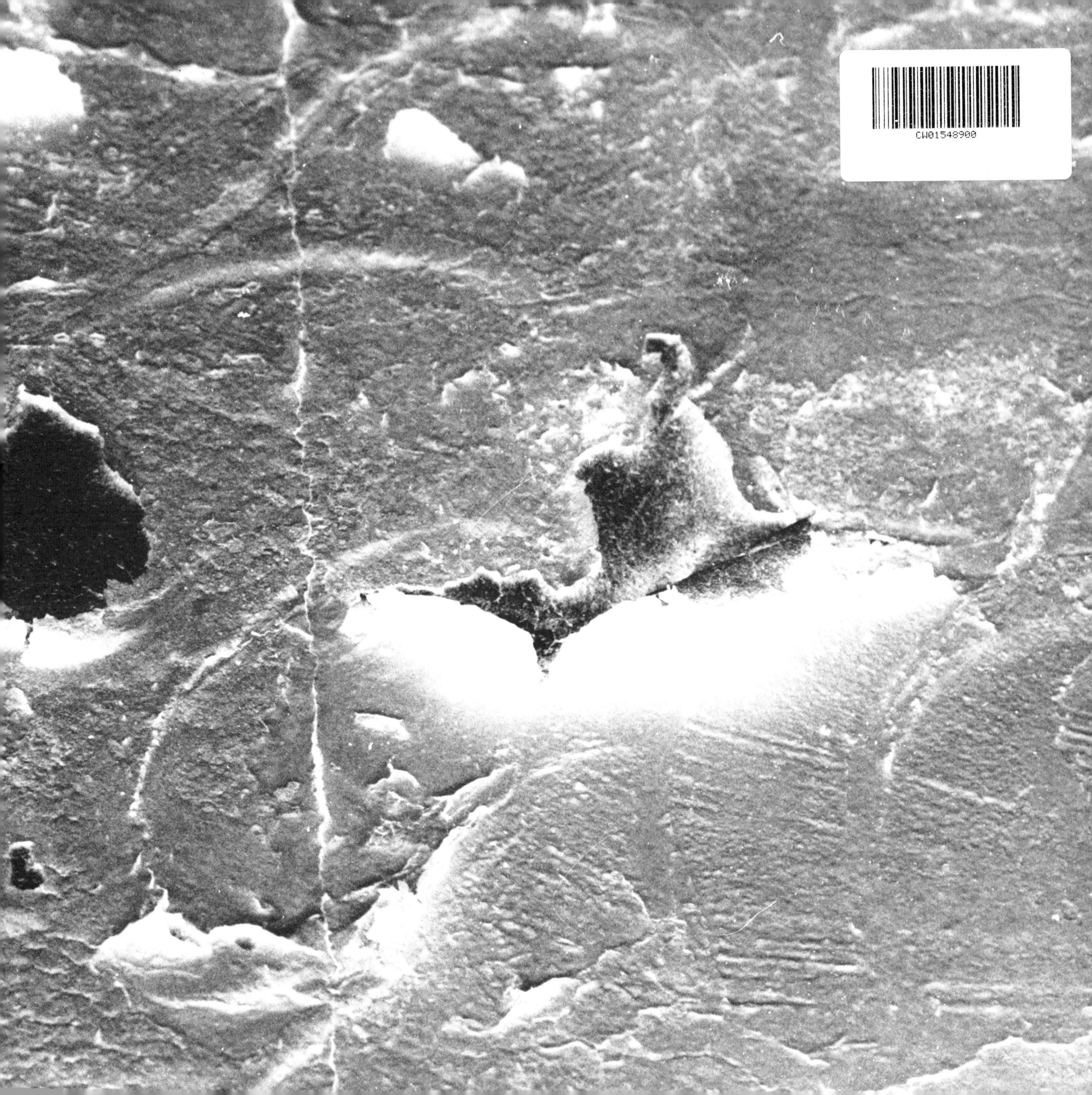

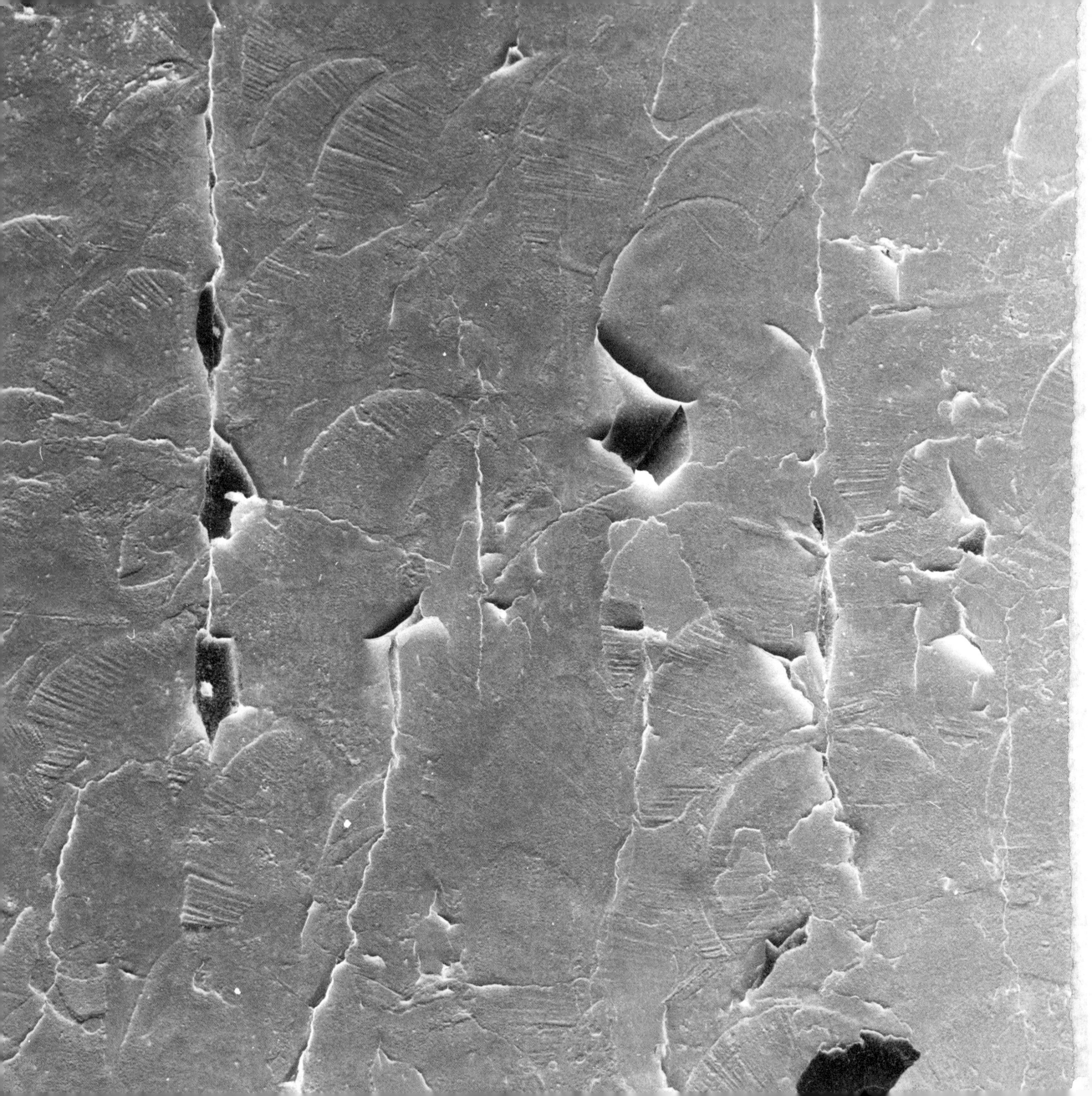

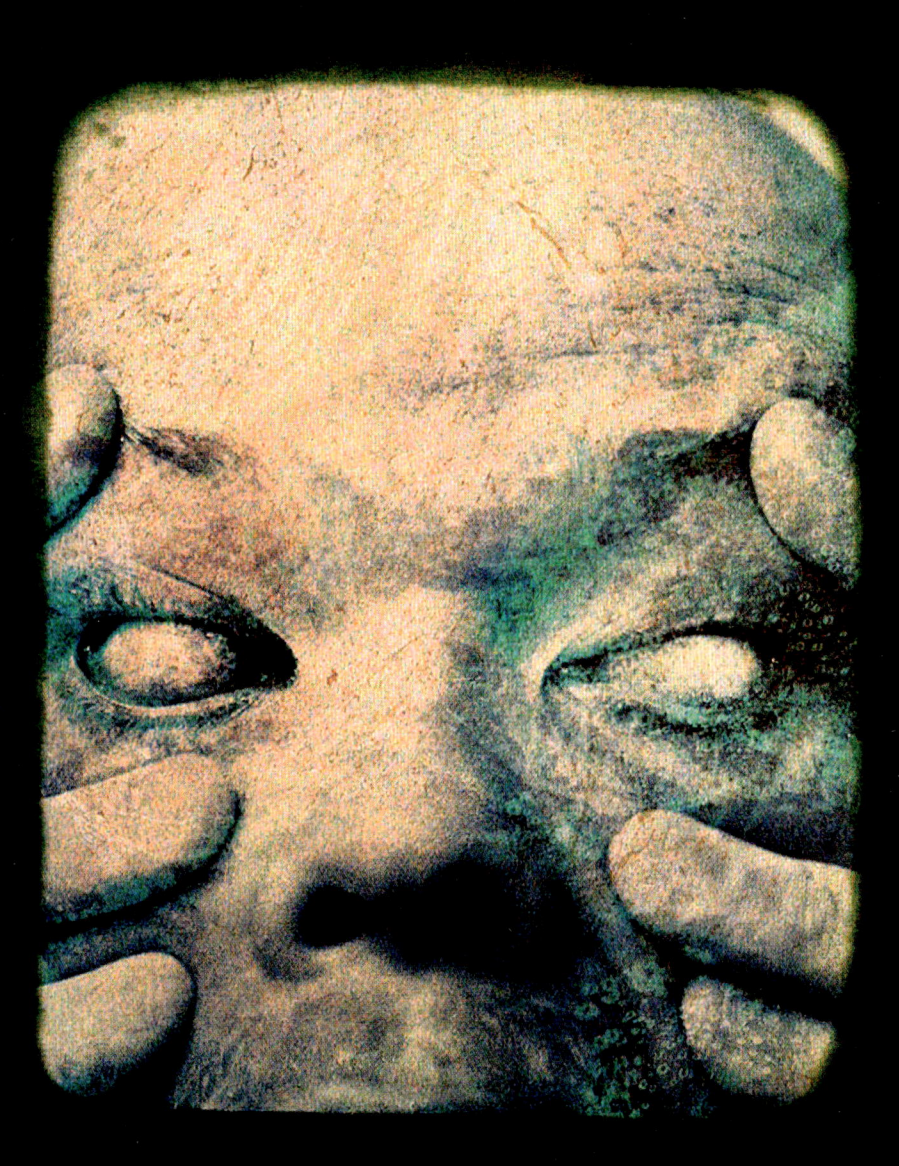

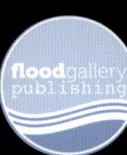

Flood Gallery Publishing
3 Greenwich Quay, Clarence Road, London SE8 3EY

www.thefloodgallery.com

First published in 2019 by Flood Gallery Publishing
Copyright ©2019 Lasse Hoile under sole license to Flood Gallery Publishing

Text copyright ©2019 Lasse Hoile/Carl Glover/Steven Wilson/Richard Barbieri/Gavin Harrison/Richard Allen/Mike Bennion where applicable

Graphic design by Carl Glover at Aleph Studio
Production coordination by Dave Evely

All rights reserved. No part of this publication may be reproduced, stored in a retrieval system or transmitted in any form or by any means, electronic, mechanical, photocopying, recording or otherwise, without the prior permission of Flood Gallery Publishing.

Printed in Italy

British Library Cataloguing in Publication data.
A catalogue record for this book is available from the British Library
ISBN 978-1-911374-09-1 (deluxe edition)
ISBN 978-1-911374-12-1 (collectors edition)

LASSE HOILE / MUZAK

INTRODUCTION

The seeds of this book were planted during a backstage conversation in 2006, where I proposed to Porcupine Tree's so-called manager at the time to do a book of my work so far – mainly covering outtakes, initial ideas and tour material. He agreed to the idea enthusiastically, and I collated a rough version of the book in a heavy A4 binder. This did the rounds of various interested parties, and was even waved under the noses of an occasional publisher. Needless to say nothing happened, and with hindsight I can say that it was probably a bit too early in my career to make any significant impact.

Fast forward to now, I can still see the DNA of that initial version in this book. It's a curious experience seeing a significant part of a life's work distilled into 240 pages but gratifying too. Most importantly, the inclusion of the live projection footage in storyboard format gives a more complete picture of the overall concepts surrounding the four albums and their associated tours.

What you are holding in your hands is a record of eight years work for what was the best band on the planet at the time. Rendered phsyical via cellulose-based pulp combined with spirit-based ink to create something for the eyes that accompanies something for the ears. Dig out your favourite Porcupine Tree album, open this book, press play and read on…

Lasse Hoile, London 2019

CONTENTS

06INABSENTIA
56DEADWING
96FEAROFABLANKPLANET
150THEINCIDENT

INABSEN
DWINGF
ABLANK
THEIN

NTIA	DEA
FEAROF	
KPLANE	
CIDENT	

Carl Glover: *In Absentia* was the first Porcupine Tree album that you worked on. Did you have a brief to work to, or was it something that emerged from conversations?

Lasse Hoile: Yes and no. I discovered Porcupine Tree via a mutual friend who acquired a CD of *Lightbulb Sun* almost by mistake - it blew us away on first listening! The internet was in its infancy so it wasn't that easy to find much information about the band, but we did discover that they were performing in a little Danish town called Odense. We immediately booked tickets and were probably the first and only ones to do so. I think there were no more than 20-30 people there, but what a gig! SW was mostly looking downwards and being a bit shy. Nobody will ever forget that night. It changed everything for us - PT was a breath of fresh air. I think I bought everything that was on sale at the show that night.

At the time I was just starting to get more into album cover art and wanted to try and make a living from it. I located Delerium Records on the internet and sent some of my photography to PT's manager at the time, Richard Allen. I never really expected a reply but he got back to me and gave me SW's email address. I got in touch and we just hit it off right away. We had similar tastes in art, books, music and movies. I didn't know that he was busy with *In Absentia* at the time, then I got a message to say that he and band liked some of the stuff I had sent, especially what ended up as the cover. This was lucky as I presented that image earlier to a local metal band who really didn't like it. Not gory enough I guess. From that point onwards we started to chat about the concept SW had in mind for the album and it's themes, which was mostly concerning what it is that creates and makes serial killers tick. It was something I also had an interest in - someone who could be a close relation, a good friend or an amiable neighbour, and so on…

Richard Allen: Steven always had very high standards for Porcupine Tree cover art and we wouldn't always agree when looking at potential ideas, but one day Lasse contacted me out of the blue and sent through his portfolio. I recall immediately being impressed with the ideas, the execution and the quality and I knew that it would probably appeal to Steven as well. I put Lasse in touch and as I predicted he liked it. I'm not surprised Lasse and Steven have had such a long association, because they are both individualists and accomplished artists with a highly recognisable style.

Lasse Hoile: We both also talked about the power of photography and the art of Dave Mckean, which I really liked at the time and still do, although SW wasn't a fan. The idea was to try and capture places and atmospheres - the aftermath of a family discovering a serial killer among them, then erasing him from their life by scribbling and tearing out his presence from photo albums. Also trying to capture the lunacy inside the head of a killer, but showing that darkness through photography and manual work instead of the easier photoshop route.

I ended up scratching negatives, burning film, adding dirt to processed film then scanning it, things I had done before but now minus photoshop - more a collage technique, but all by hand. I think it helped shape me, by keeping everything real and simple in a twisted way. The music, I think, was 'upbeat' in a certain way, the lyrics were occasionally dark, but with incredibly catchy music. I think the dark images gave it an interesting balance. The power of real photography gave it an organic quality, and the imagery is not what you would expect for a band that was labeled 'progressive rock'.

In Absentia really took shape from thereon. I think it worked great and still does, it was a combination of material I already had, but taken further and elaborated on.

Richard Barbieri: My initial impression of Lasse's work was that it was very striking and immediate. Quite influenced by film I thought, though I might be wrong. There seemed to be a great balance between beauty and the grotesque. The *In Absentia* album was a great vehicle for Lasse to start a relationship with the band. Groups are quite insular and managers, agents, promoters, record label or any outsiders are often not usually welcome into the inner workings of the band, but Lasse quickly became a presence that we were happy to have around and could even ignore, which is a good sign. This led to better photographic documentation of the band at work than conventional 'photo sessions'.

Carl Glover: Was there any particular reason for using yourself on the cover of *In Absentia*?

Lasse Hoile: I needed a few pictures of eyes for another project and that was the best I could do as I didn't have proper macro equipment. I had to make good use of the small amount of film that I had at the time, I played around with the image a bit using some burnt film and it became the cover image. Very simple really, but it had a vibe.

Carl Glover: Having occasionally used myself on an album cover, it's usually to illustrate an idea which, almost by mistake ends up as the finished article because the client likes it as it is. Sometimes the budget/deadline makes it hard to find a suitable model.

Did you have a feeling that *In Absentia* was going to be something special? It did seem to mark a change of direction toward something much darker.

Lasse Hoile: When I heard the music I knew it was going to be special. Coupling the cover image to the album was obviously a risk for the band and its label, but the image was effective, even from afar. I think it summed up the album pretty darn good. It was bold and risky but paid off long term, which is what it's all about. Over the years a lot of people who ended up as PT/SW fans have told me they only got to listen to the music because of seeing the *In Absentia* cover and wondering what the album was going to sound like.

Carl Glover: Could you tell me about the live background films for *In Absentia*, Would I be correct in saying that at this point they were effectively atmospheric slideshows?

Lasse Hoile: Yes exactly! There wasn't really a budget to do much, so we had to make the most of everything - it was still expensive to rent proper video cameras in those days. I animated still images made for *In Absentia* combined with other pictures that I had. It was quite experimental but seemed to work. We also had a tiny 4:3 screen and a low end projector, so to make it all work we had to squeeze the tiny screen in where we could on the stage. The *In Absentia* tour played at mainly small venues and bars, except for the bigger cites. I had to run the films from a DVD - we had two DVD players set up and a little vision mixer. I had to try and synchronise the films by pressing play manually, hoping that they were in time somehow whilst also doing the lights!

I think it worked well back then, as the visuals were not the usual backdrop films one saw those days. The projections had a dark atmosphere to them which worked as a great contrast to the music. People seemed to respond well to them at least.

Carl Glover: What was touring with Porcupine Tree like?

Lasse Hoile: I think I joined the crew on the second leg of the *In Absentia* tour, which was in the USA with Opeth, and then through part of the *Deadwing* tour. I was working a day job too and sadly couldn't get any more time off work to complete the *Deadwing* tour. I never got to do more after that.

It was also at a time where the band couldn't afford to bring their own lights, so we had to make the best use of whatever the venue had. I filmed documentary footage and took as many still images as possible, as there were always promo shots needed. I also had to haul equipment in and out, set up the screen, then focus lights. It was hard work, but also an exciting crazy big adventure. I miss it every day still. It's hard to work so long on a show and then say goodbye!

Carl Glover: I think it was on that tour where I first met you back in 2005 at The Astoria London after the show. It was a very intense concert!

Lasse Hoile: Yes, I think it was The Astoria where we first met.

Carl Glover: Did doing the tour give you a greater insight into what was required for the backdrop projections?

Lasse Hoile: We were trying to come up with new ideas for the films, like holographic projections, having our own lighting, putting small projectors in Gavin's drums and finding ways to get the films in proper sync without using DVD players. Everything was expensive at the time so we never got to do a lot of stuff that we thought up. In the end it was just a lot of hard work. It didn't help having to juggle a day job on top while doing band visuals on the side.

Carl Glover: The powerful-yet-disturbing look of *In Absentia* hasn't diminished over time. I feel that what helps is that it avoided the pitfalls of early digital photography whilst embracing film – a medium that was beginning to be seen as outdated. Was this a conscious decision?

Lasse Hoile: It was deliberate in that at the time there were no decent digital cameras around capable of producing images in a useful resolution. Most importantly you can't beat the grain in film, the surprises and imperfections are what makes film so damn good. Film was the only medium I had to work with via a decent scanner. I think the limitations of working that way teaches you a lot and is also healthy, as you have to improvise more while keeping it simple. I didn't have the means or access to swanky gear to do whatever I wanted.

Carl Glover: Digital photography was quite horrible at that point but huge amounts of people were leaping into it, just for the novelty I guess.

Lasse Hoile: Digital was nastily compressed then - like most mobile phones today but slightly better quality. It doesn't matter so much now as most things seem to be viewed on a mobile phone... sadly.

Carl Glover: Did anybody else in the band have a say regarding your work at the time of *In Absentia*?

Lasse Hoile: No, it was a dialogue between SW and me. I think he shared the images he liked with the band for approval.

Richard Barbieri: The initial collaborations were primarily between Steven and Lasse since obviously the lyrical content and concepts are all important at that stage. Any misdirections or misunderstandings would've been addressed at that point. The rest of the band would then critically look at the art direction and make comments and suggestions.

Looking at the body of work he has produced for these four projects, it's astounding and exhausting. There is a lot of power in these images, again disturbing and beautiful at the same time. I love the nostalgic sadness of aspects of the *Deadwing* and *The Incident* albums and the gritty literal contemporary feel of *Fear of a Blank Planet* but my favourite overall project is *In Absentia*. It's brutal and relentless in it's depiction of disturbed minds and evil persona. Porcupine Tree's career jumped massively with this release and Lasse was on the trip with us - to the end.

Carl Glover: When did you first start using moving footage for the projections?

Lasse Hoile: I guess it was with *Deadwing*, I was able to borrow a DV camera and record some stuff while doing pictures at the same time. I was also using it for recording a documentary which we started at the end of the *In Absentia* tour, the recording of *Deadwing*, and the beginning of the *Deadwing* tour.

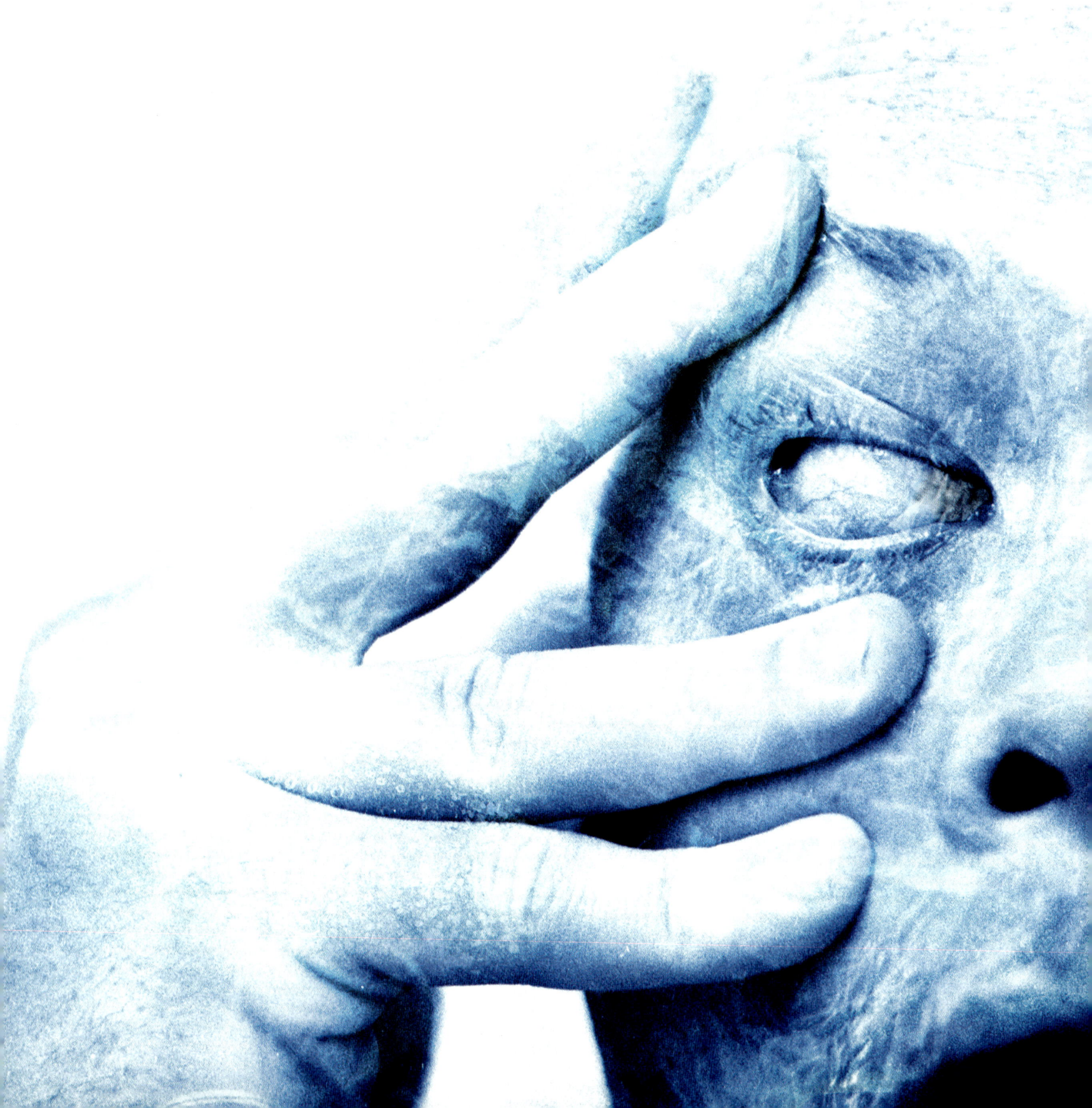

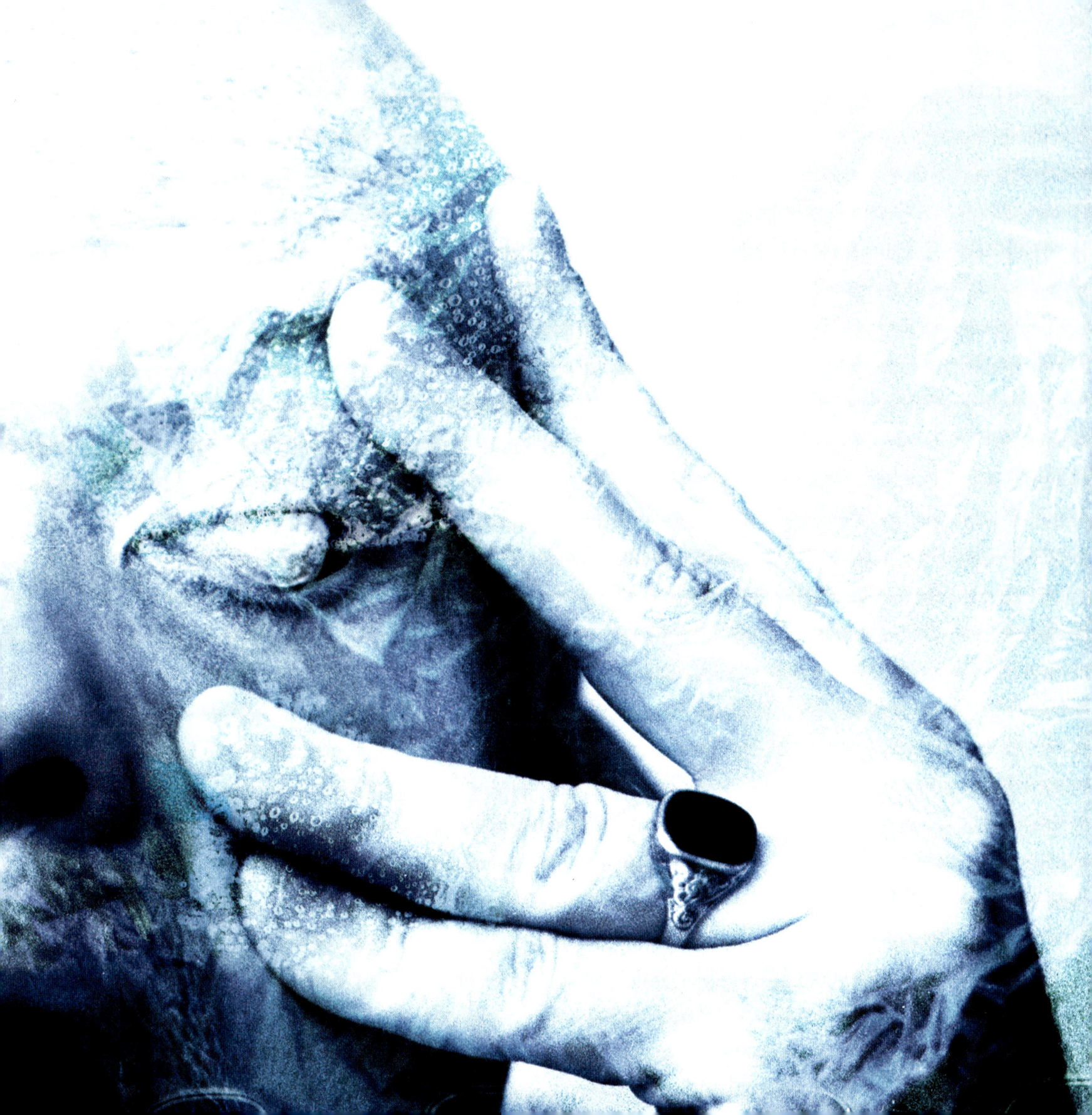

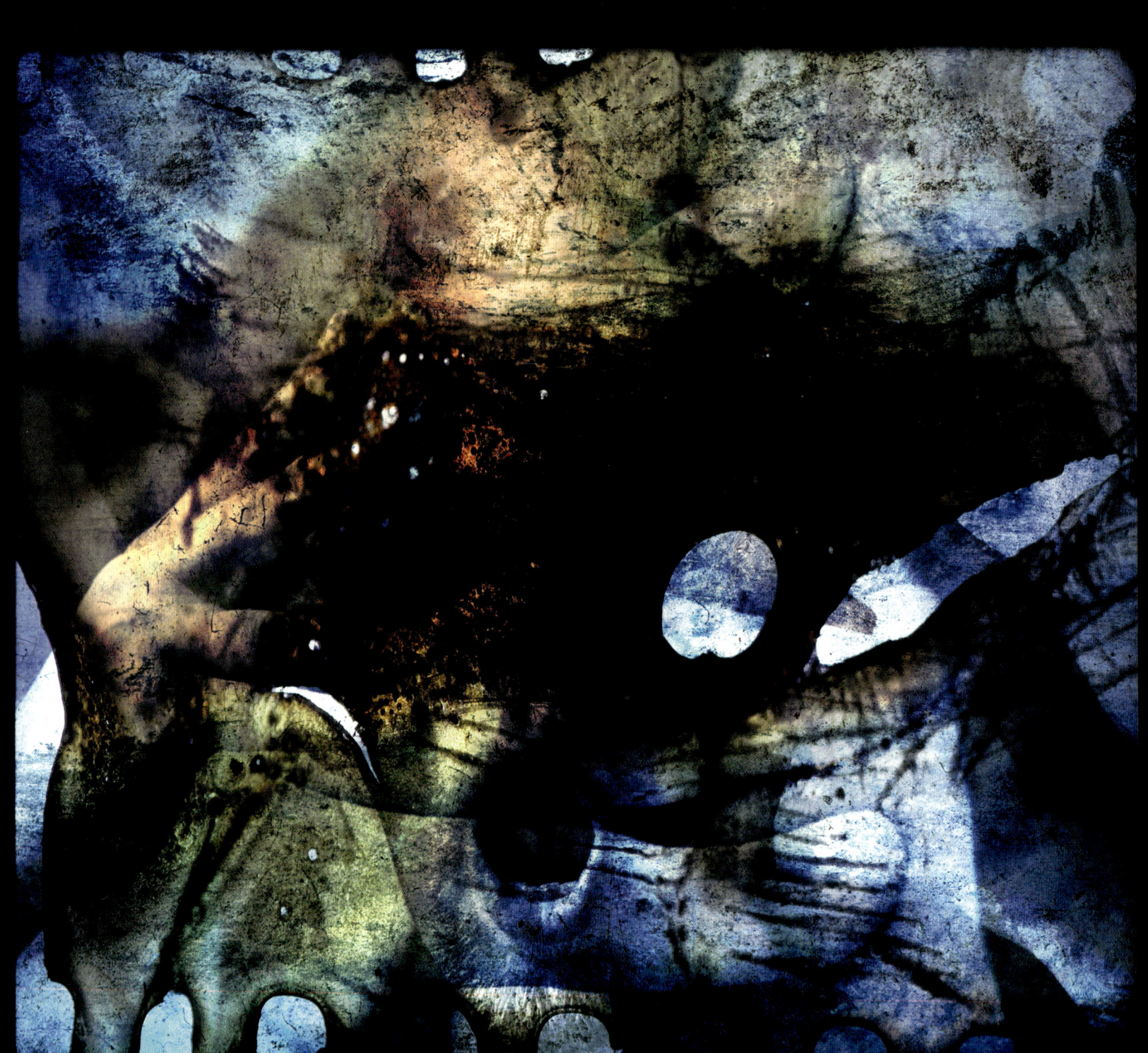

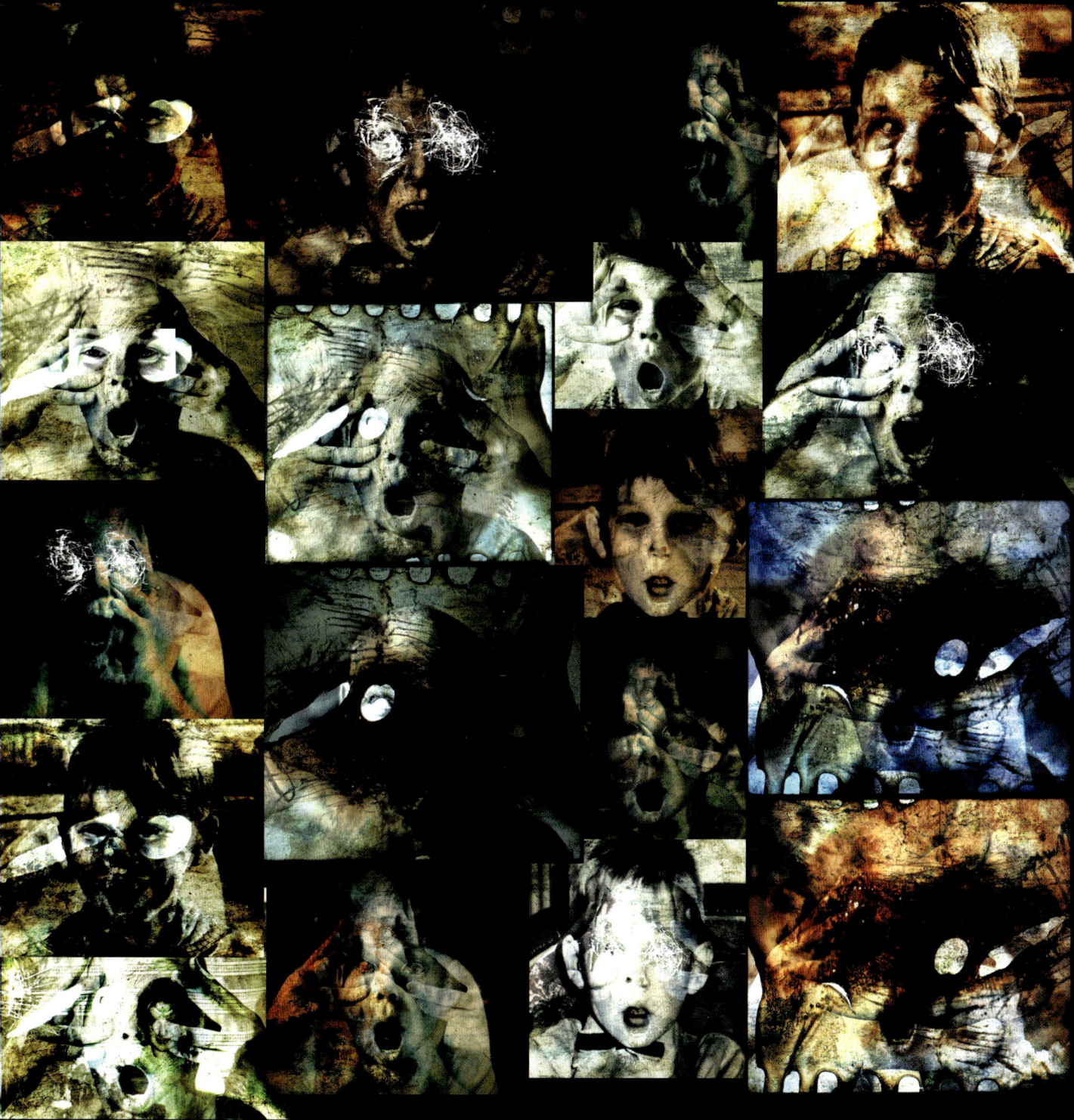

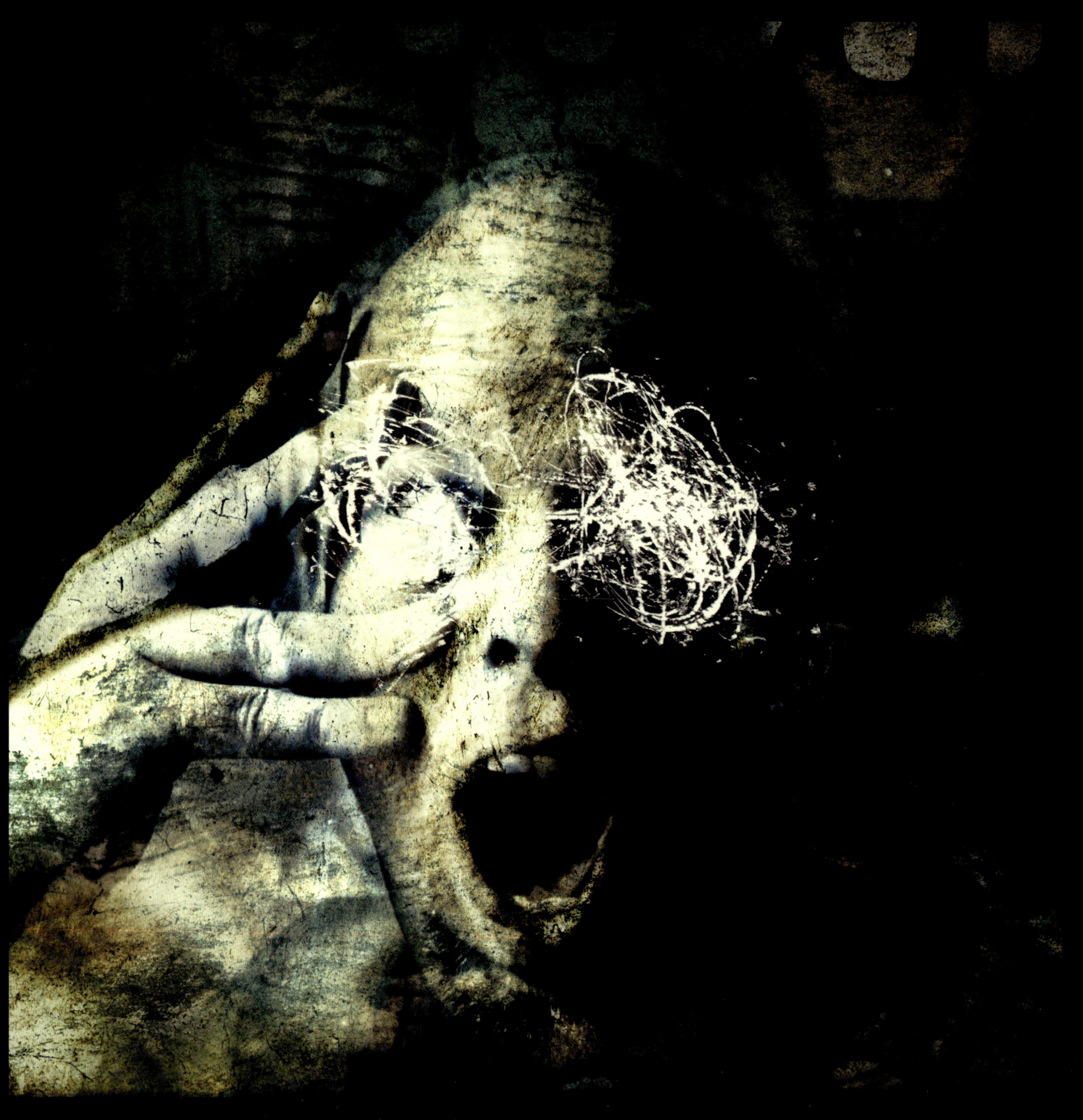

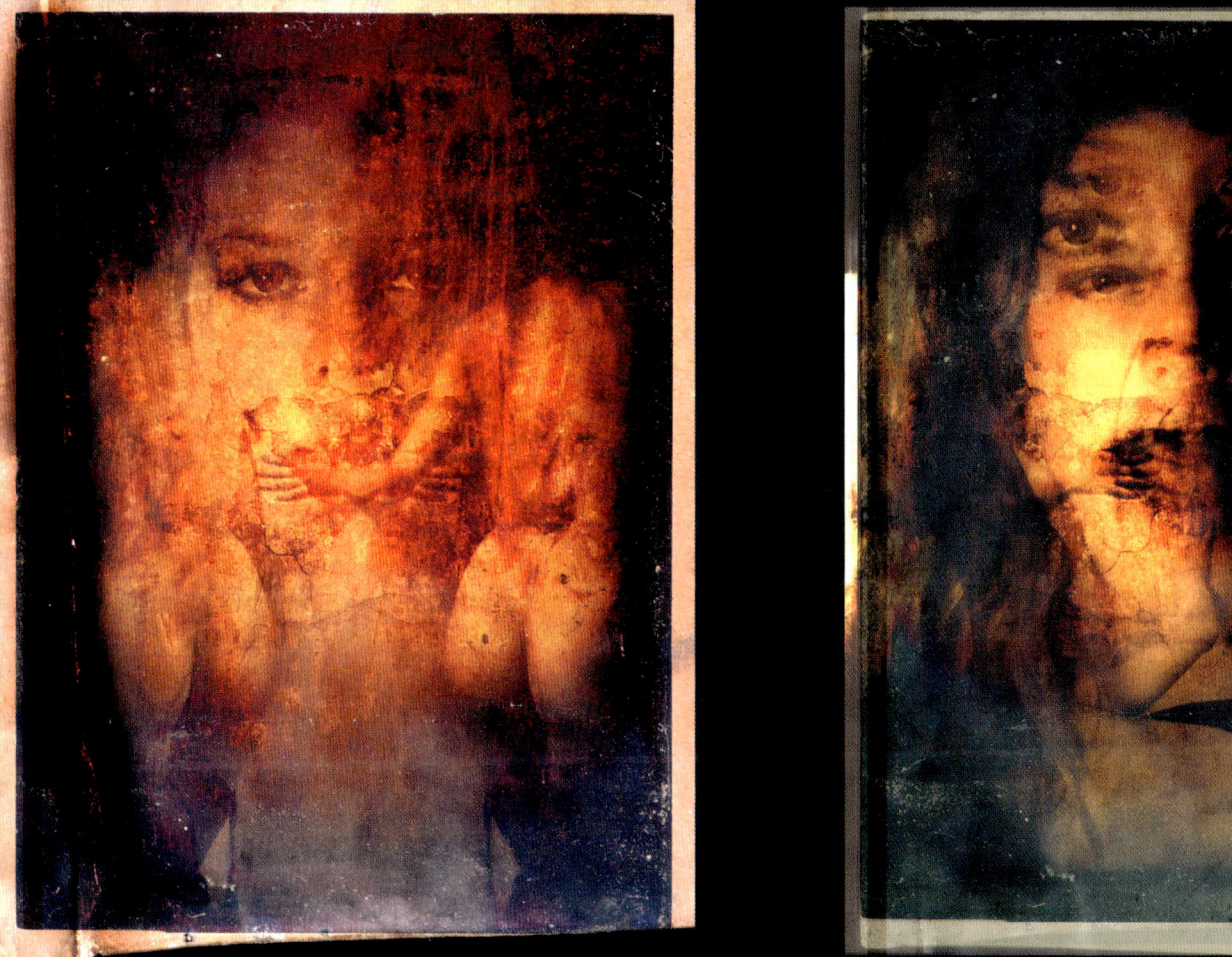

BLACKEST EYES 2002

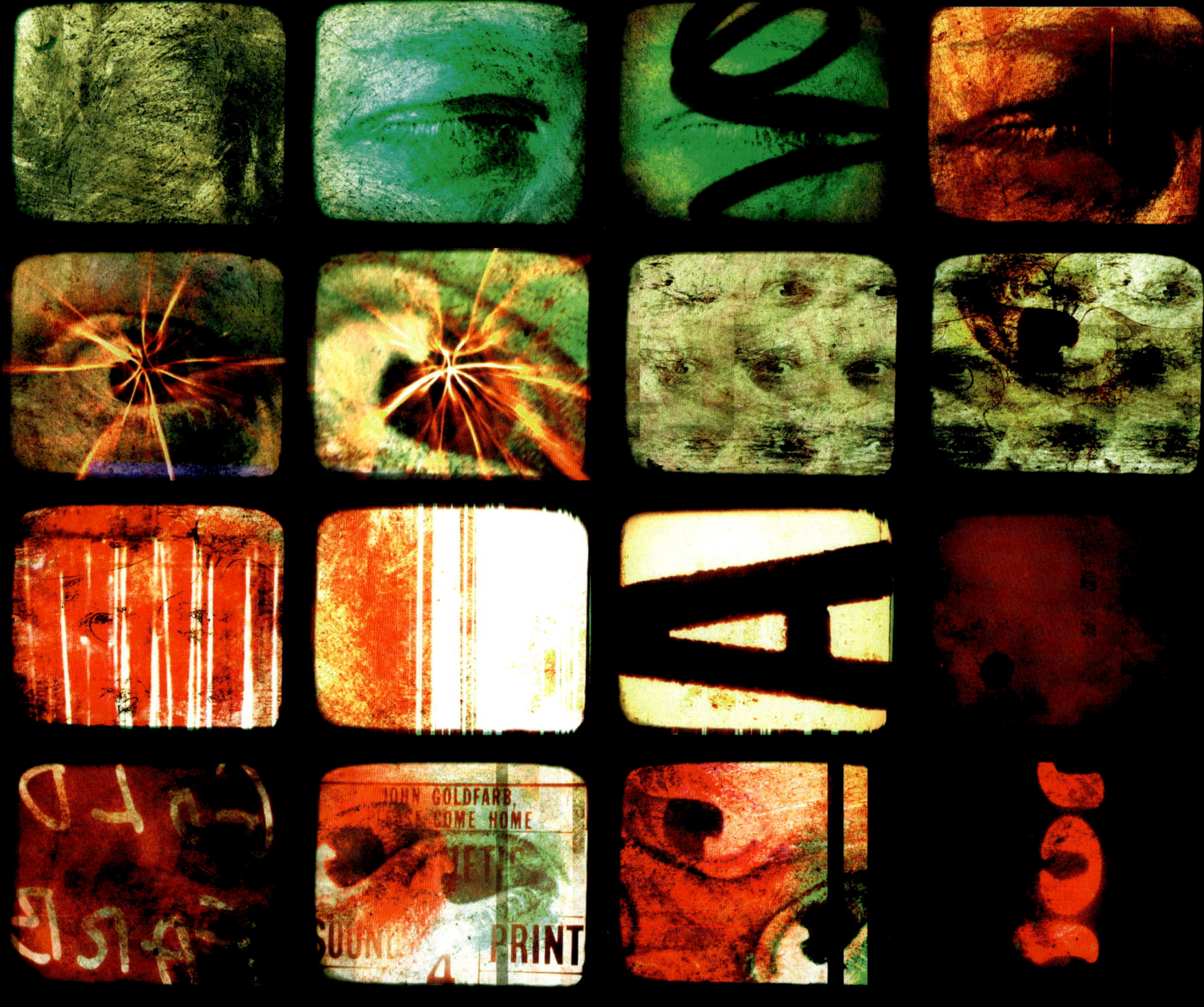

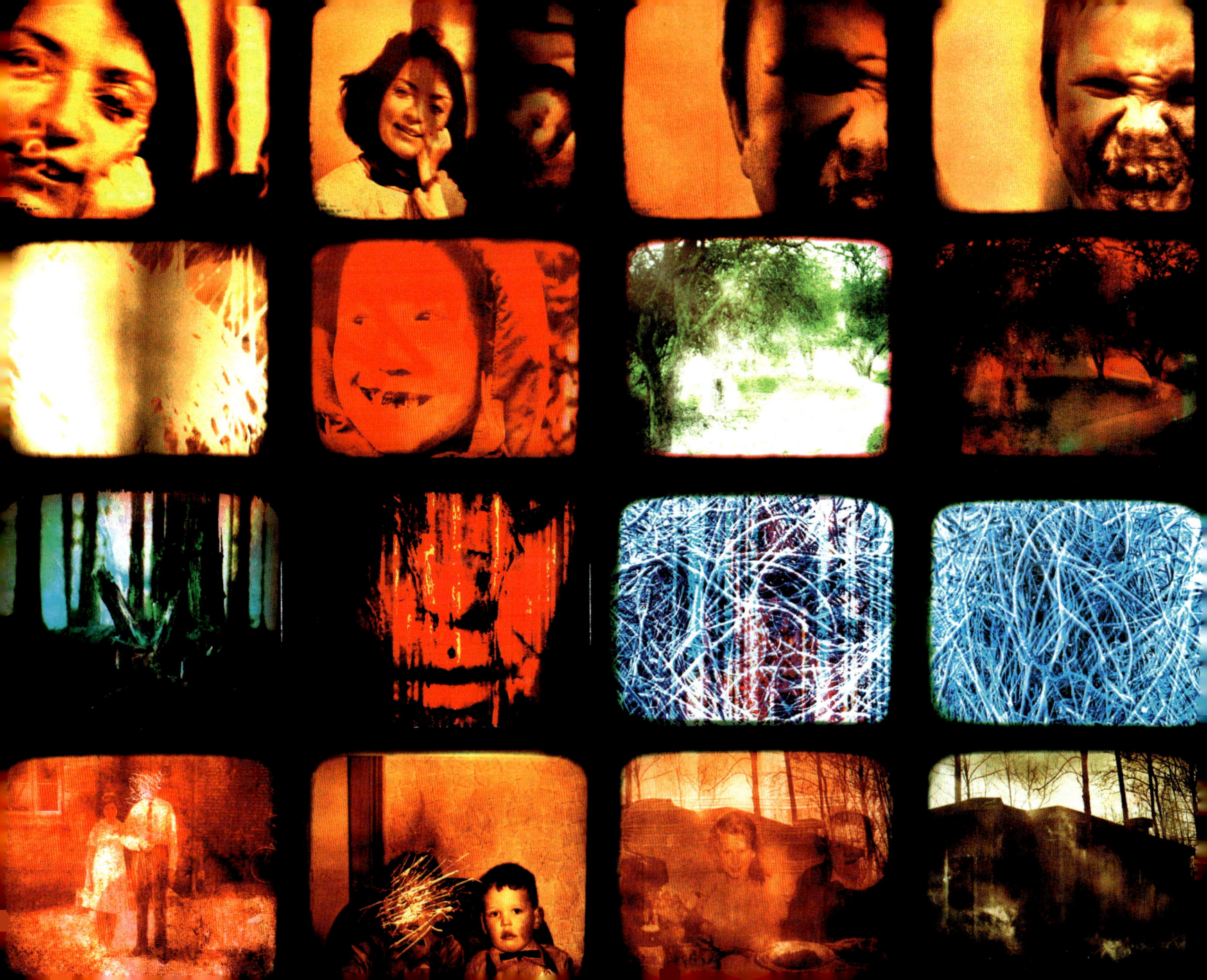

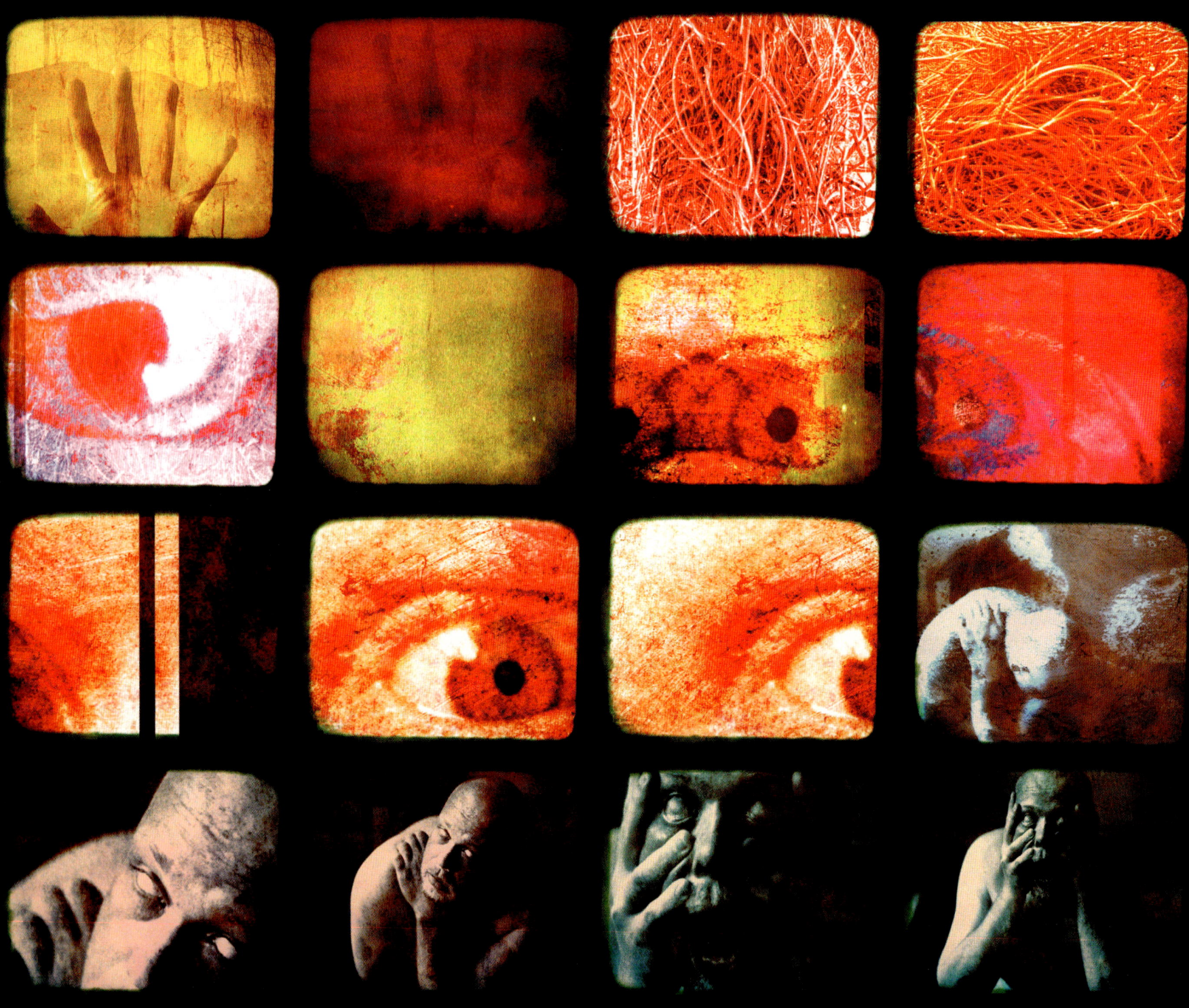

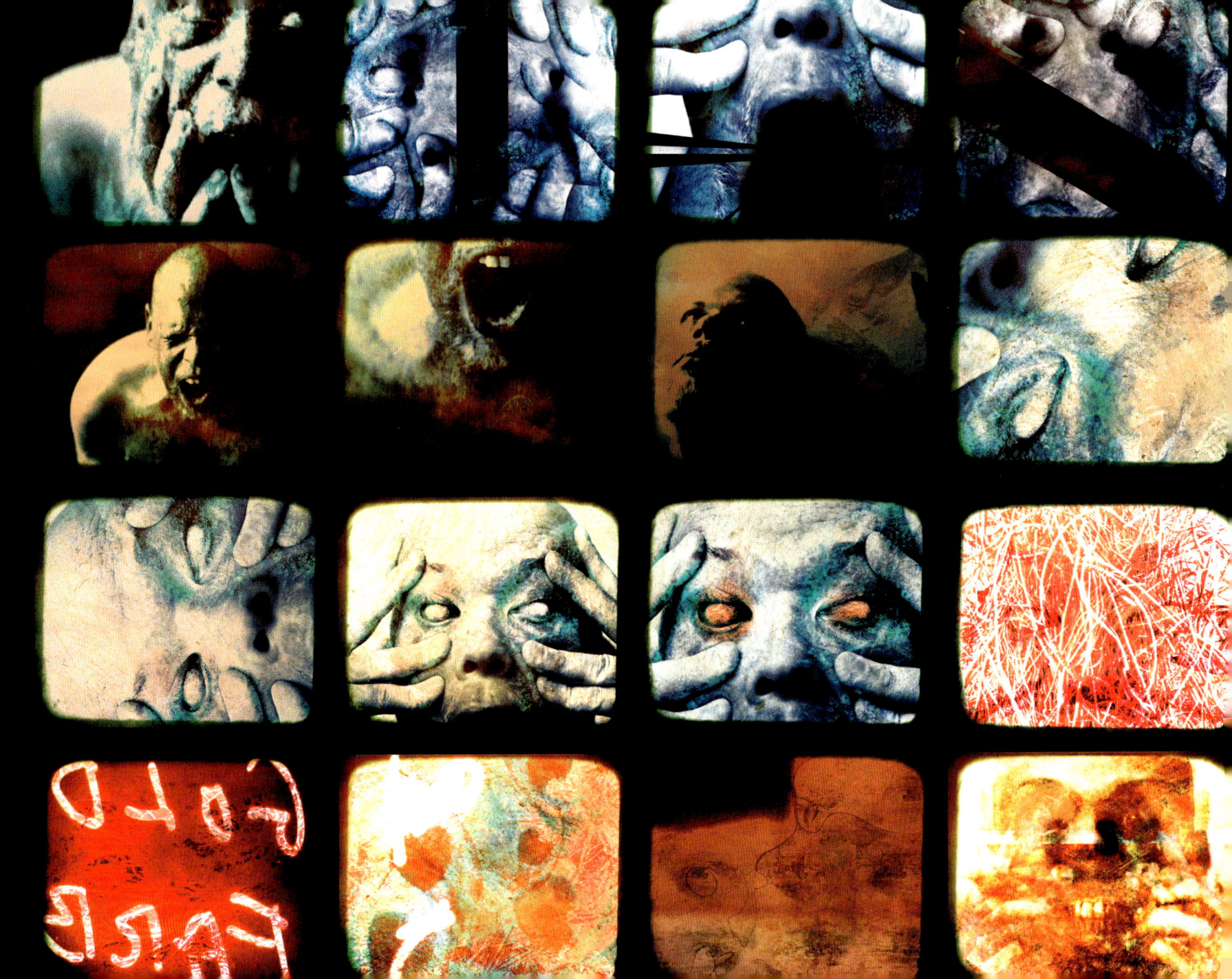

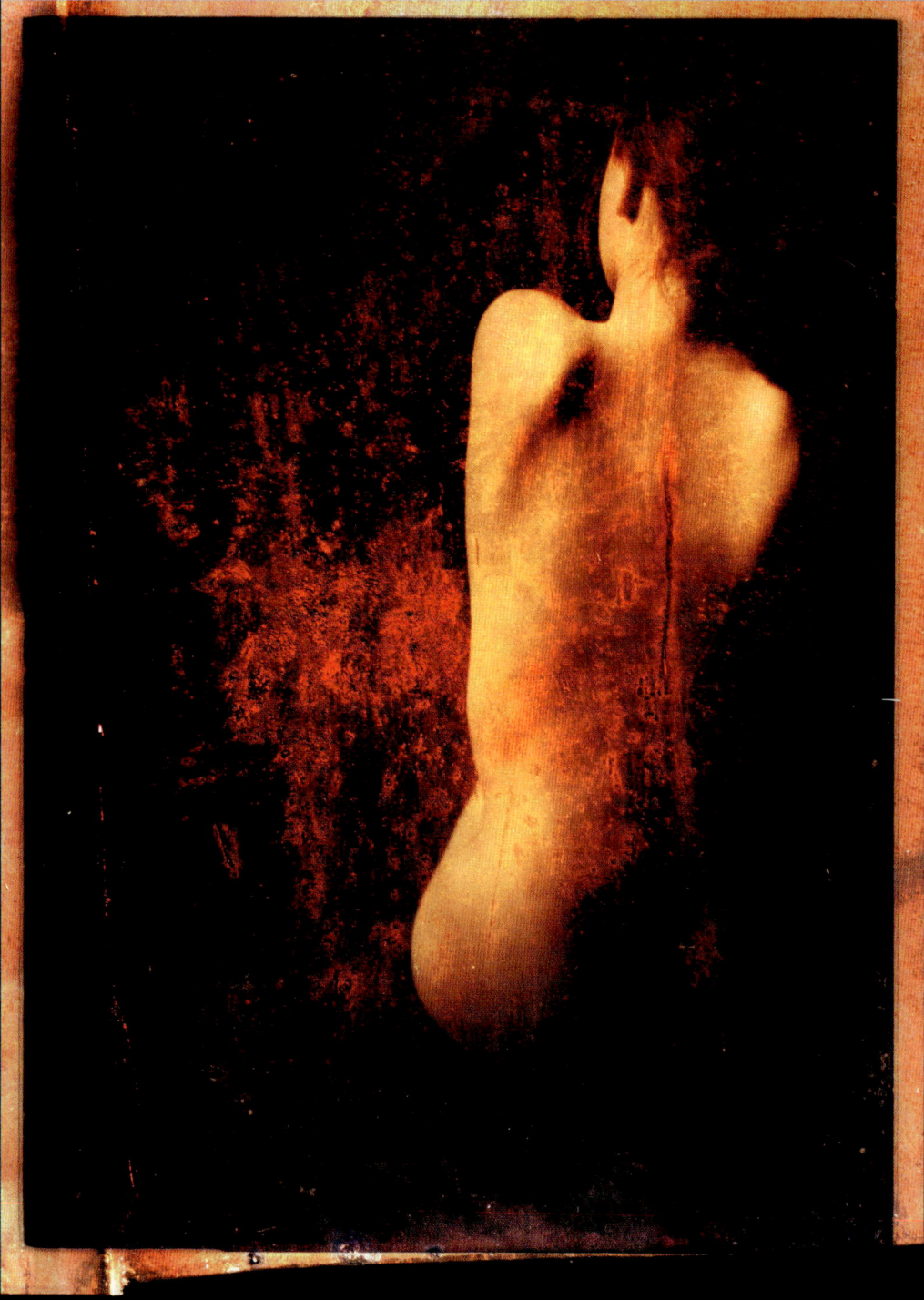

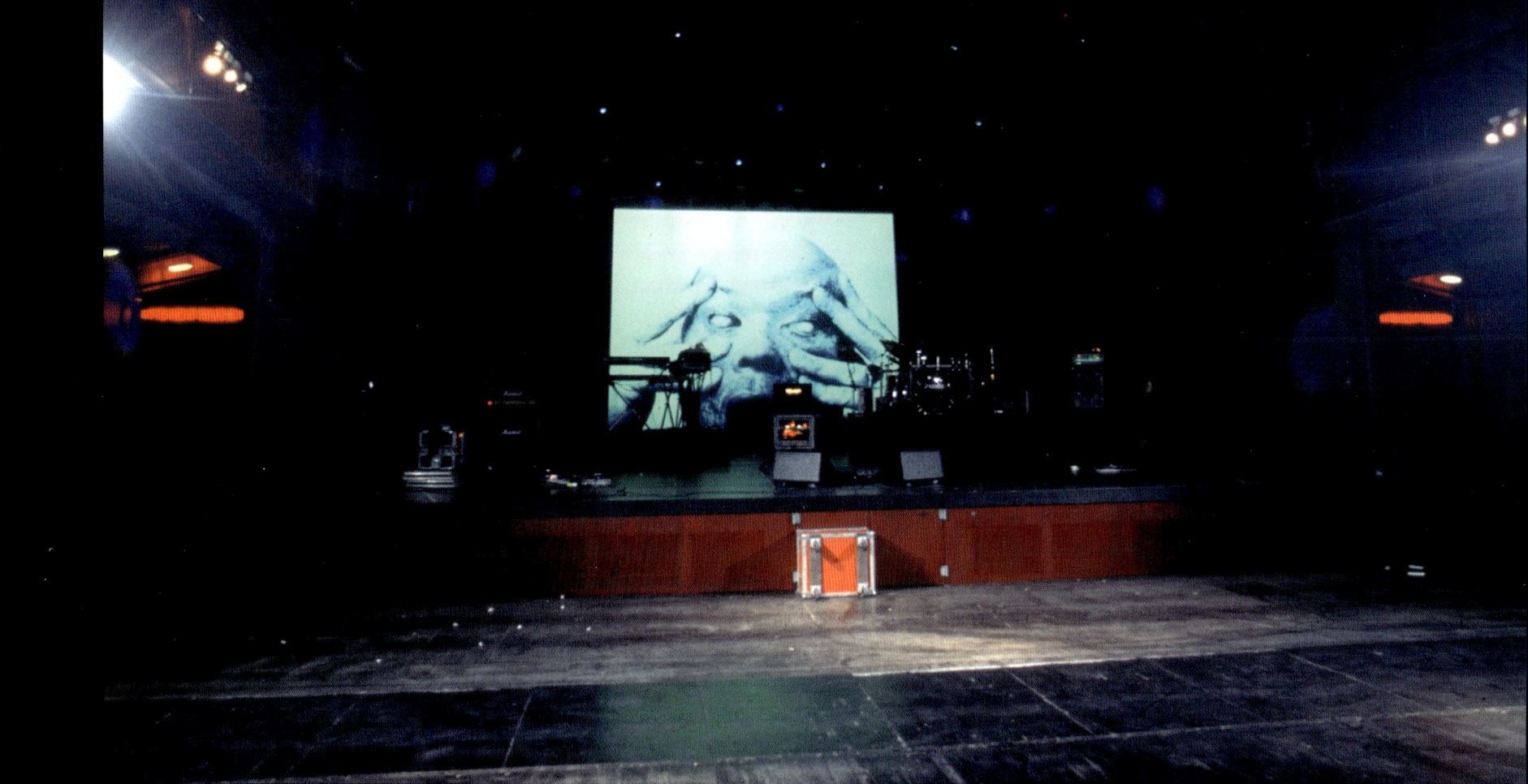

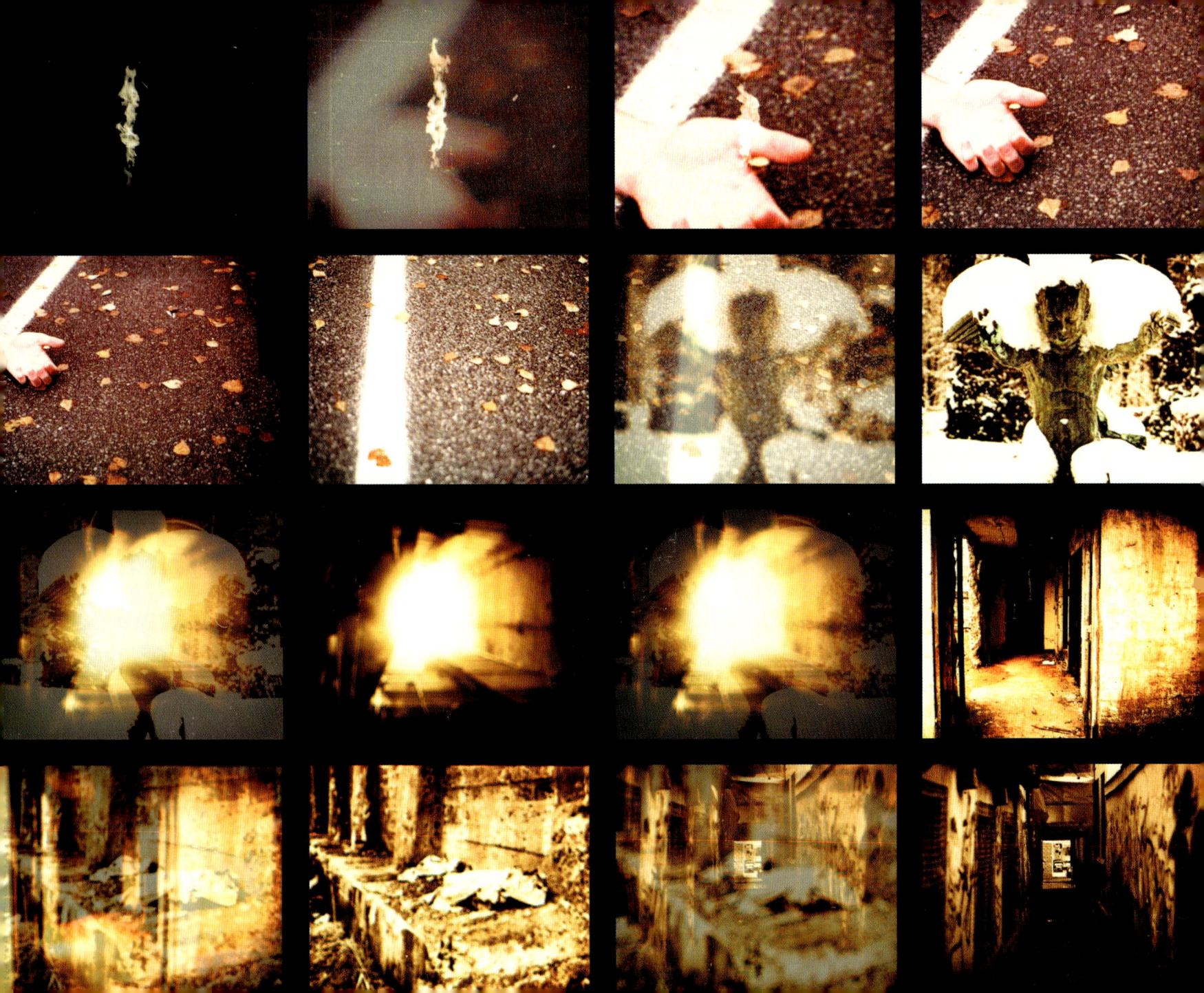

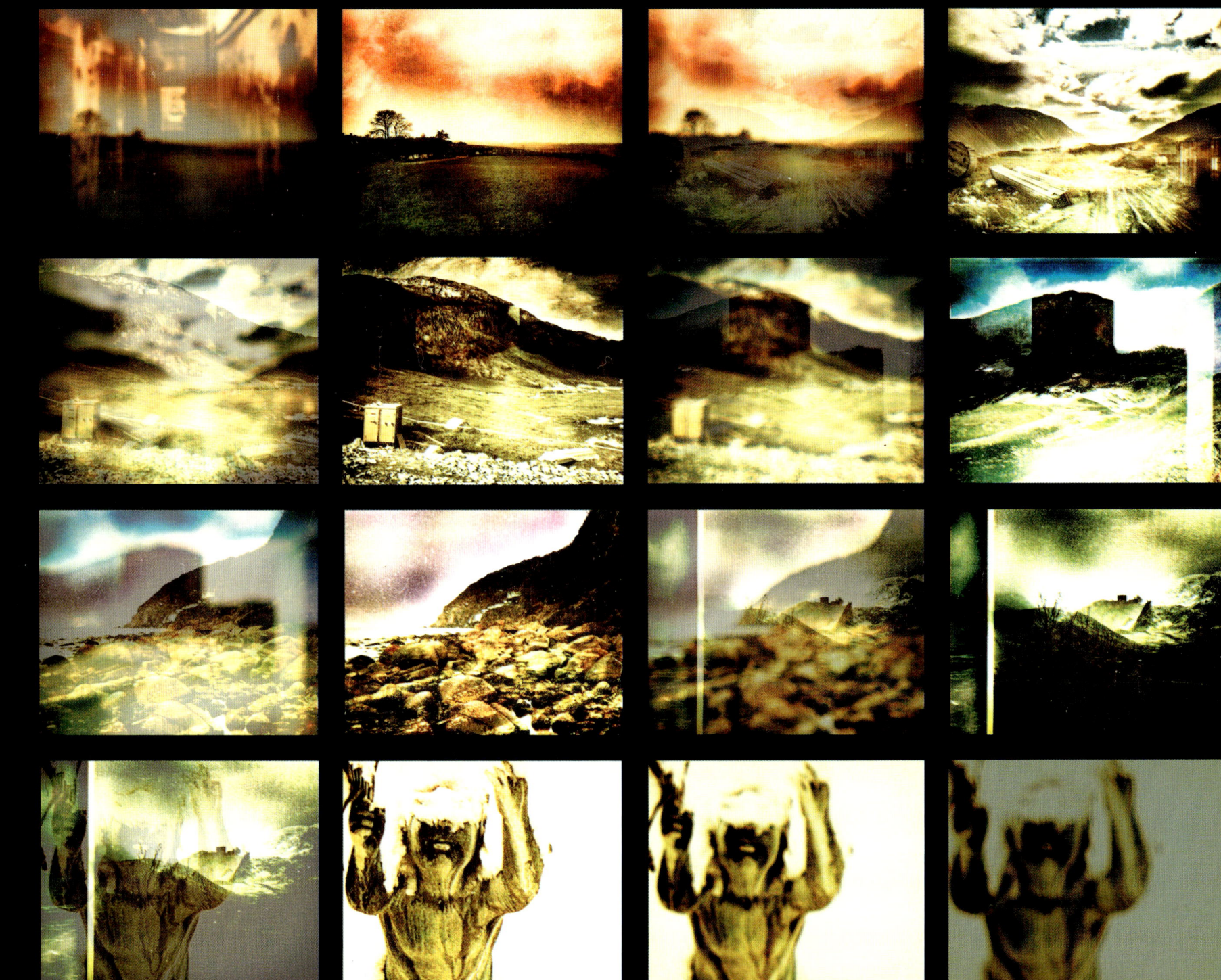

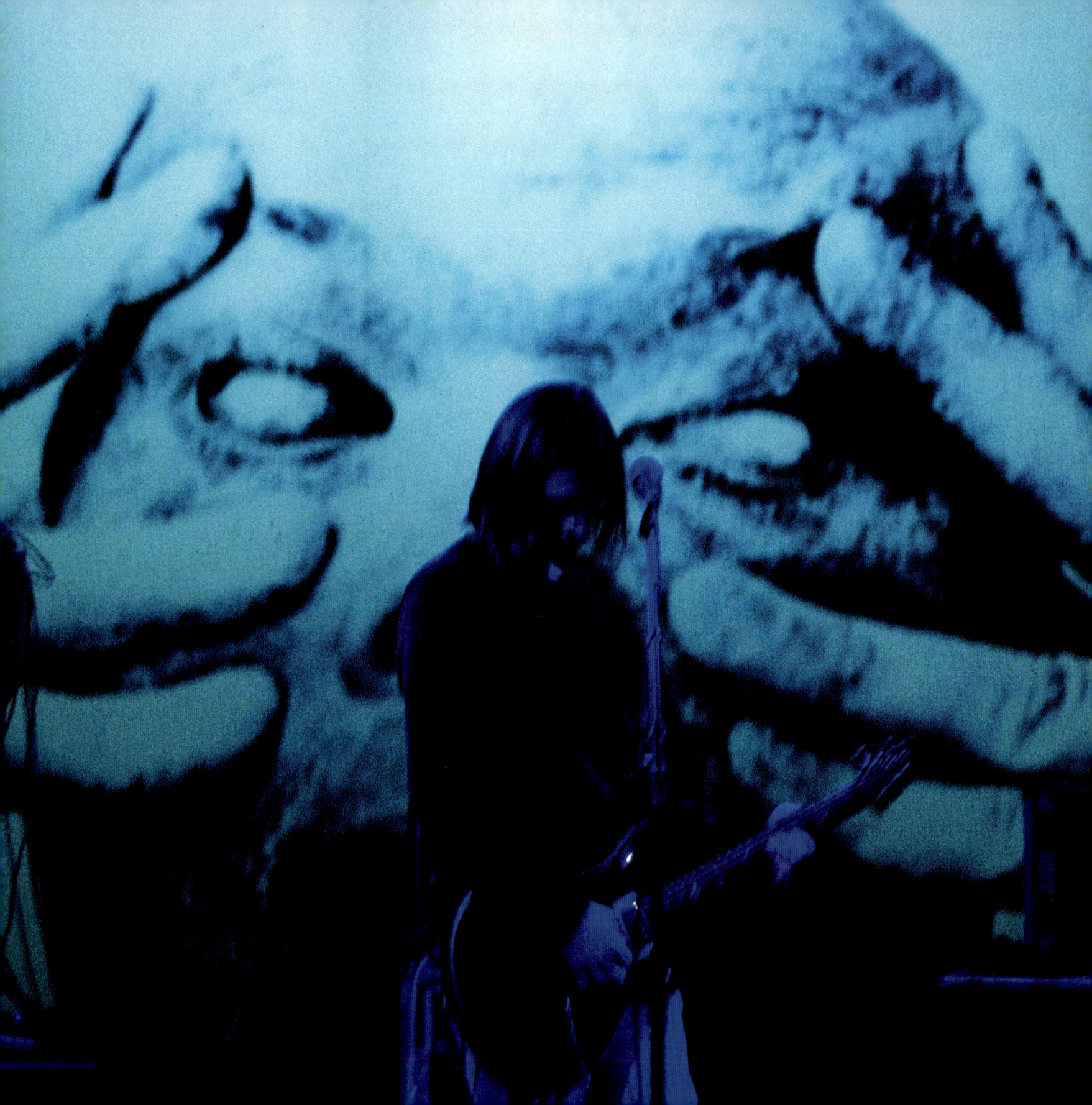

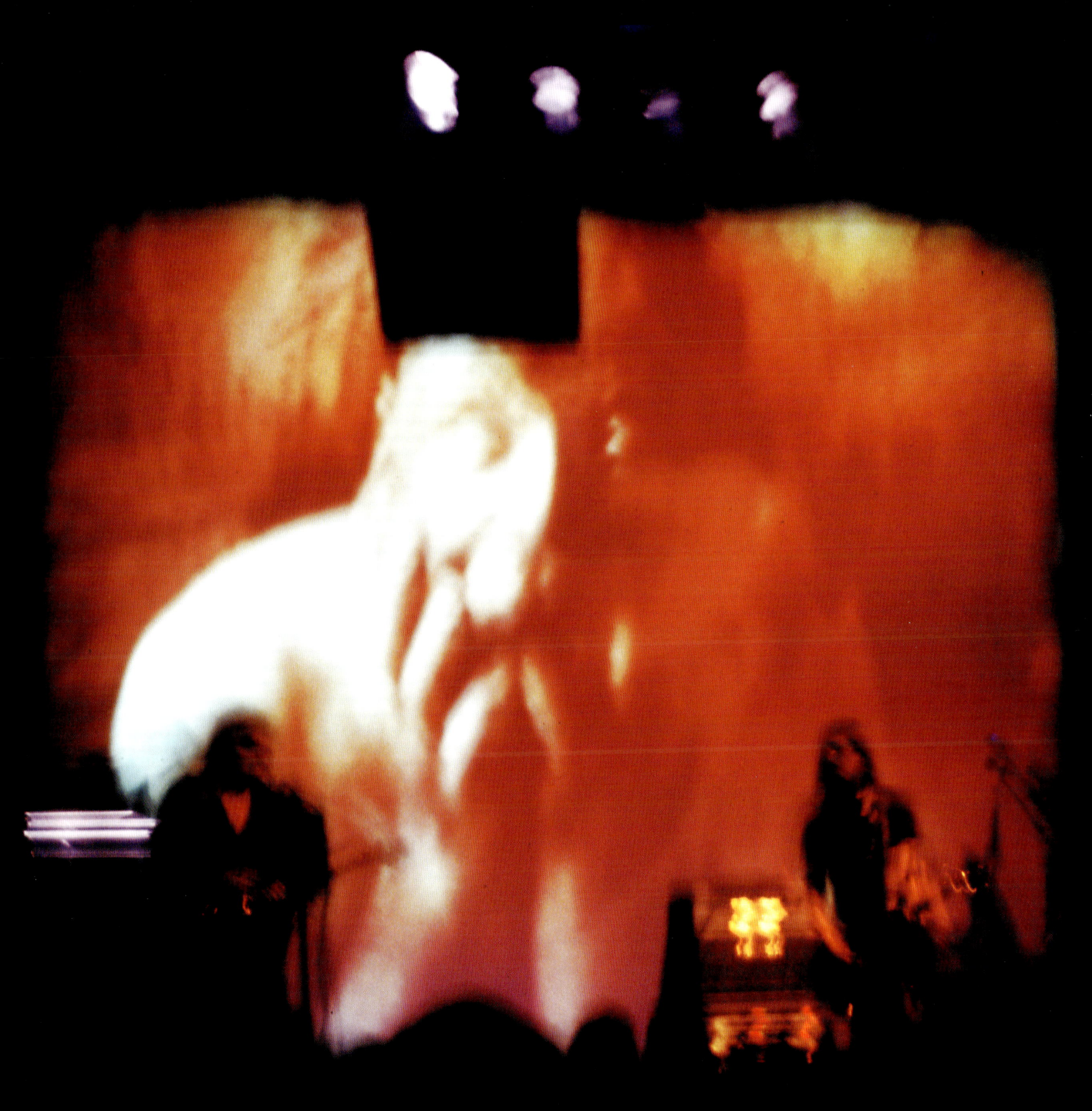

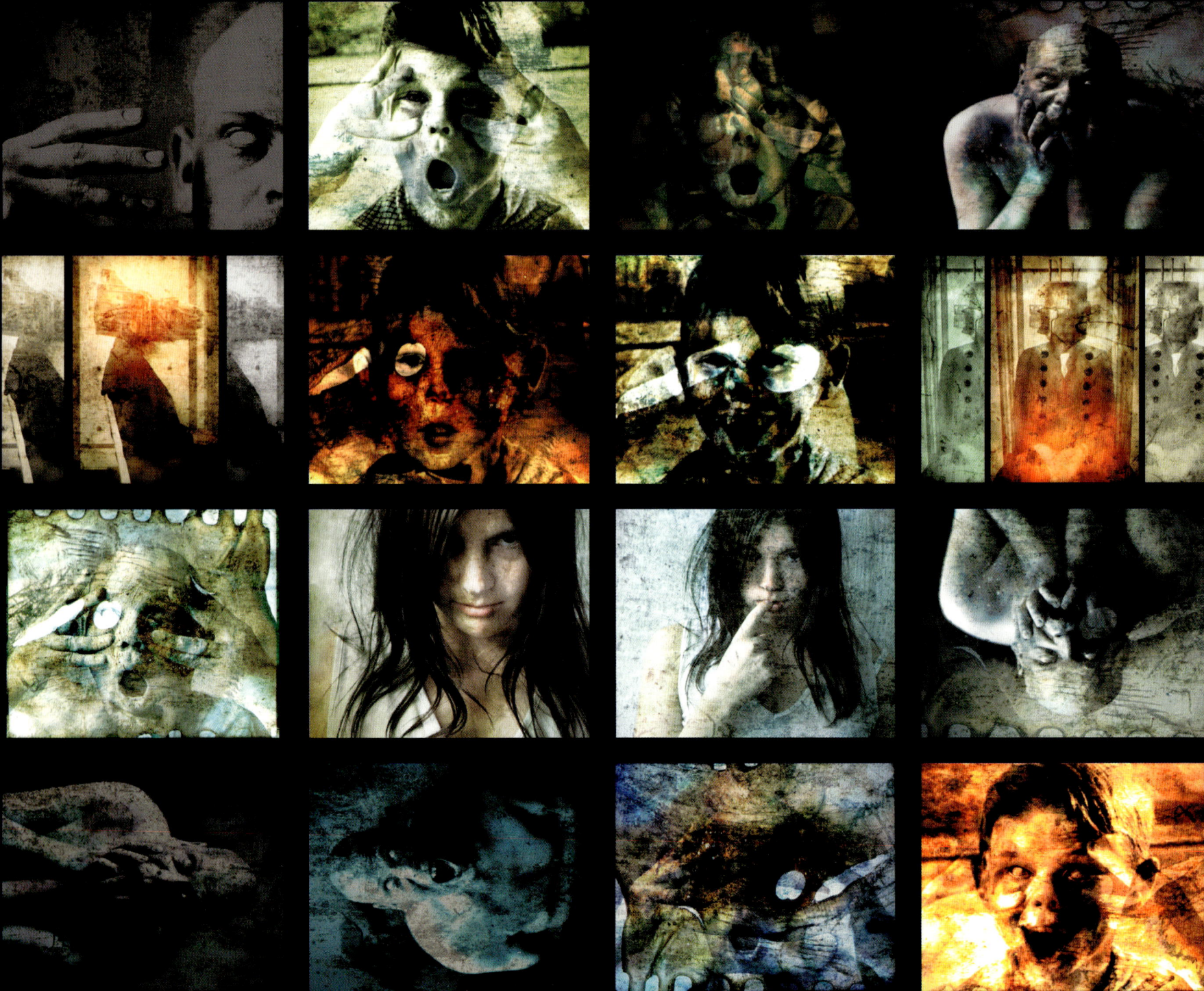

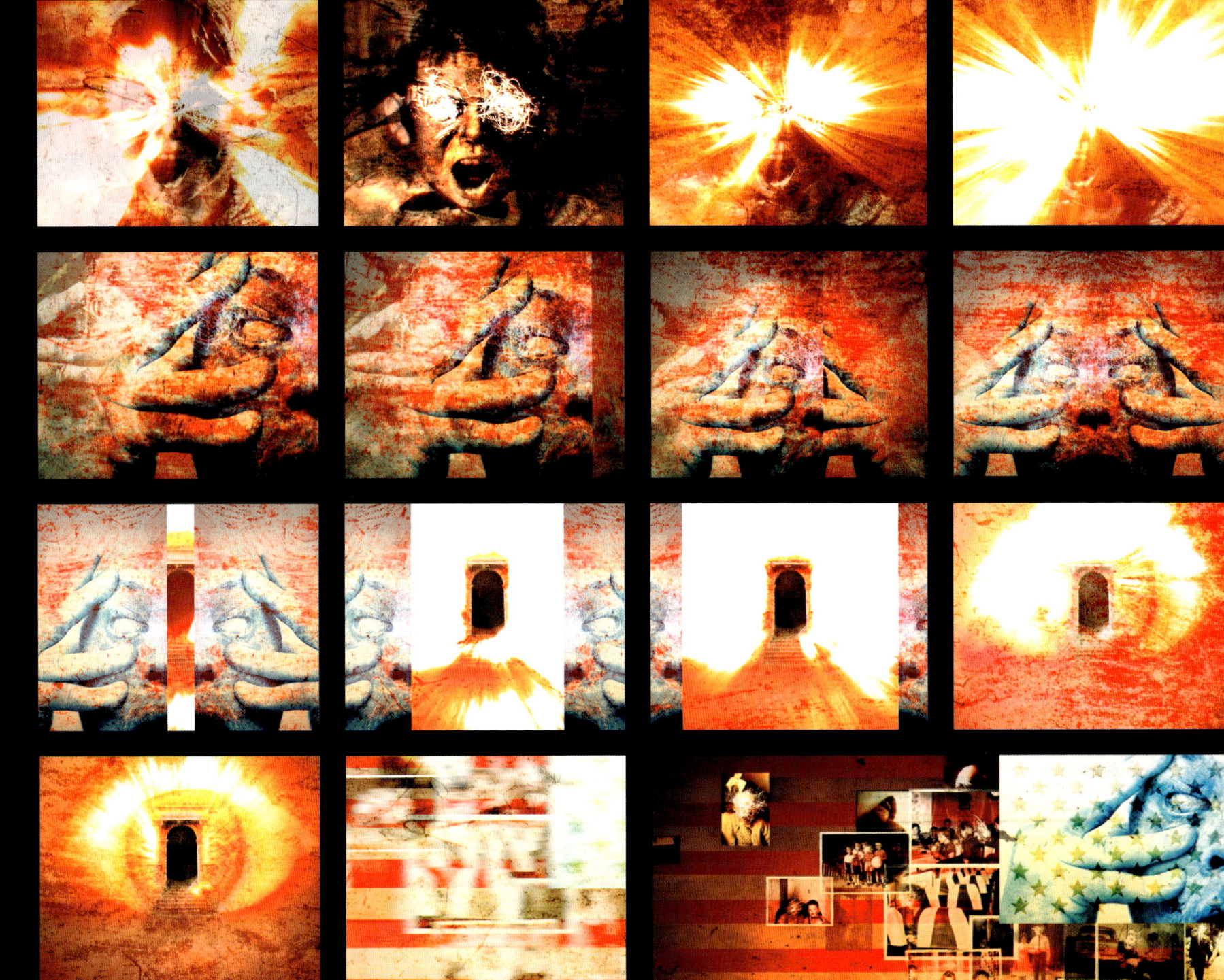

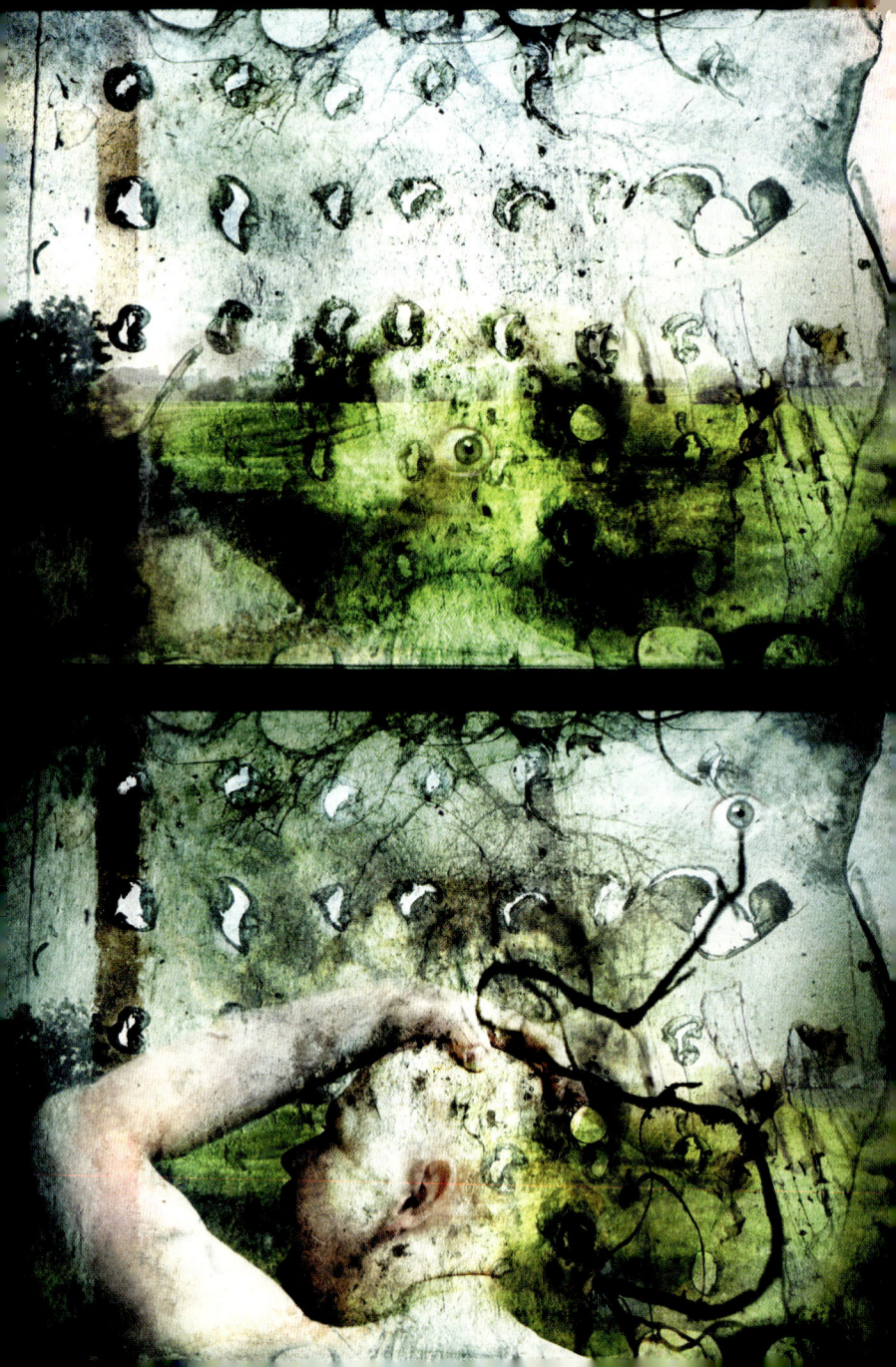

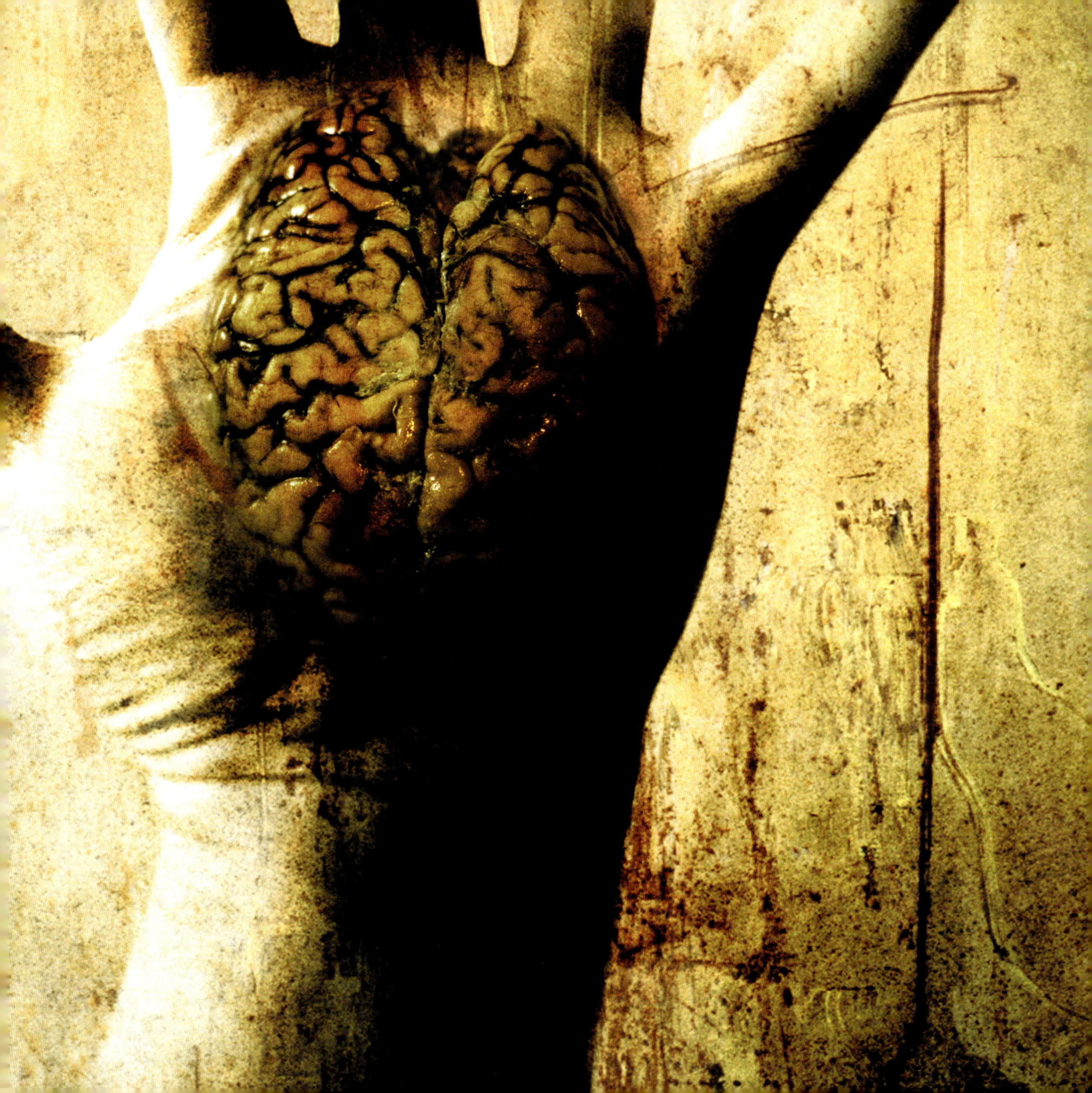

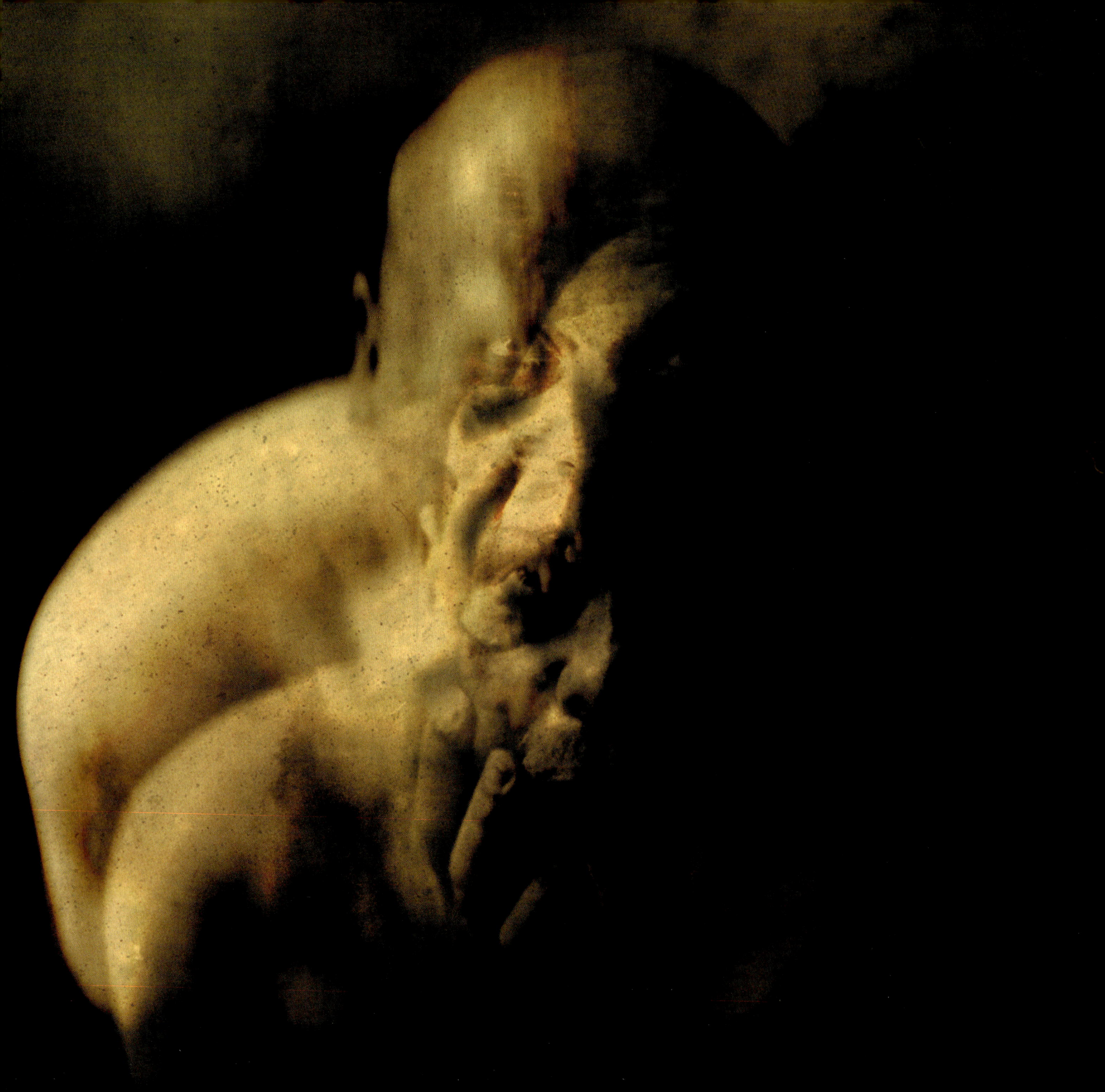

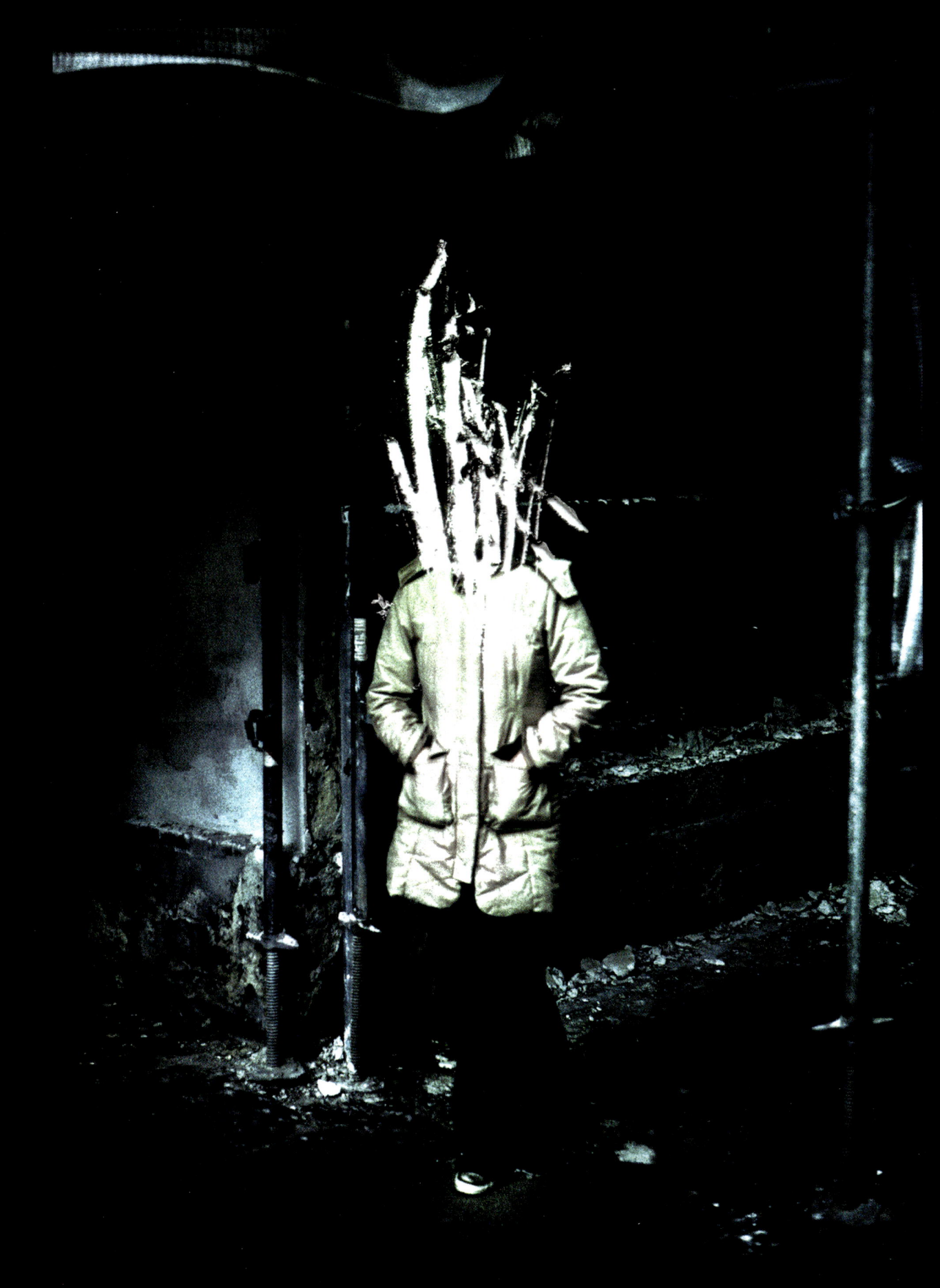

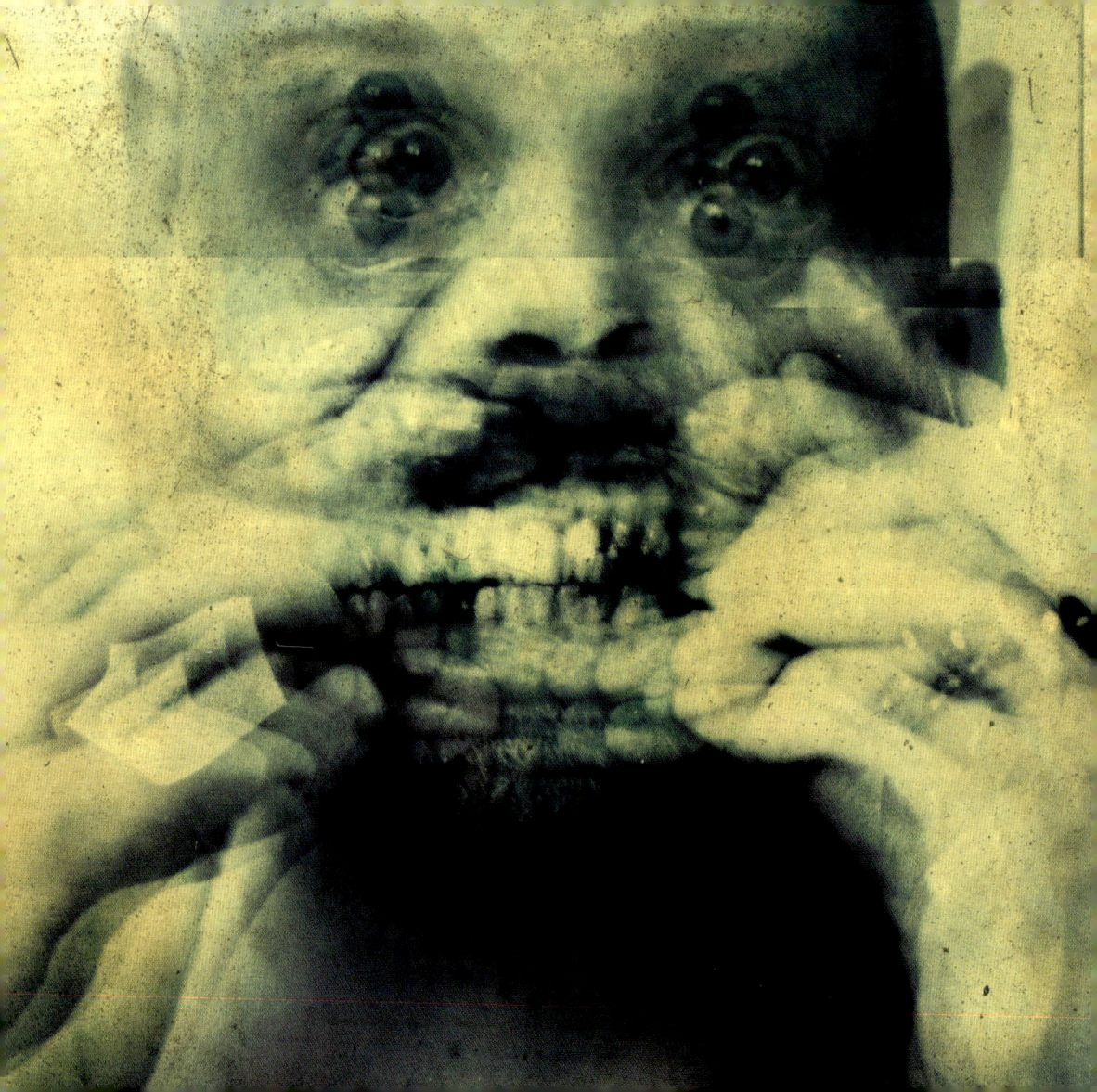

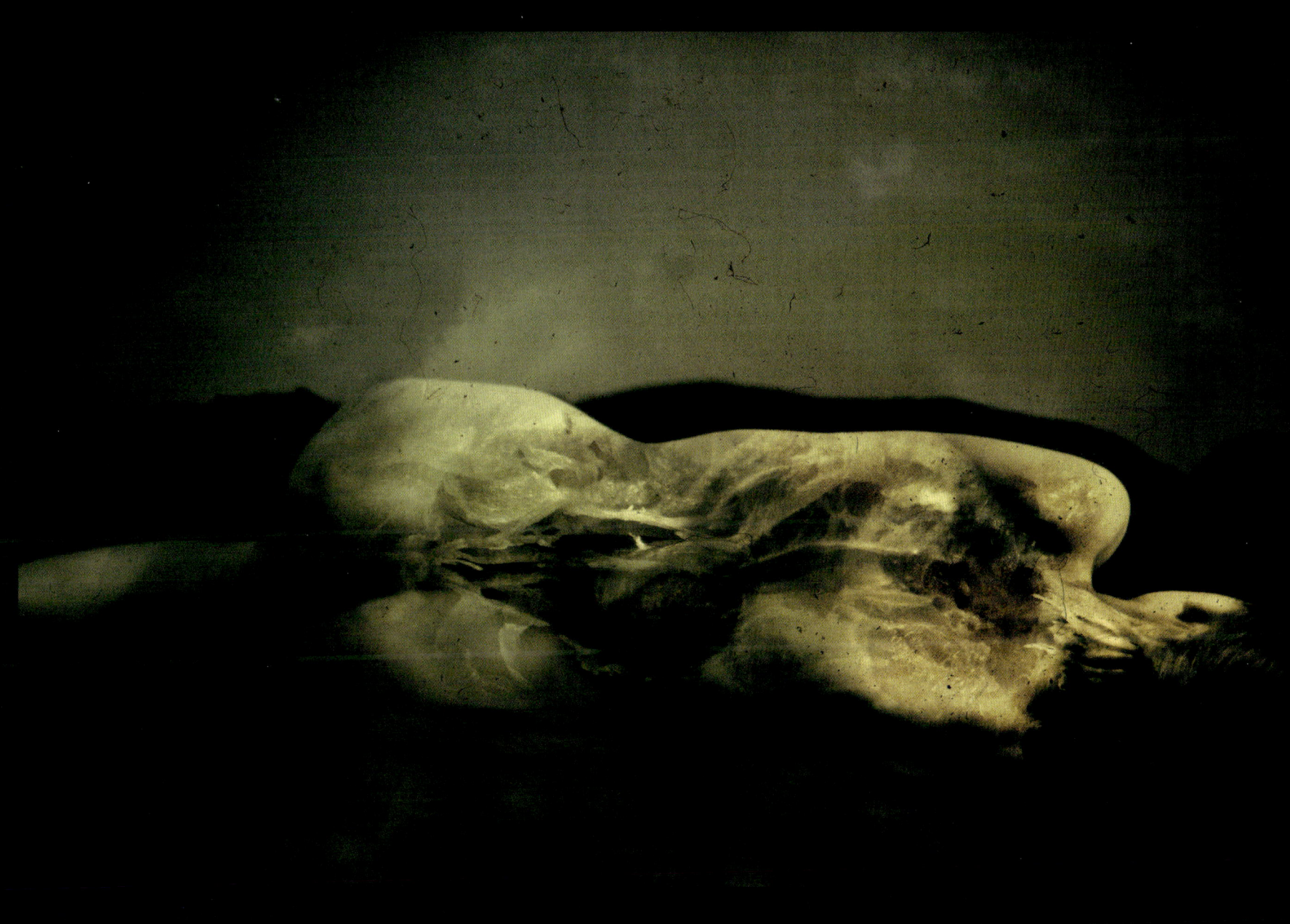

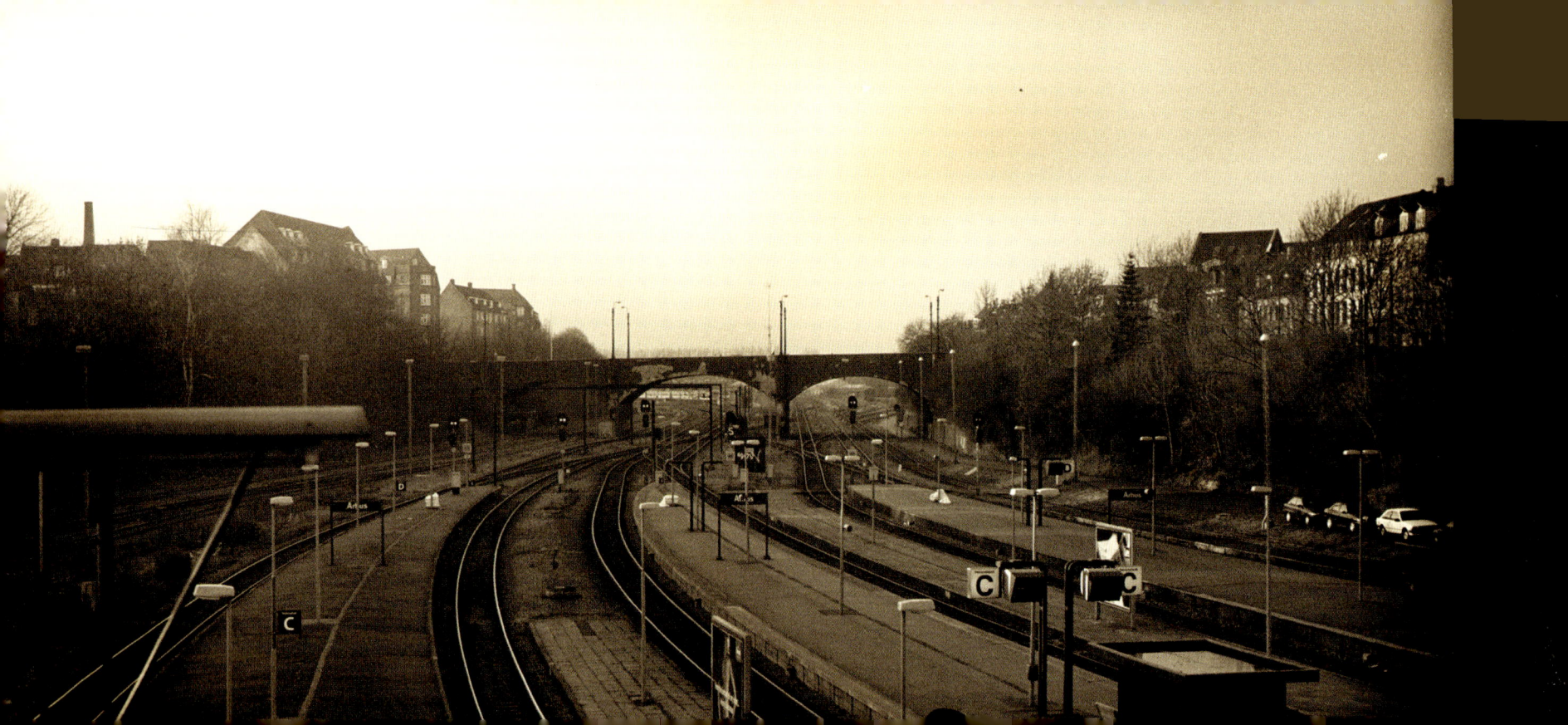

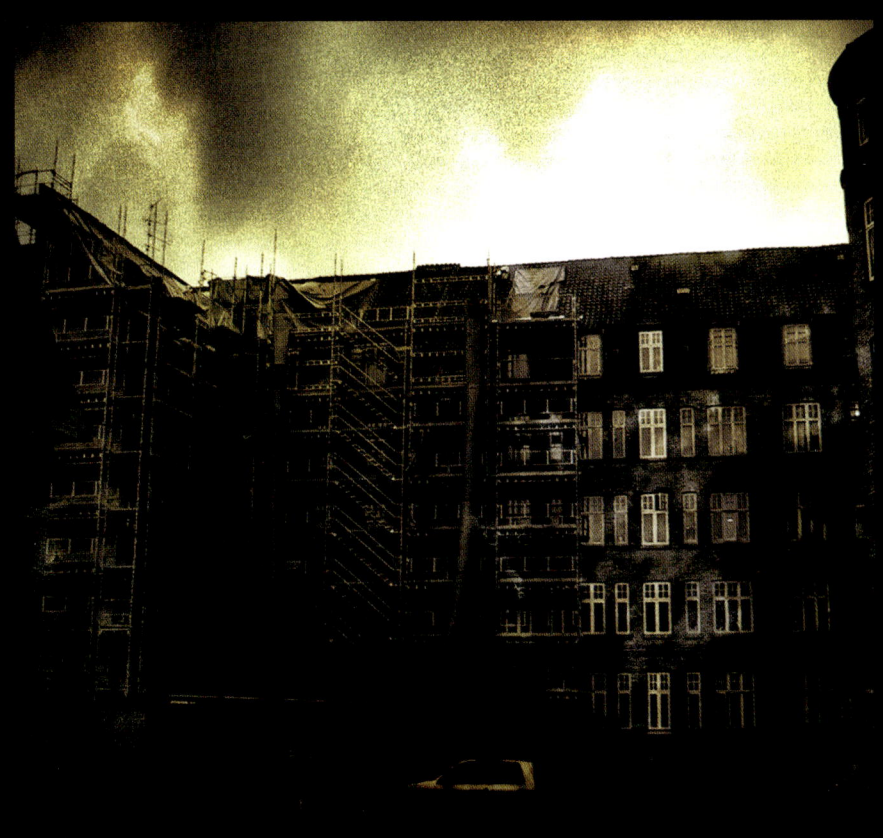
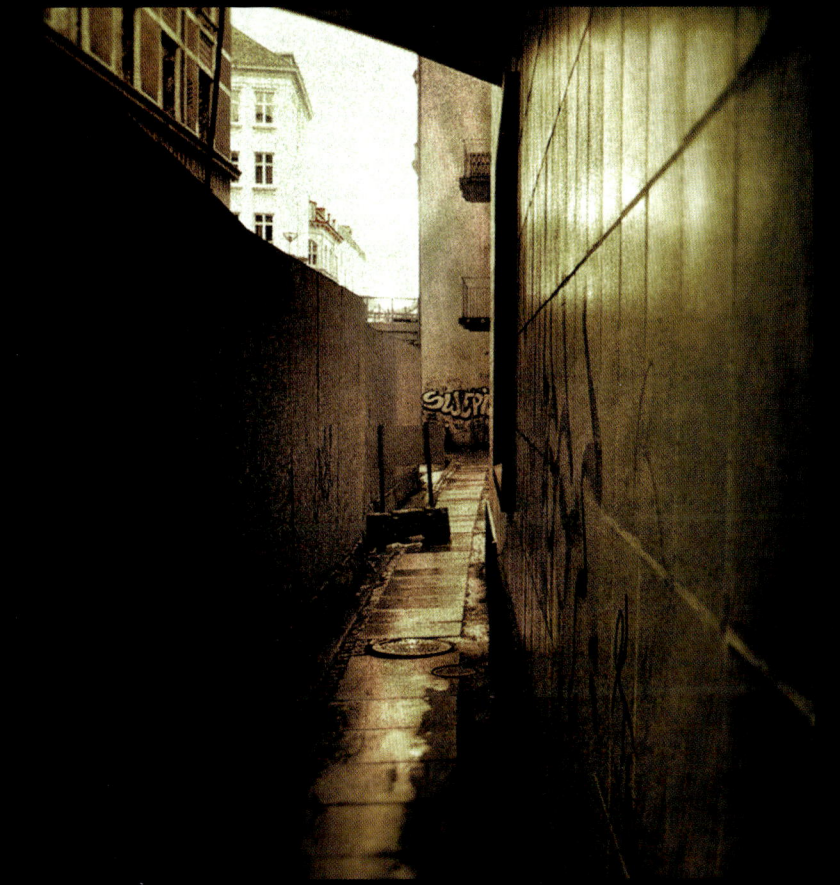

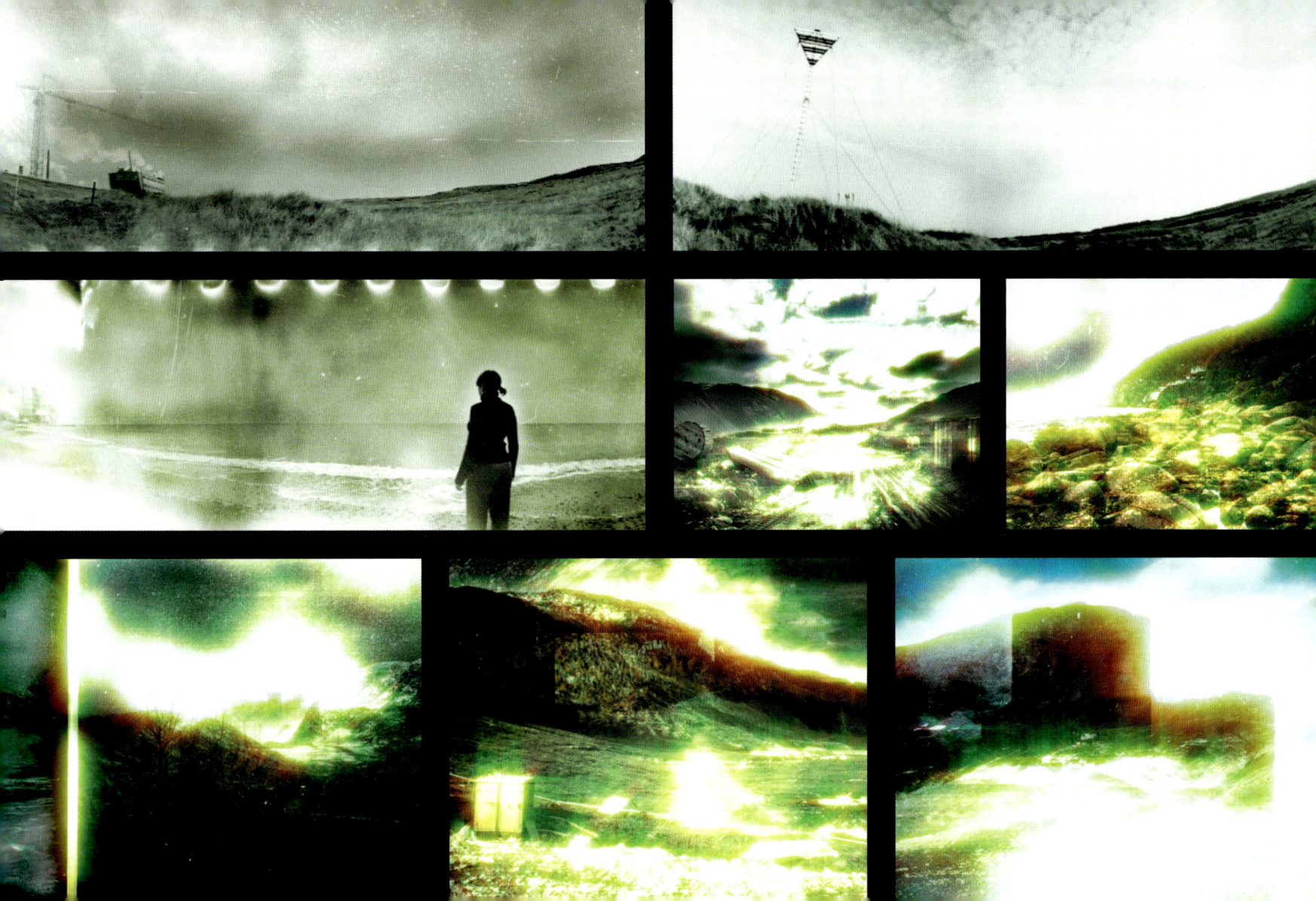

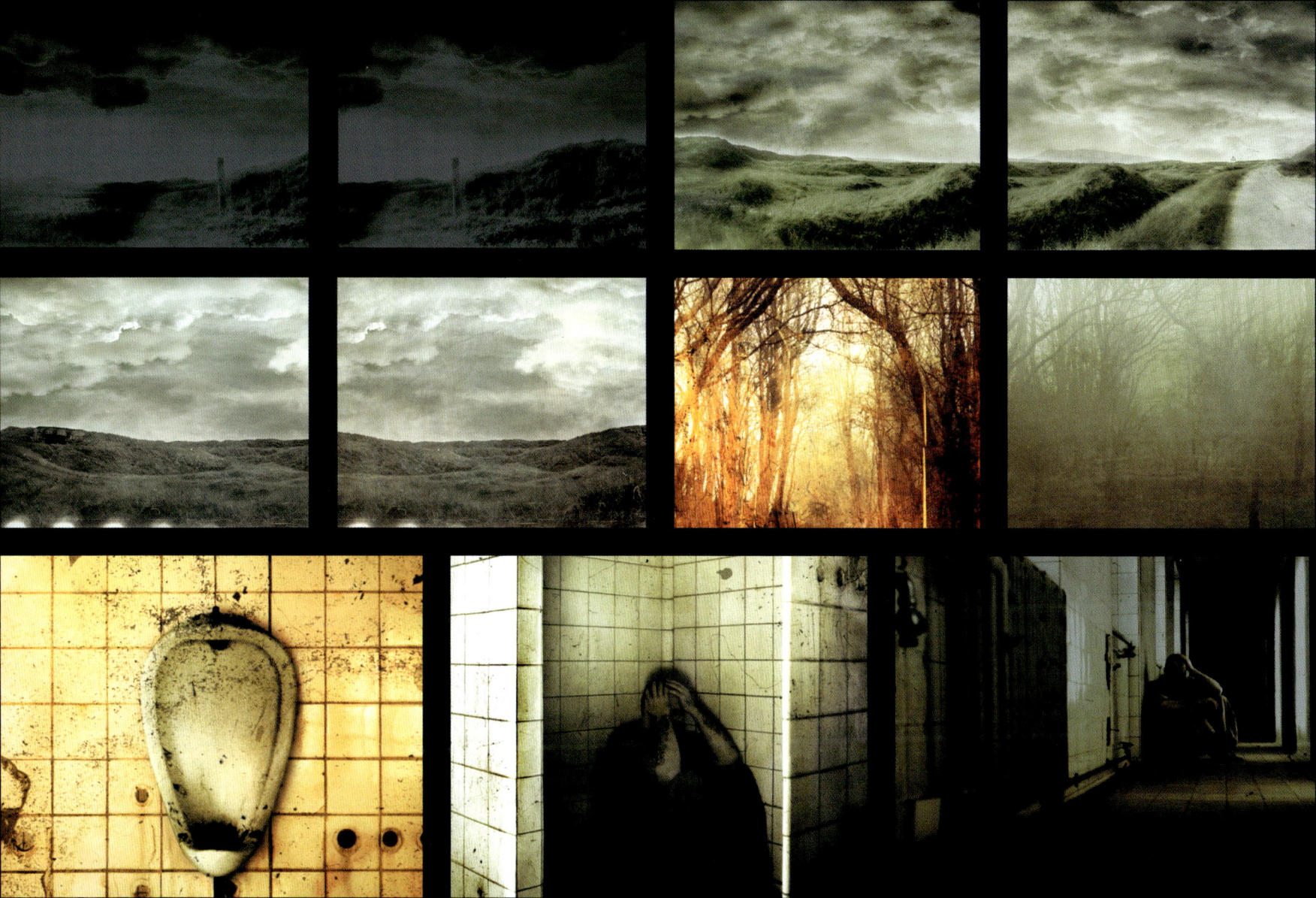

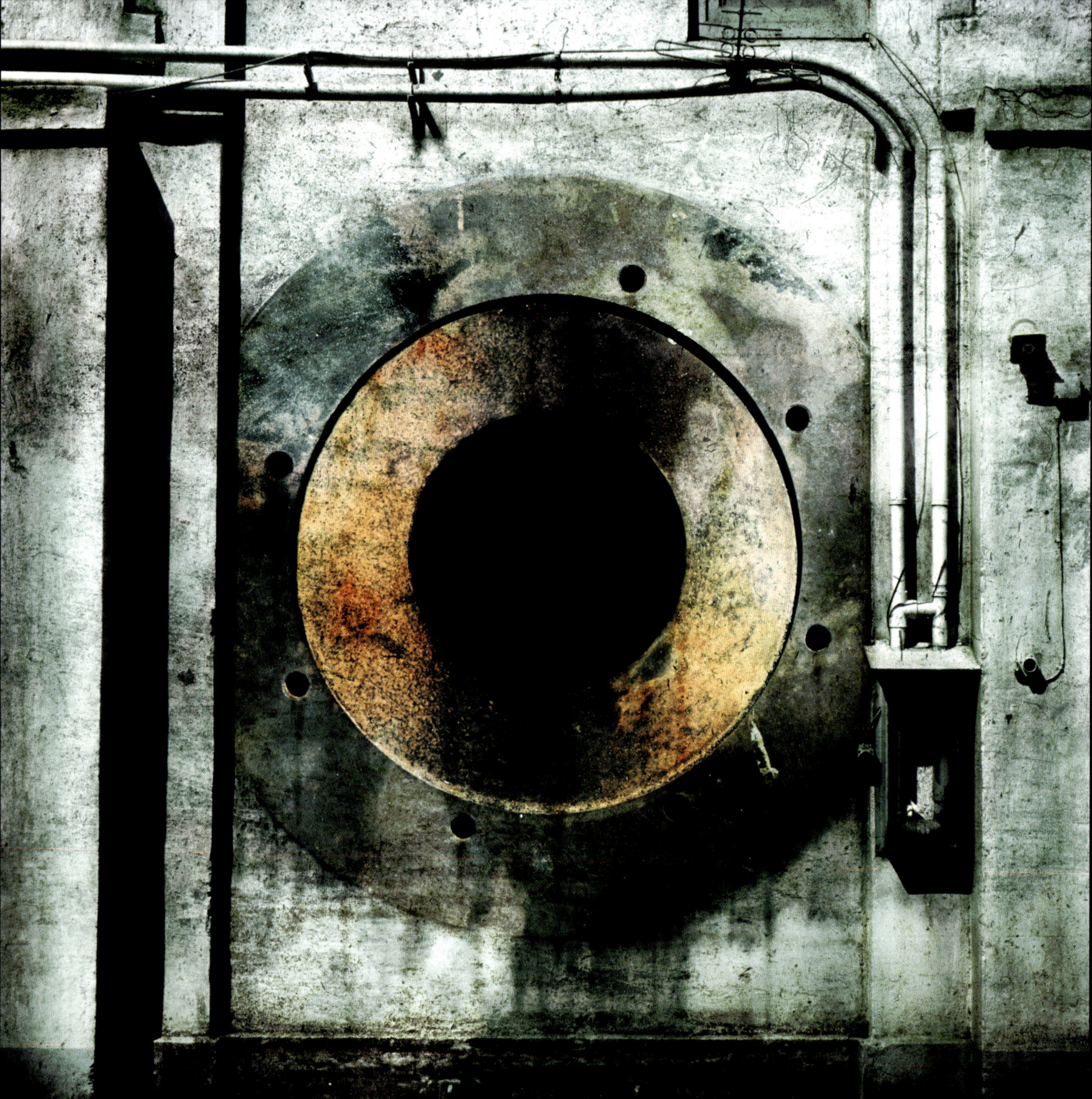

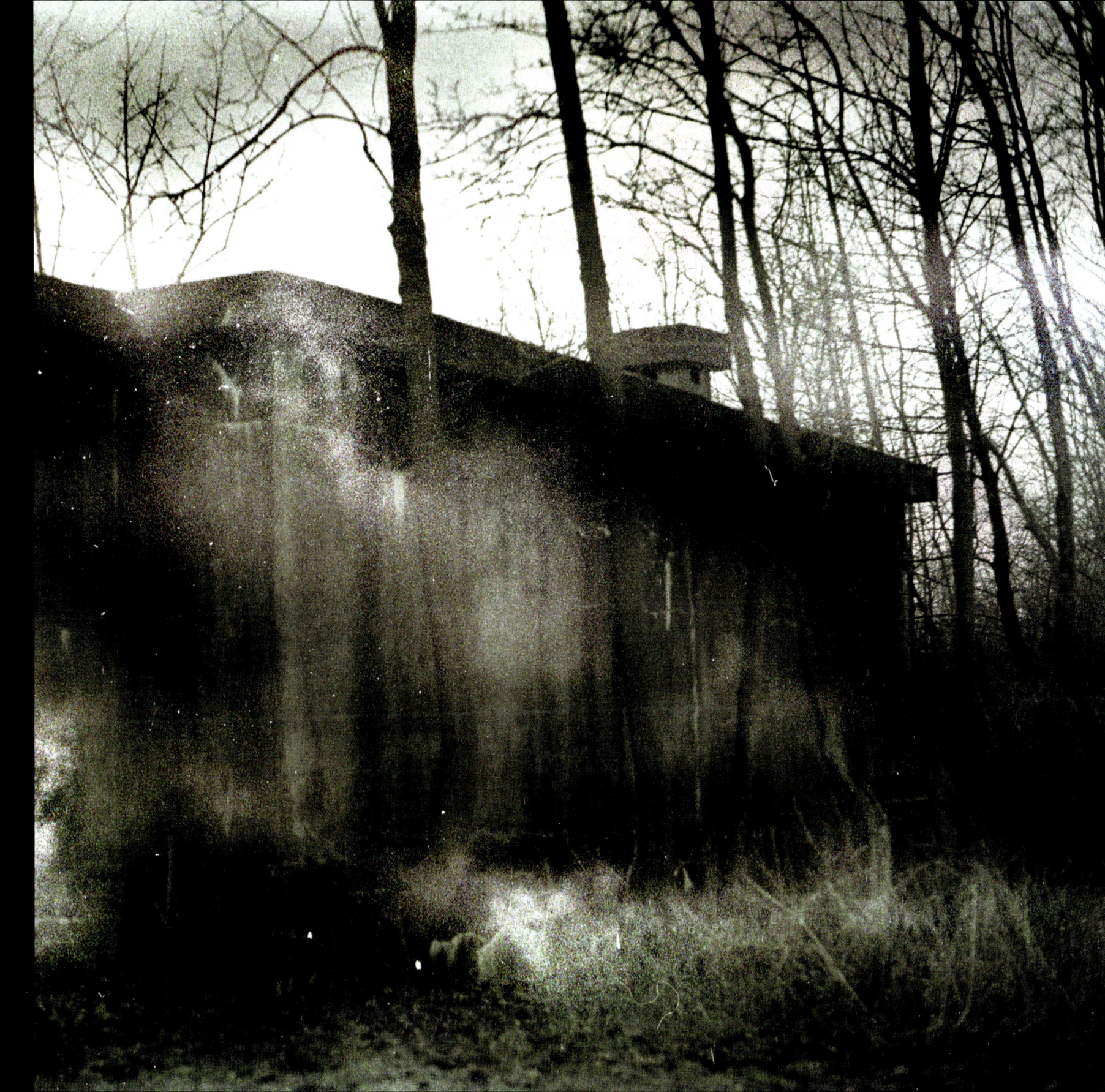

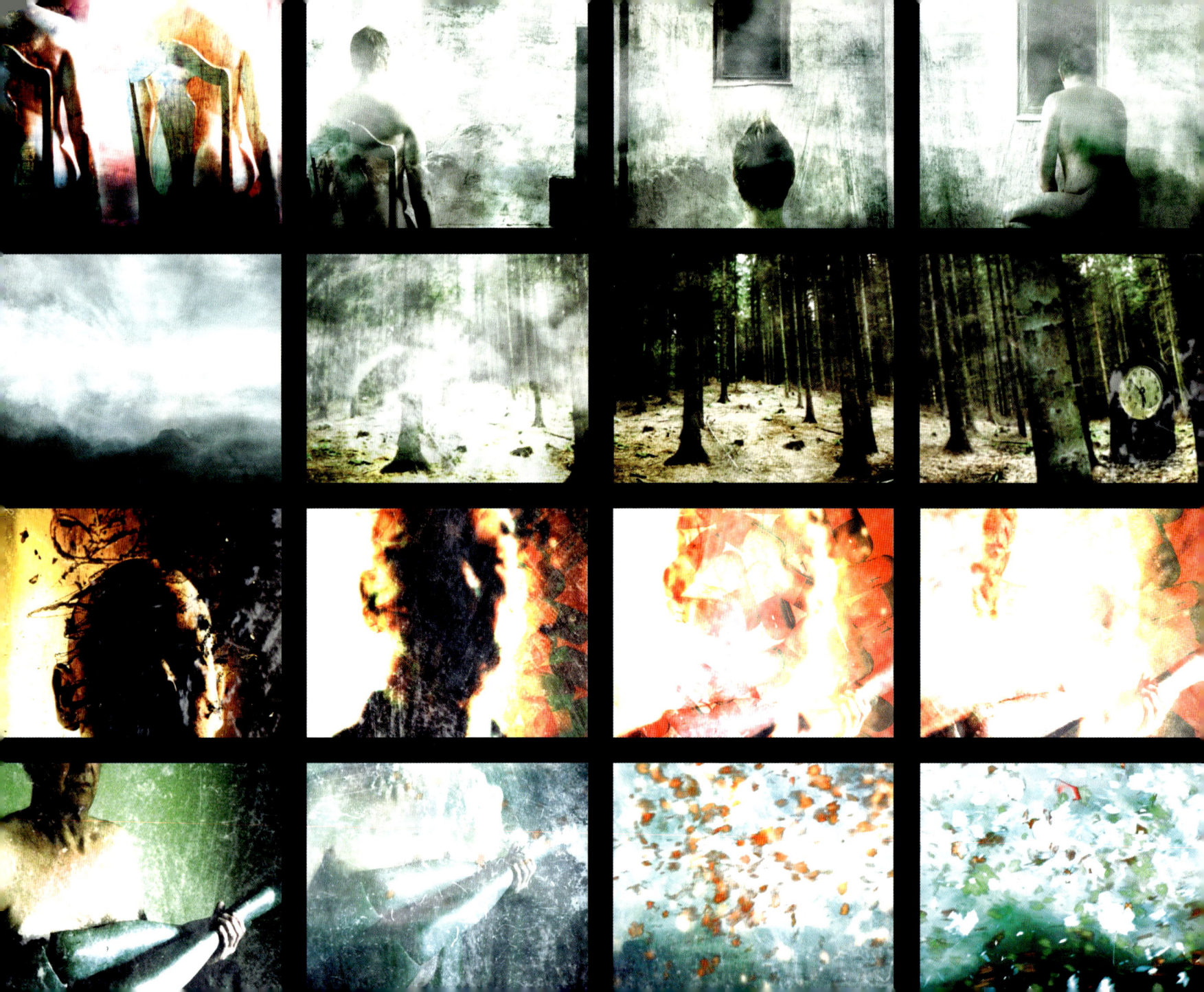

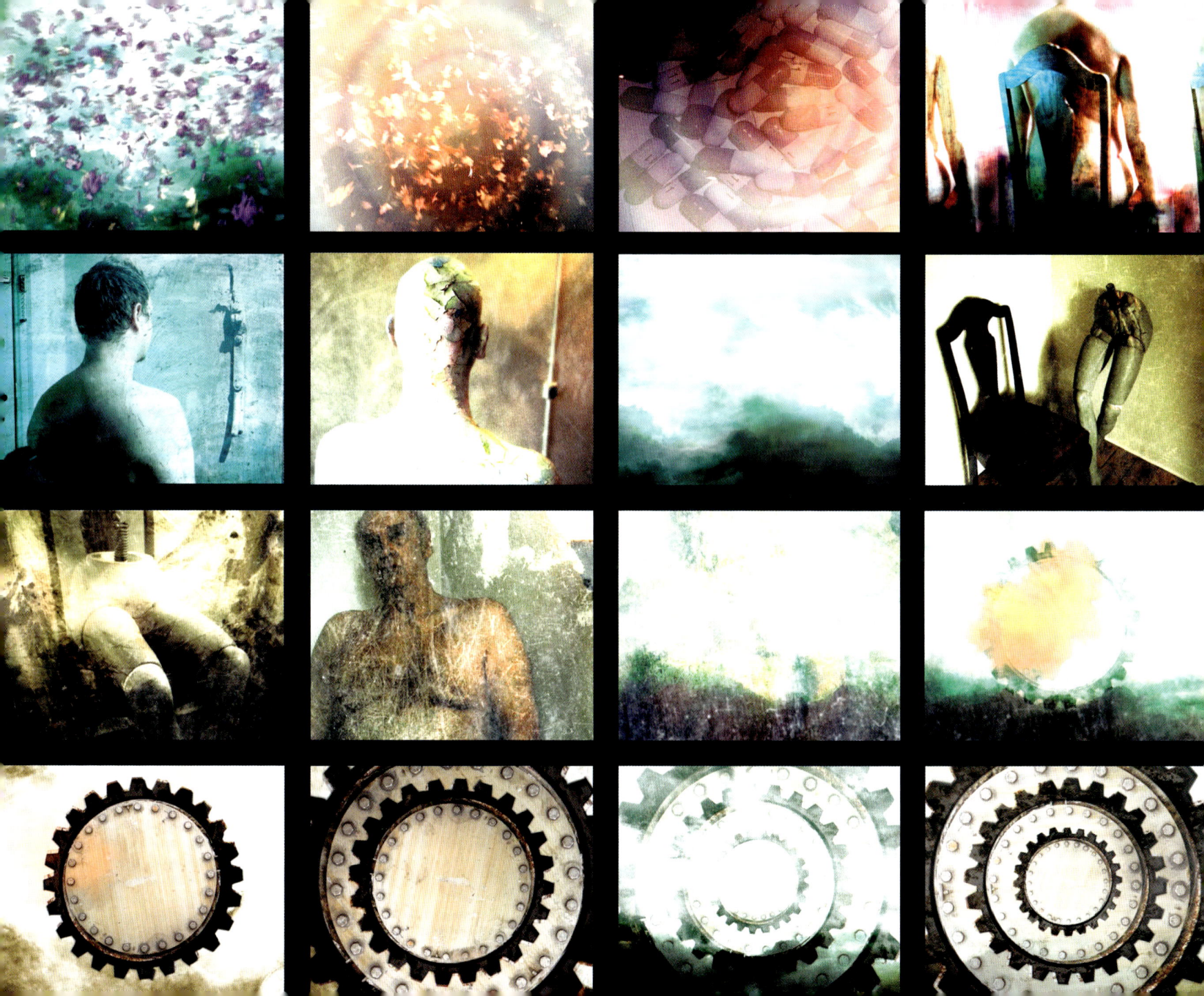

INABSEN
DWING
ABLANK
THEIN

INITIAL IDEA
FEAR OF
BLACK PLANE
INCIDENT

Carl Glover: Bearing in mind that the theme of the album is based on a movie script by Steven Wilson and Mike Bennion, were you following the story as part of your brief?

Lasse Hoile: Somewhat yes, but the project was shared with Mike who was creating the collages for the album, and not all the music related to the script. It was more about the mood of the potential film and the environment the main character would have grown up in. Myself, SW and Mike took a trip to Wales to scout some locations which were quite beautiful and desolate. It was a dull and rainy day but we tried to capture as much atmospheric stuff as possible.

Carl Glover: One of the components from the Deadwing project that works well is the Halo series of images. How did you get to the idea of the circular neon tube surrounding the head but covering the eyes?

Lasse Hoile: It was an idea I had for a long time because we were using these ring-lights, which were originally for places like toilets, repurposed for use in music videos. If you put one over a lens you can light a face pretty good and get a circular reflection in the eyes. It was also about how religion blinds people. Not being religious myself, it was something that I had wanted to do for a long time.

Before Deadwing happened, I was doing a video for a Danish metal band and took a few photographs using the ring-light which turned out pretty good, so I tried a few more at another session later on. I would have liked to have done more with a group of people simultaneously, almost like The Last Supper but there was no budget. Later on I used the pictures for Halo, they worked well in the live projections.

Carl Glover: Deadwing was also the first time you started using a significant amount of models. Did it take time for you to locate the appropriate people for the photography?

Lasse Hoile: It was friends, family & friends of friends who were willing to spend a little time with me.

Carl Glover: Deadwing seems to be the album with the least amount of outtakes when it comes to imagery, almost everything seemed to get used at some point. In my experience this is quite a rare occurence. Was there anything particularly different in working on this album compared to In Absentia?

Lasse Hoile: The idea was for me to provide images for Mike to use in creating the collages. Mike would use different media that would also relate to the script. With In Absentia I had many images from the previous 2-3 years and was able to make more once I knew more about the direction SW wanted to take.

Carl Glover: How was the Glass Arm Shattering film done? It looks quite difficult to do knowing how tricky lighting can be for underwater photography.

Lasse Hoile: We rented a public swimming pool for the evening. One of my friends was a skilled diver and photographer, we also had a safety diver to make sure everything would be ok. We had a 5K (I think) HMI light aimed directly down into the pool and was lucky to find two people willing to be naked who could swim. For some unknown reason the girl decided to cut her long hair off the day before the shoot. It was too late to find a replacement, the film would have looked dreamier if she had kept her hair long. It turned out well considering the budget was about £900. Most of the other projections for DW were made with stills and some video that I was able to shoot, with a little stock footage thrown in.

Carl Glover: Even though it is filmed underwater, the couple seem airborne to me, it's the black background I think. Certain scenes in the film 'Under The Skin' have parallels with what you were doing all those years ago.

Lasse Hoile: It was what I saw in my mind when hearing the song for the first time, it was this floaty kinda thing for me. I think it fitted the tune well despite the last minute hair loss! It took a week or so to finish since I still had to juggle my day-job at the same time. I didn't sleep much, I was working similar hours, if not more on the live films than the regular day-job routine. It was more fun inventing stuff from almost nothing. I became incredibly antisocial from that point on…

Carl Glover: The films for the songs Deadwing and Halo are quite image-heavy. How long would it take to do something of this nature?

Lasse Hoile: When you get the idea in your head and have the visuals you need, then a couple of days, followed by getting away from it for a couple of days, before returning to it with fresh eyes to make some adjustments. We also had to reuse and repeat a little to make the most out of what was available at the time.

Carl Glover: Were there any other ideas for the cover or was it something that was instantly liked?

Lasse Hoile: It was one of the scenes from the script (I think), SW had a pretty good idea what he wanted for the cover which is what we ended up with.

Carl Glover: What is your most vivid memory of working on Deadwing?

Lasse Hoile: There were so many, it's so hard to single out one specific moment as I think the whole experience from ending the In Absentia tour to filming a documentary about the making of Deadwing, staying in the UK for a period to do some filming, meeting everybody, discussing ideas and concepts. Also making the live visuals and images for the album, to touring it a little bit. It was a good time, I felt that things were going onwards and upwards.

Mike Bennion: I have fond memories of me, Steven and Lasse driving around Wales looking for suitable images that would tie in with the Deadwing project. We had a specific set of images in mind but Lasse always put his own stamp on them. He says relatively little but it would always make us laugh when he'd come out with something. He does take up a lot of space in a small car though!

Carl Glover: I guess it also marks the end of the 'slideshow' era as you do more moving footage for the projections.

There aren't any films by you made exclusively from still images after Deadwing. Some may feature occasional stills but are supported by moving footage.

Lasse Hoile: Yes, the budget increased a bit when the venues got larger which was good to see. I guess being a photographer at heart I still like the power a still image can have. Perhaps more than ever now because of lower attention spans - a simple image can do more than a fast cut edit.

Back then Gavin and I would talk a lot about ideas to enhance the synchronisation of the films to the music, trying do new things and build it all up more. It's a bit ironic that Gavin now plays with King Crimson who have perhaps the most minimalistic rock show on earth, though I think Neurosis also only used white light and nothing else. It seems to work really well, it's not about anything else except for the music.

Carl Glover: What films did Gavin have a say in? I'm guessing Halo is one of them, as it looks like it's edited on the beats.

Lasse Hoile: I really just did what came to mind, presented it to the band and either got the OK or suggestions. With Gavin it was more about technically how we could do it, not the content itself.

Gavin Harrison: On our early *In Absentia* tours Lasse triggered the films from a DVD player. It was completely manual and of course impossible to be in perfect sync. We hadn't figured out a way to do that with the equipment we had available to us at that time. When *Deadwing* came around our tech Jason Birnie, Lasse and myself worked out a system of triggering the films from a laptop that could receive midi notes. That way it encouraged Lasse to compose films that could do dramatic things exactly in time with powerful events in the music - which was much more effective and impressive from the viewer's perspective.

Carl Glover: What was Lasse like to tour with at the time?

Gavin Harrison: A fucking nightmare. He never stopped moaning or eating Chocolate Oreos.

Carl Glover: Whilst putting together and artworking the various formats of *Deadwing* at the time, Mike and Steven came round to my place and we planned the 72 page CD/DVDA special edition on the living-room floor. Mike had 35 A4 sheets with his collages on, some of which incorporated your photographs. It was a memorable day. Mike was definitely involved regarding the packaging, but was he involved in the decision making process for the projections?

Lasse Hoile: Not really, I think Mike was busy with something else at that point. *Deadwing* was very much based on the film script/project written by SW and Mike, and since Mike is a very capable artist and SW had some ideas for the special edition, I didn't have that much input since it was their baby.

Mike Bennion: Lasse is gifted at complementing the music with his images, not overpowering the band. And a more loyal, hardworking collaborator would be hard to find. The guy deserves a medal.

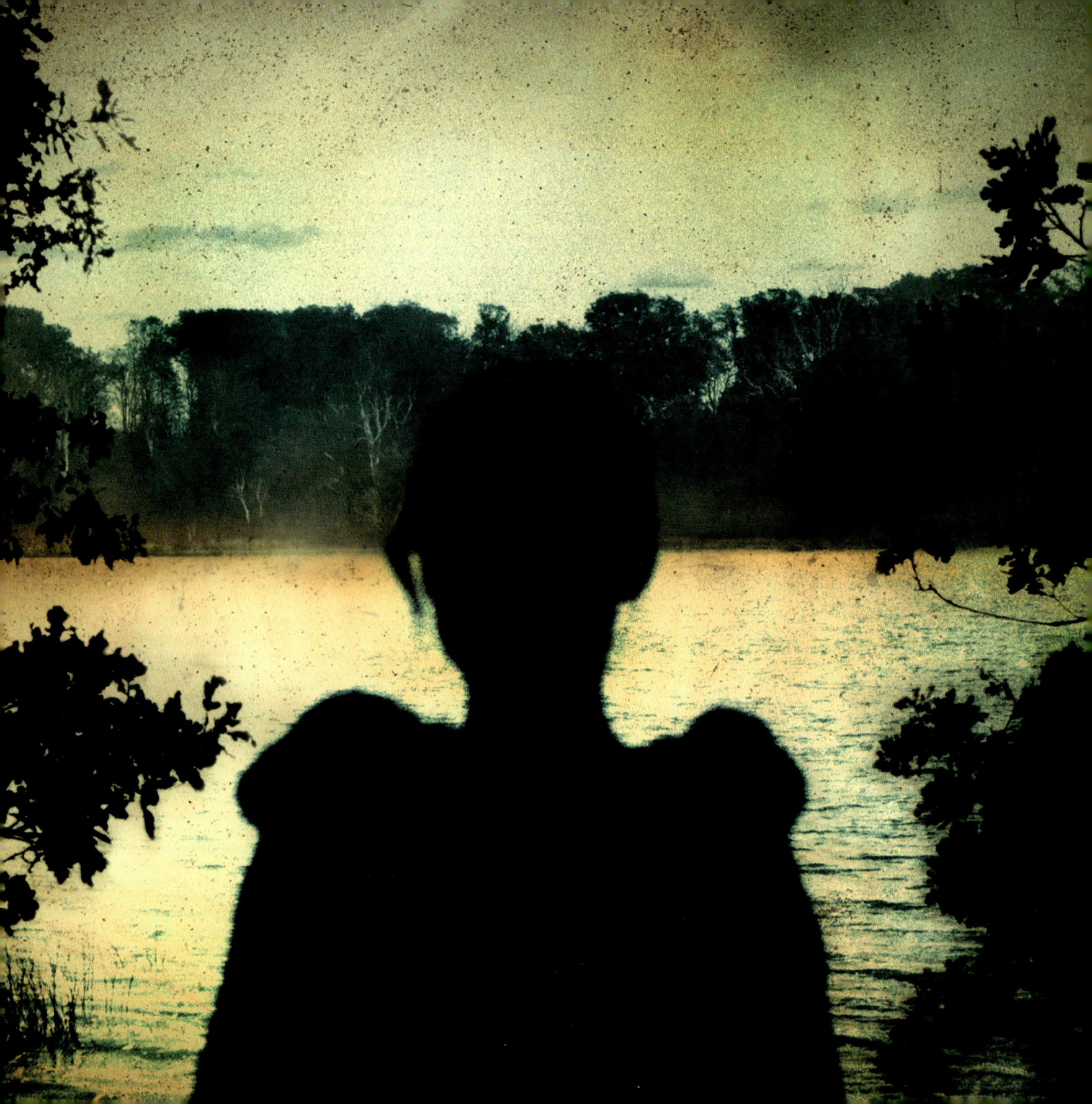

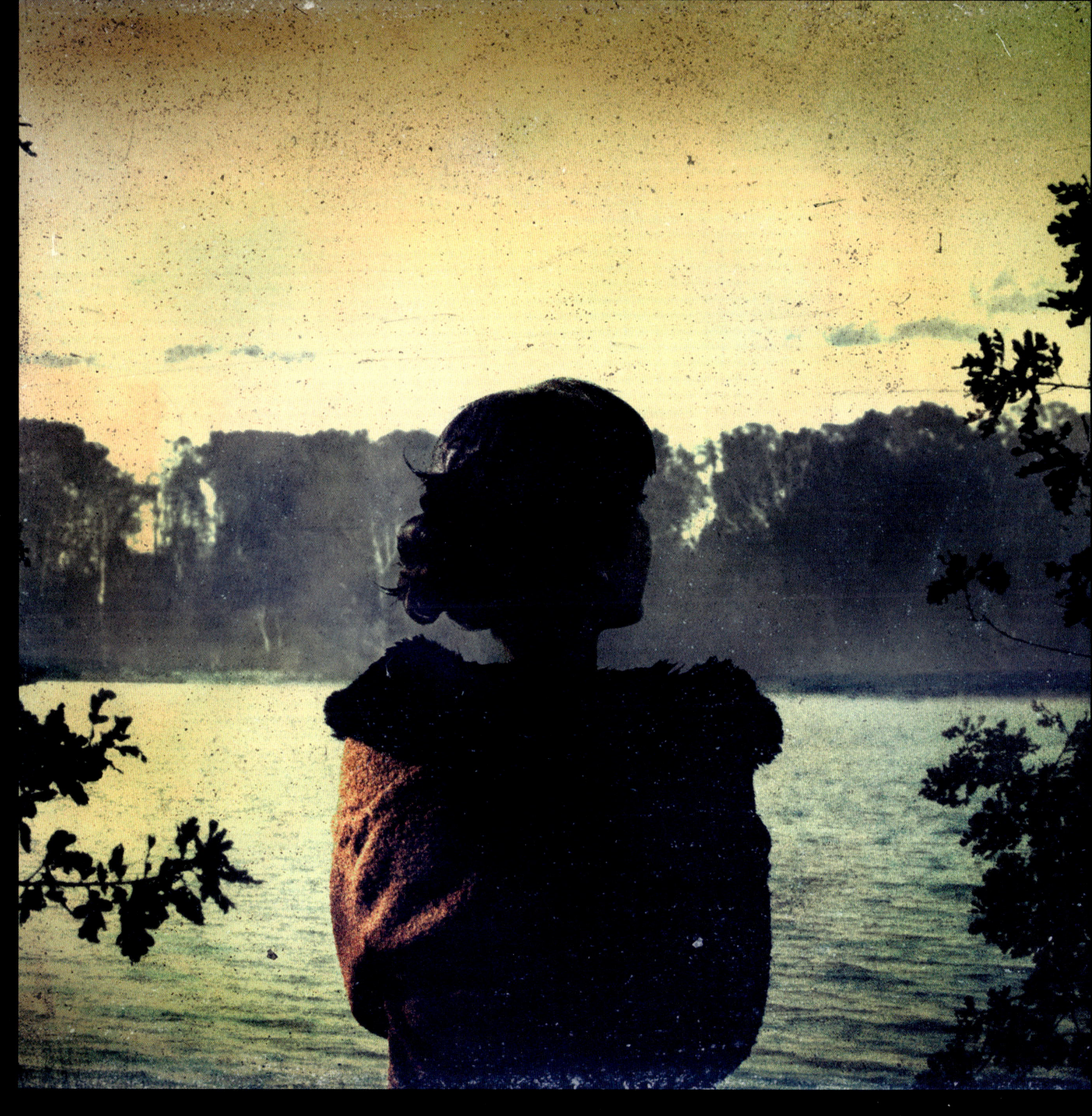

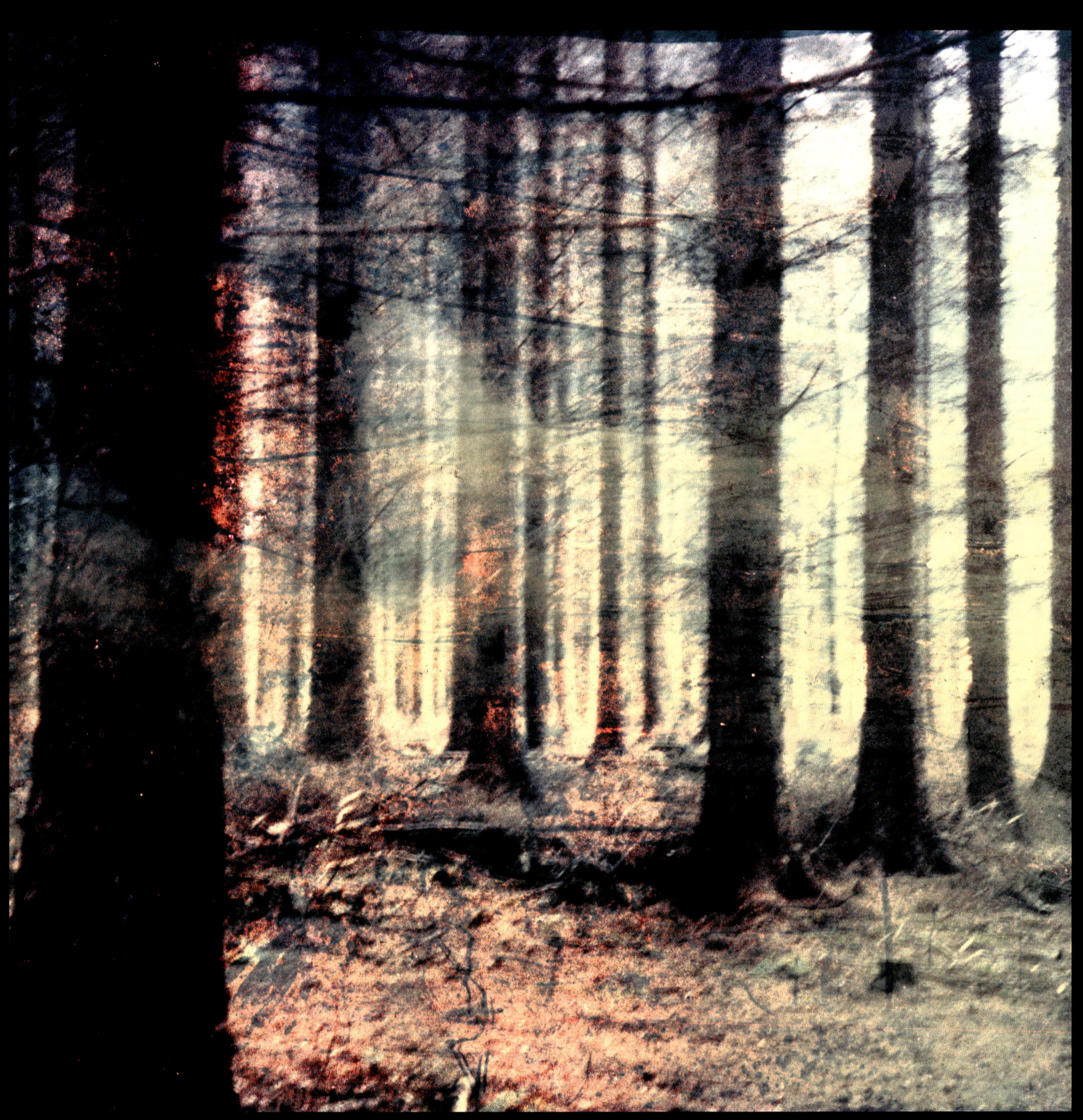

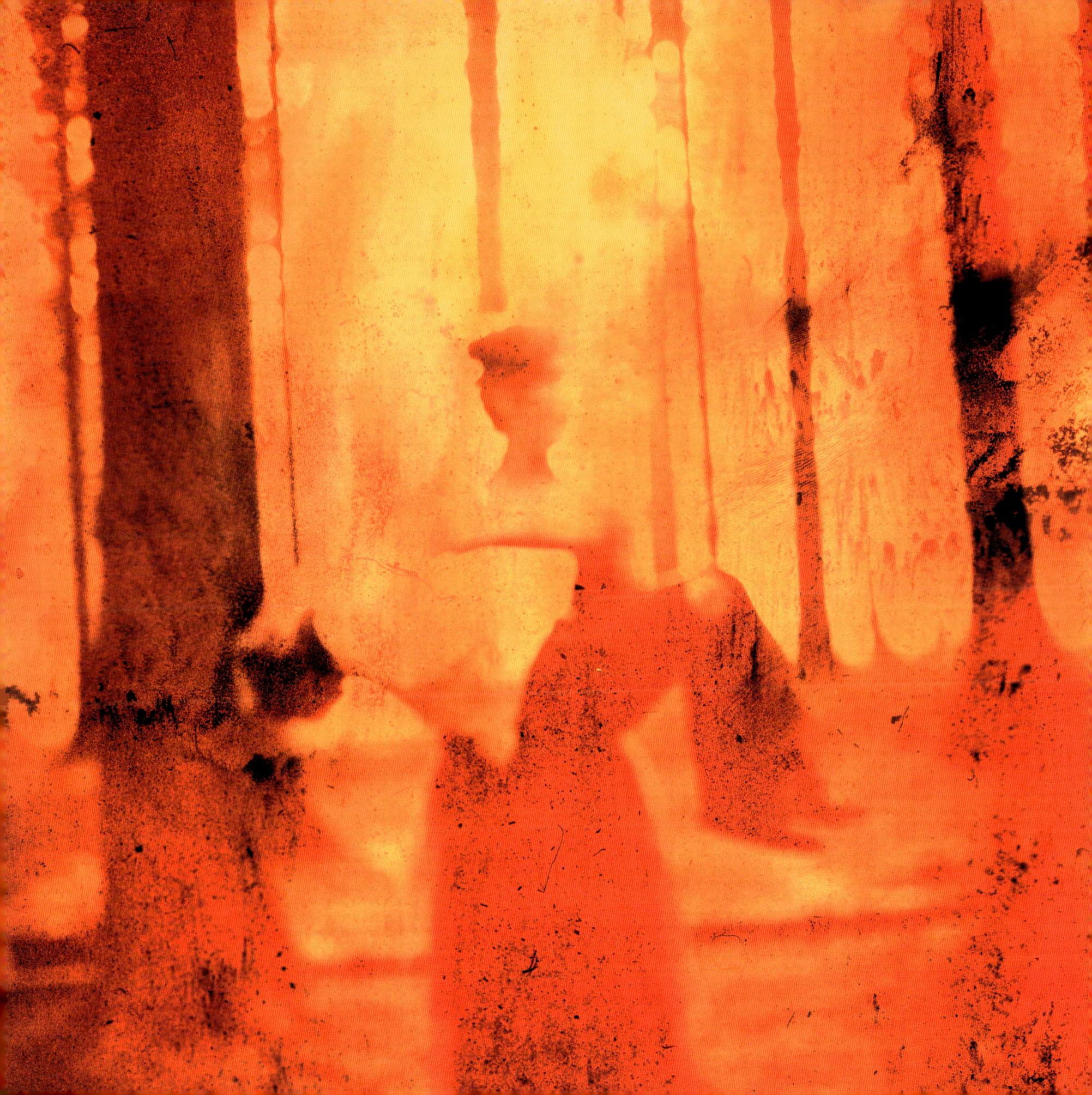

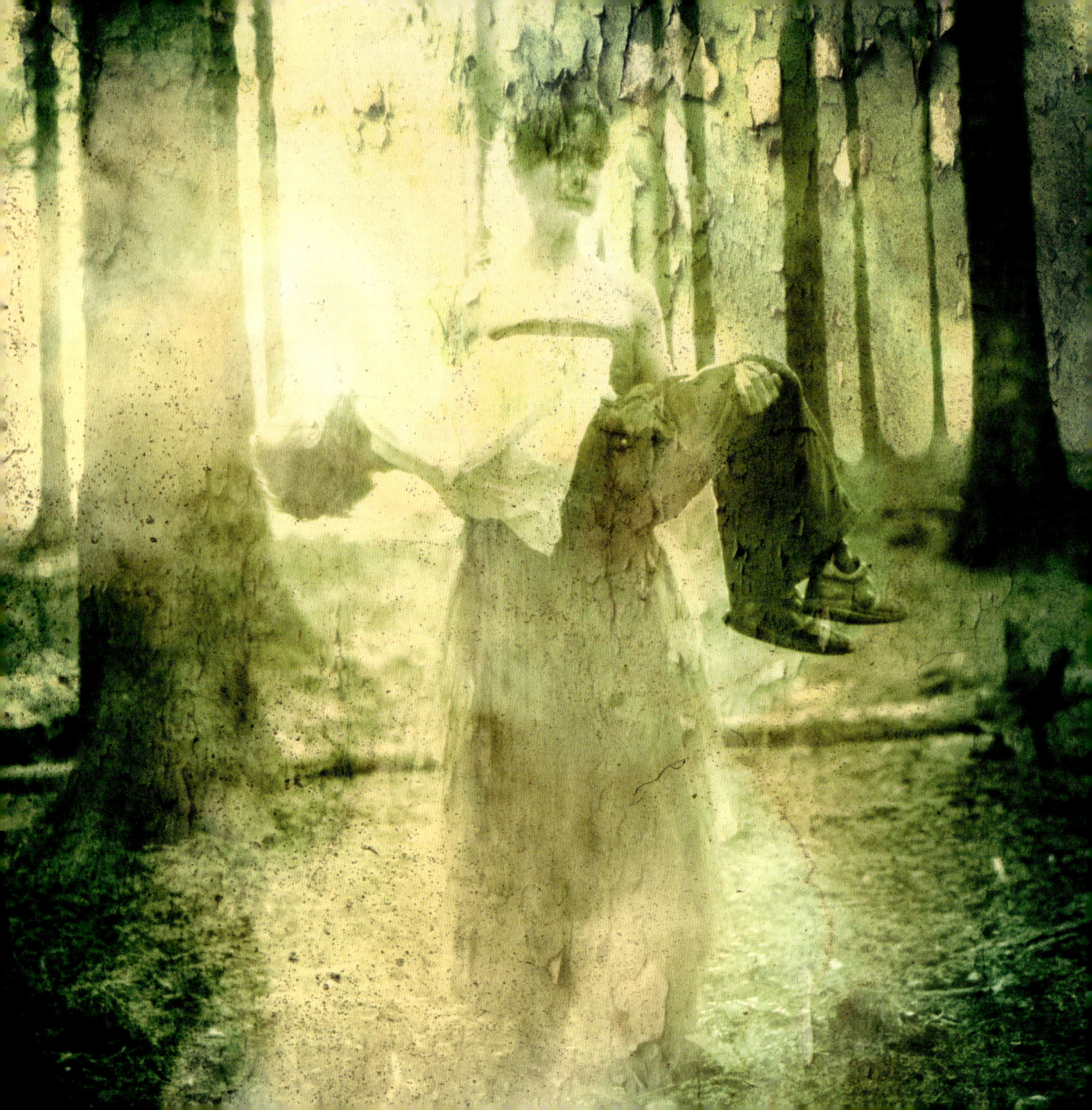

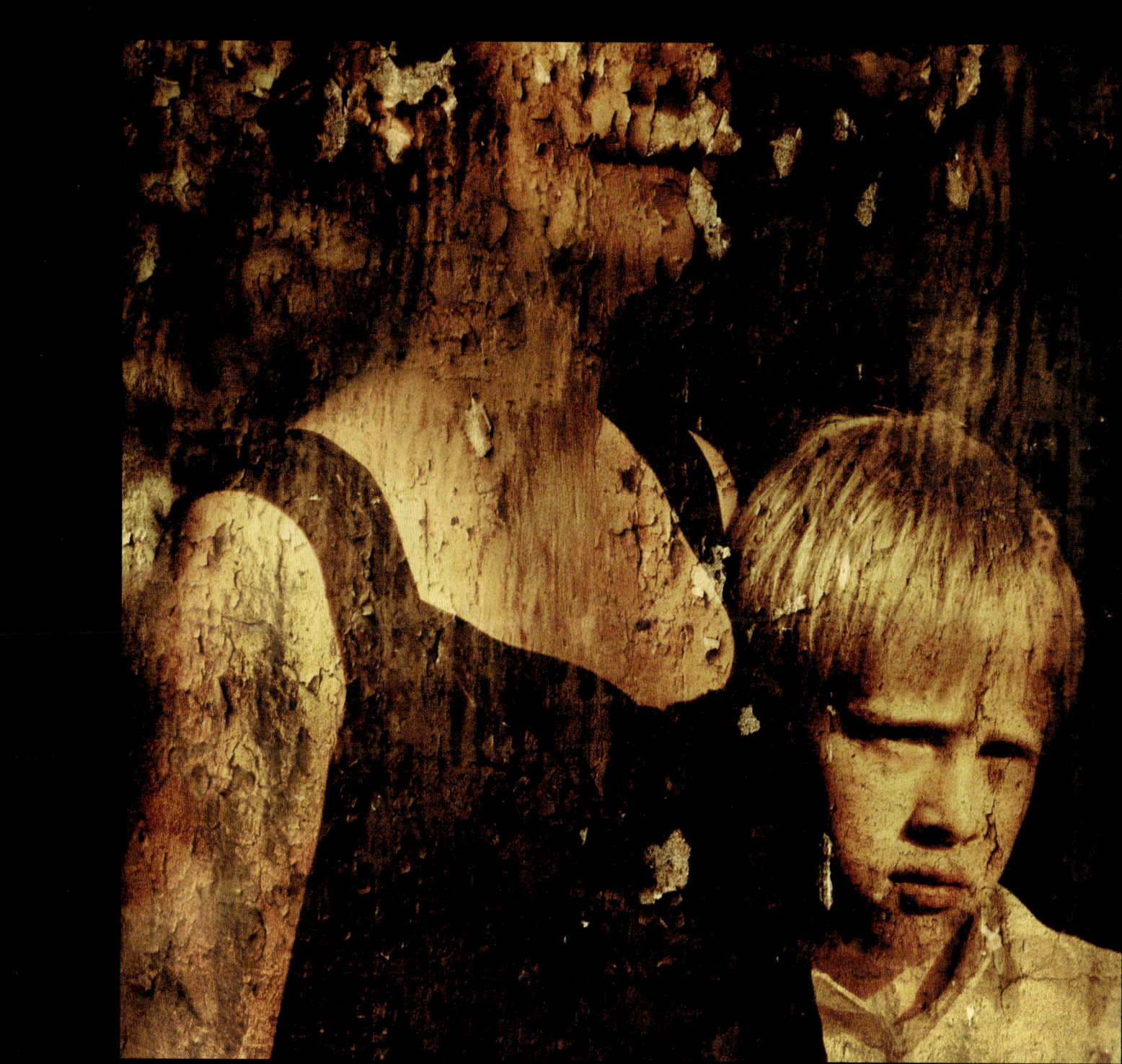

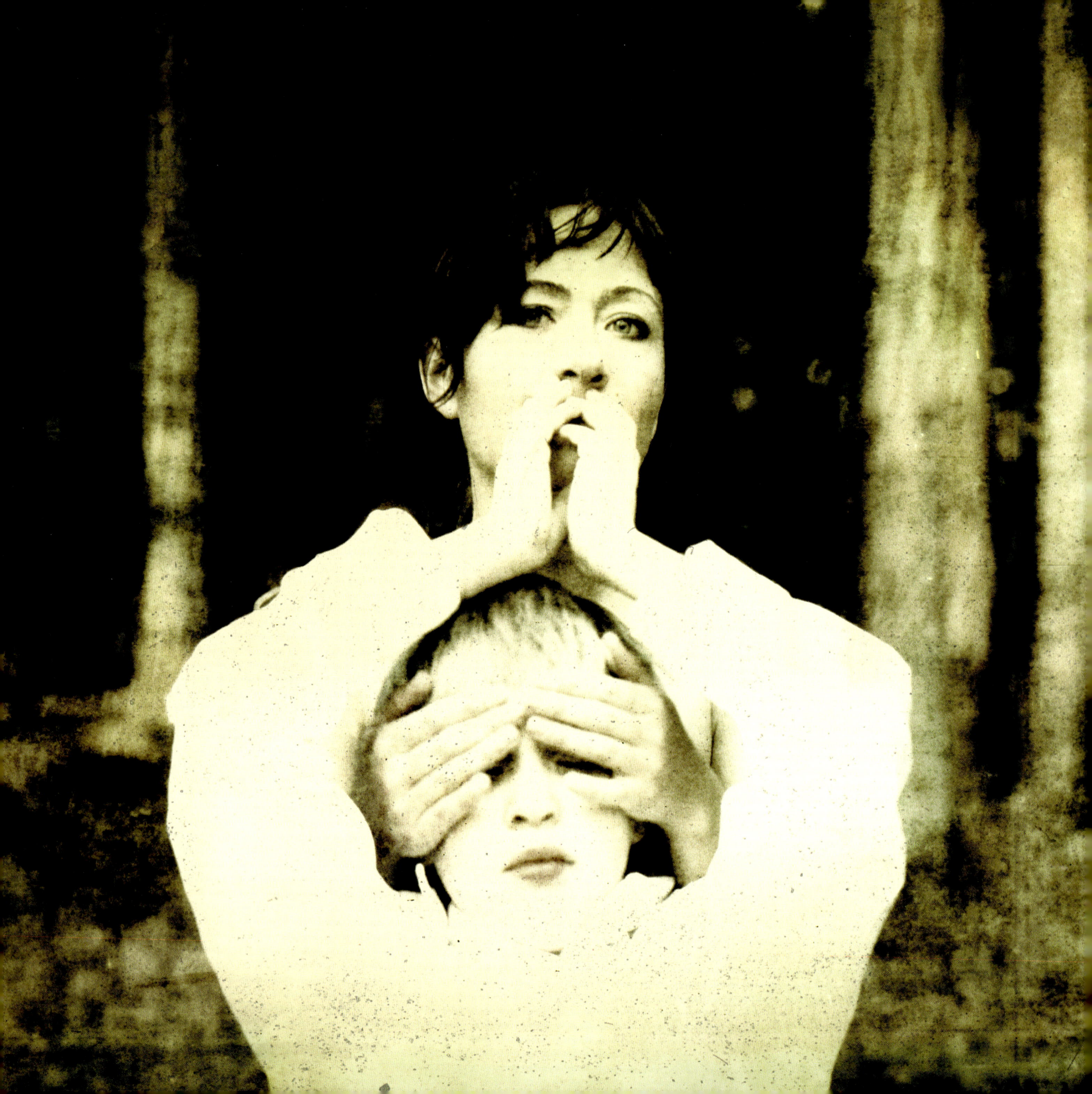

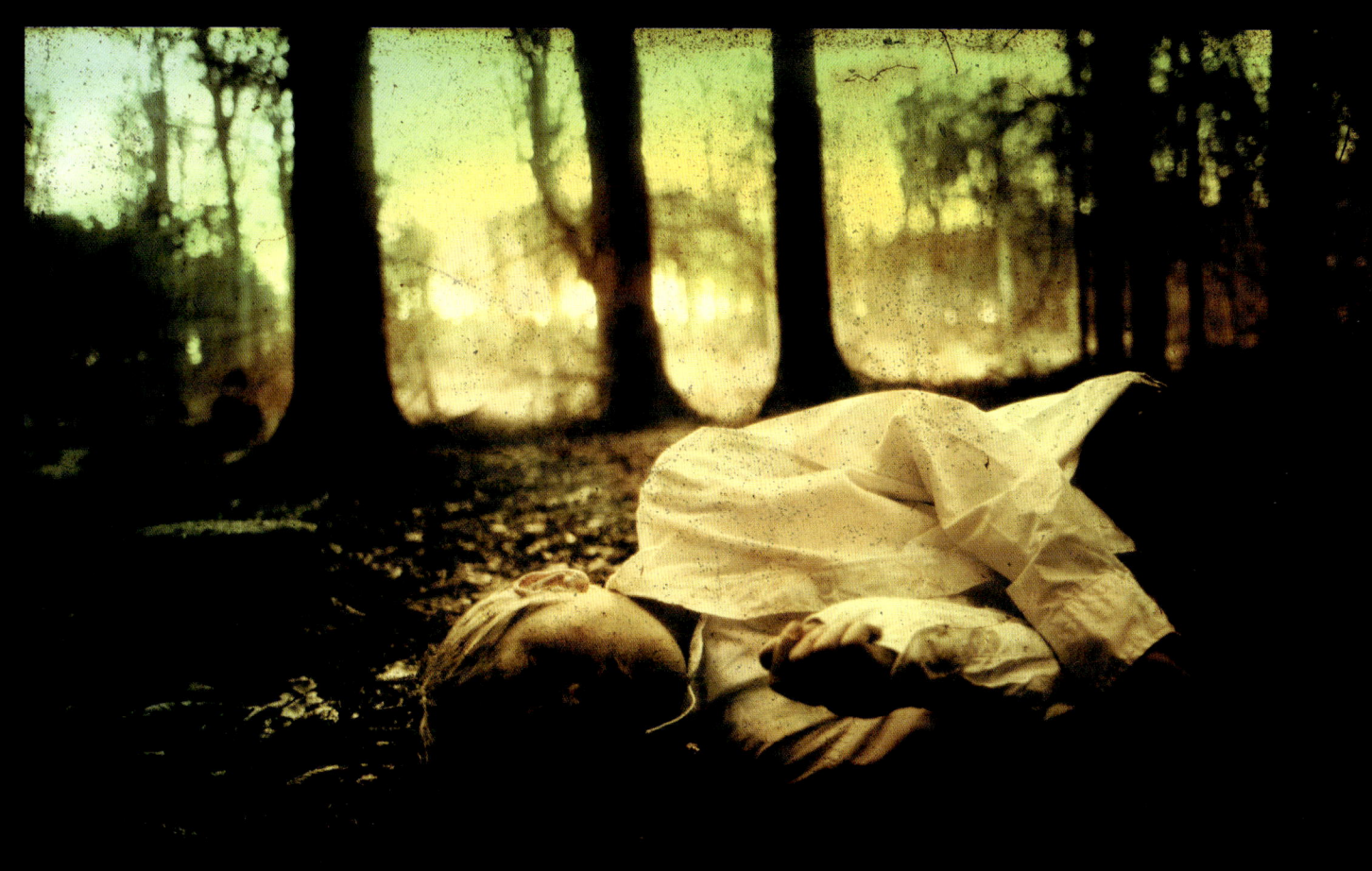

DEADWING 2005

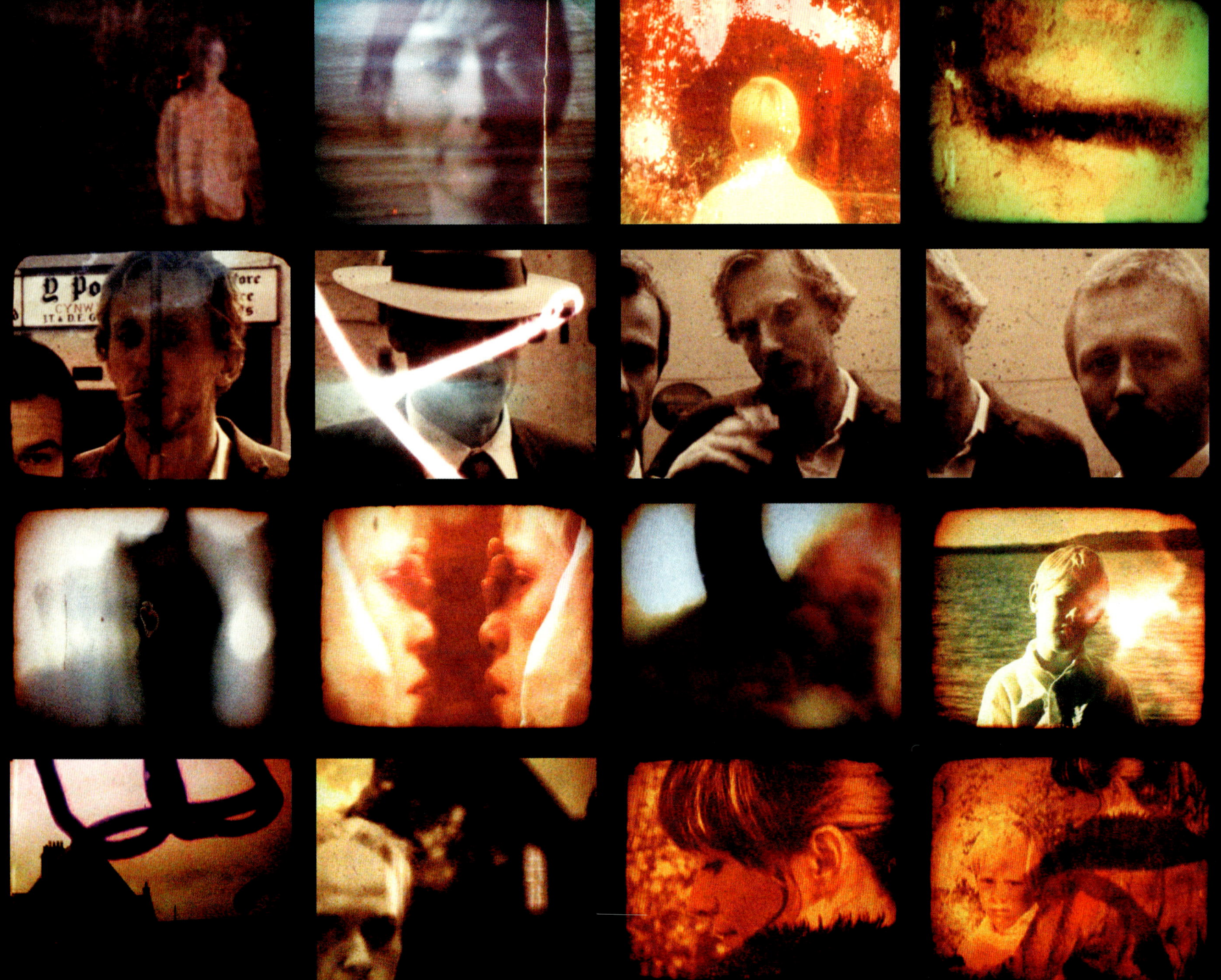

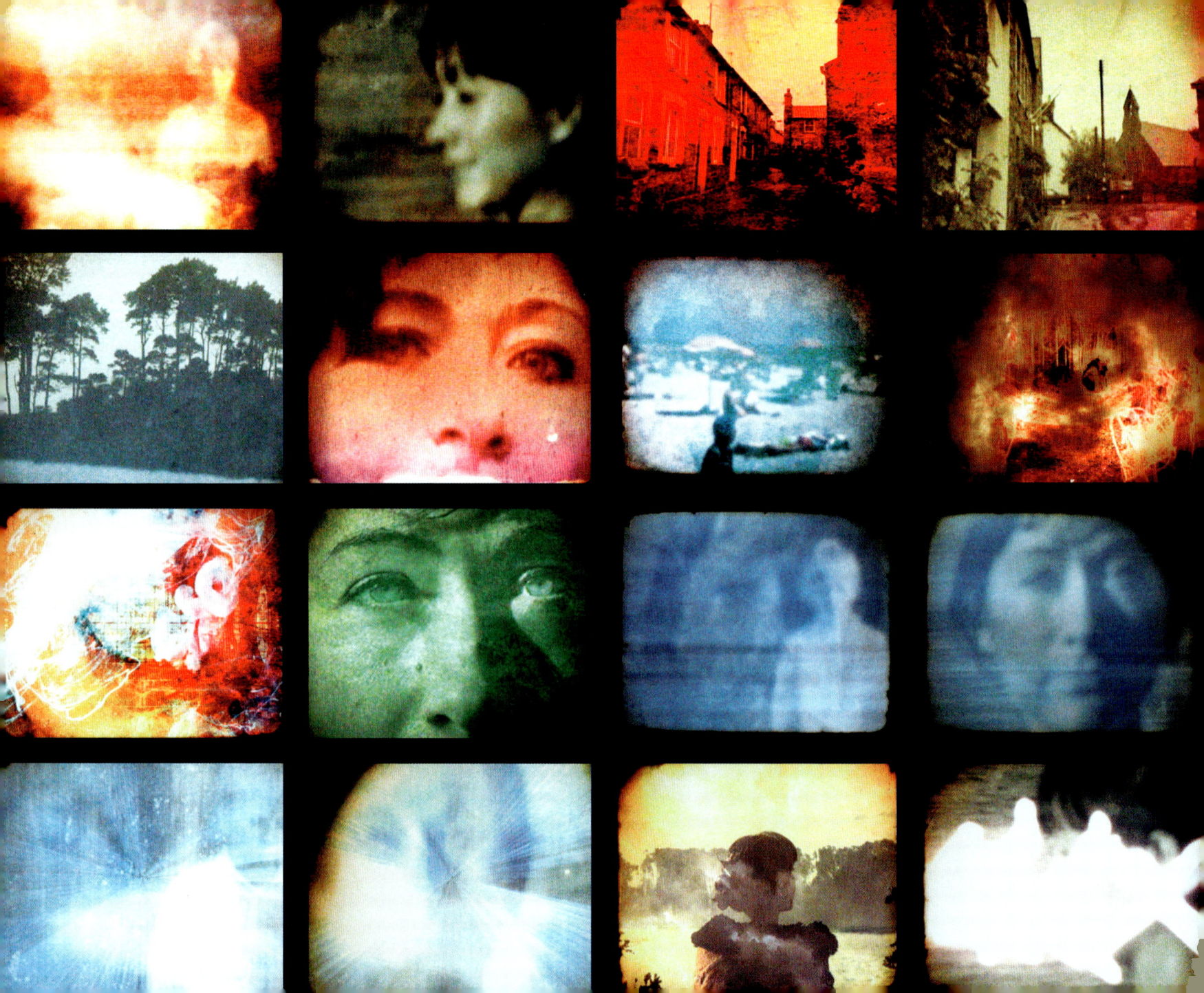

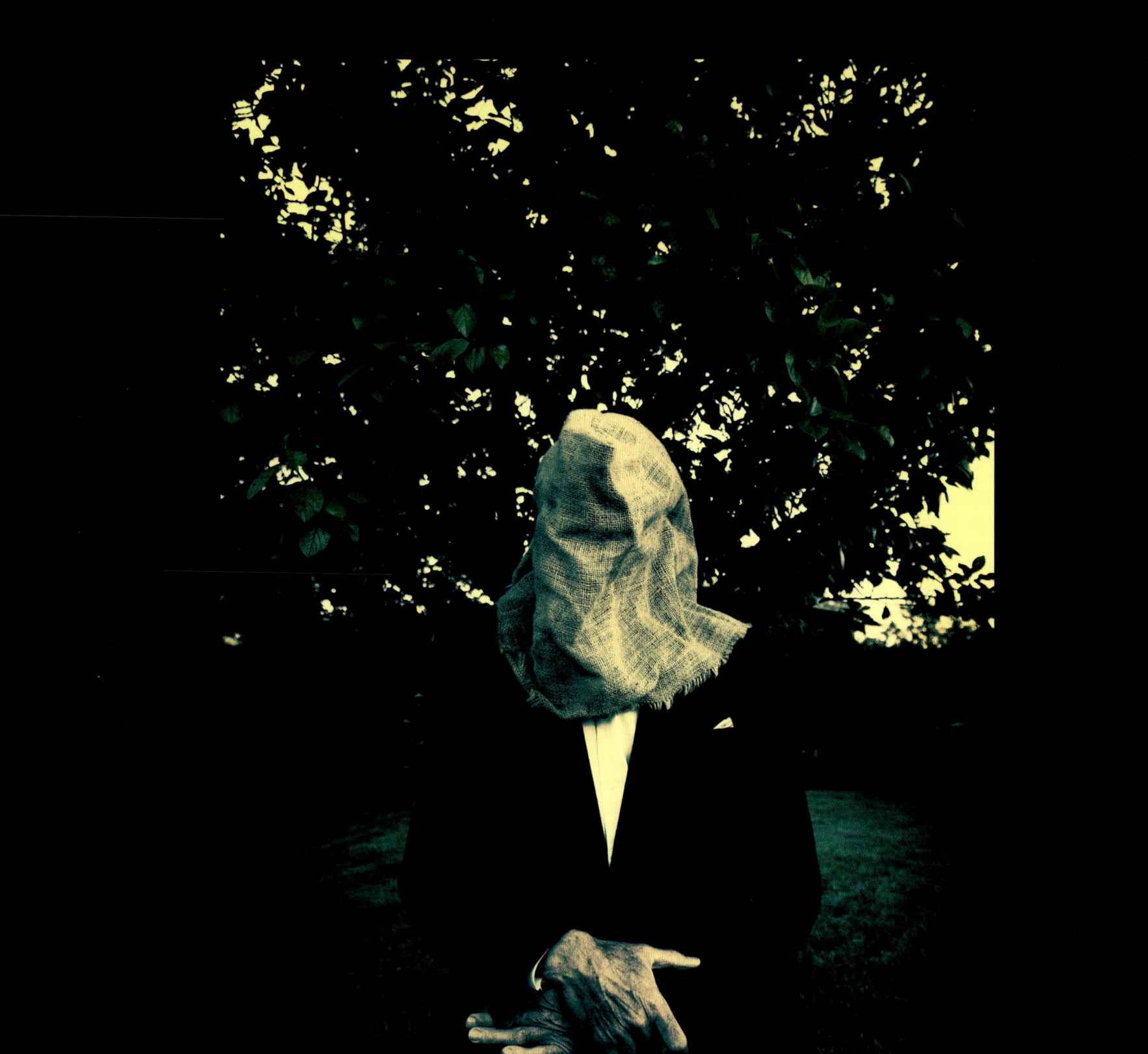

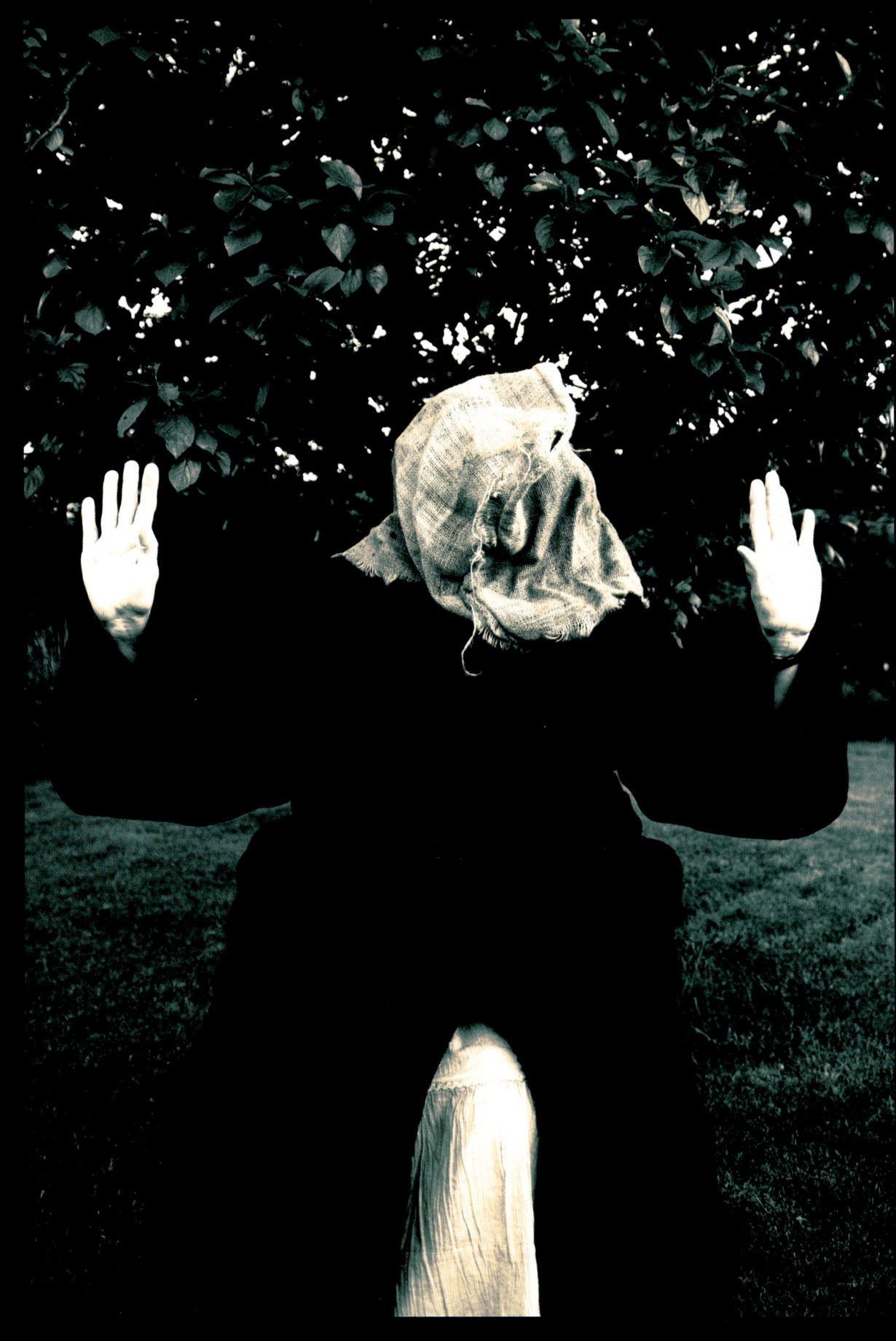

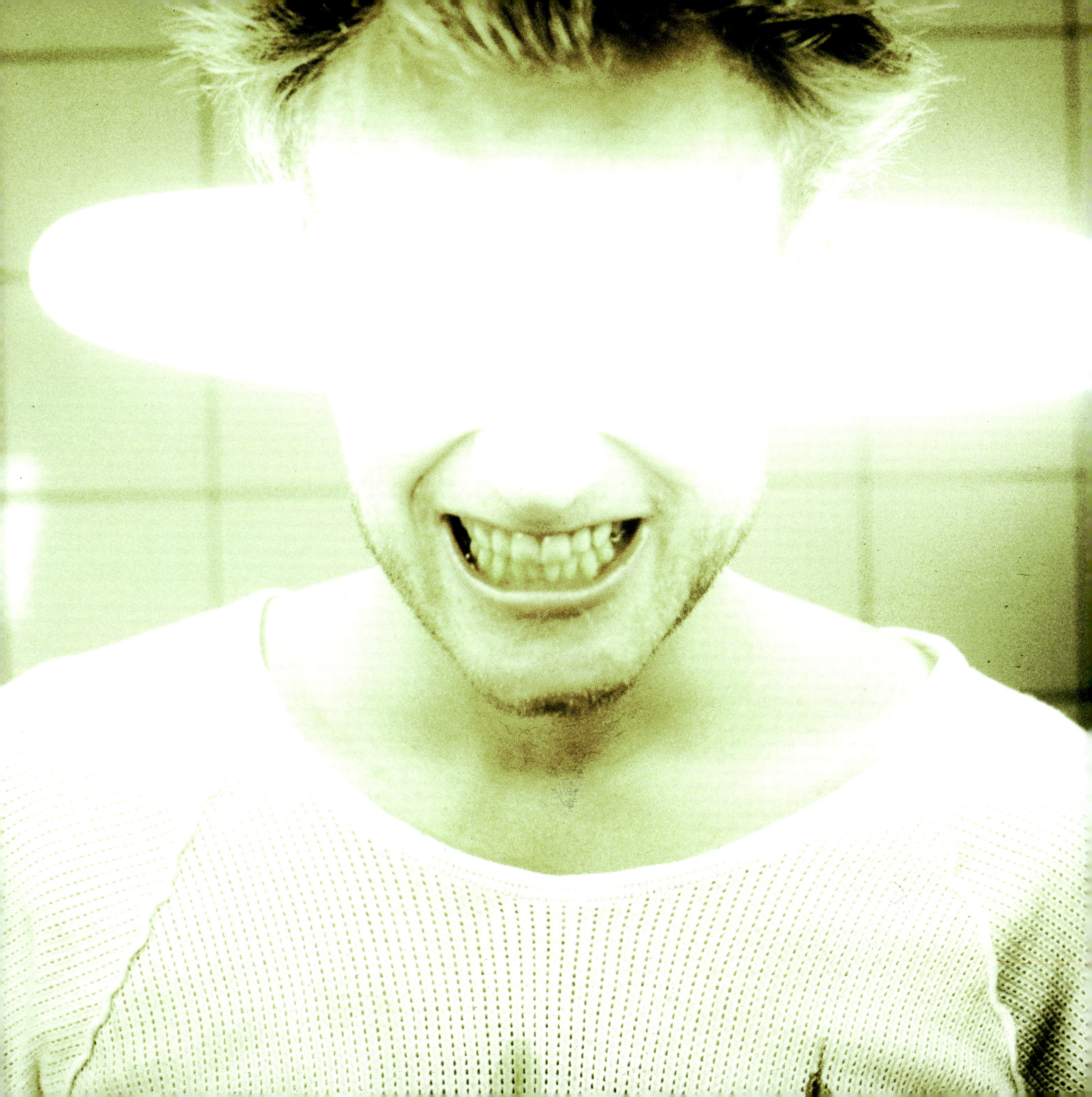

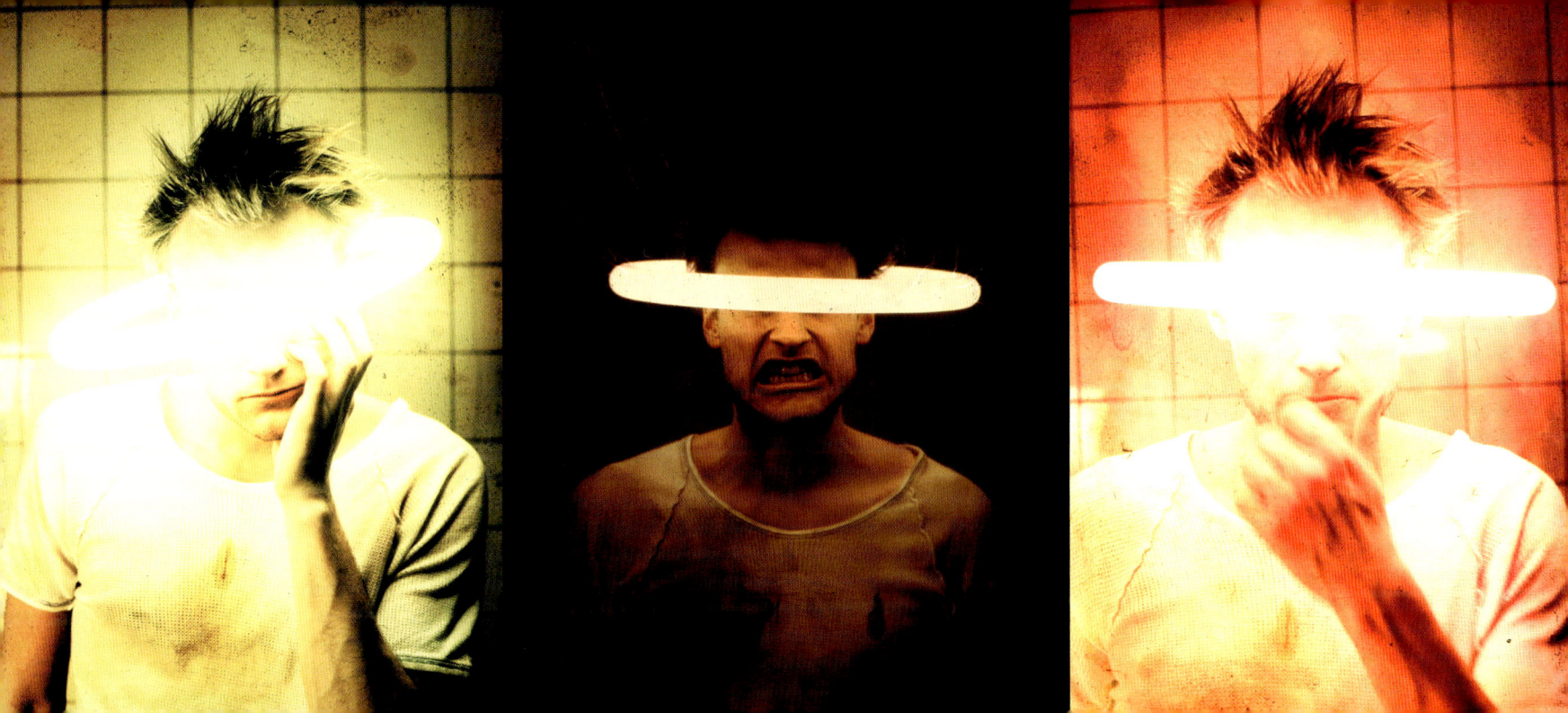

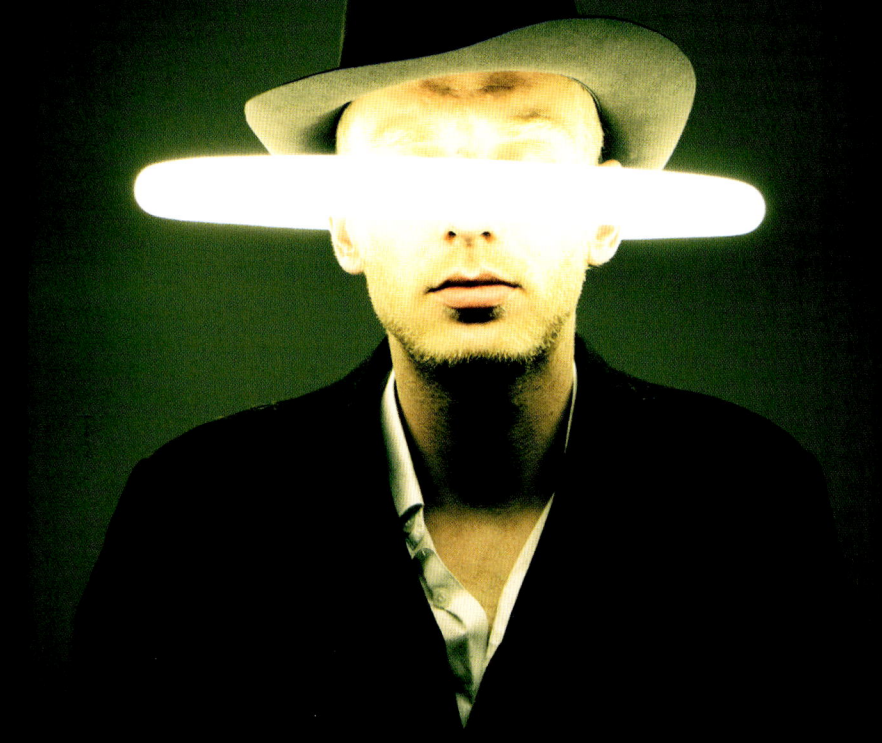

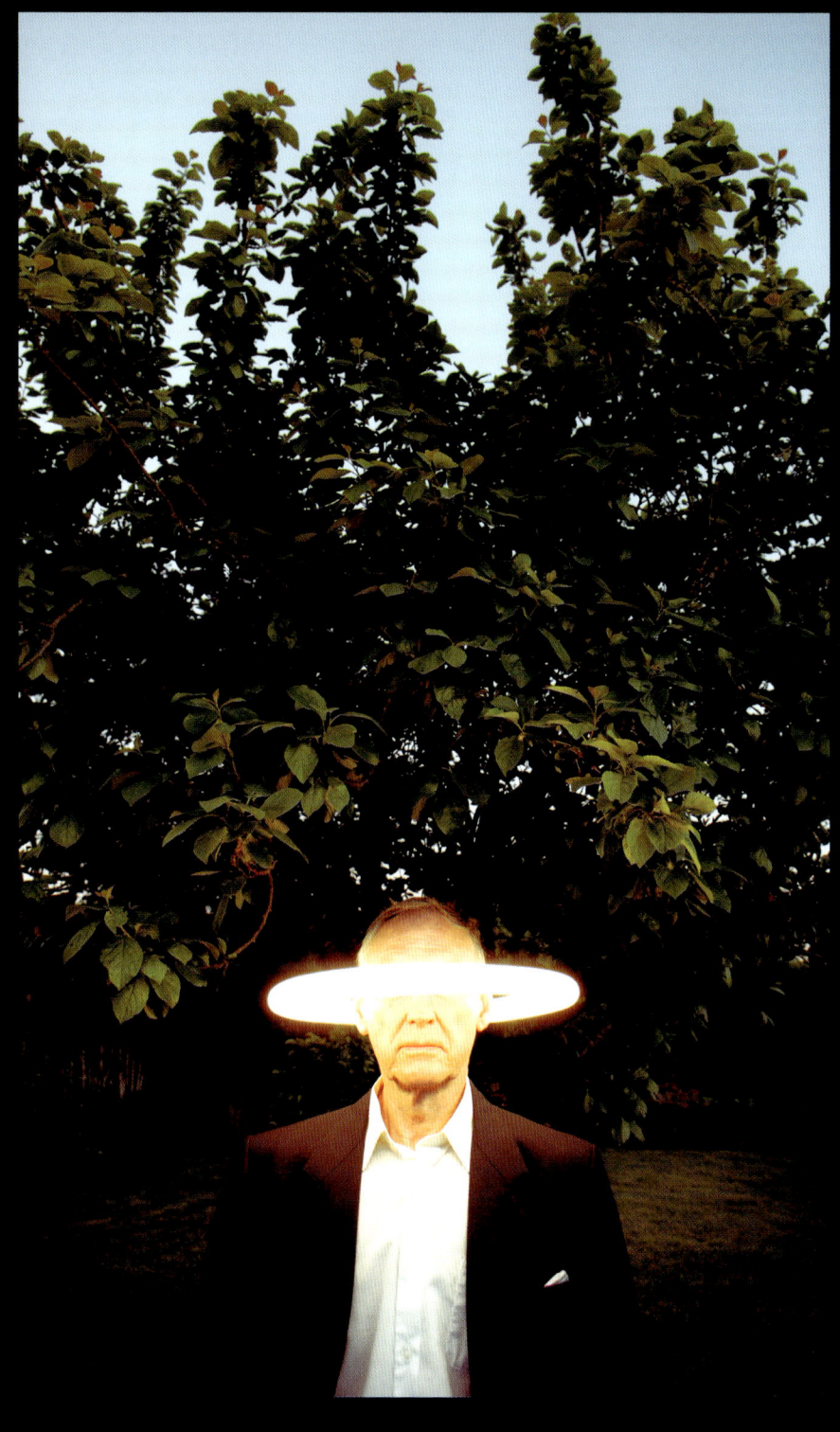

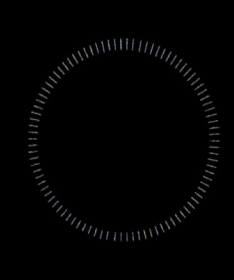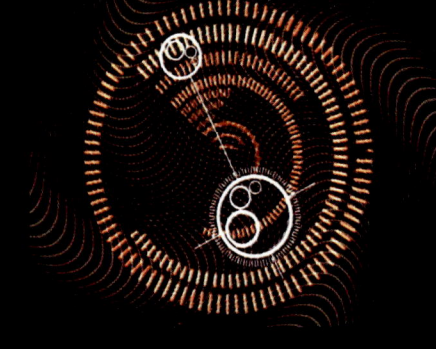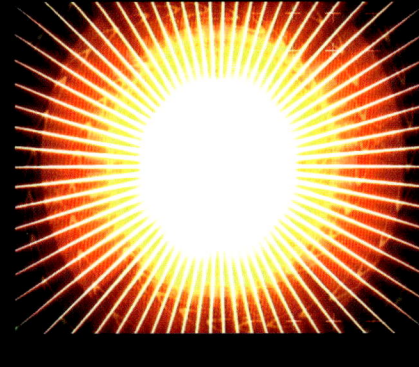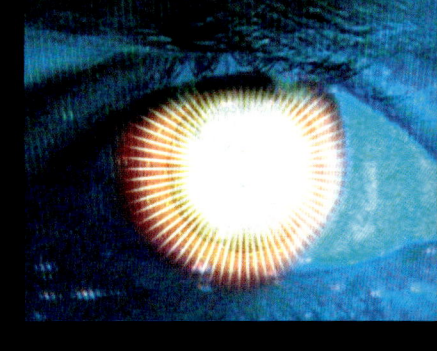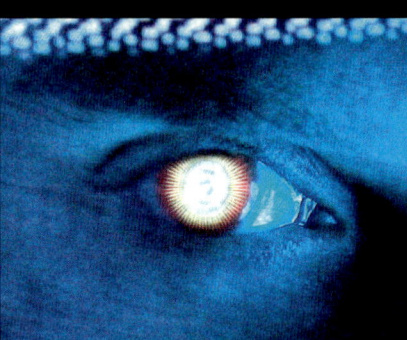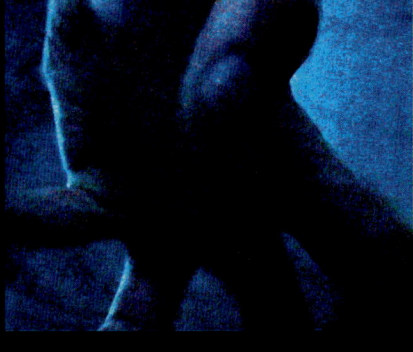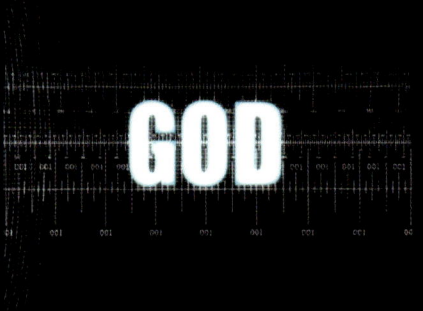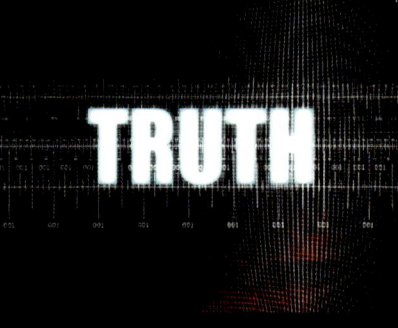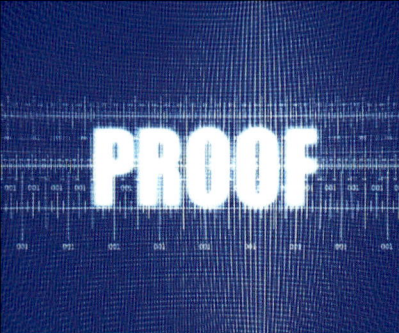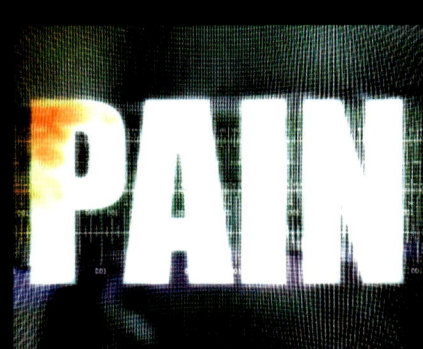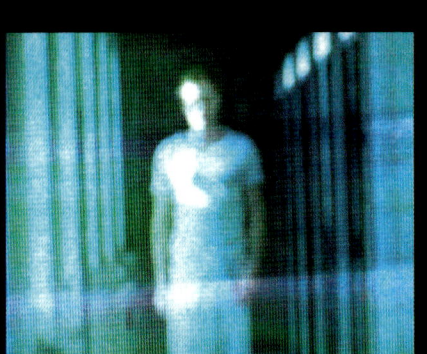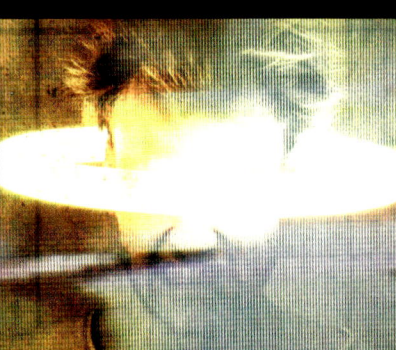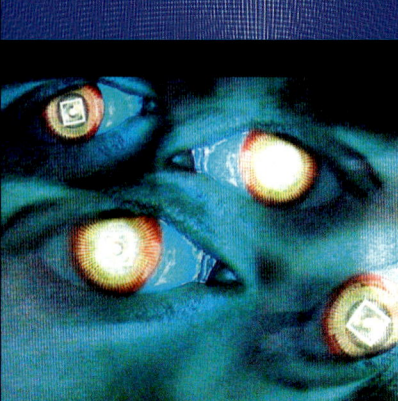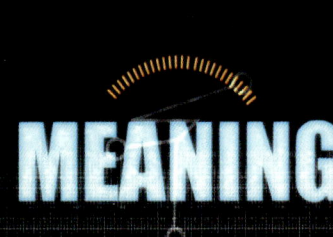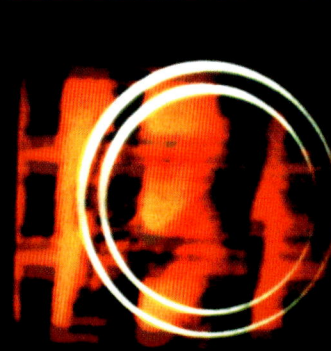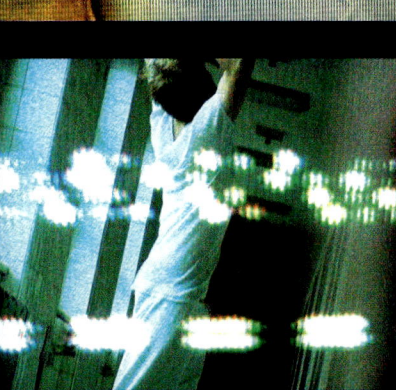

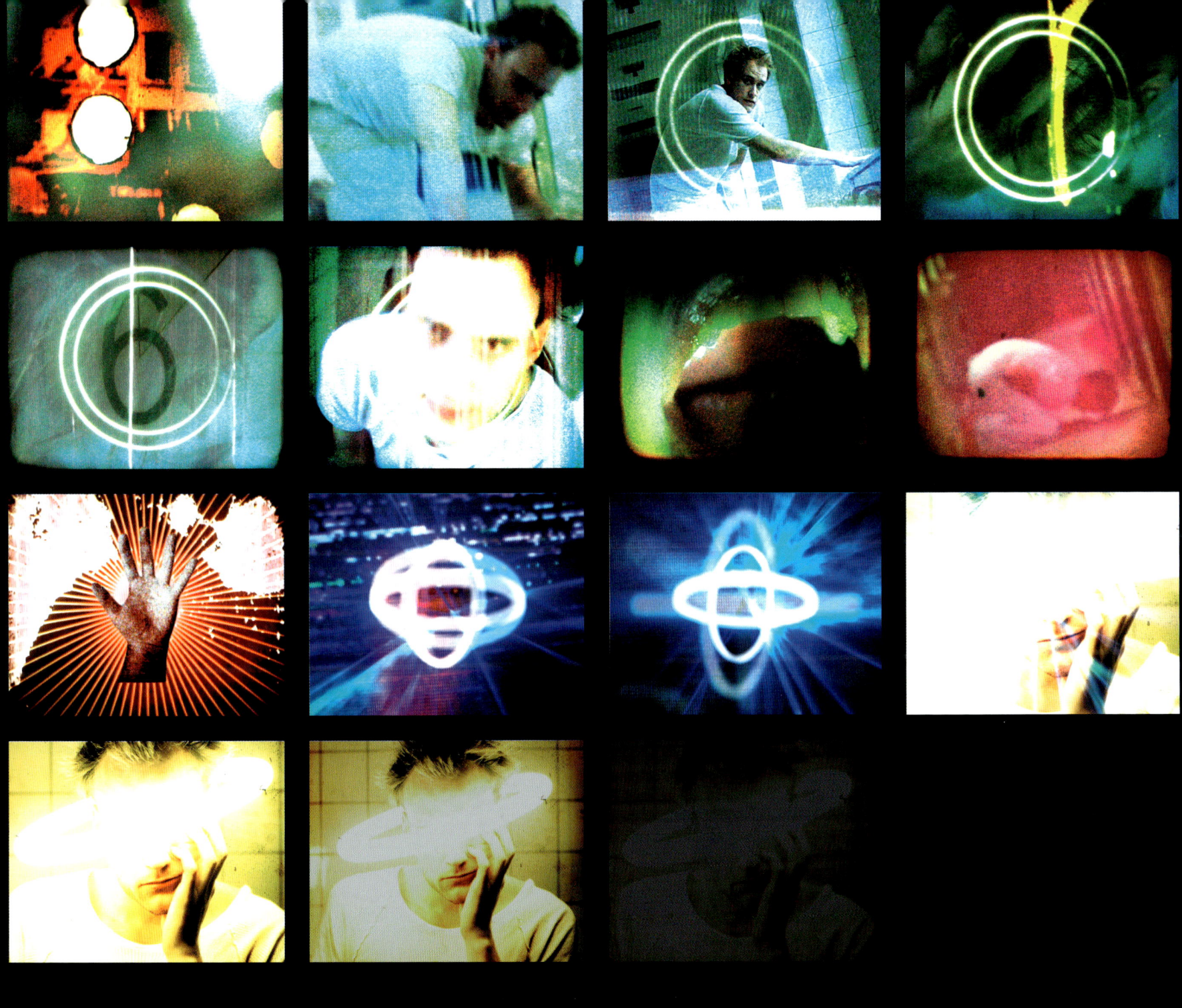

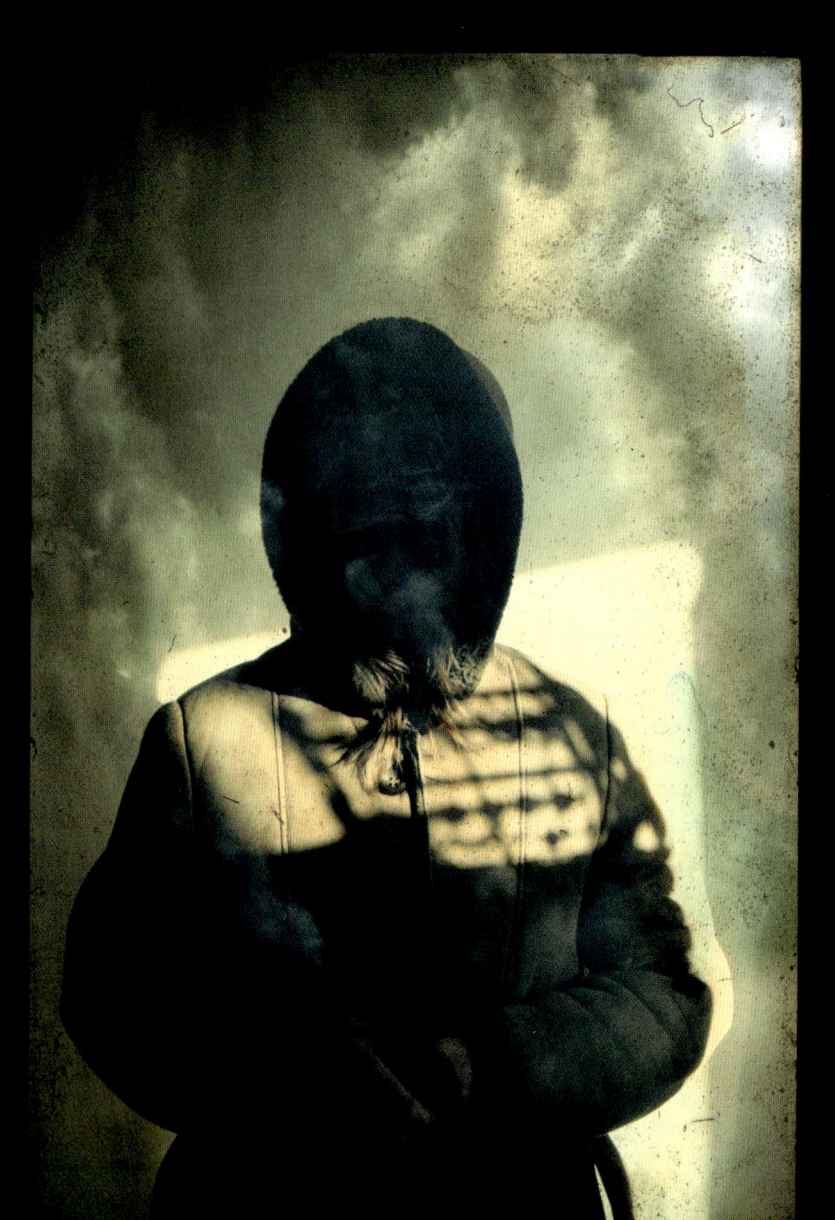
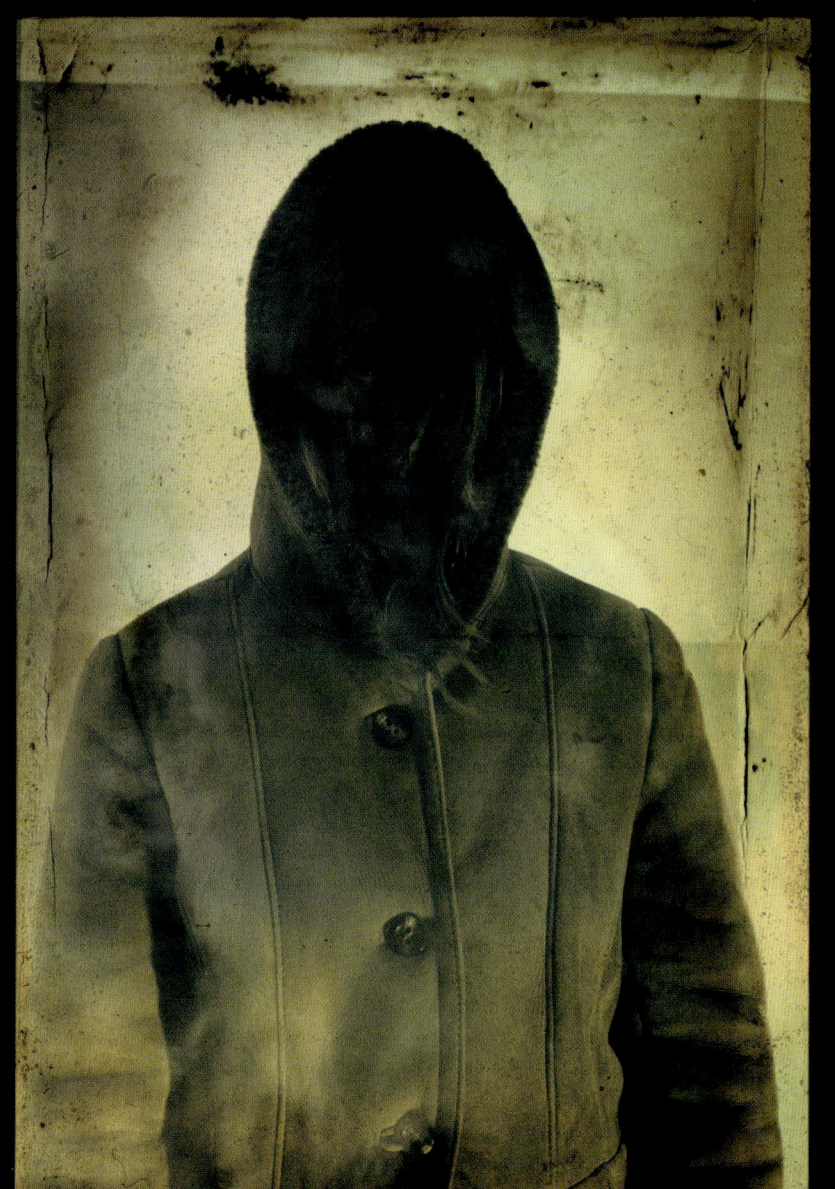

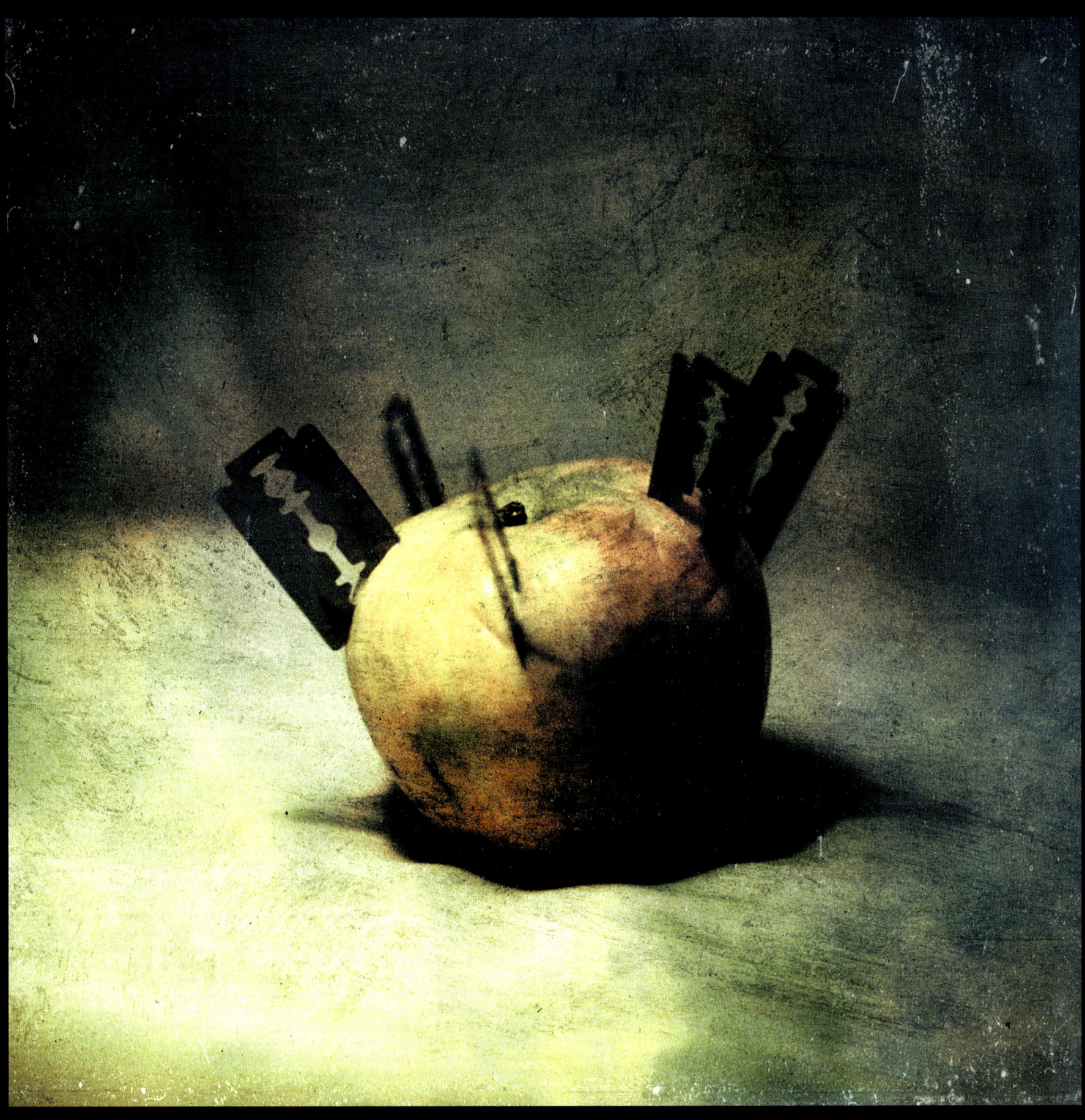

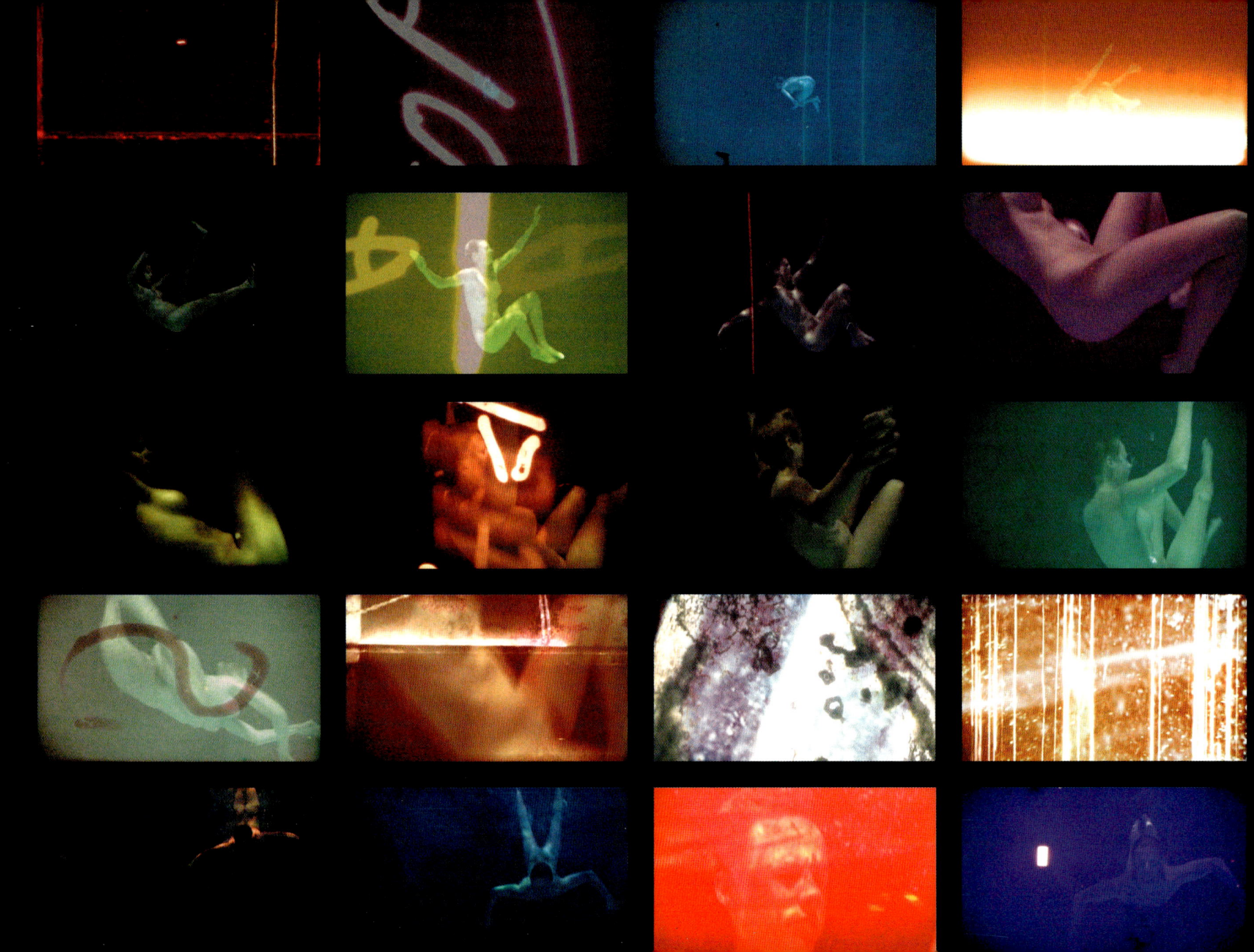

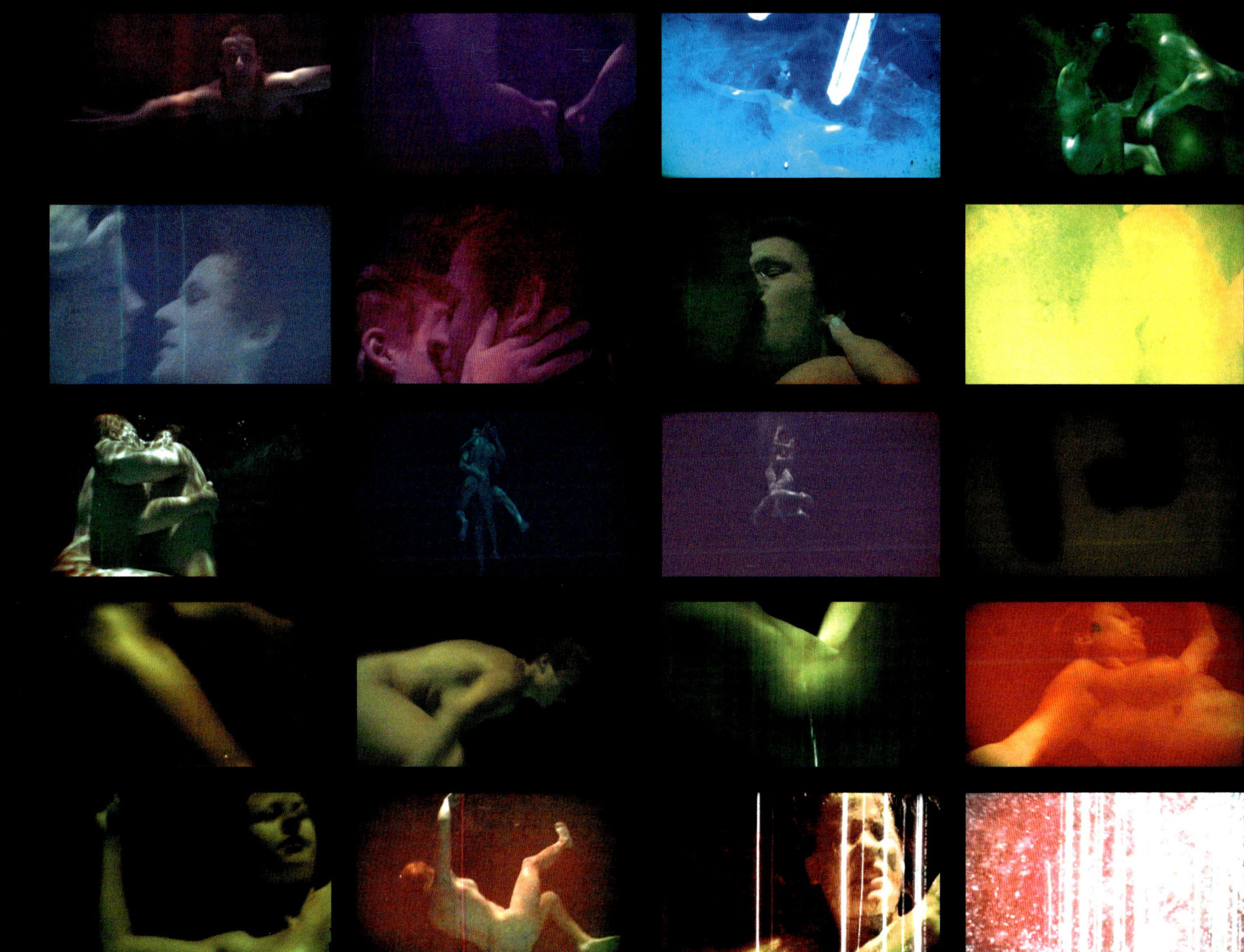

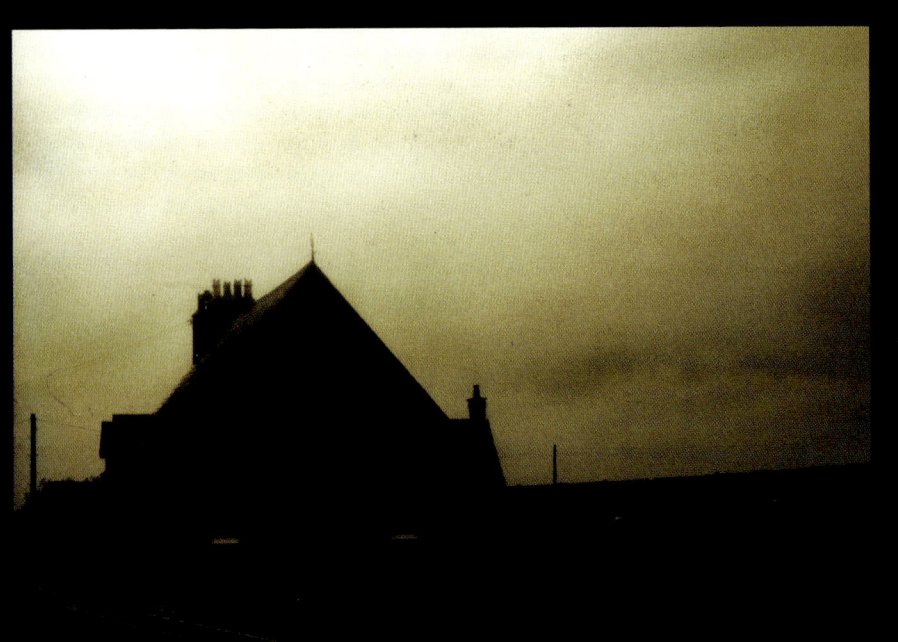
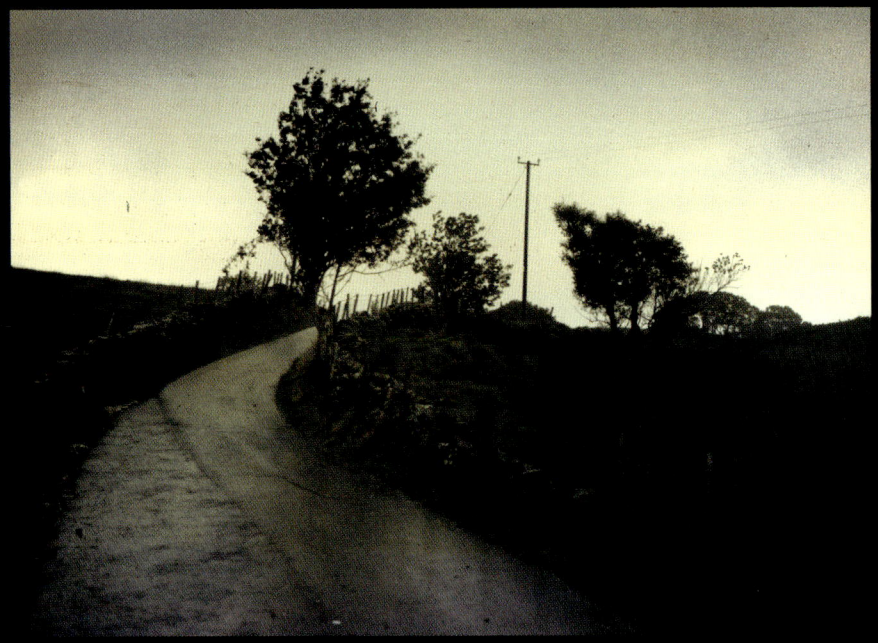
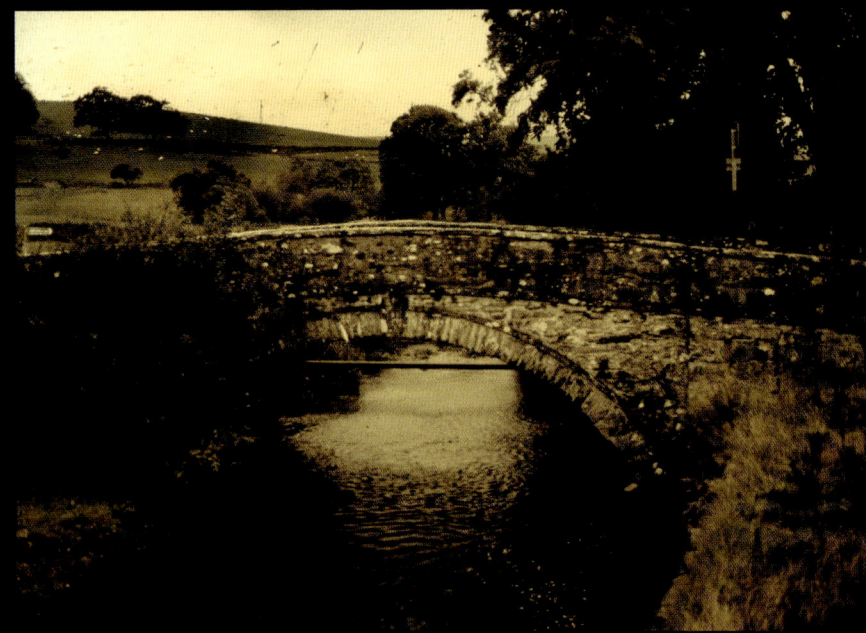
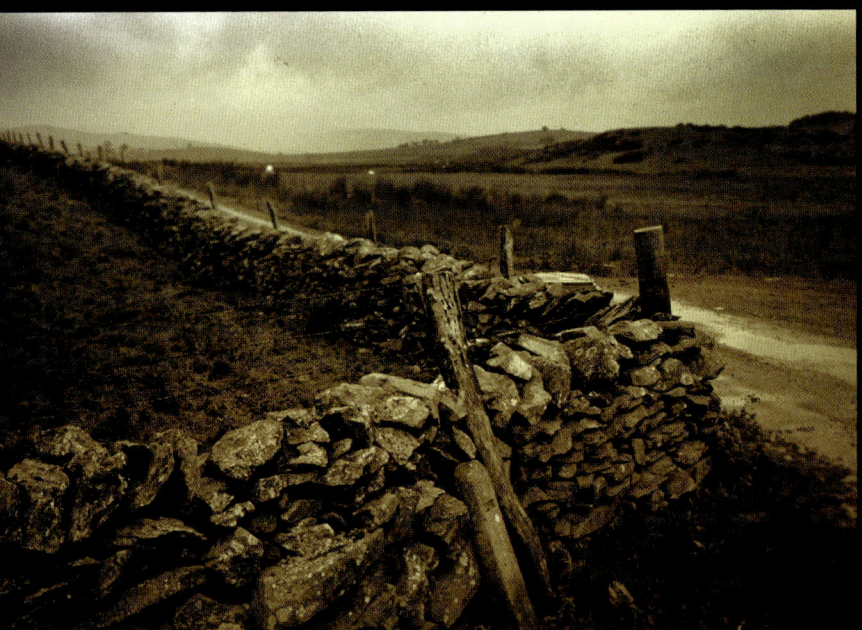

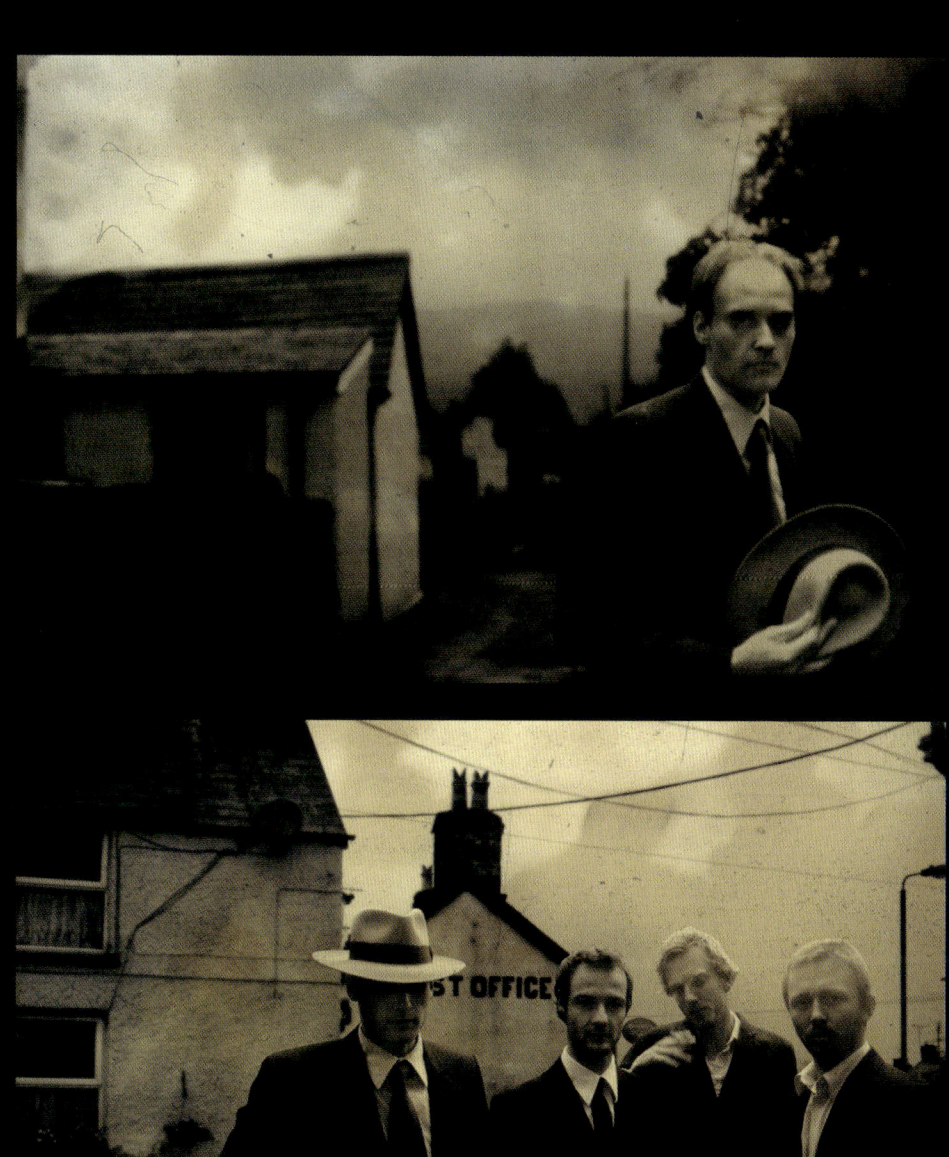

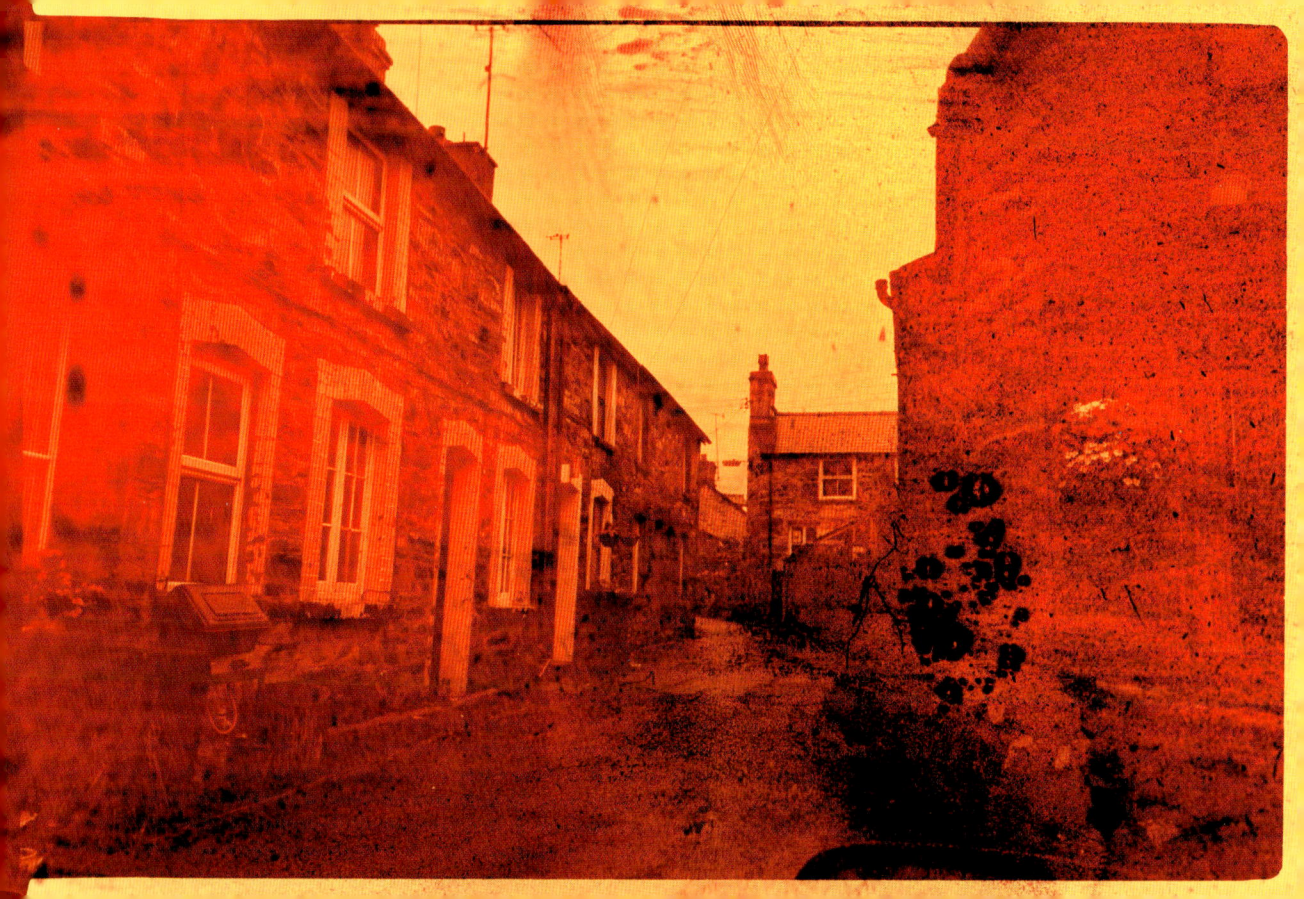

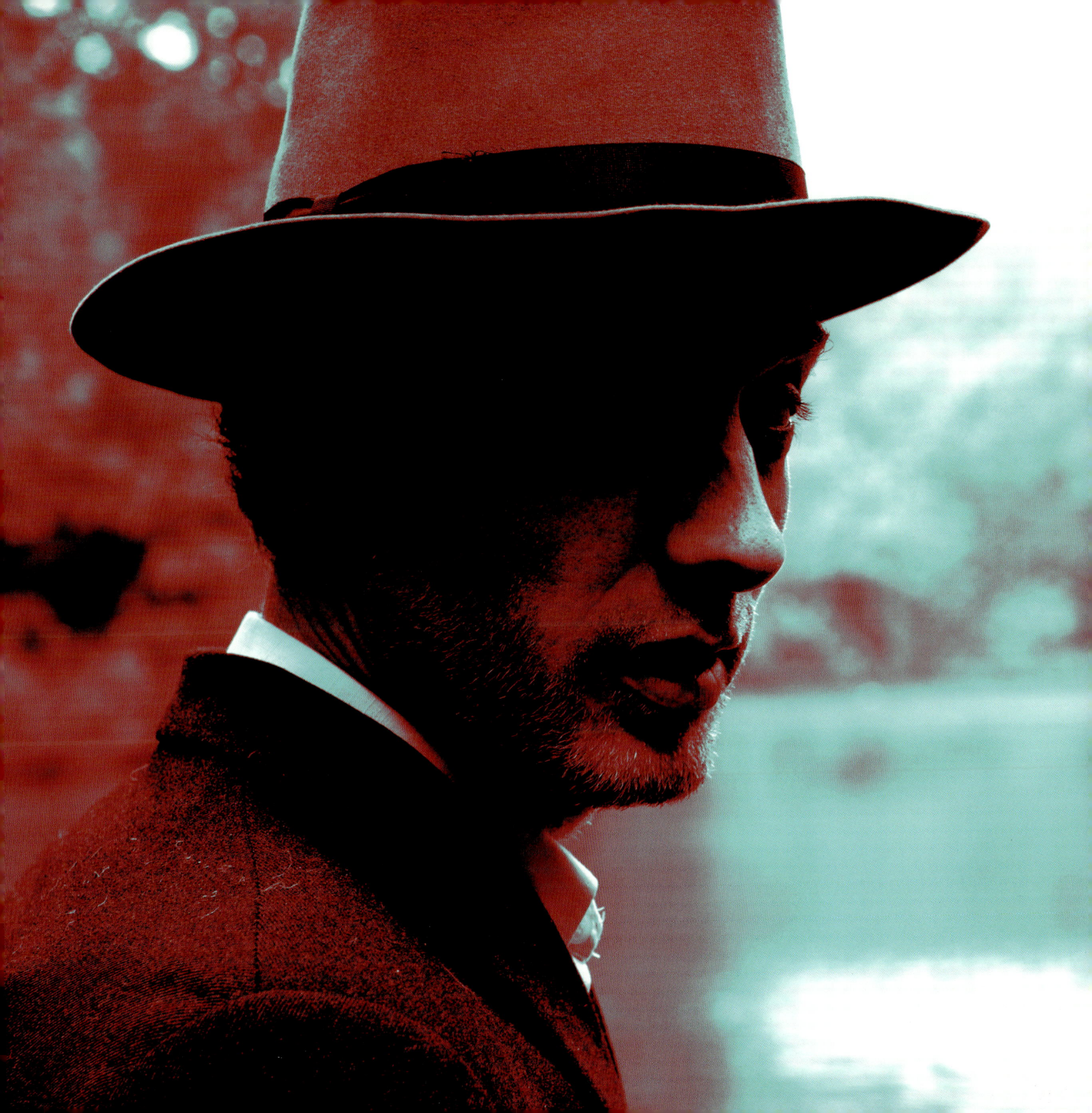

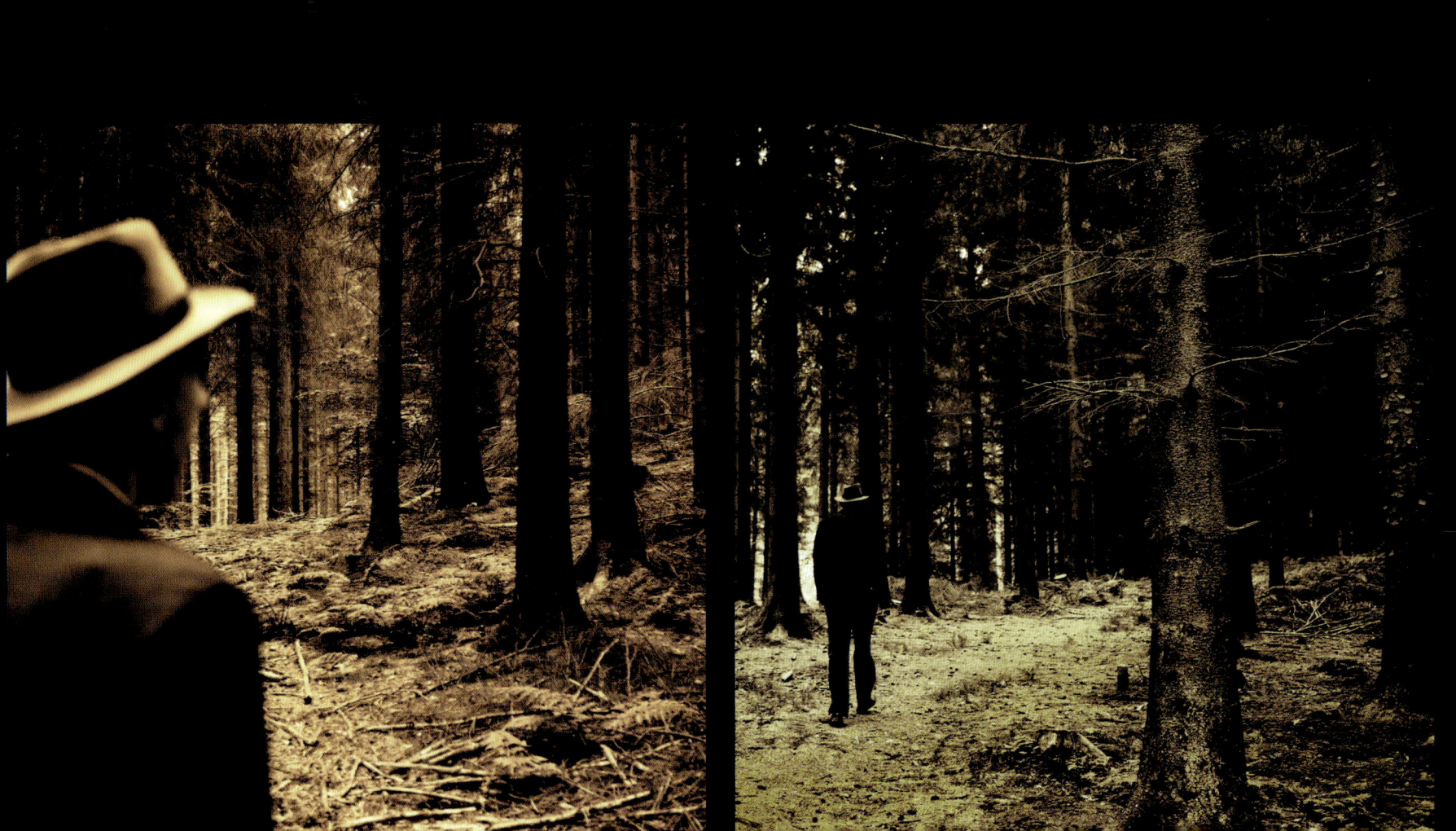

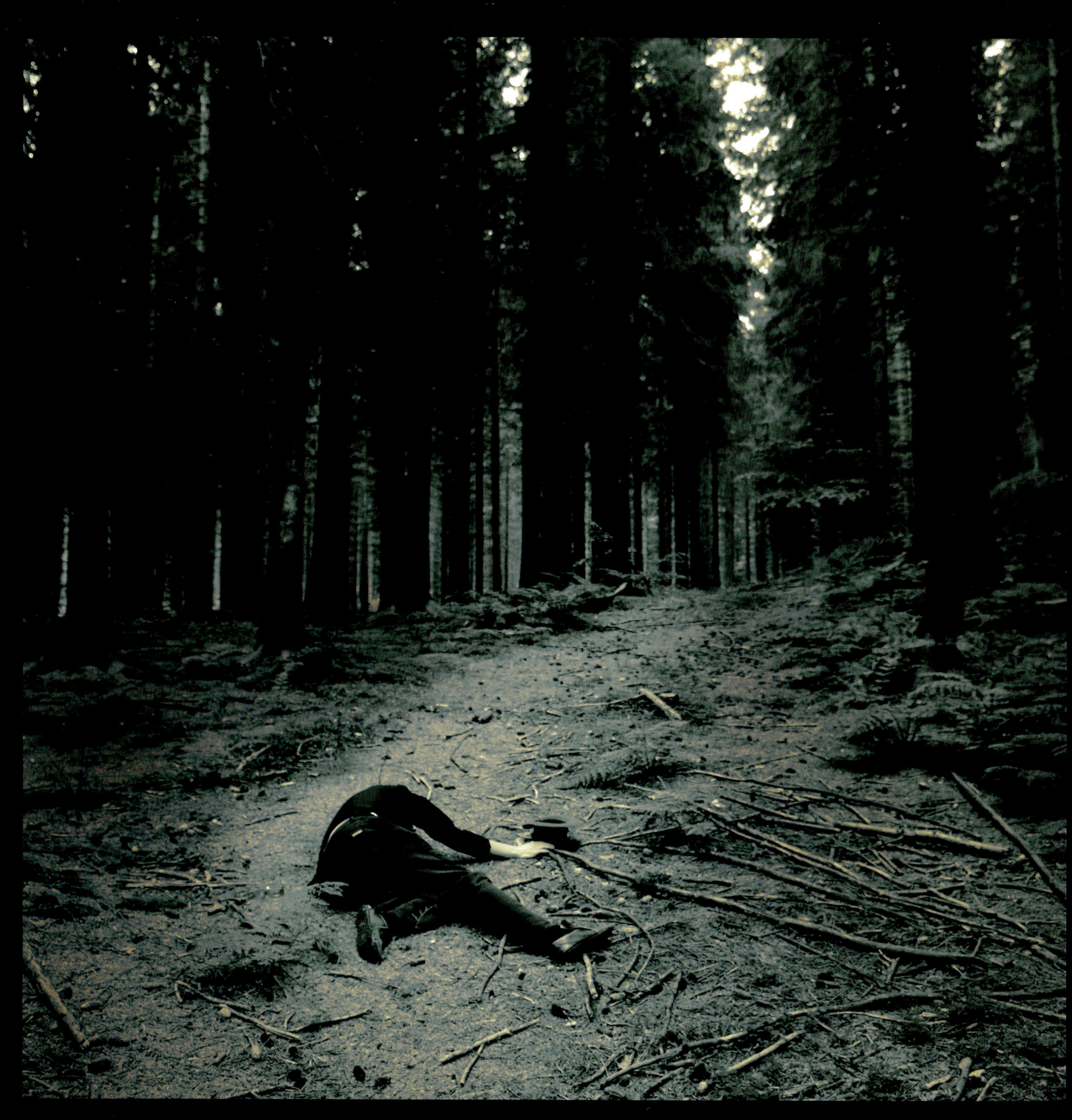

REVENANT (SHOW INTRO) 2005

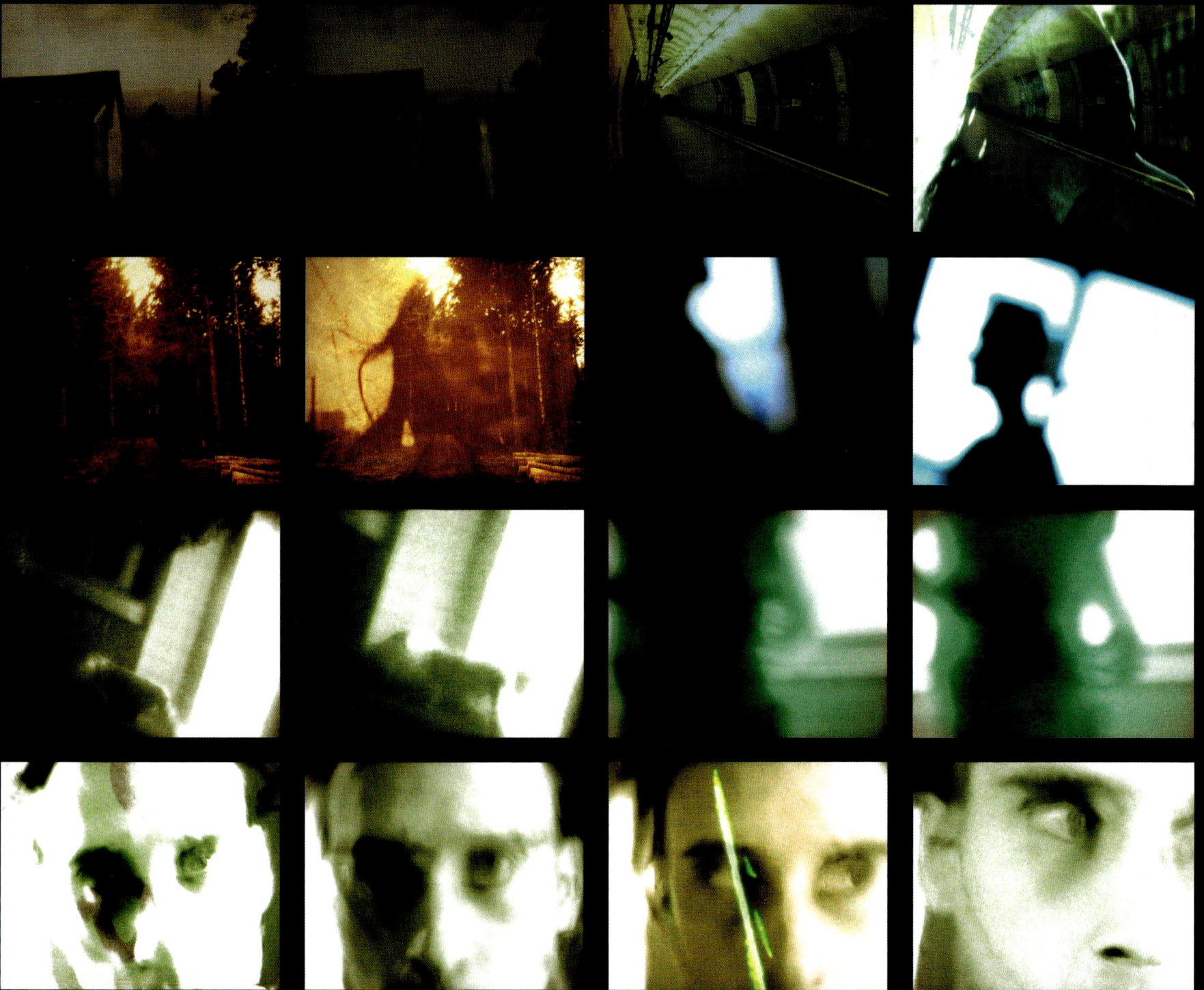

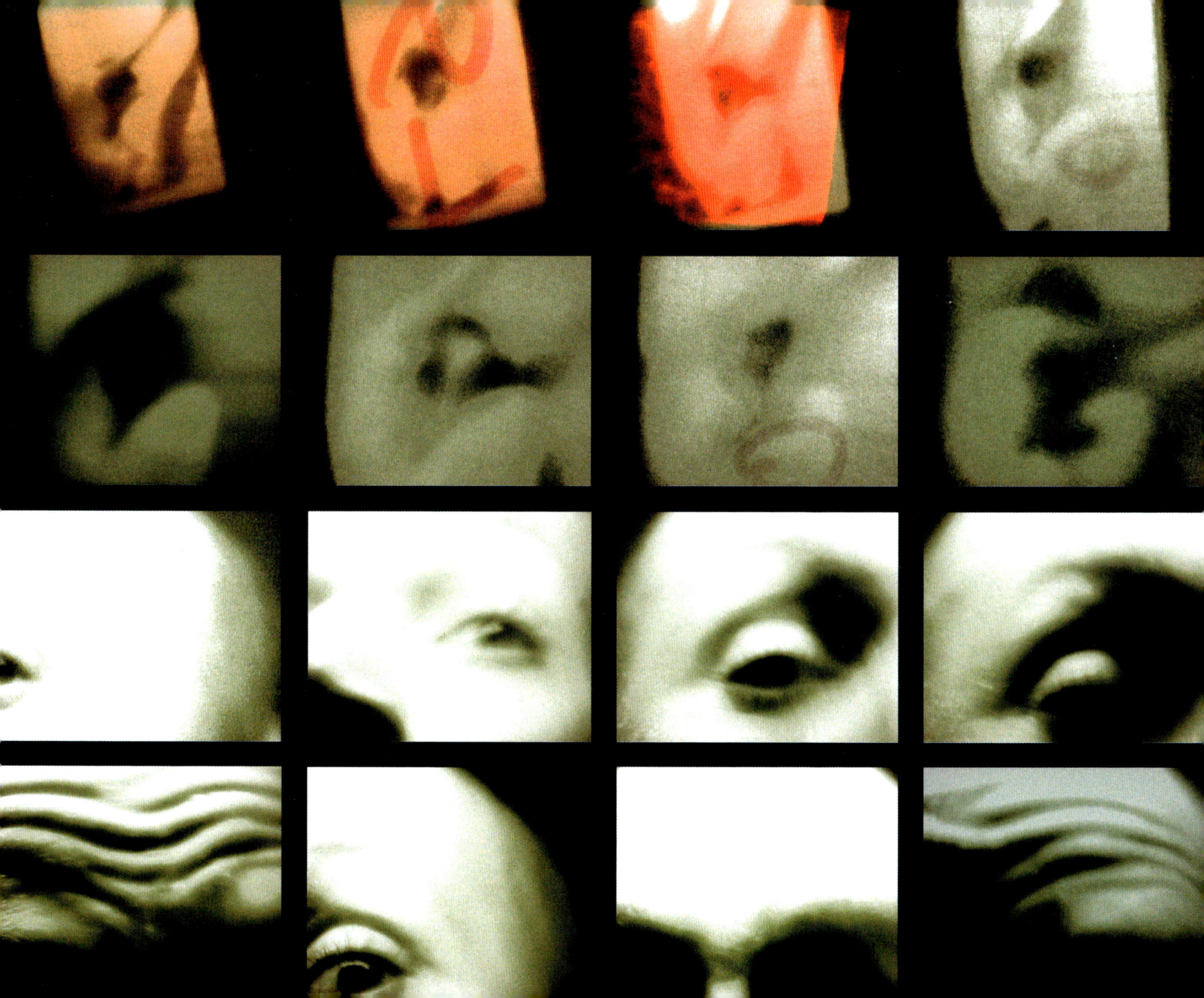

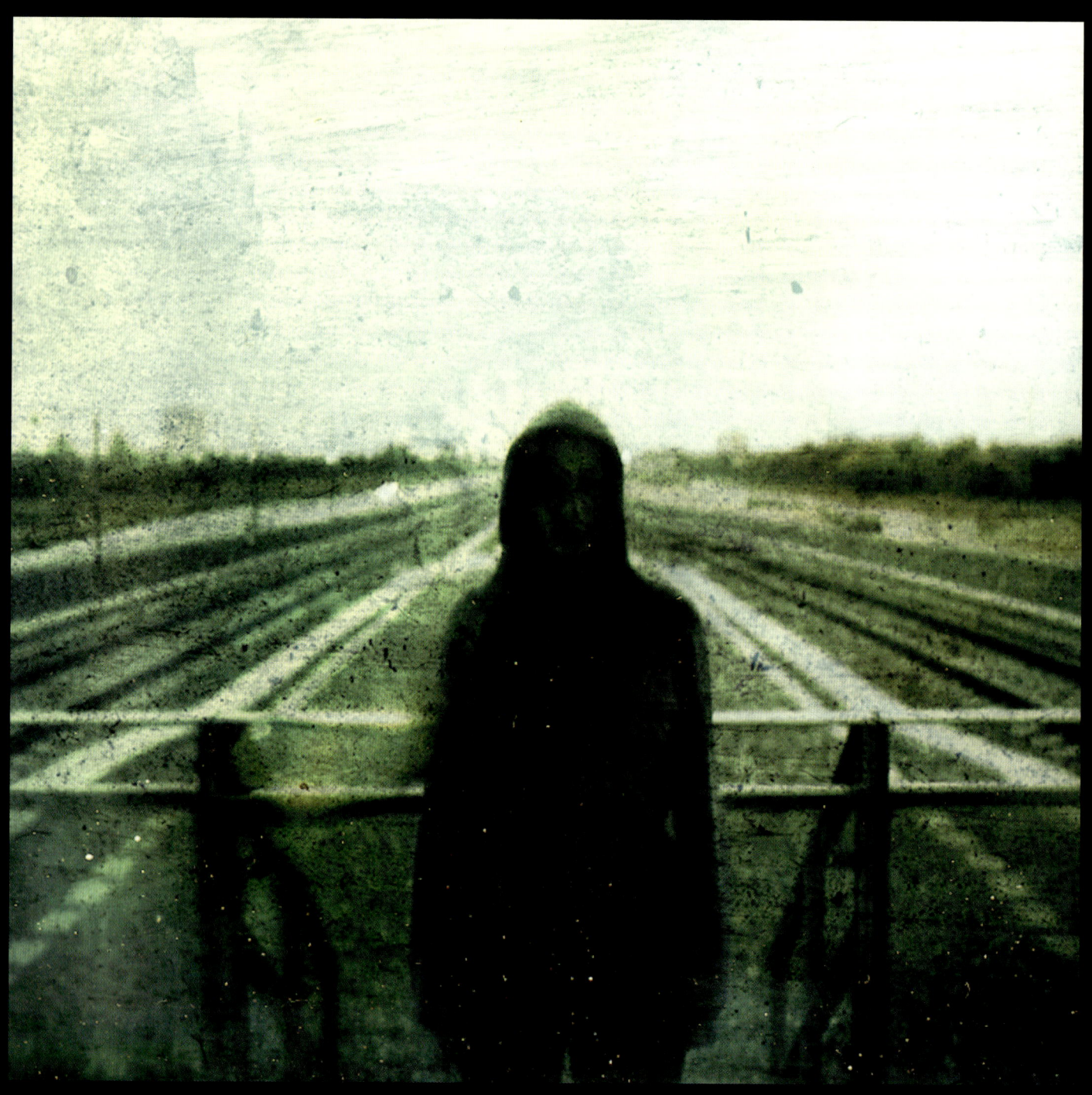

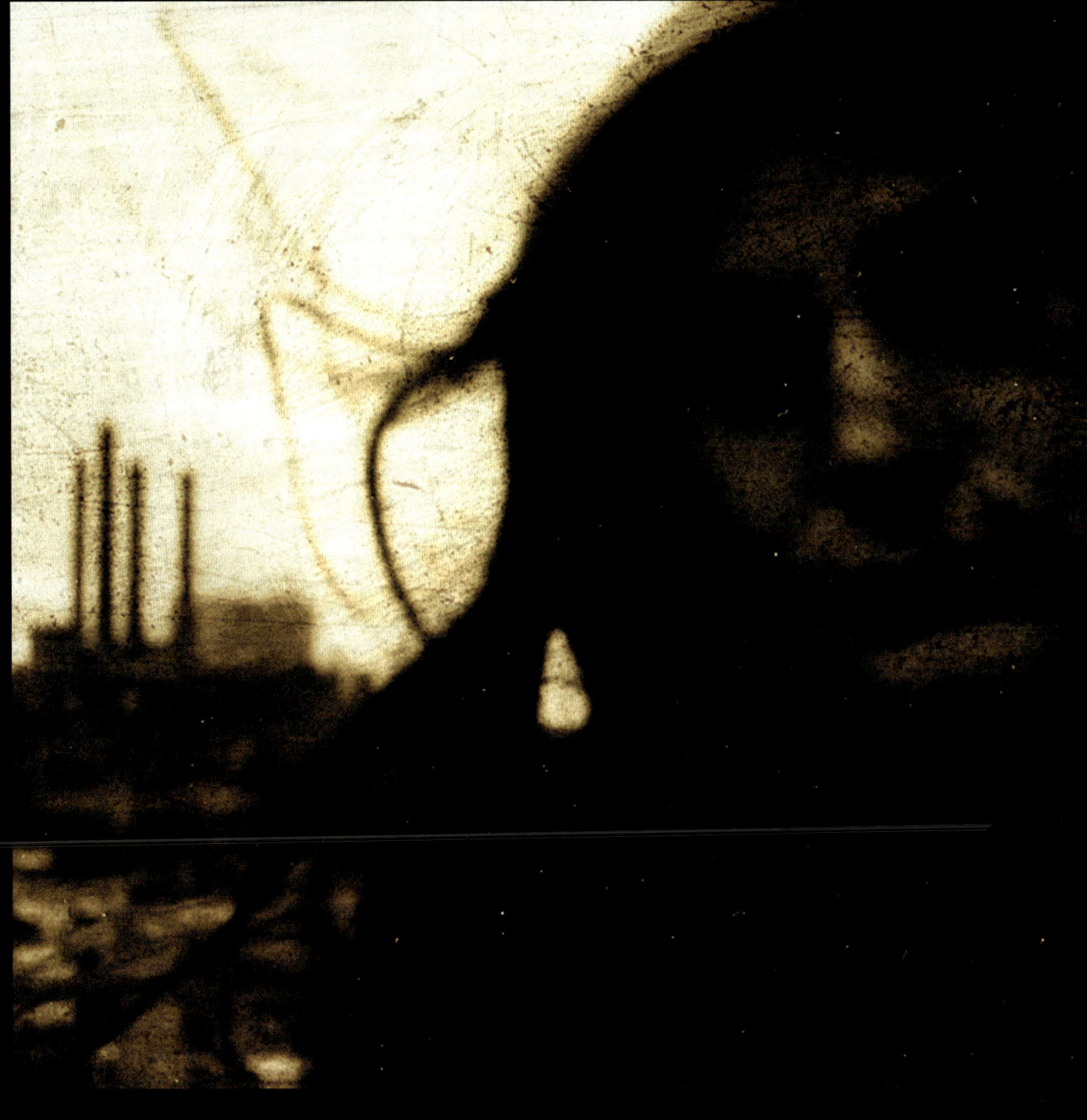

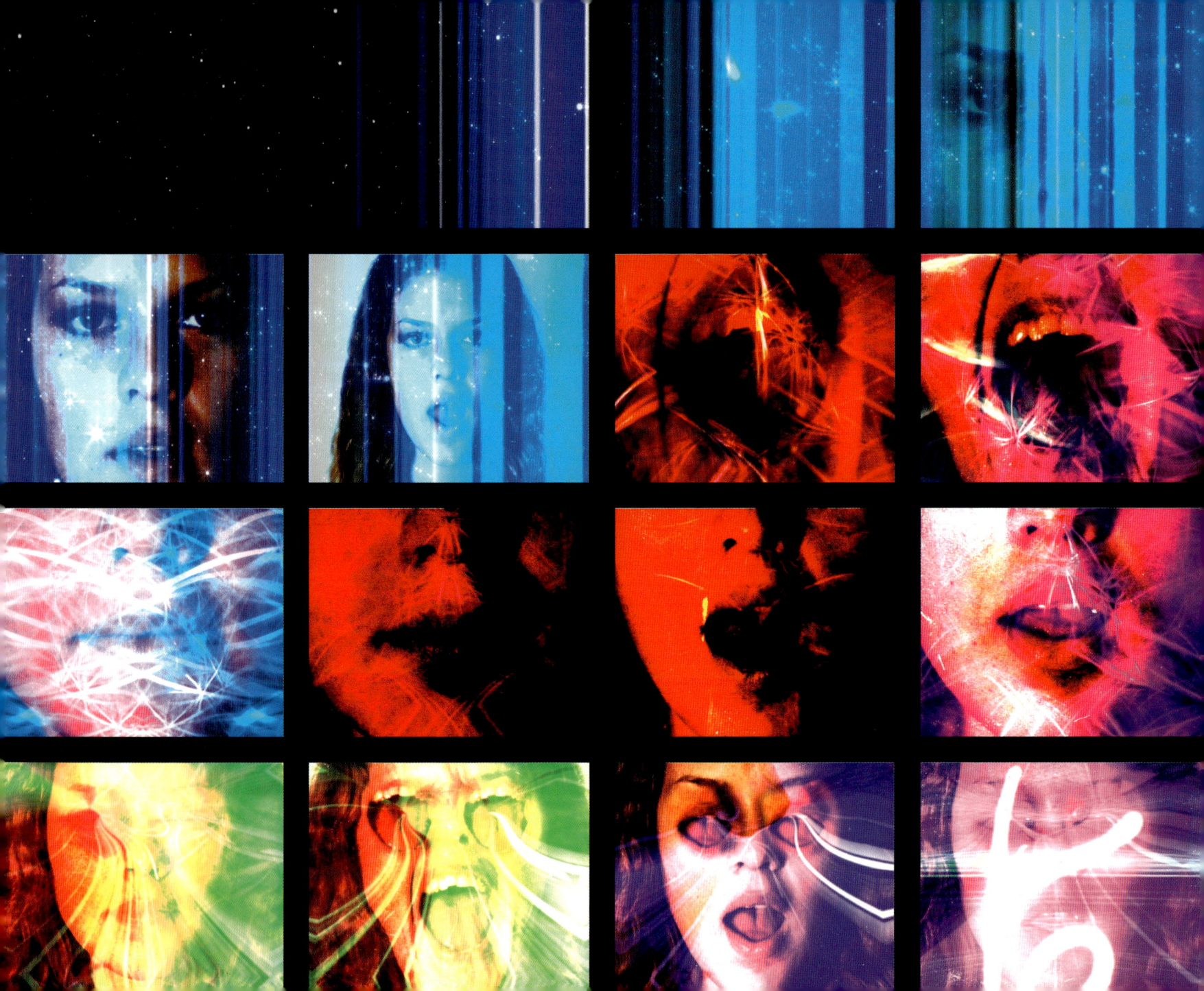

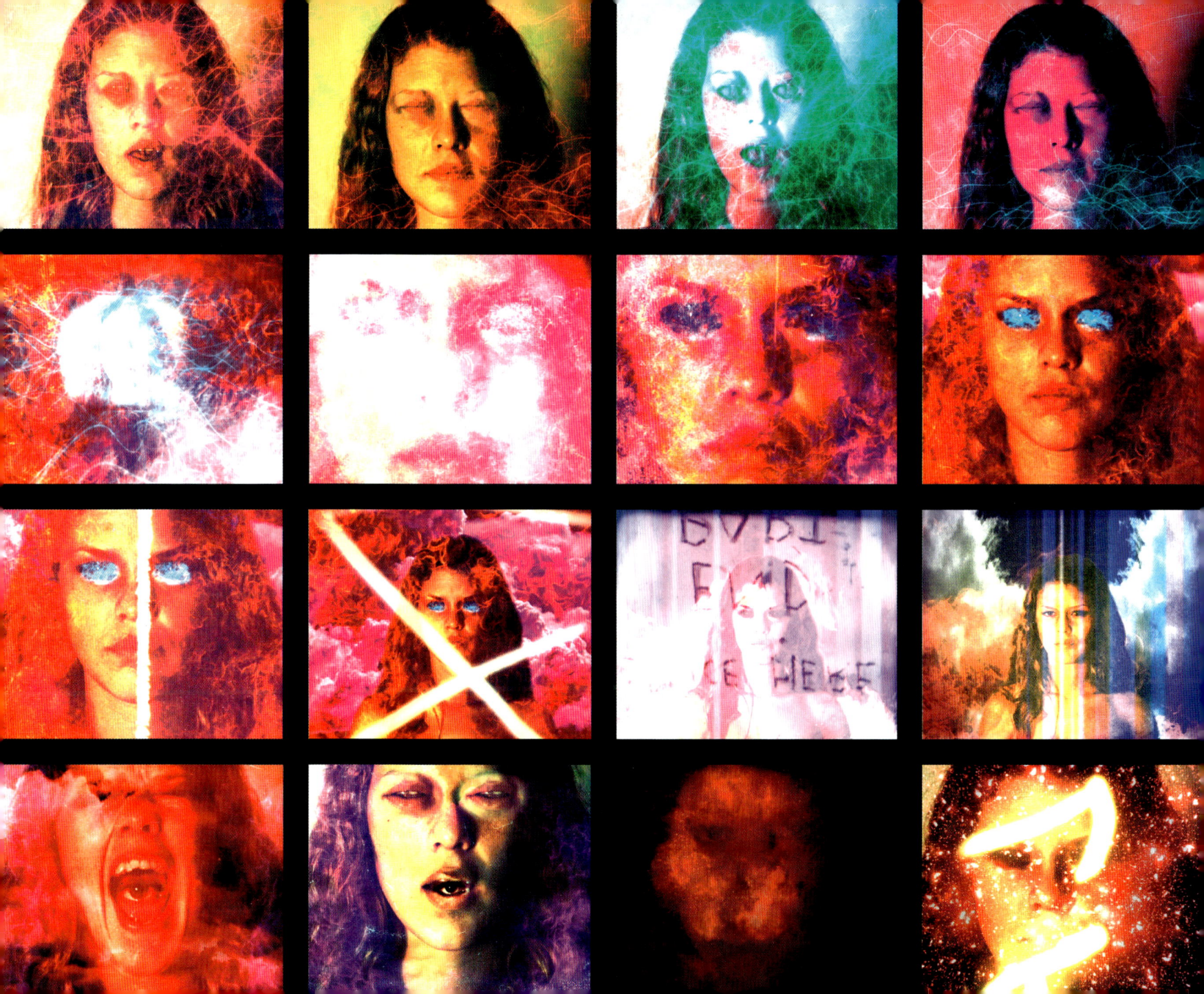

MOTHER AND CHILD DIVIDED 2005

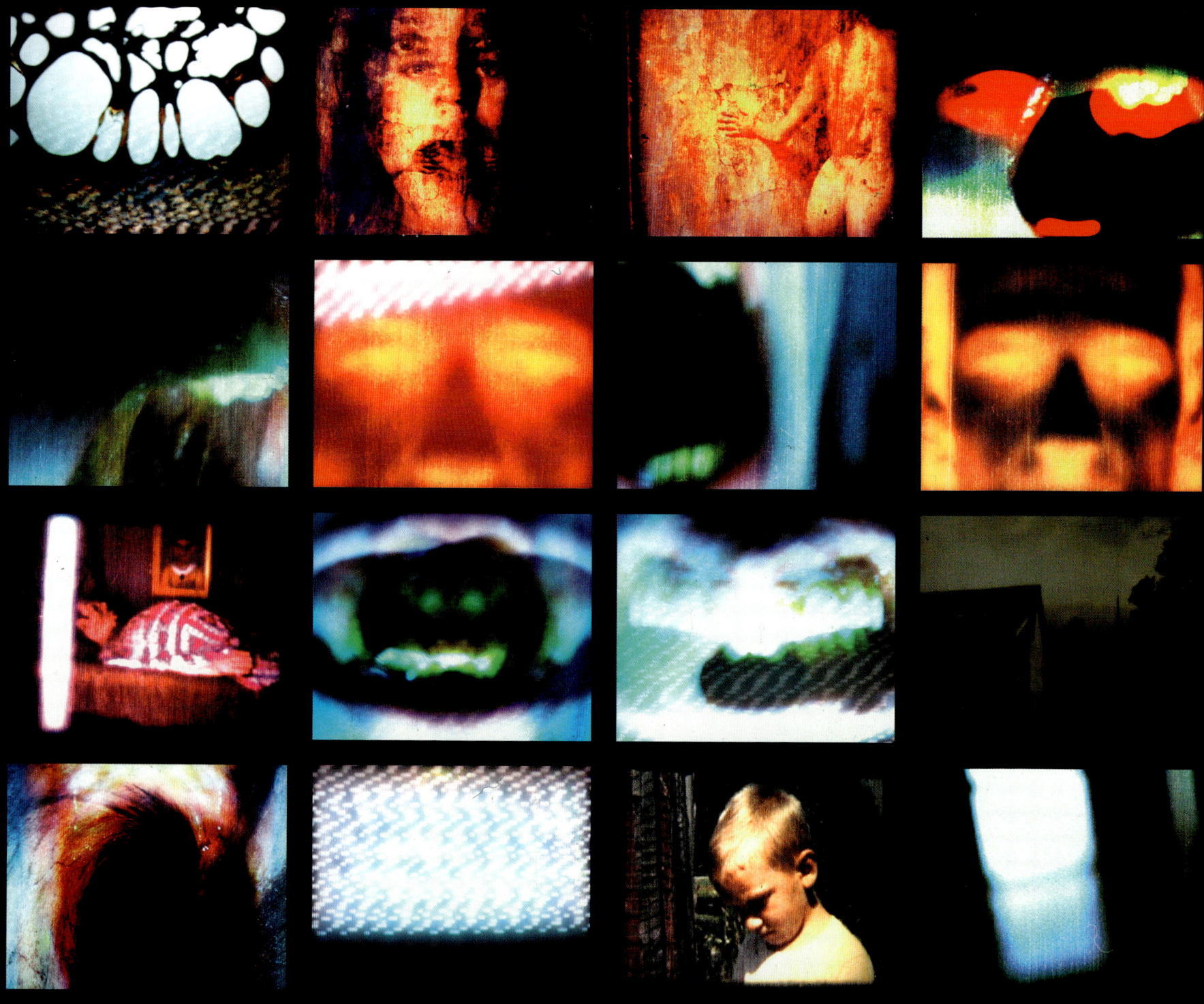

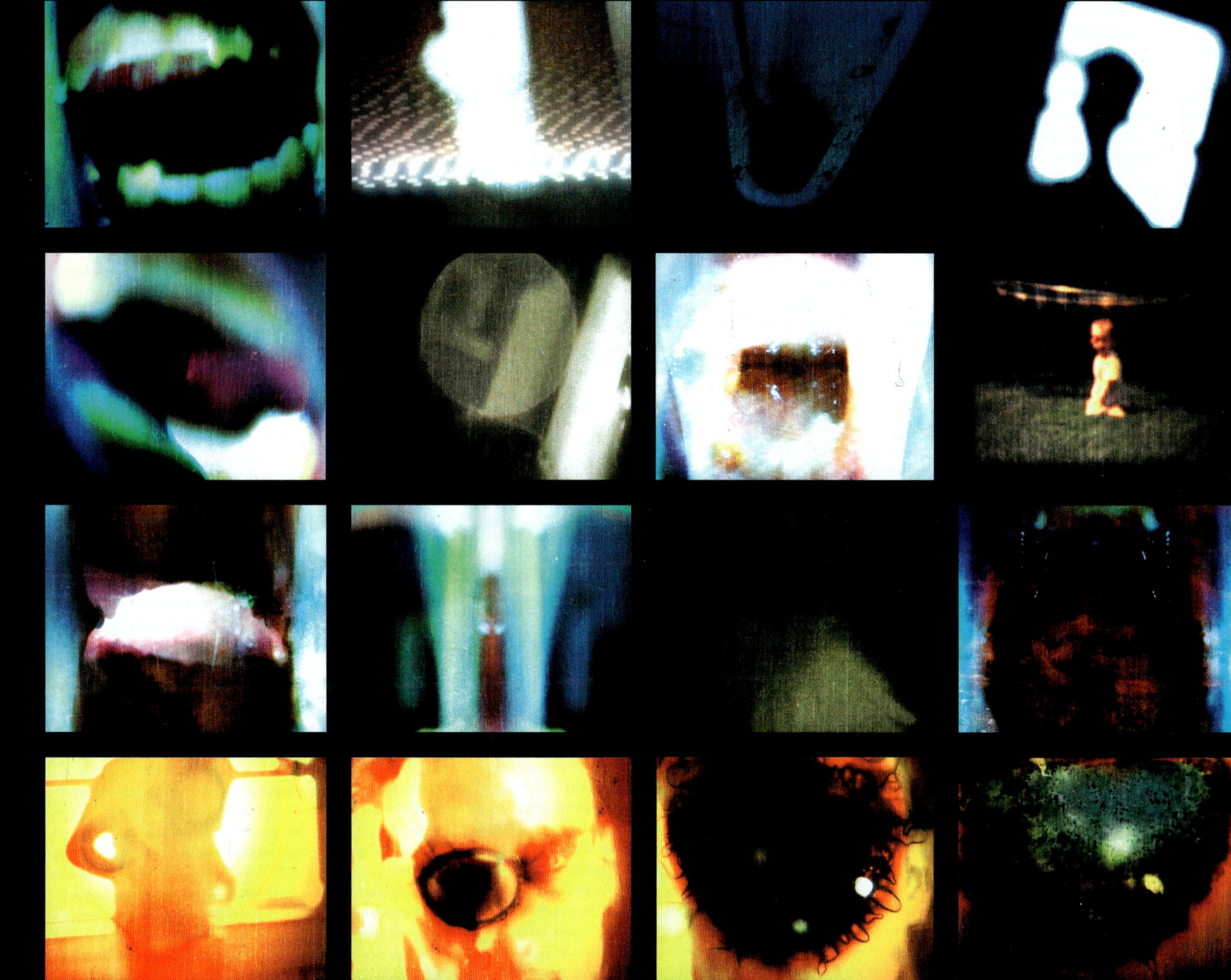

INABSEN
DWING
ABLANK
THEIN

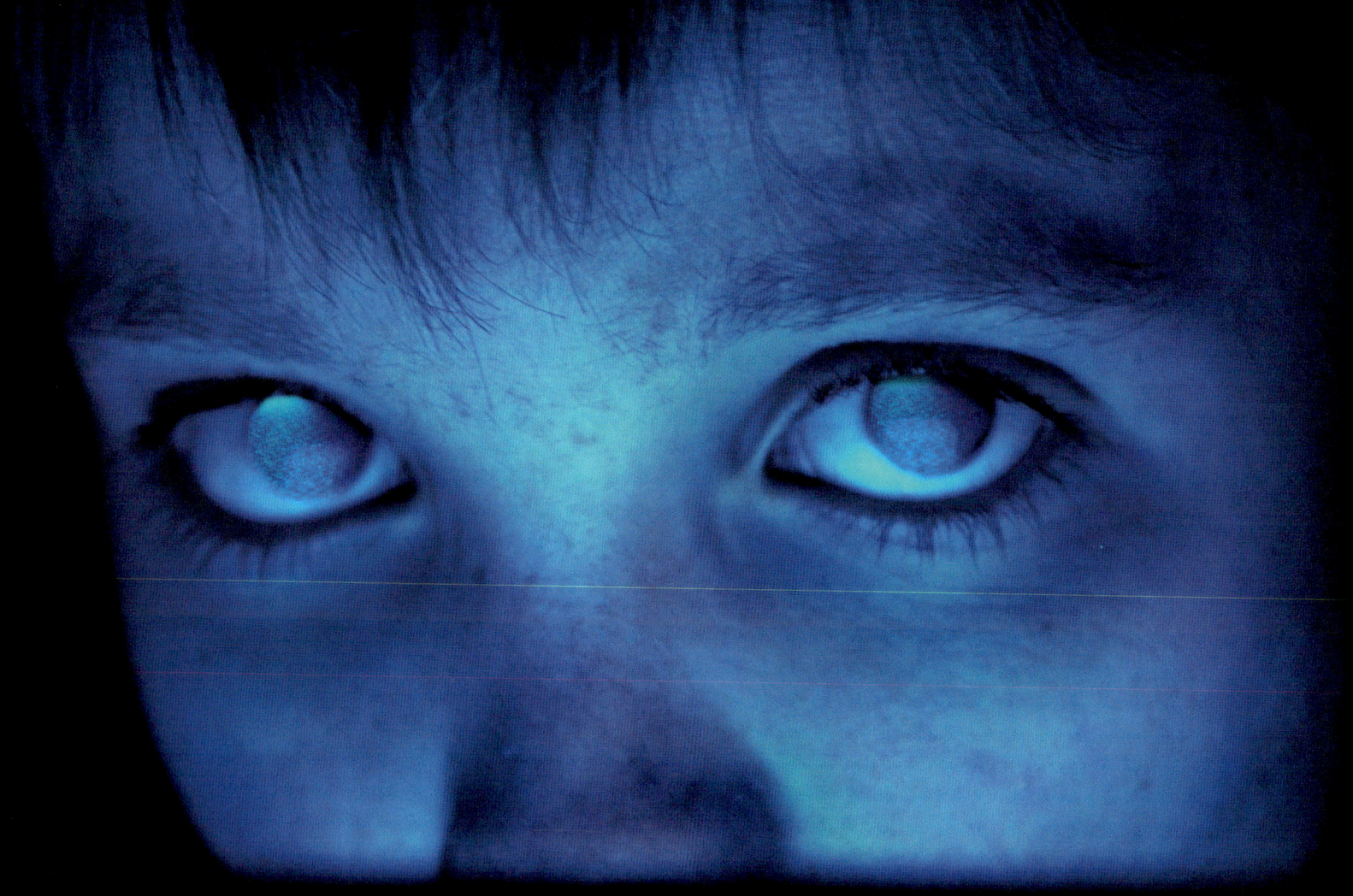

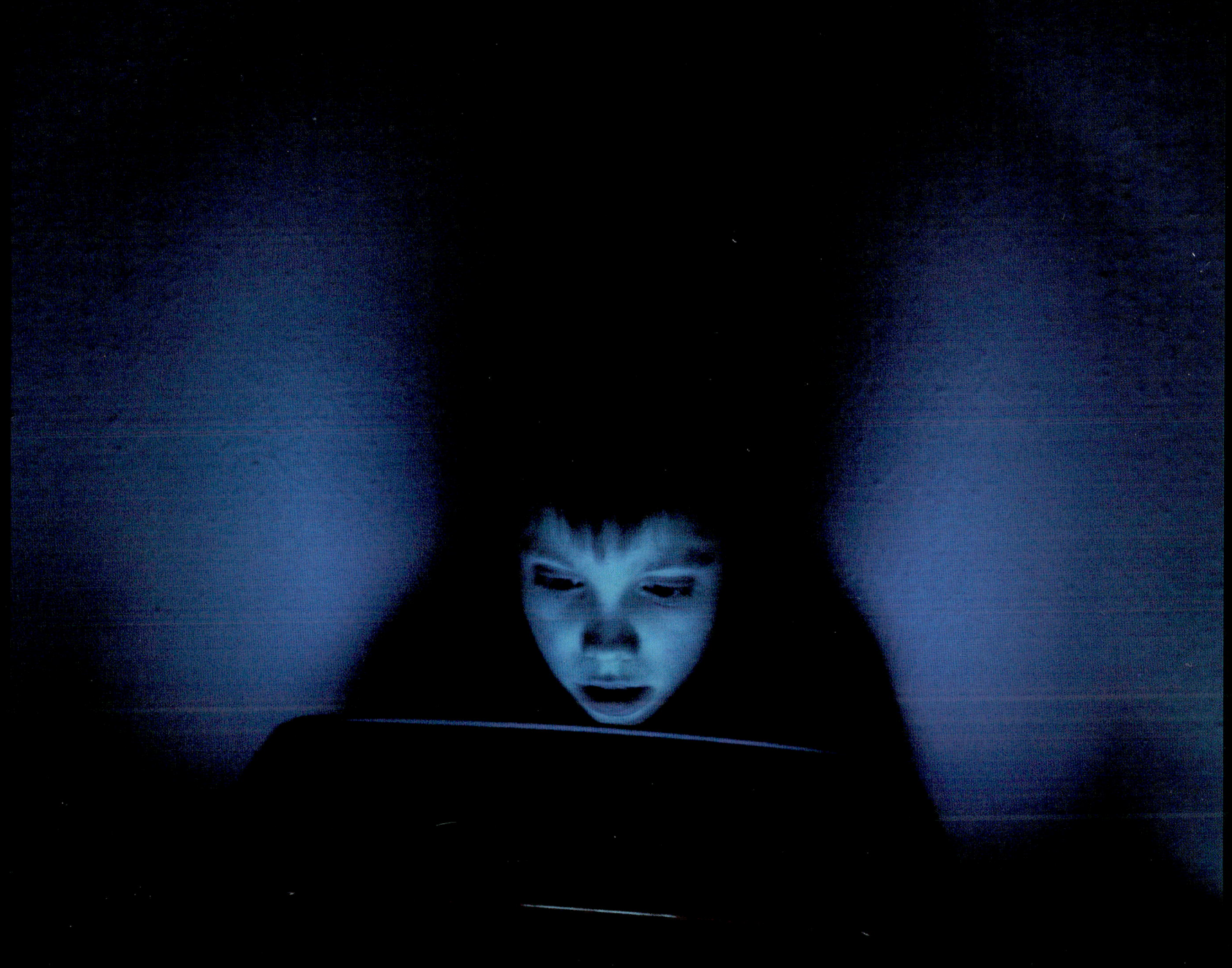

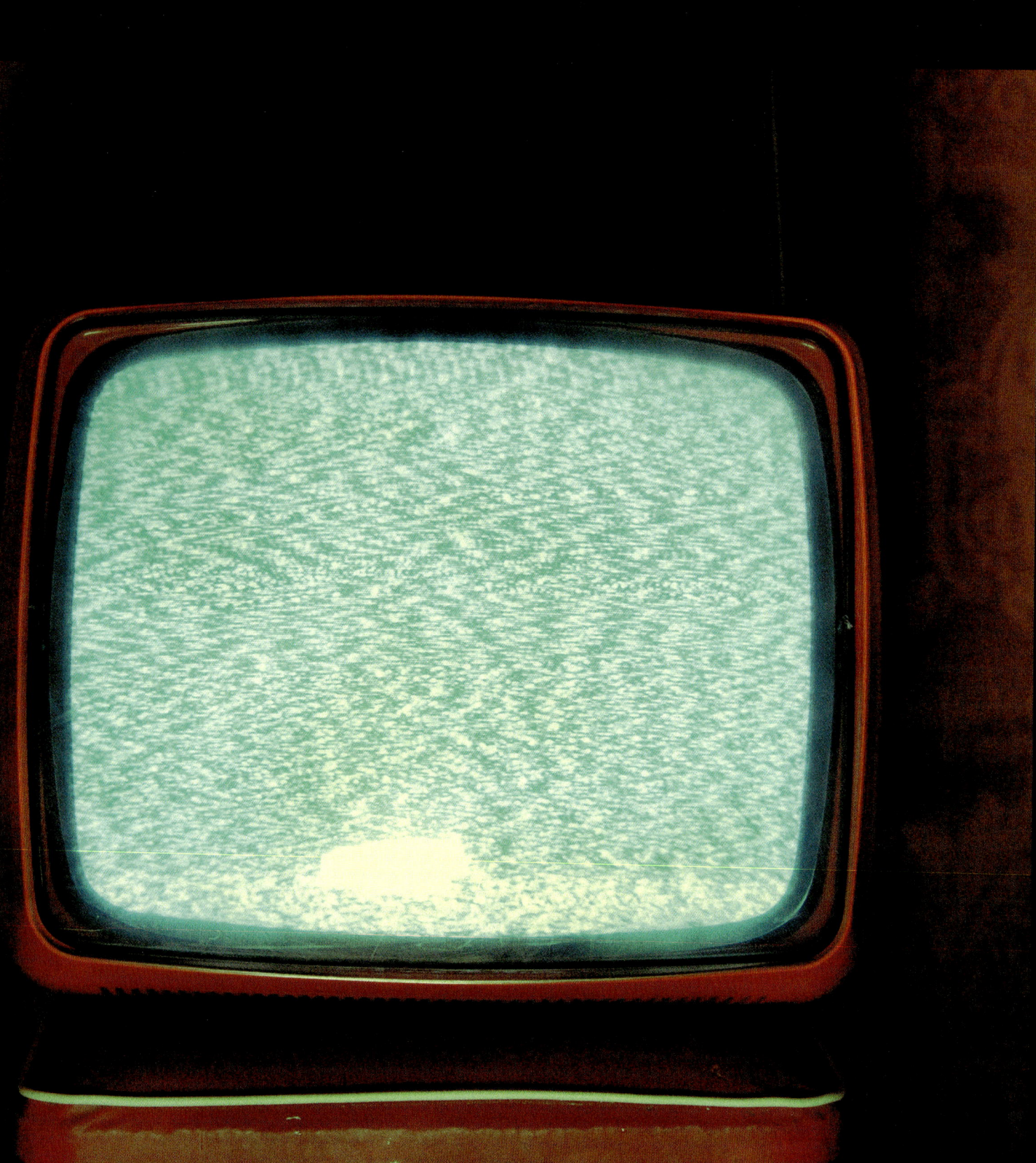

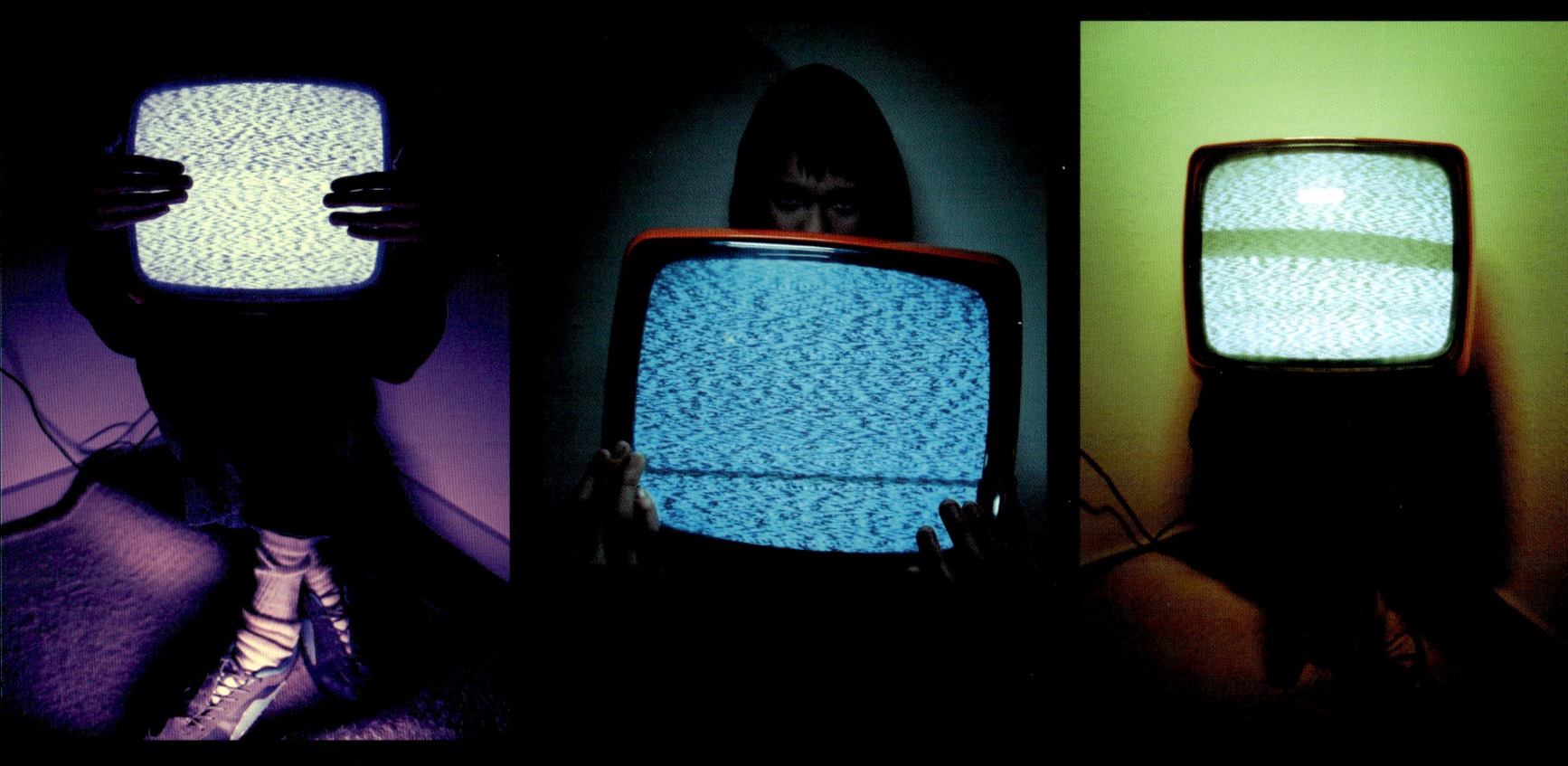

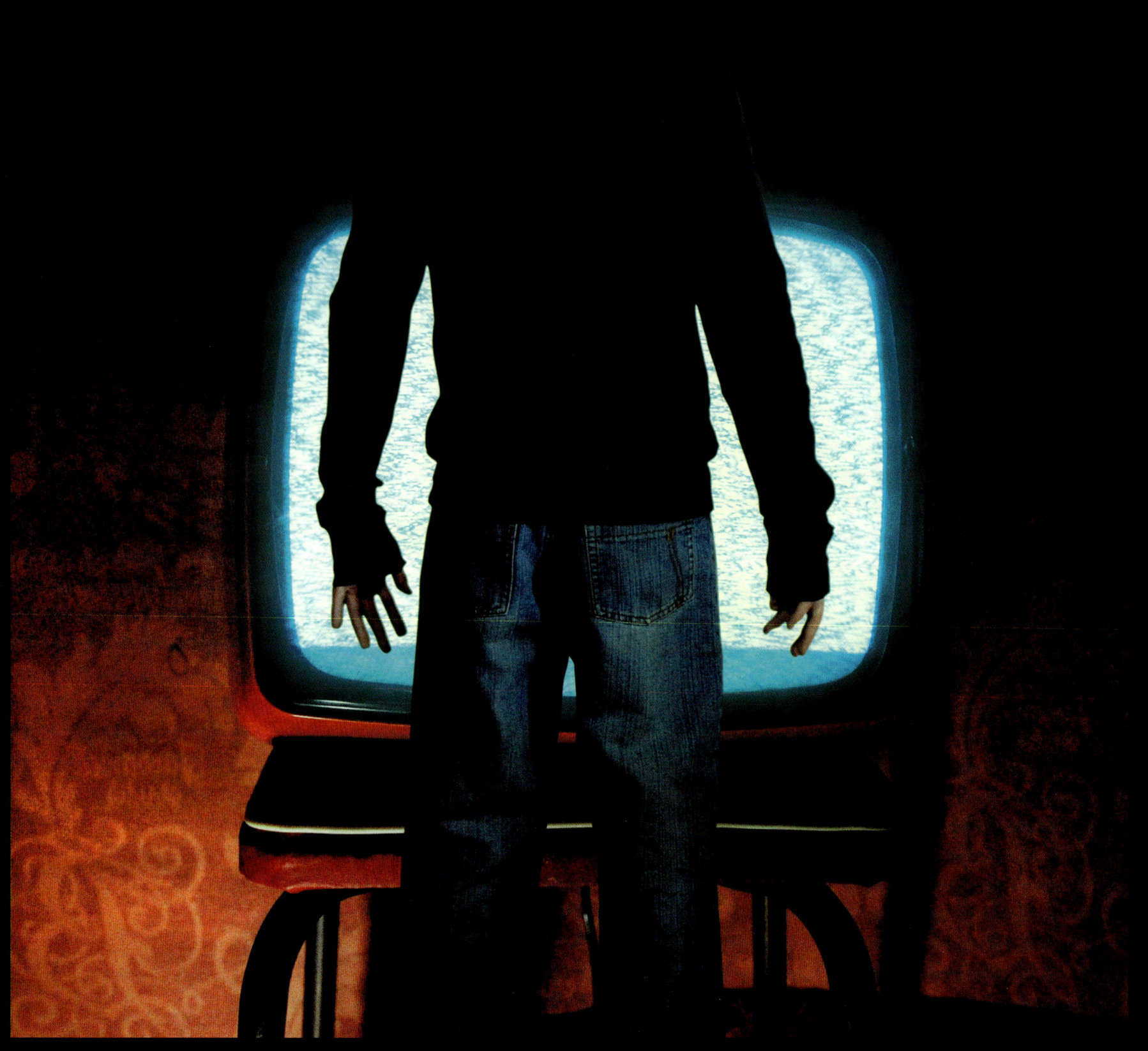

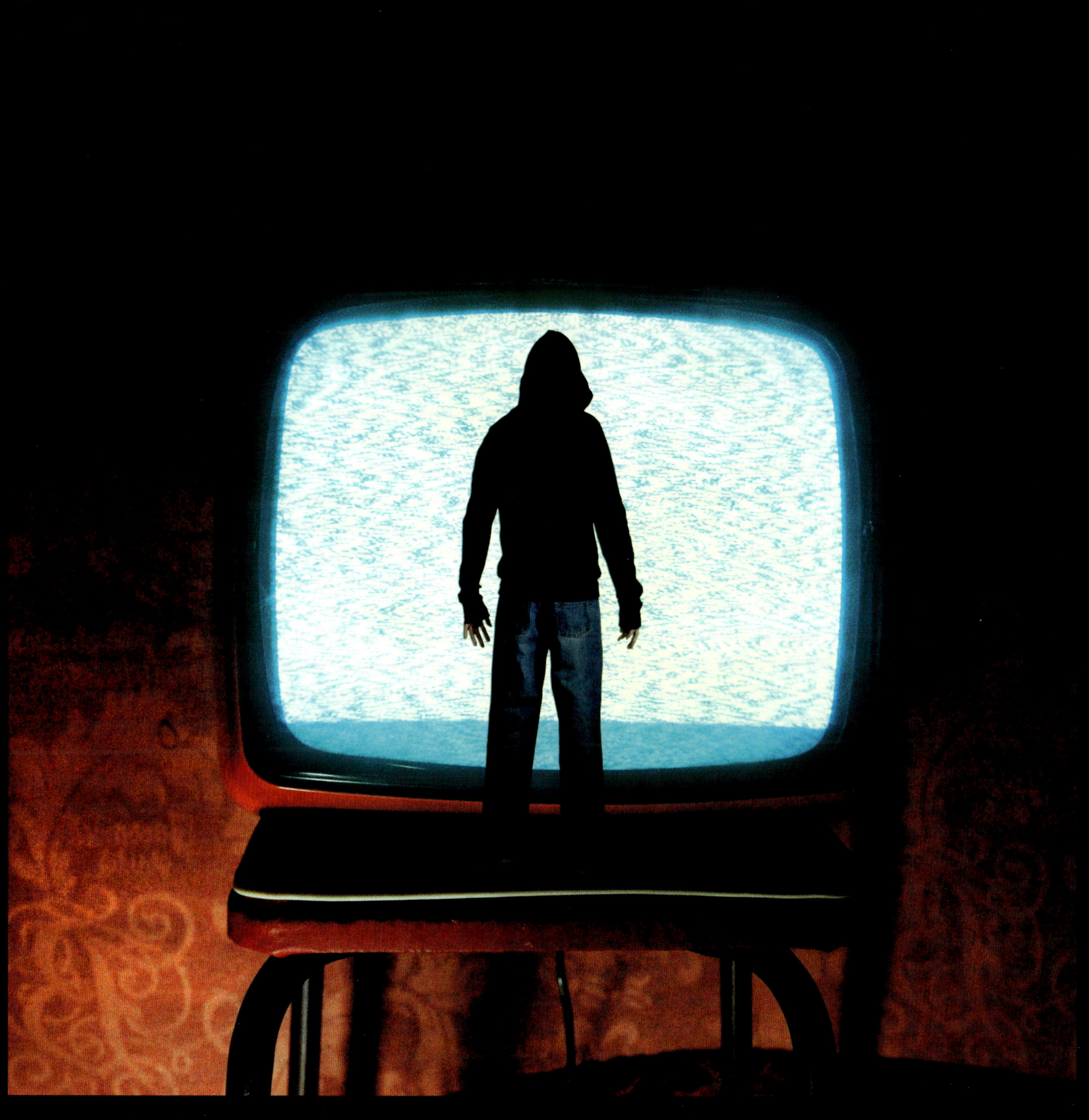

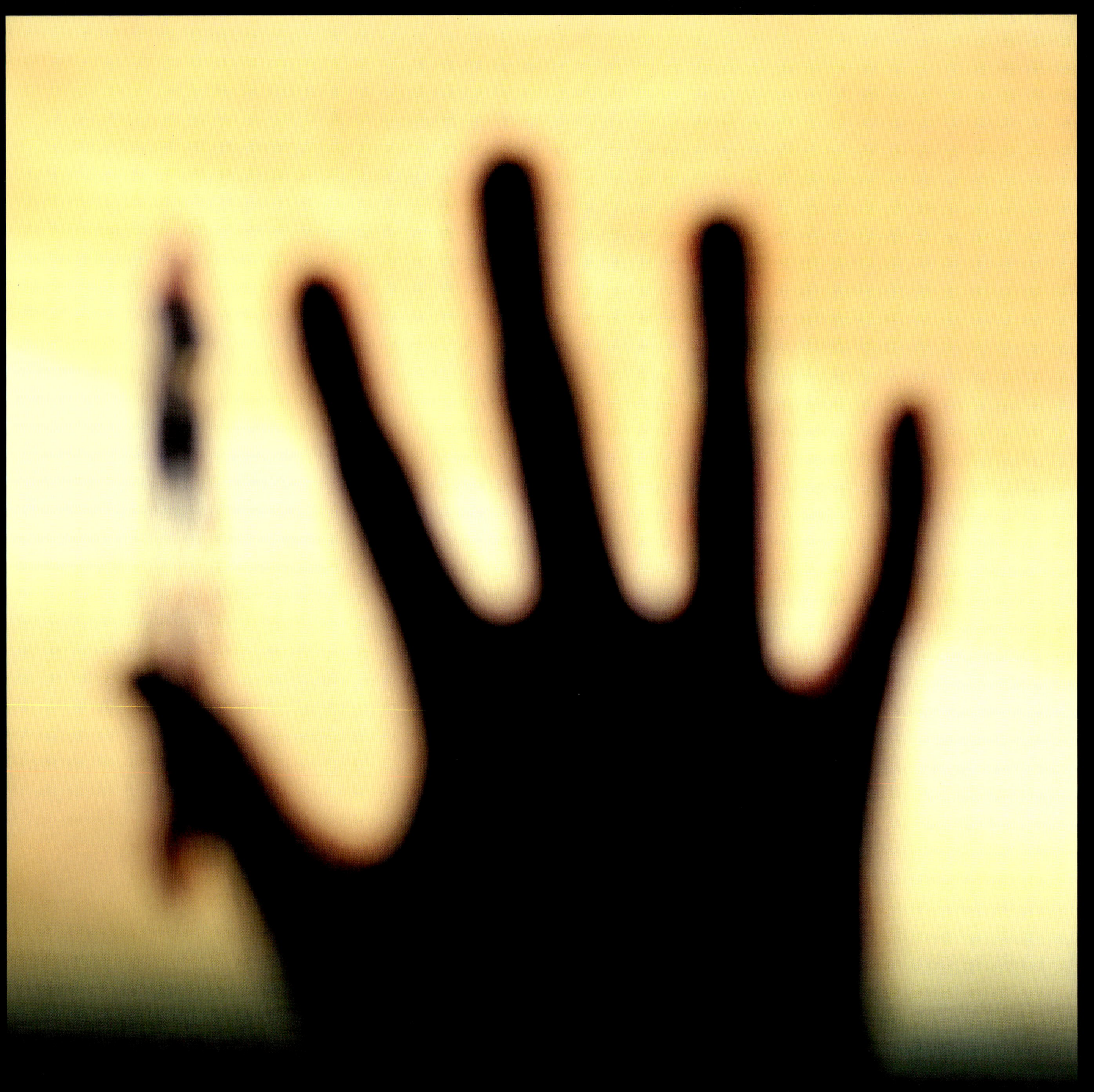

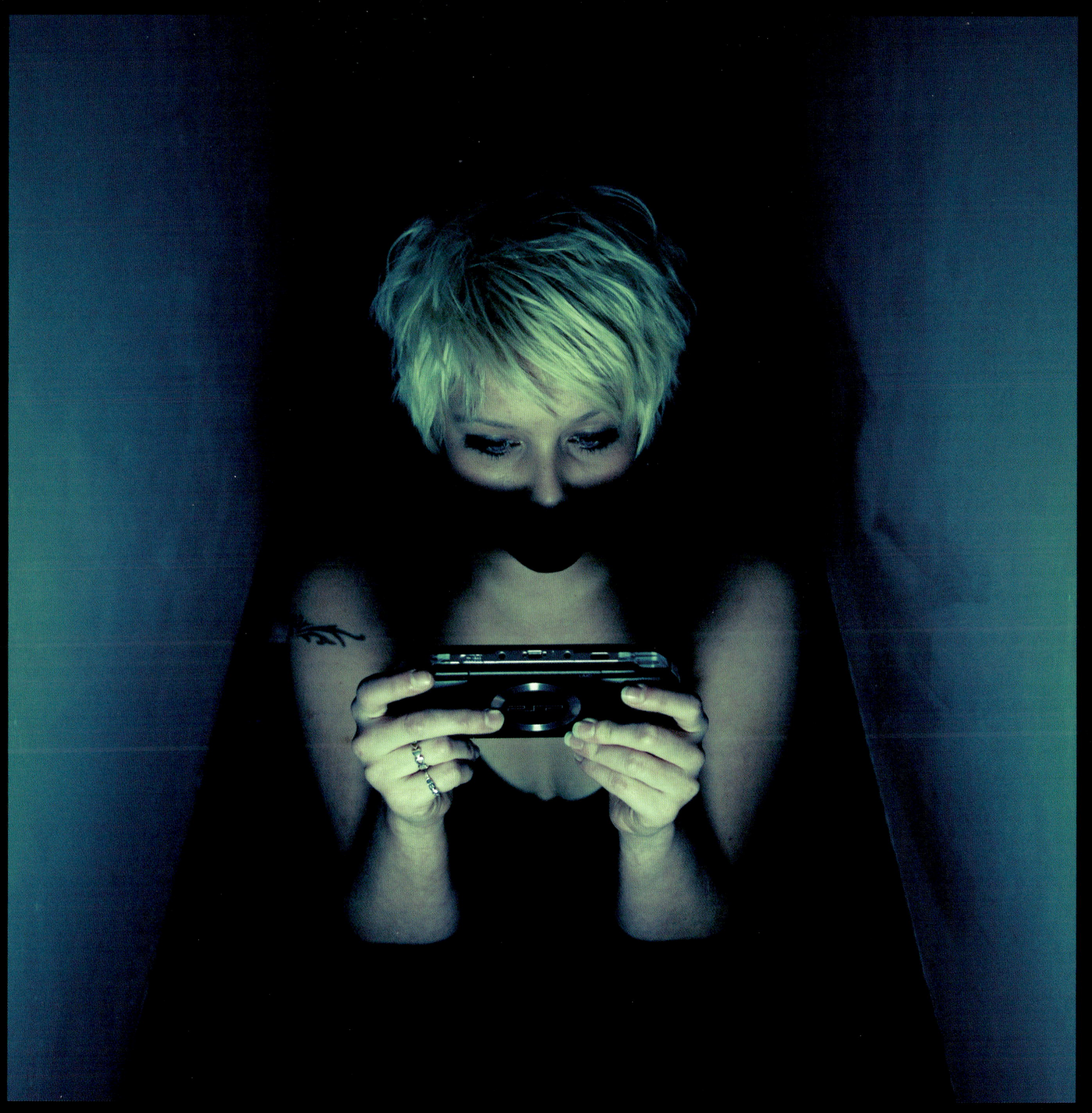

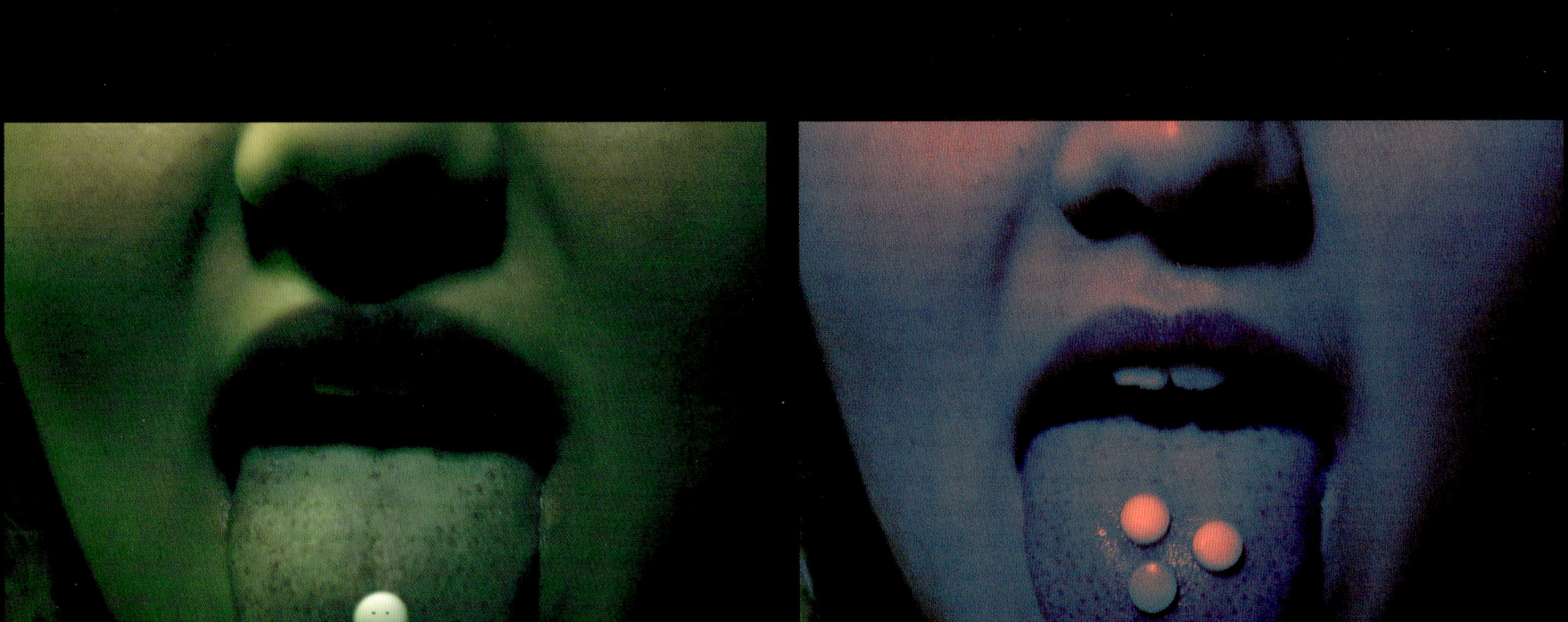

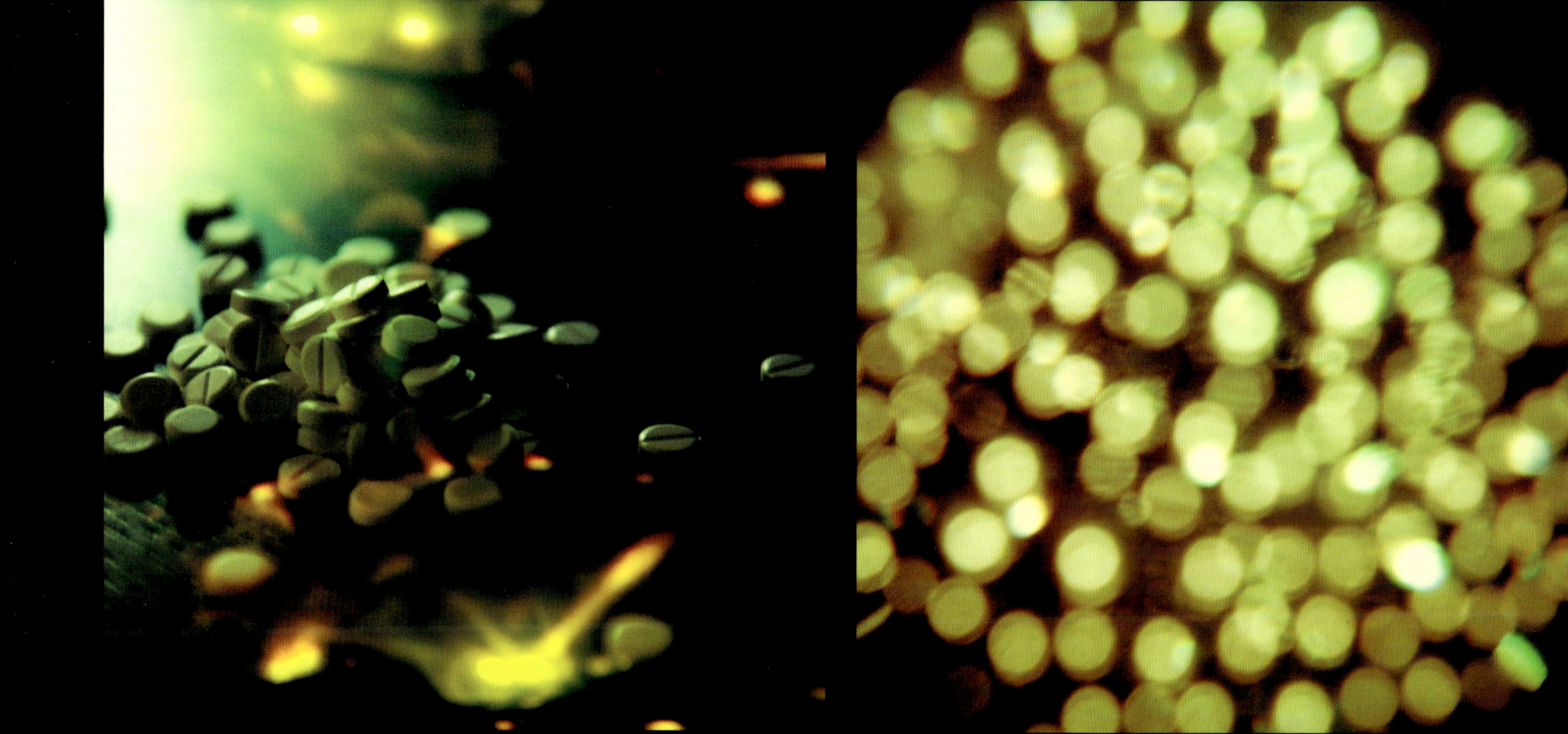

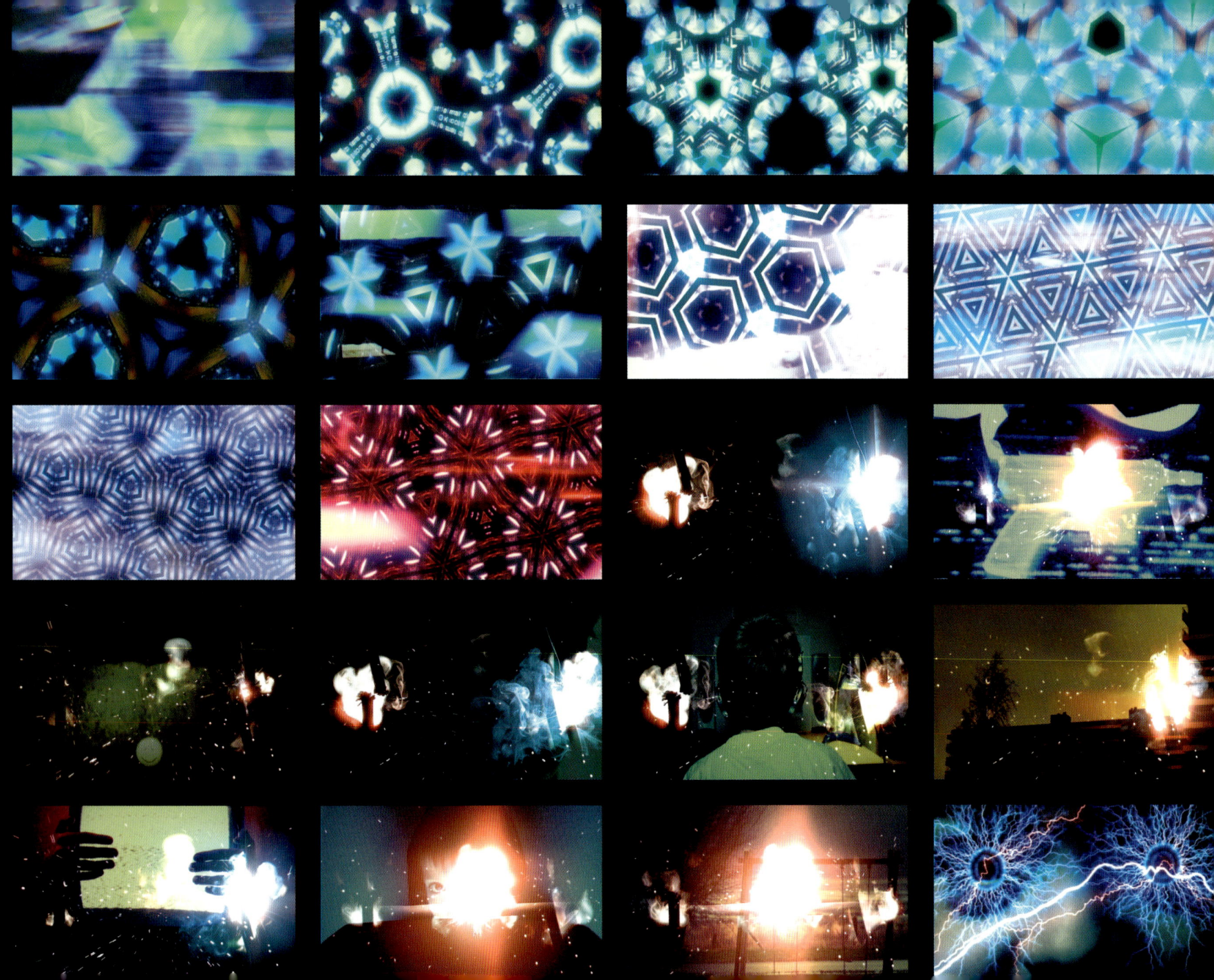

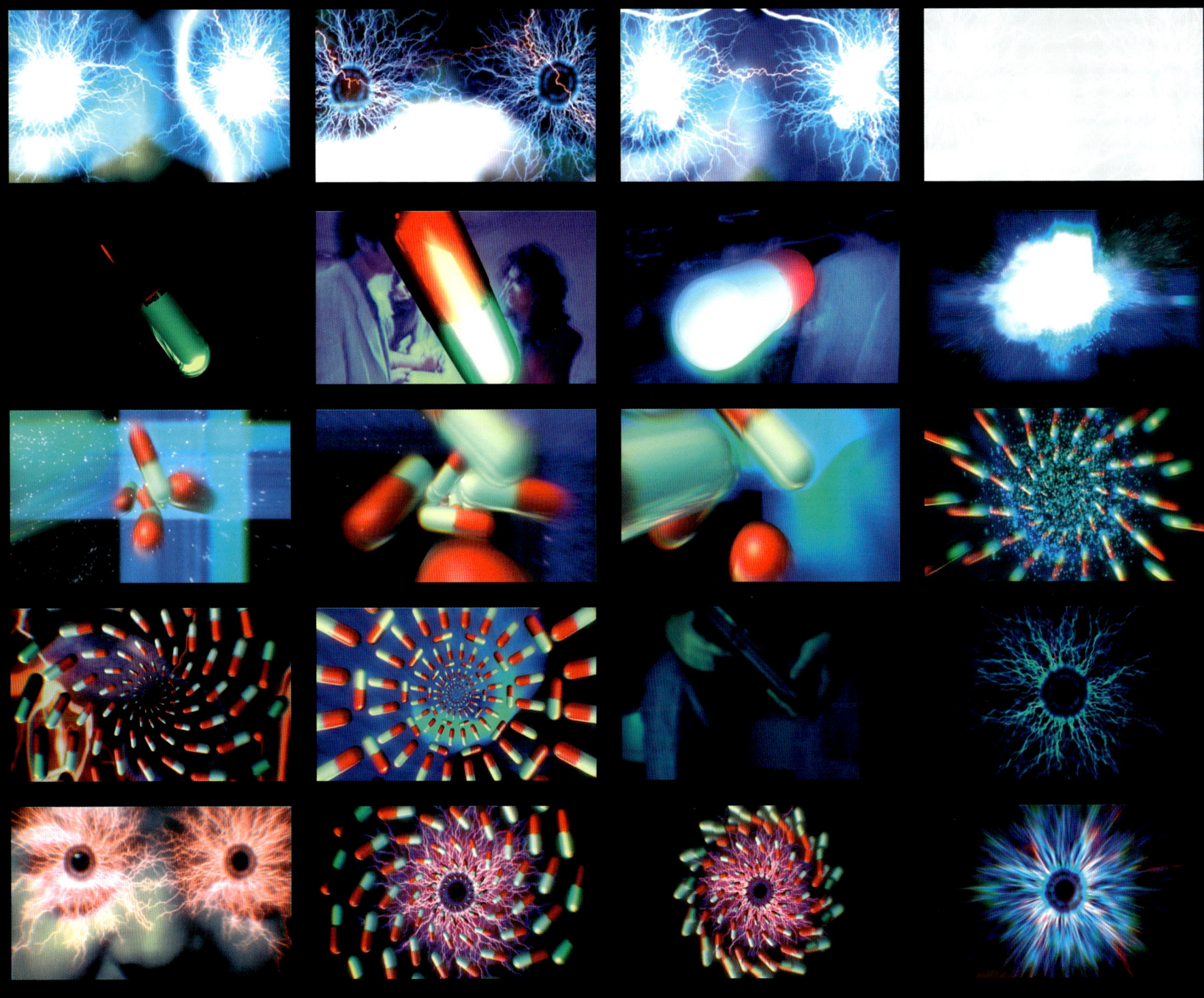

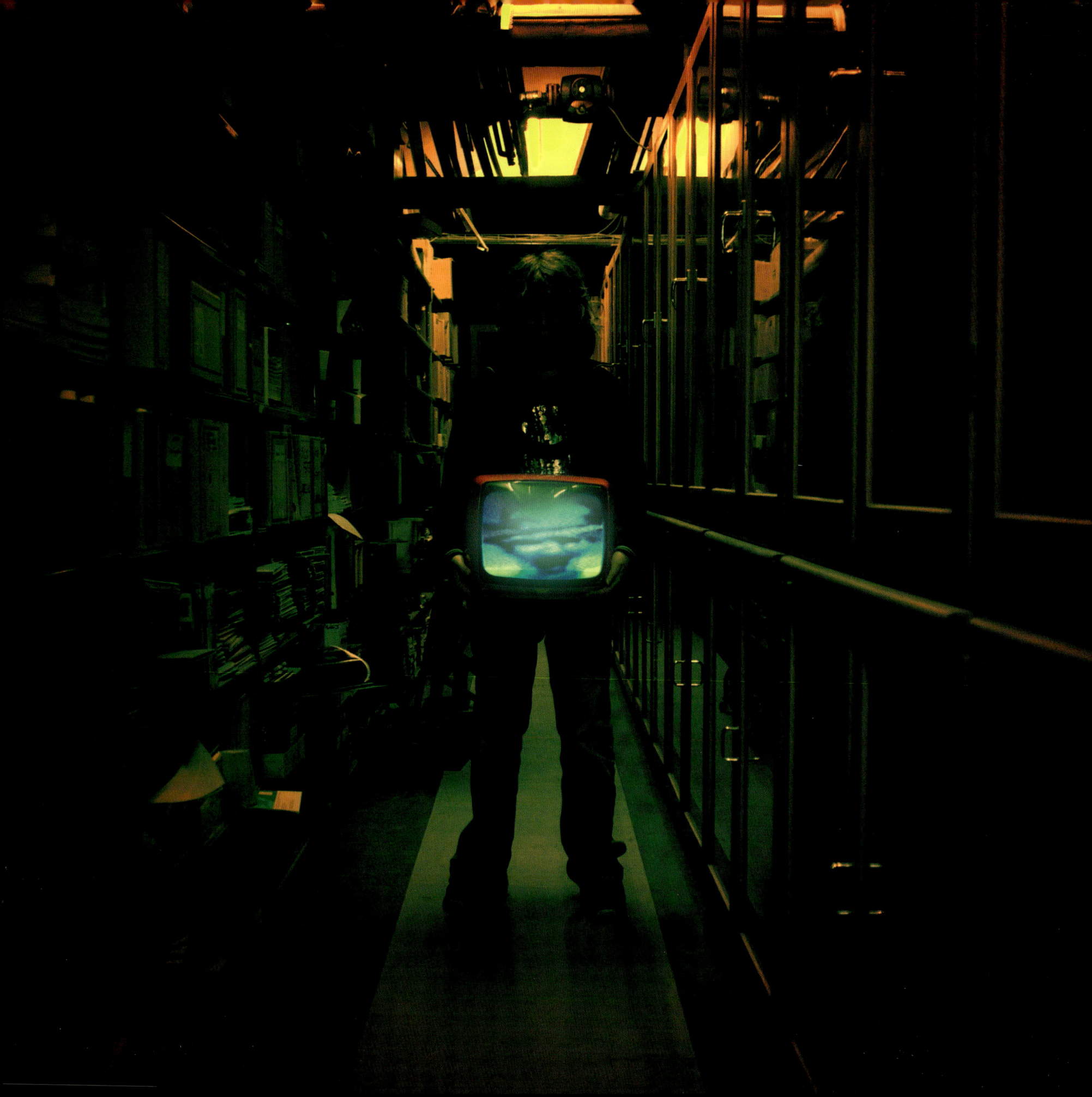

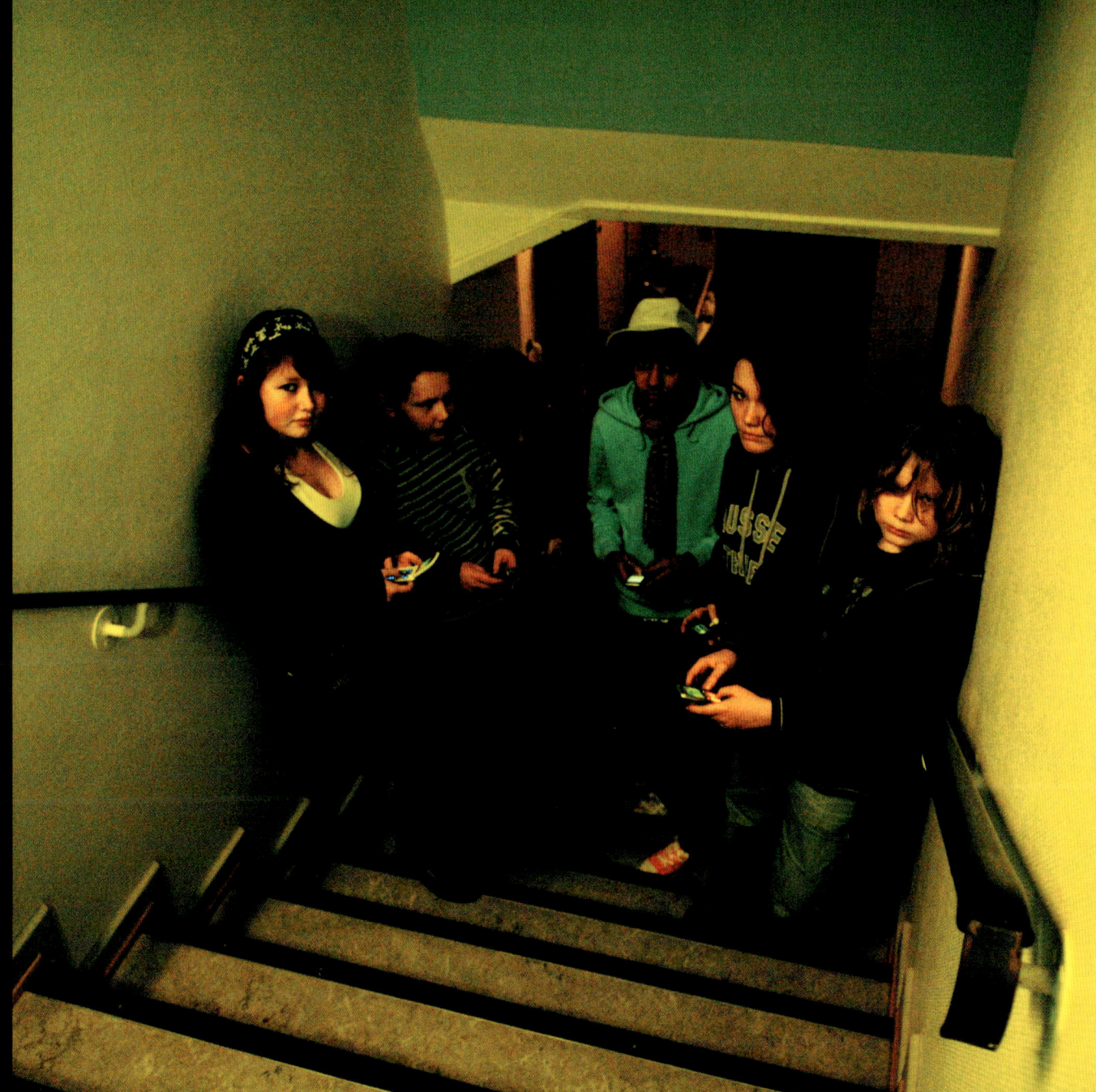

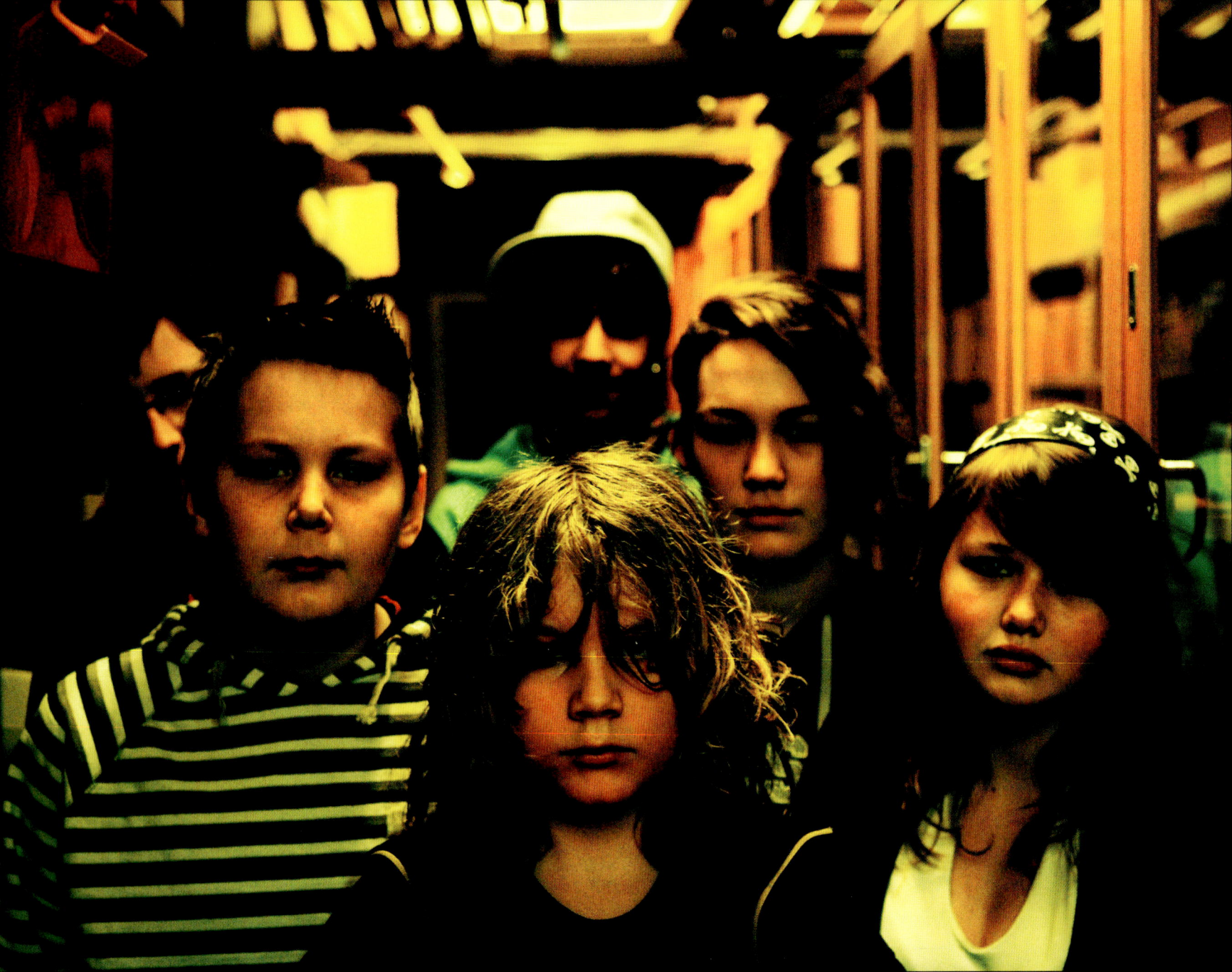

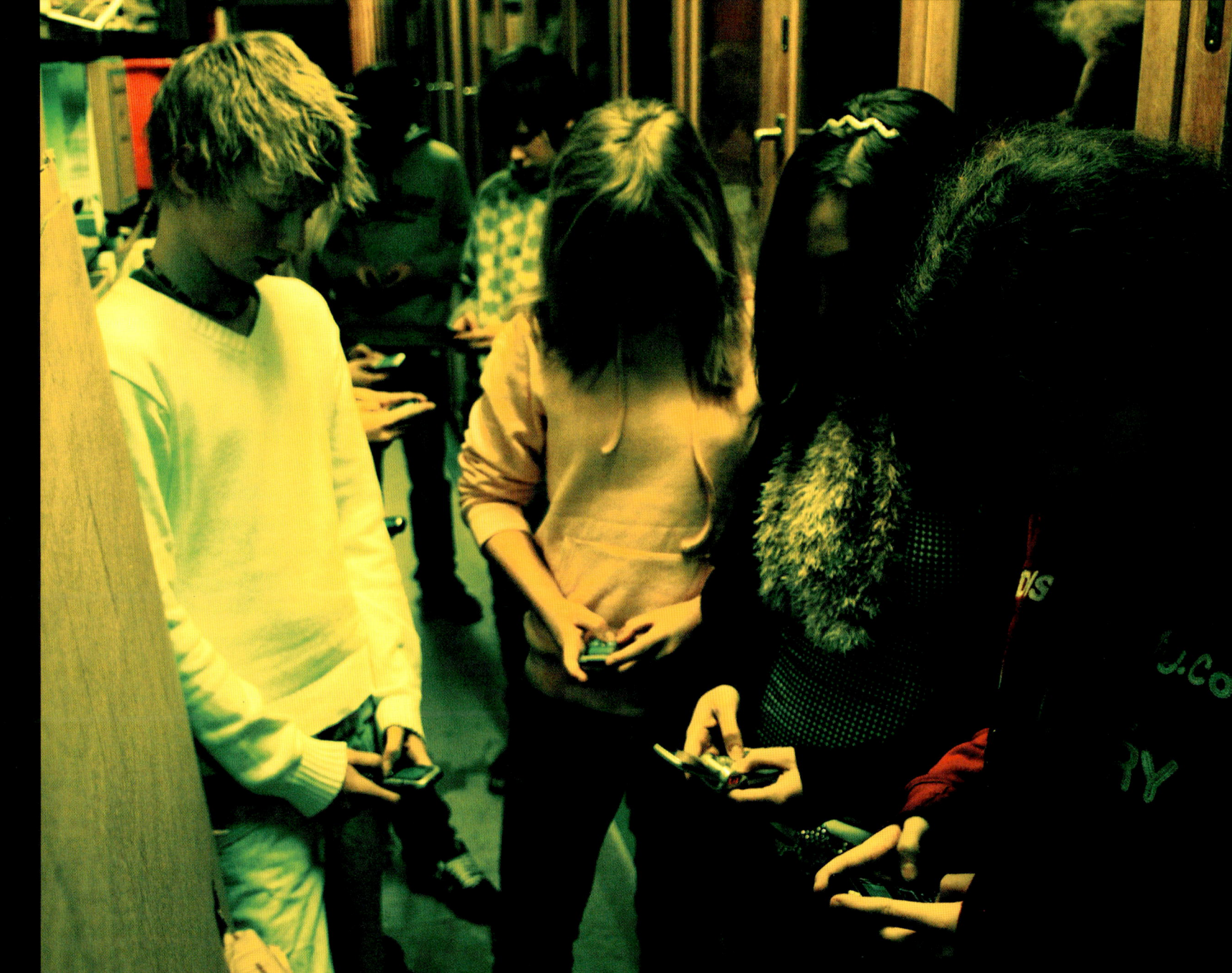

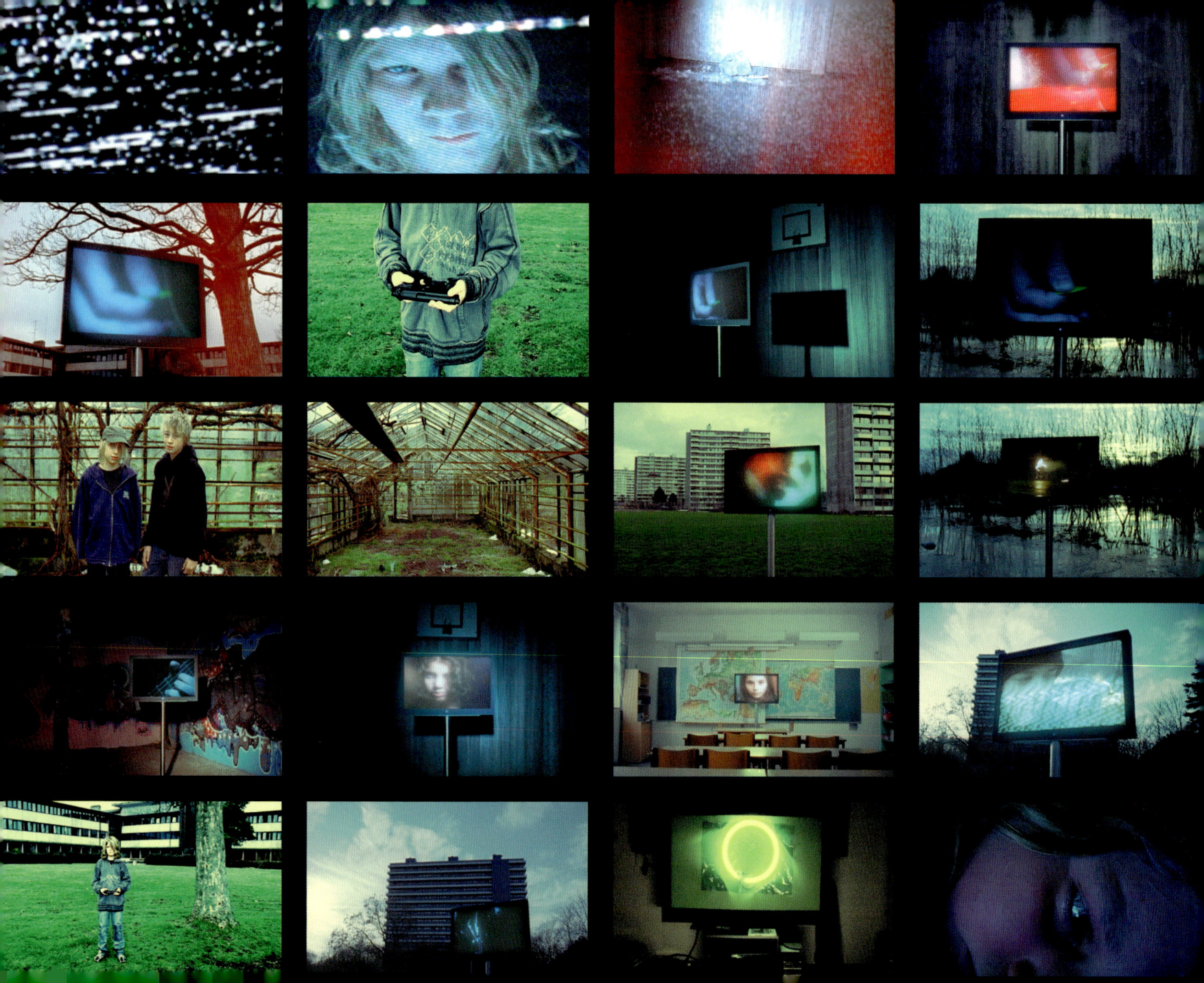

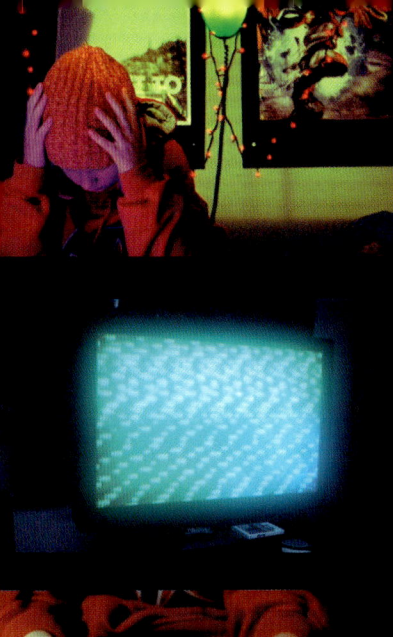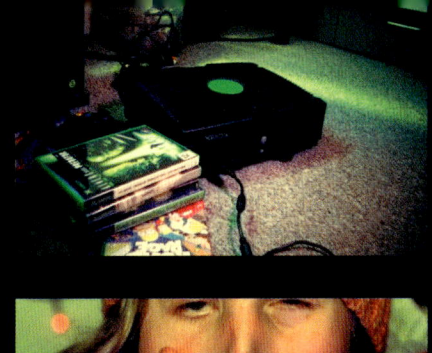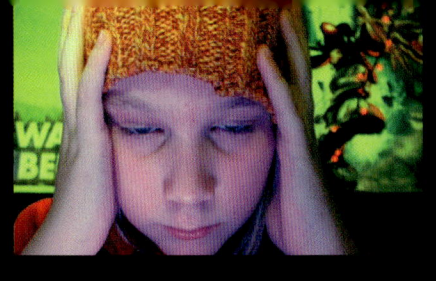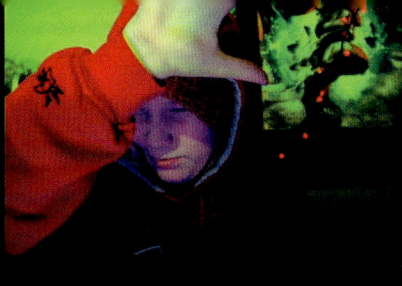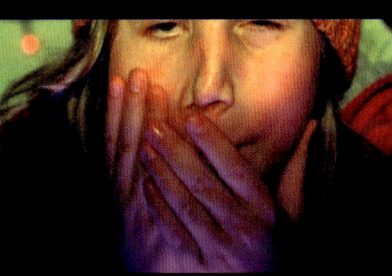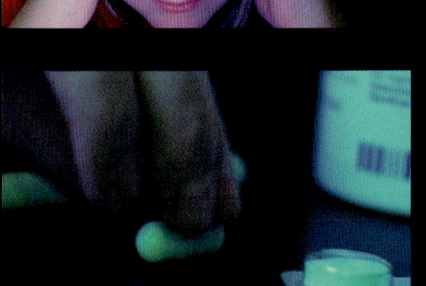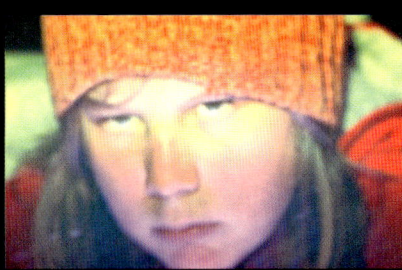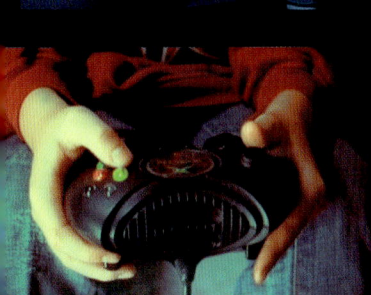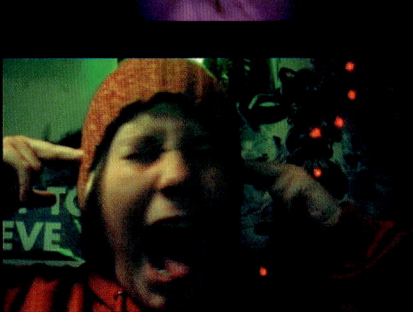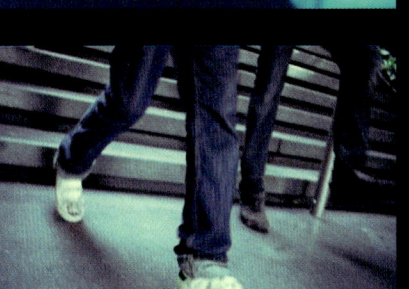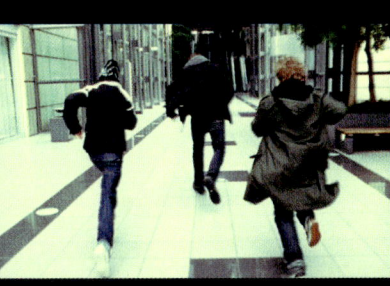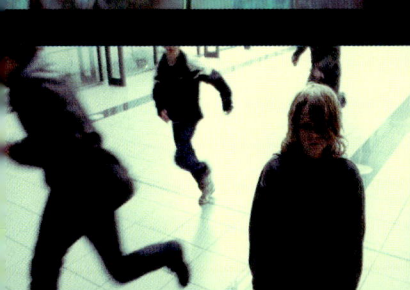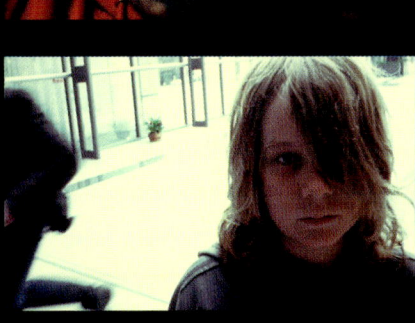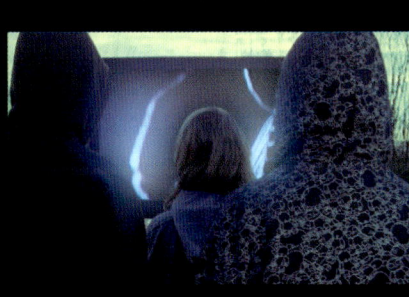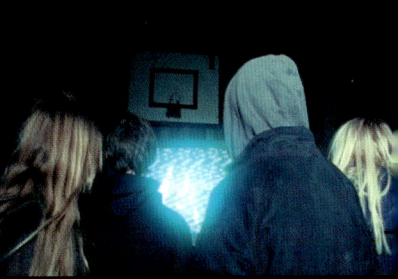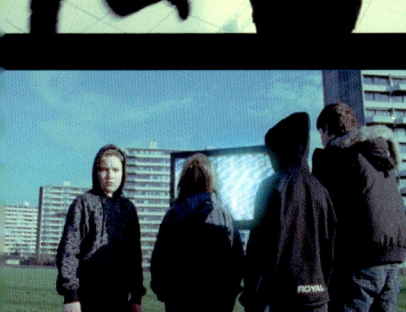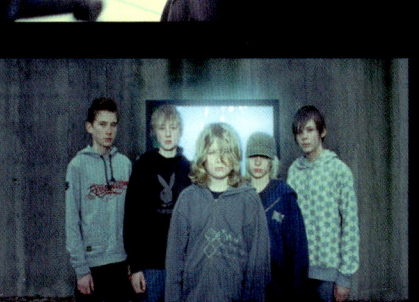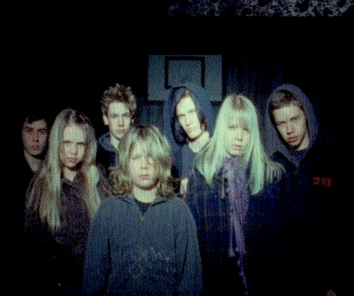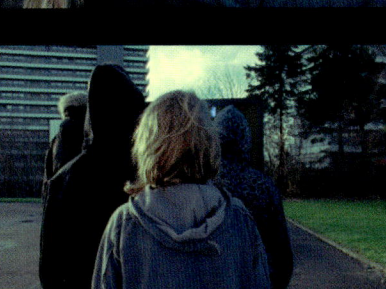

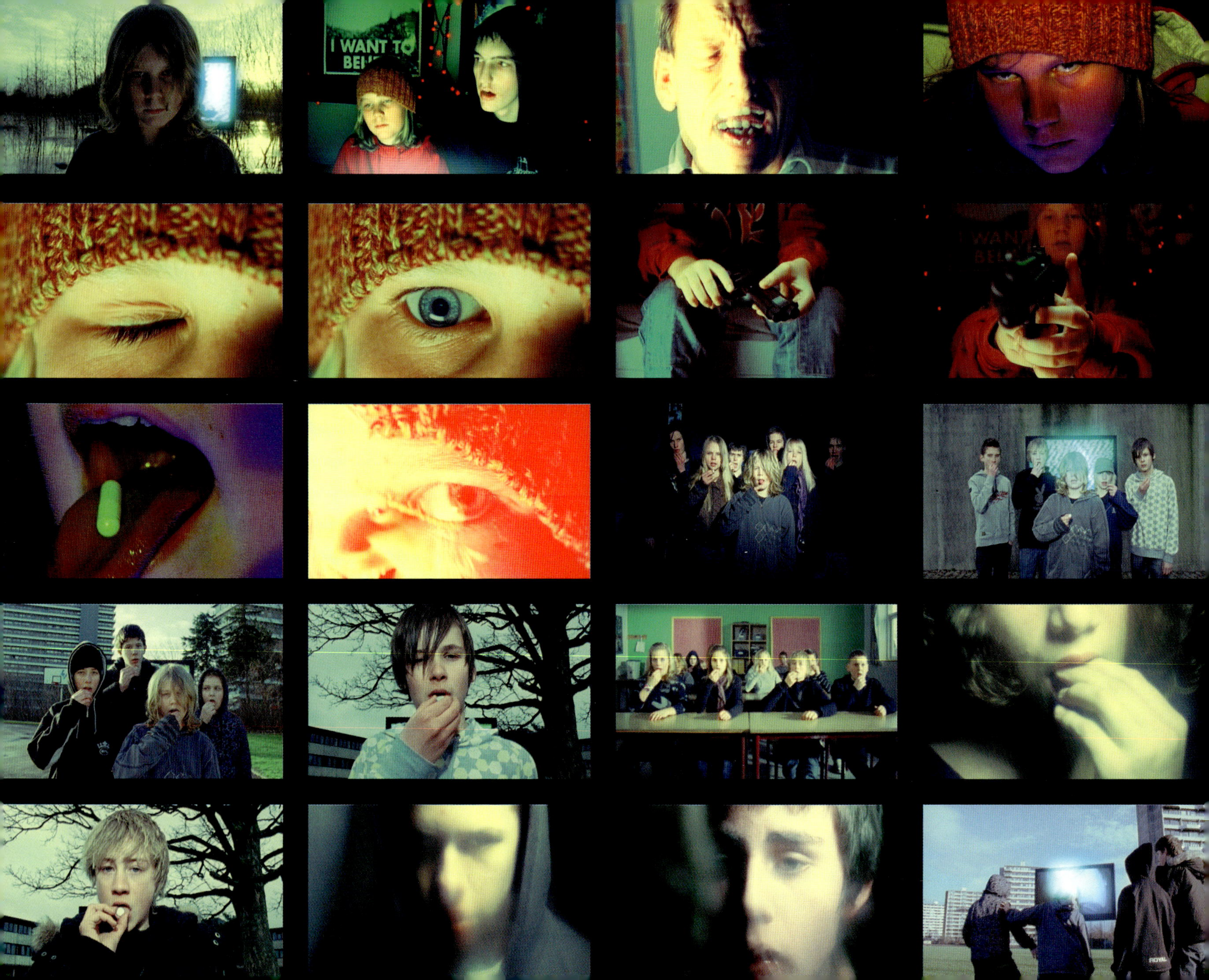

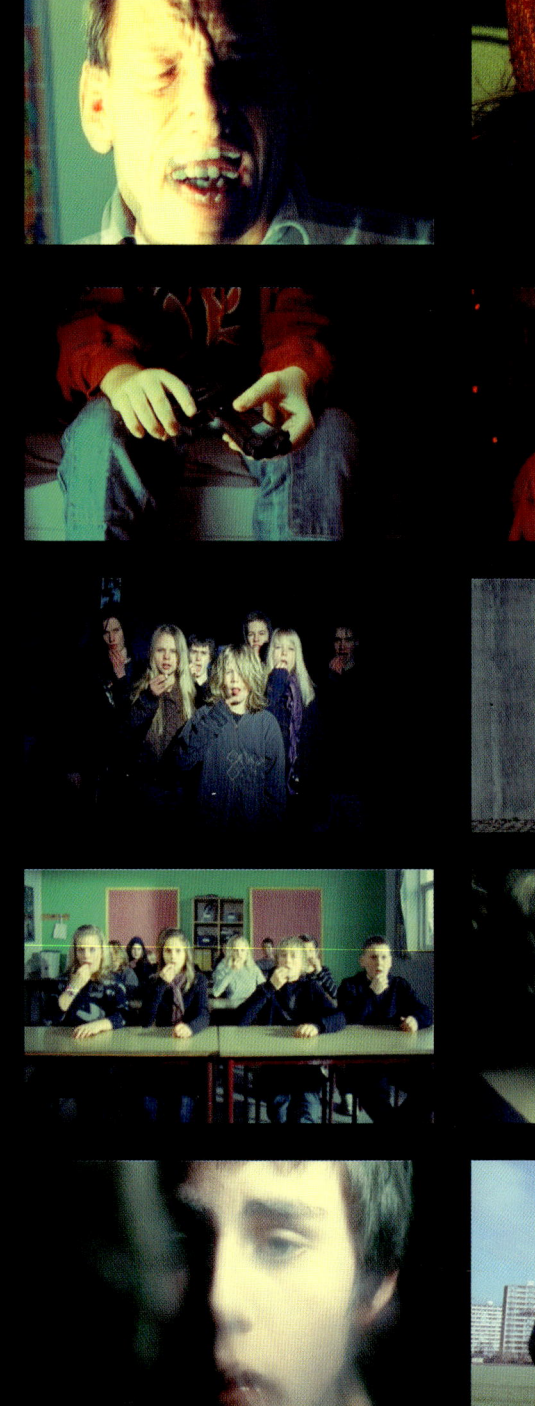

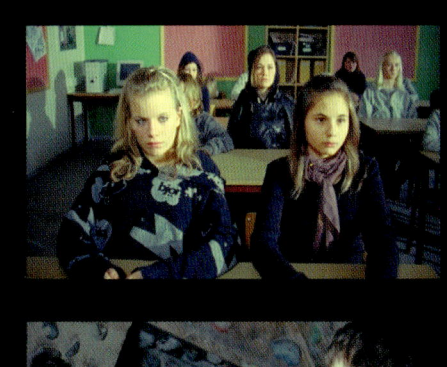 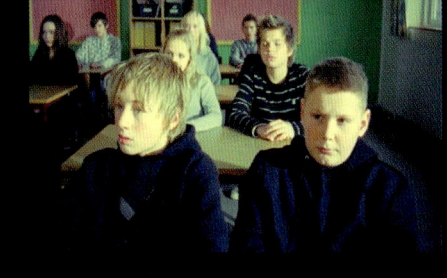 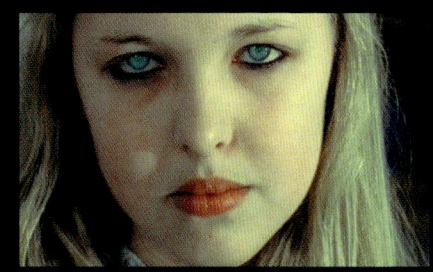 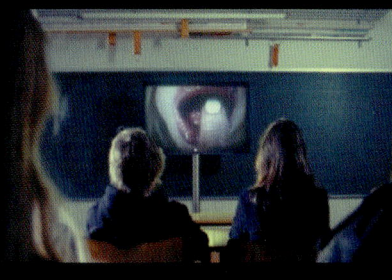
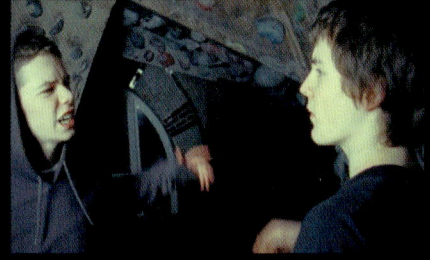 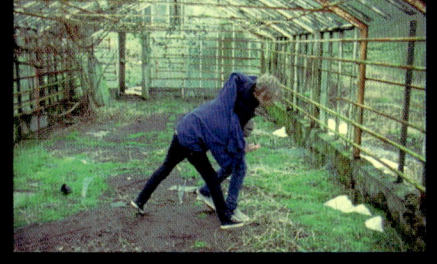 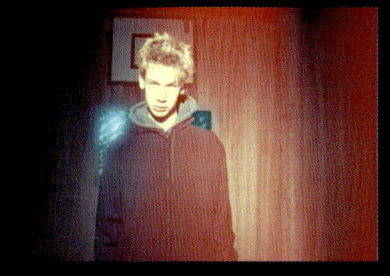 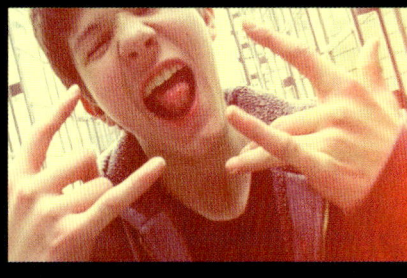
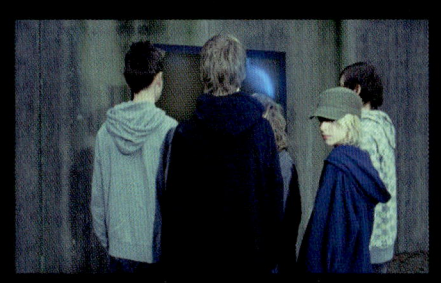 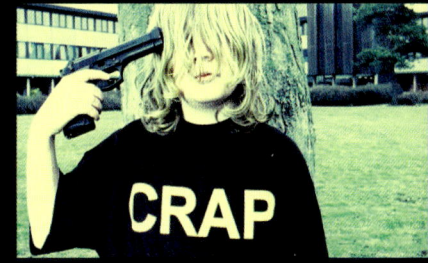 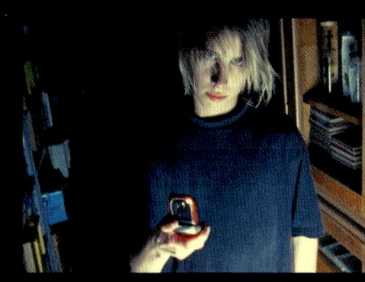 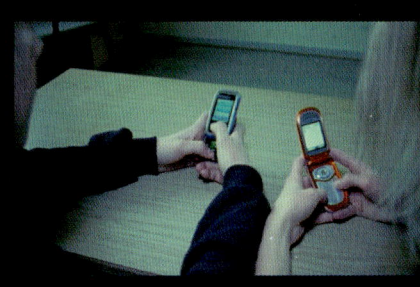
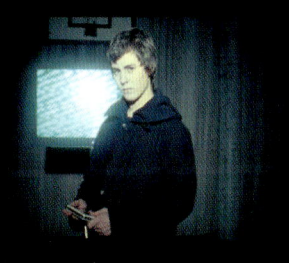 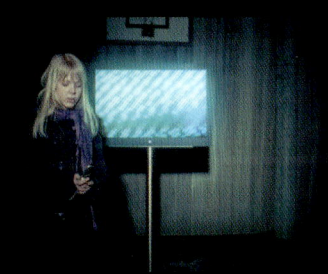 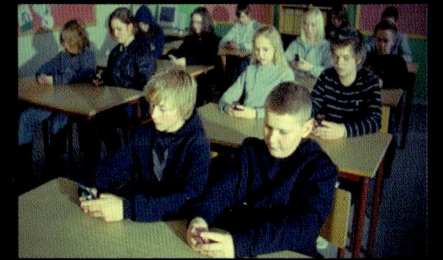 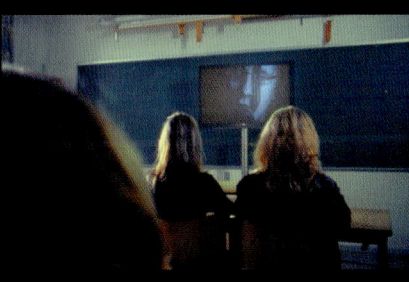
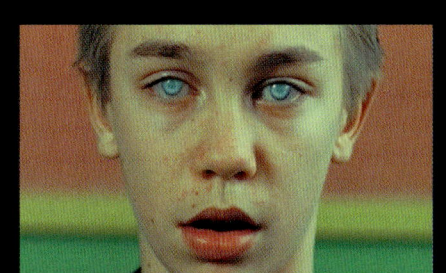 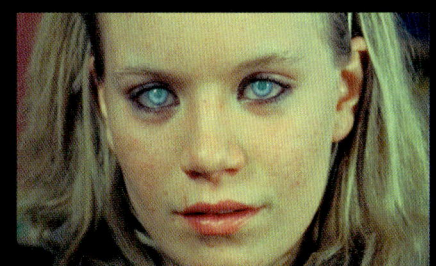 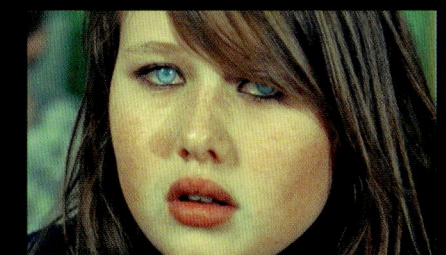 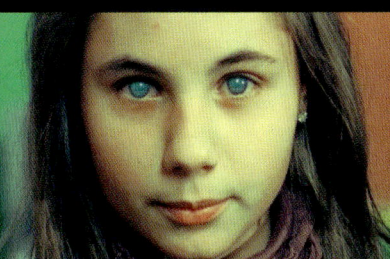

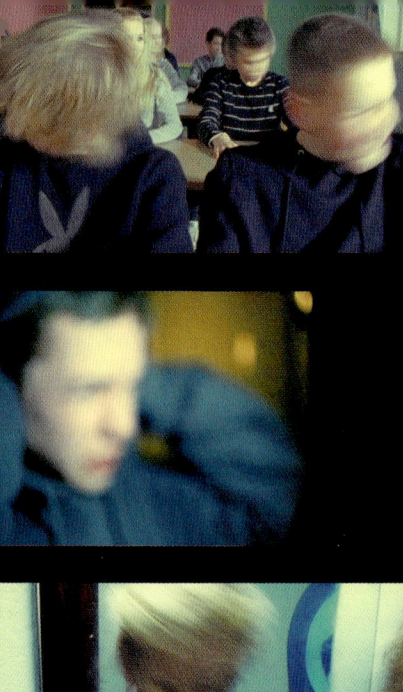
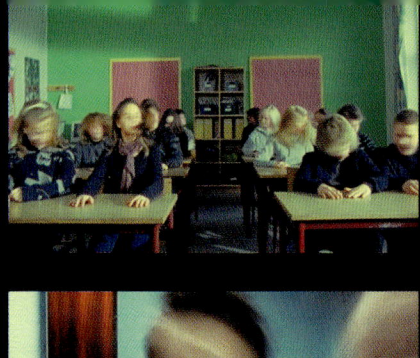
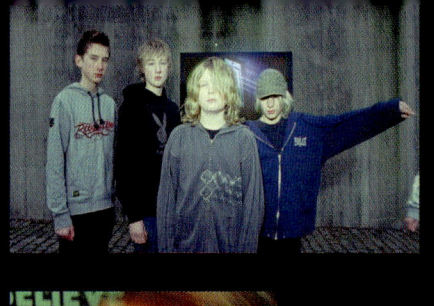
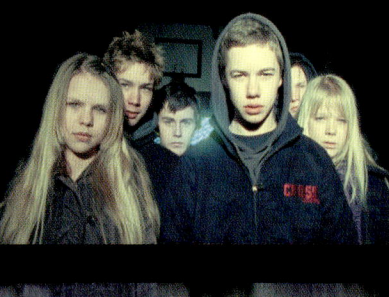
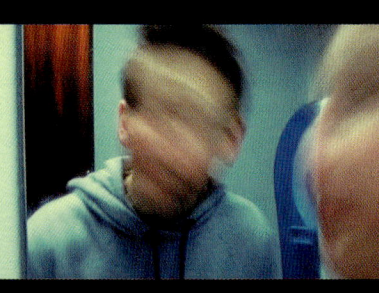
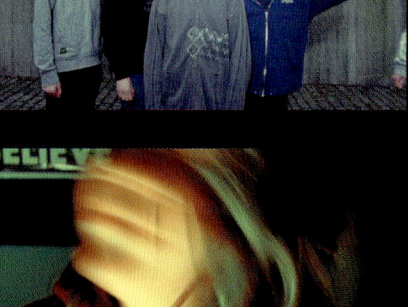
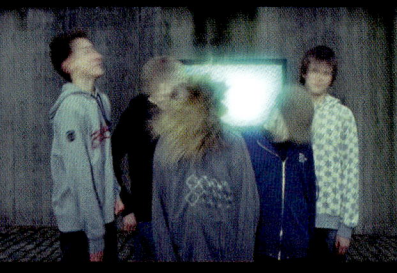
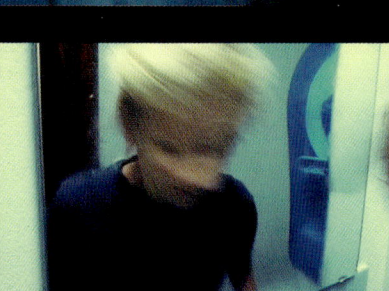
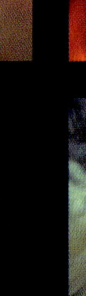
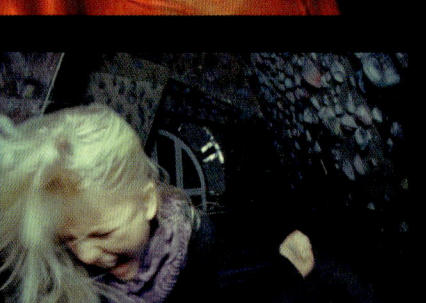
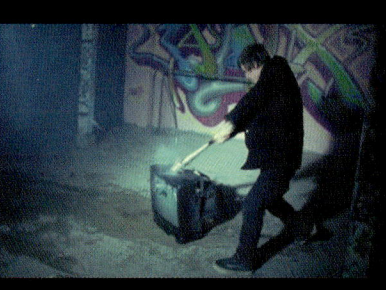
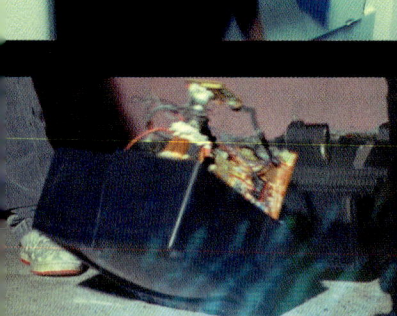
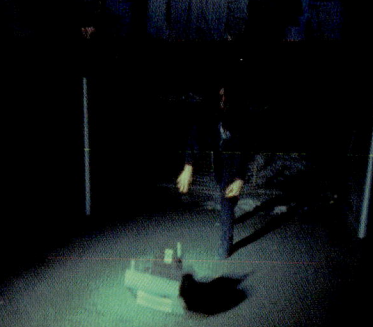
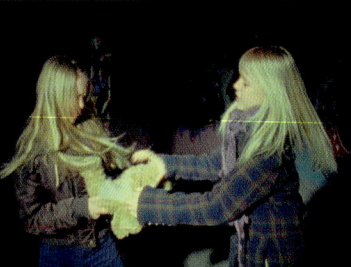
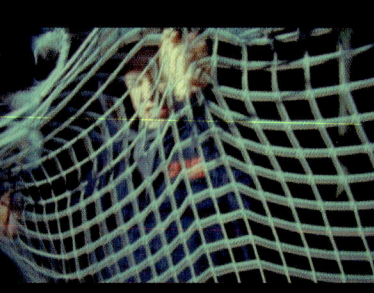
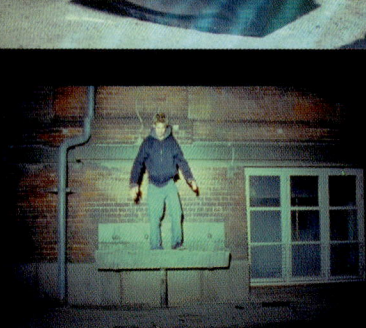
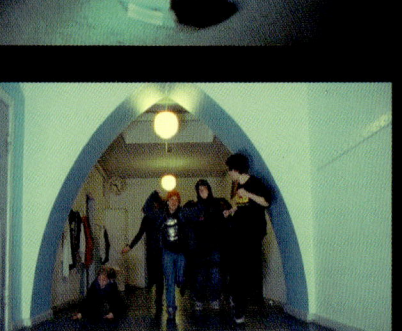
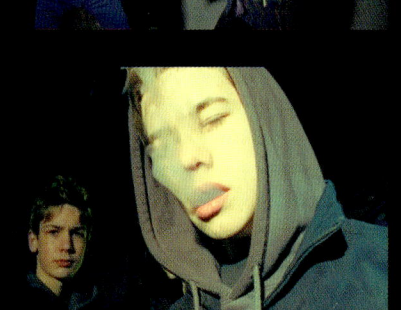
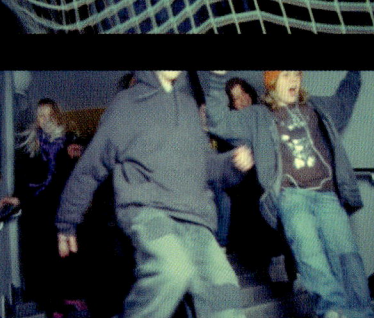

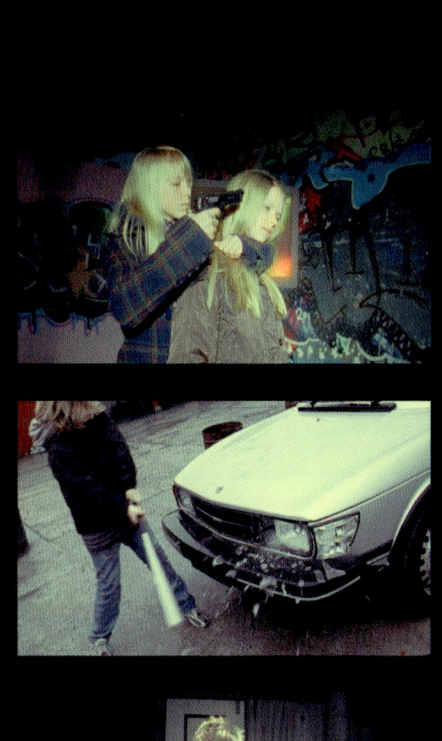
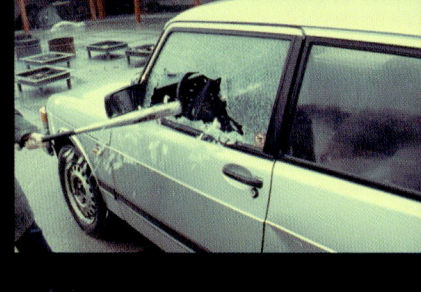
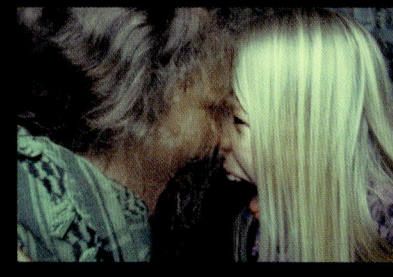
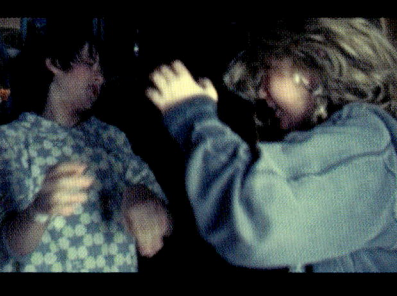
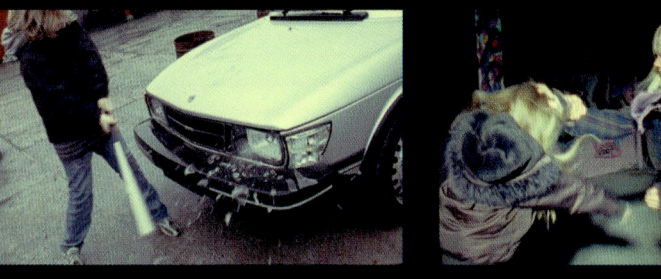
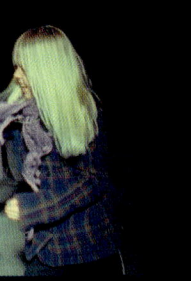
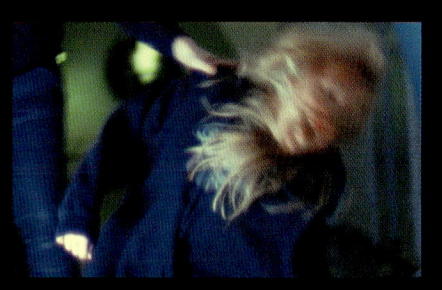
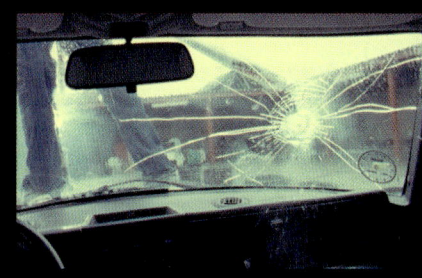
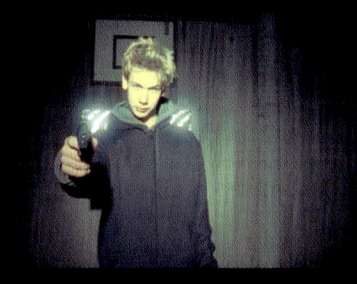
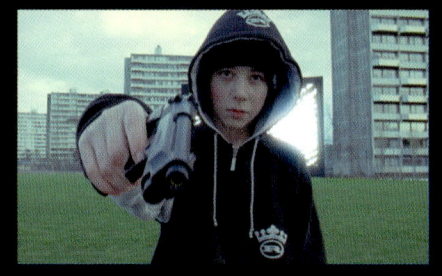
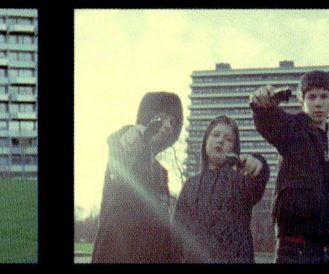
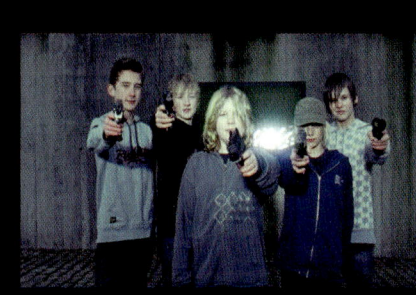
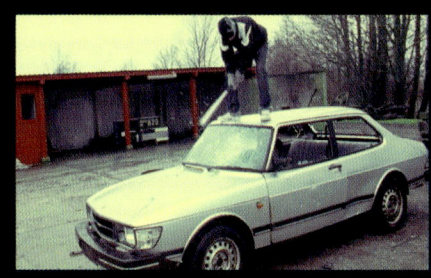
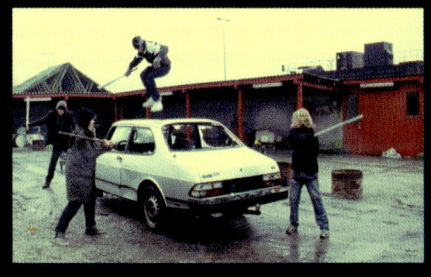
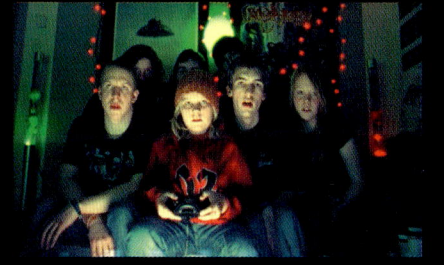
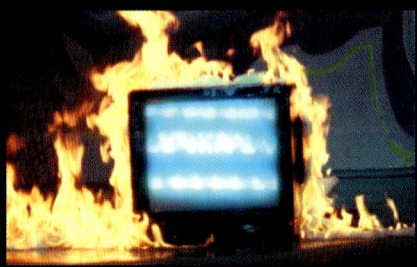
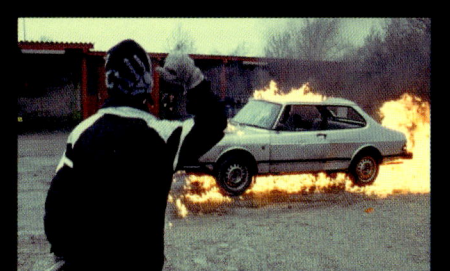
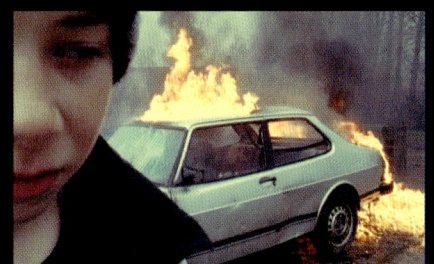
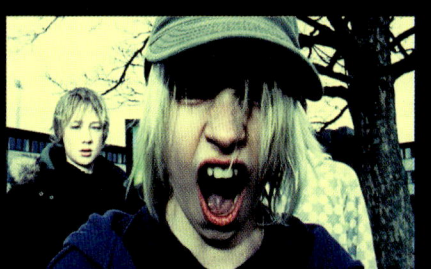
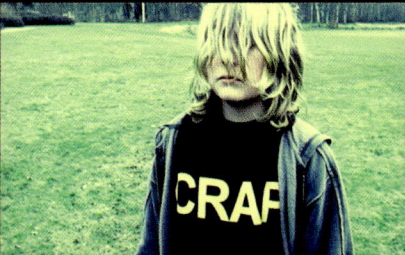

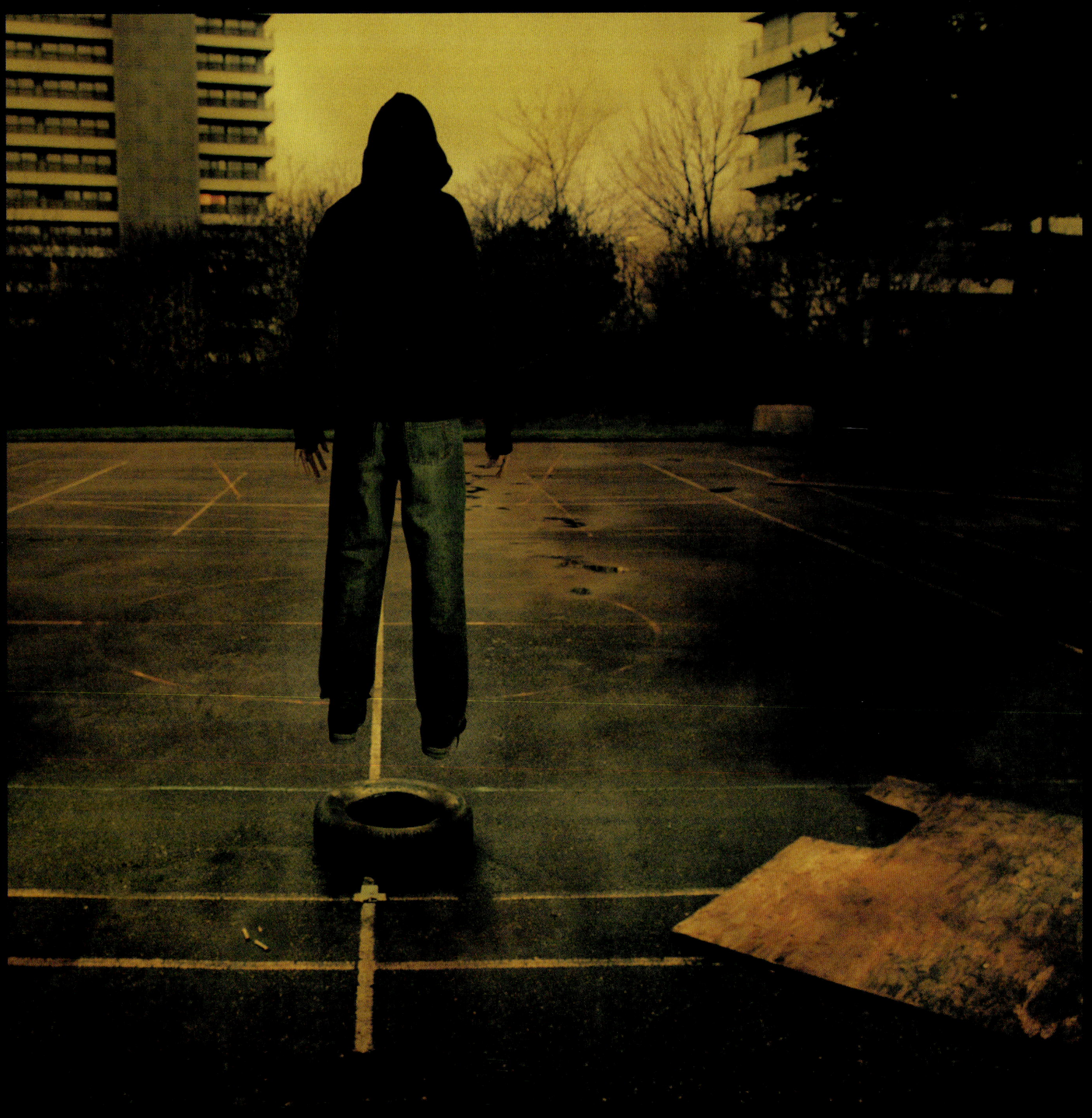

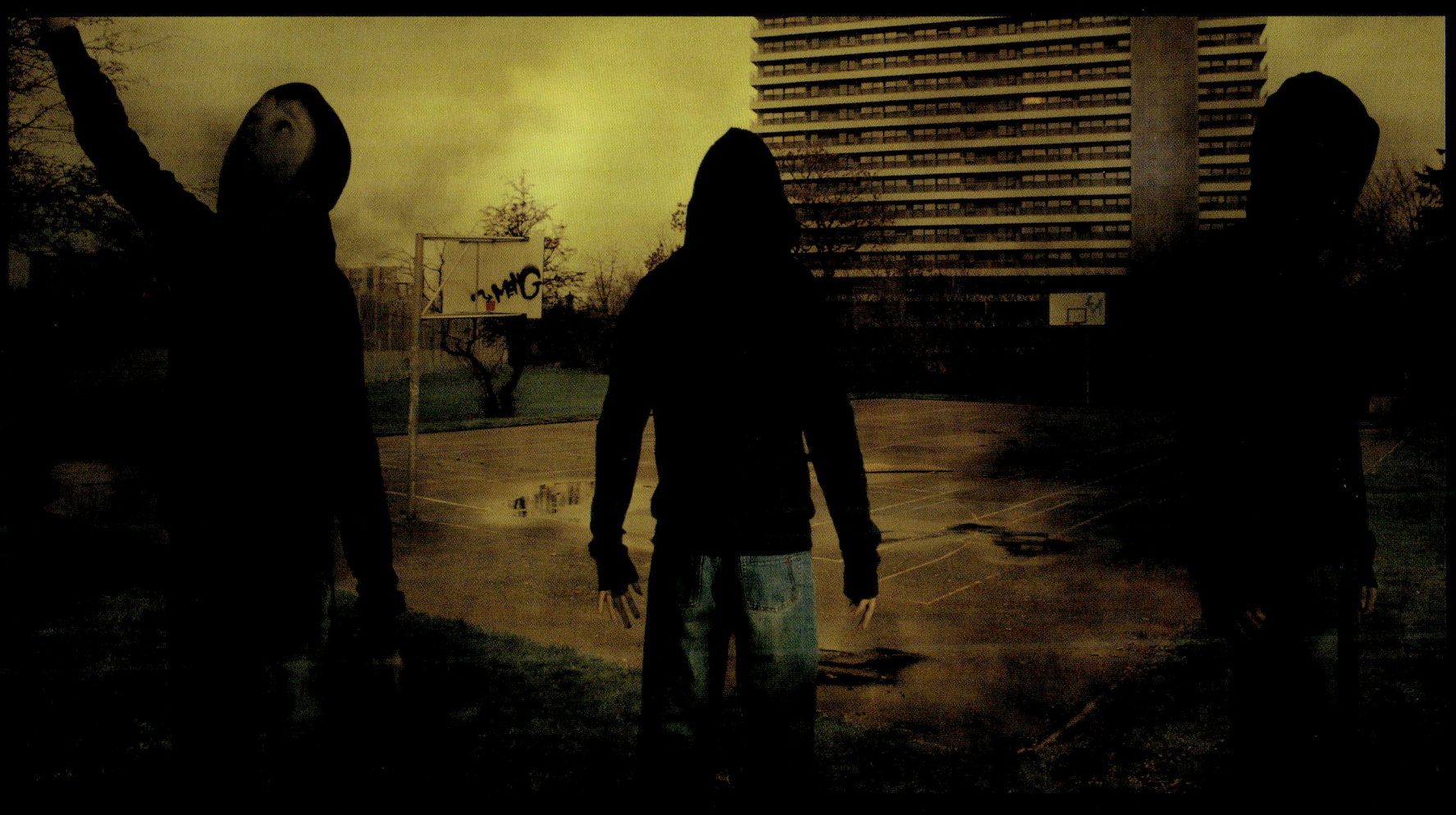

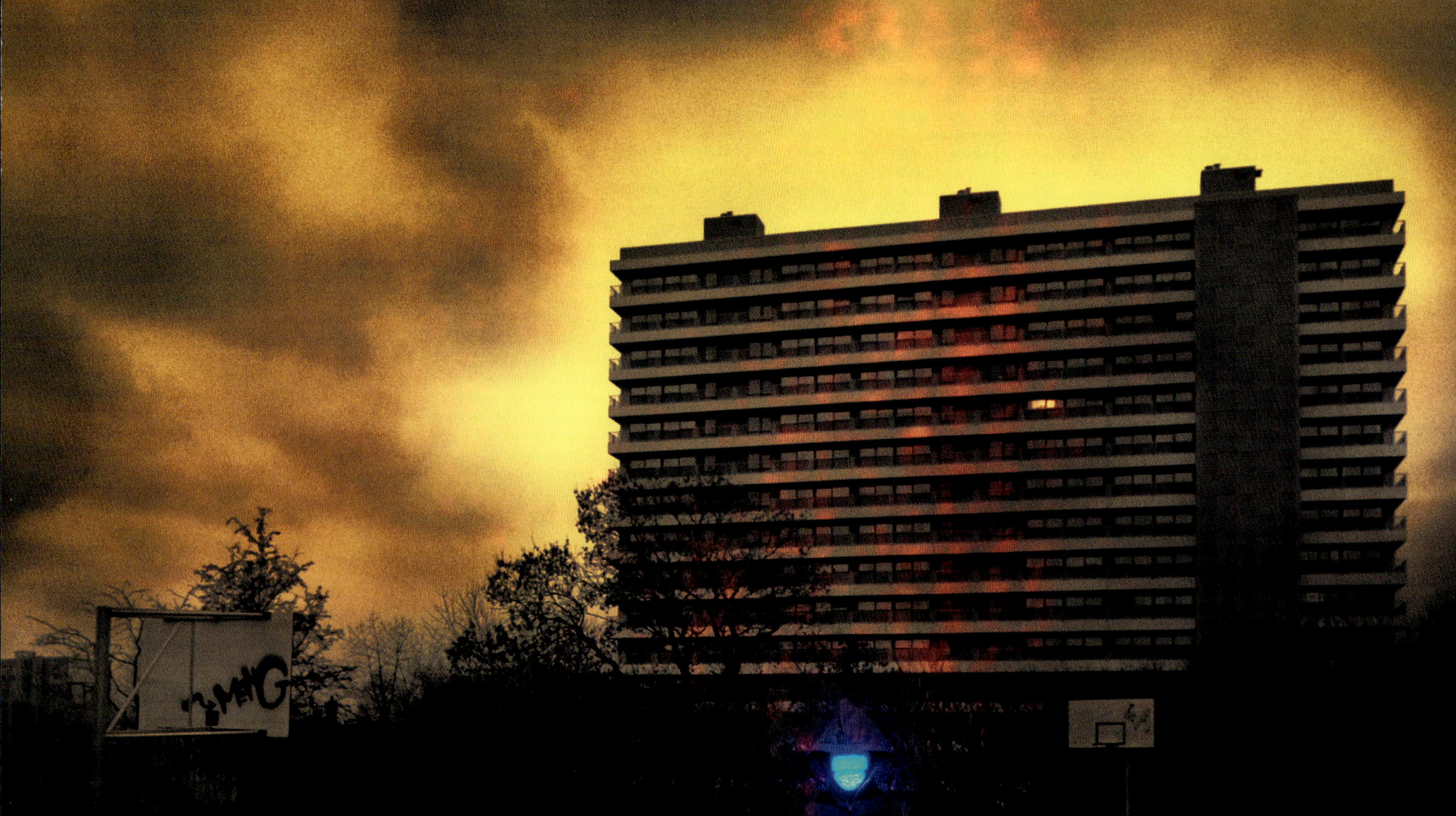

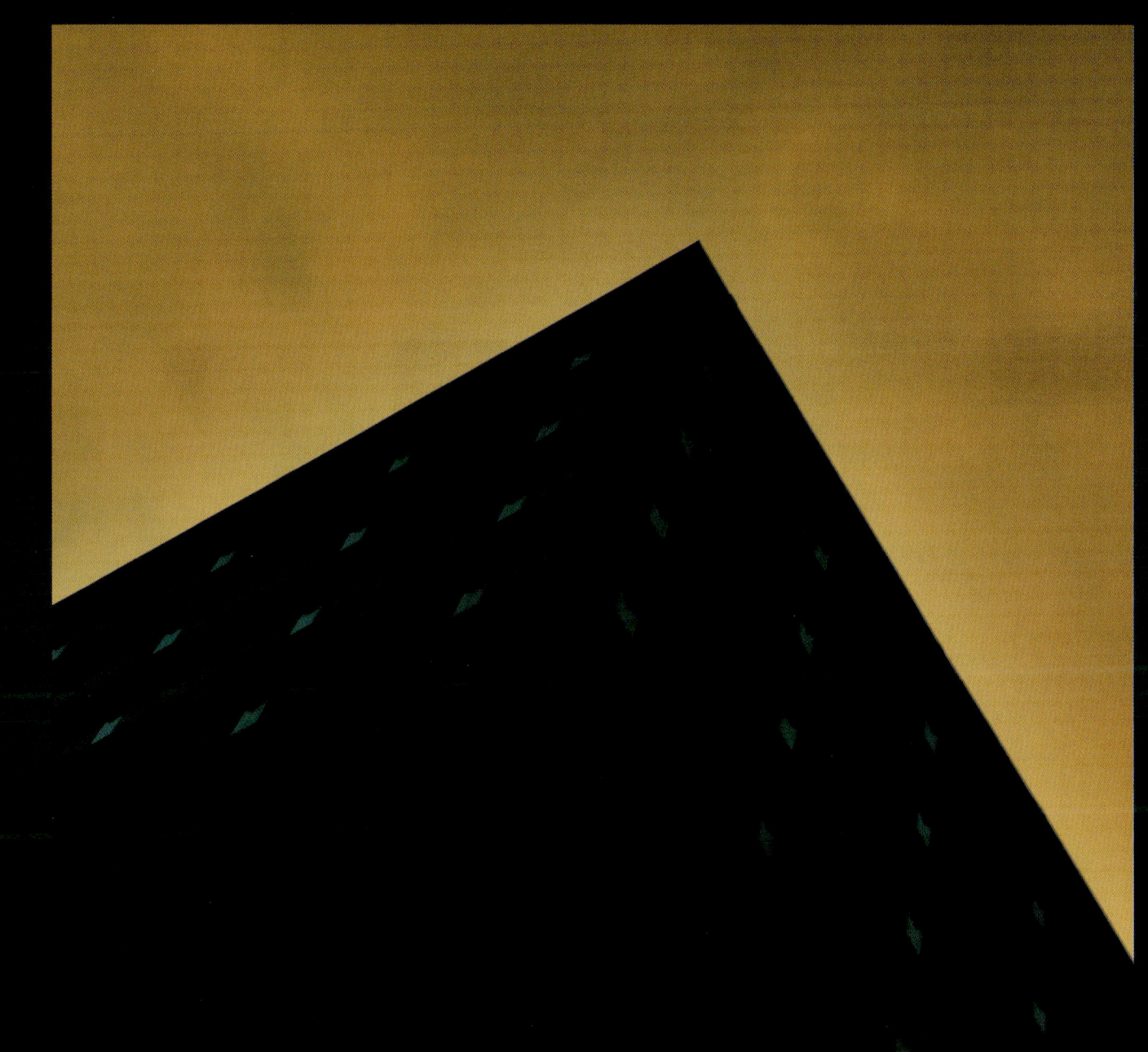

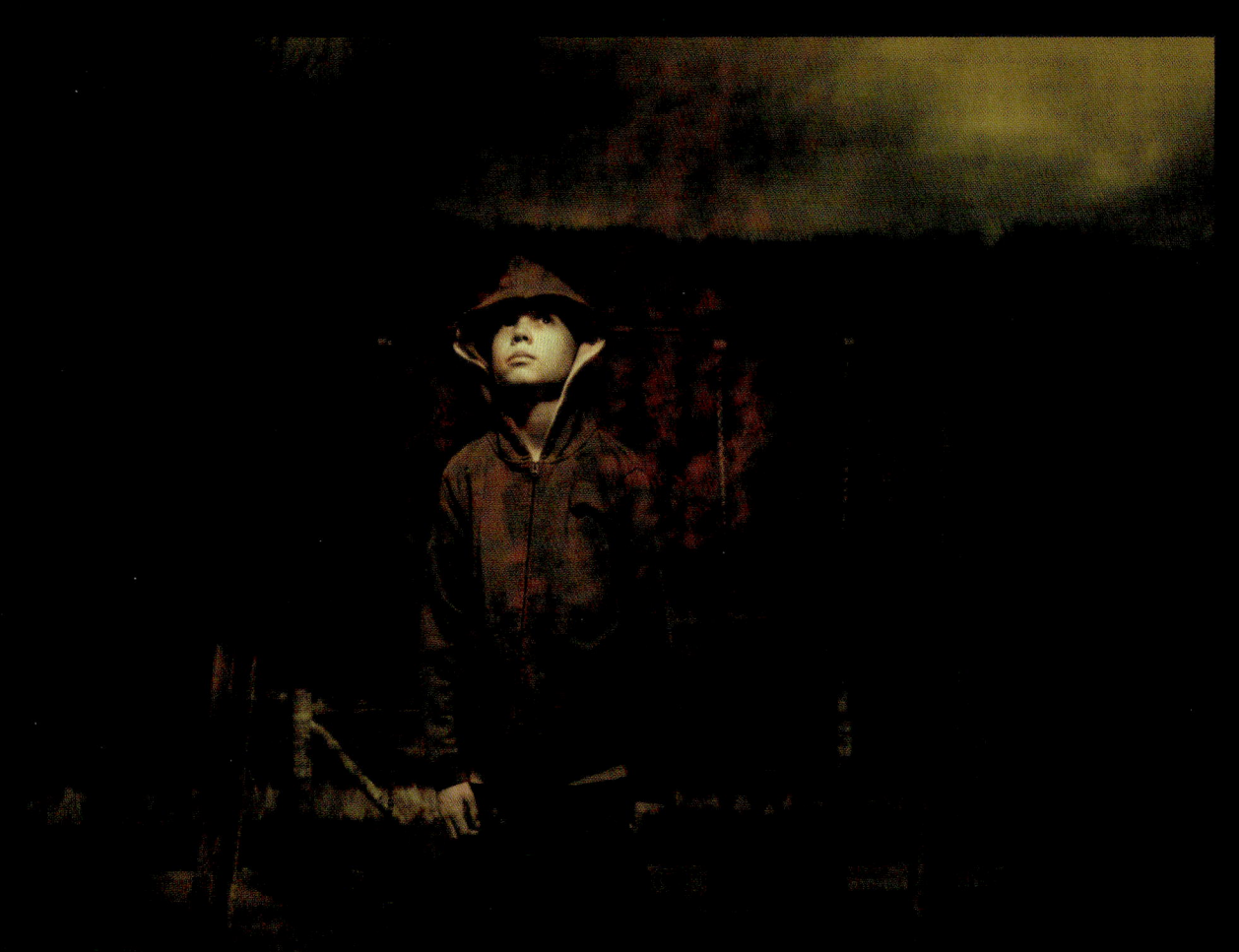

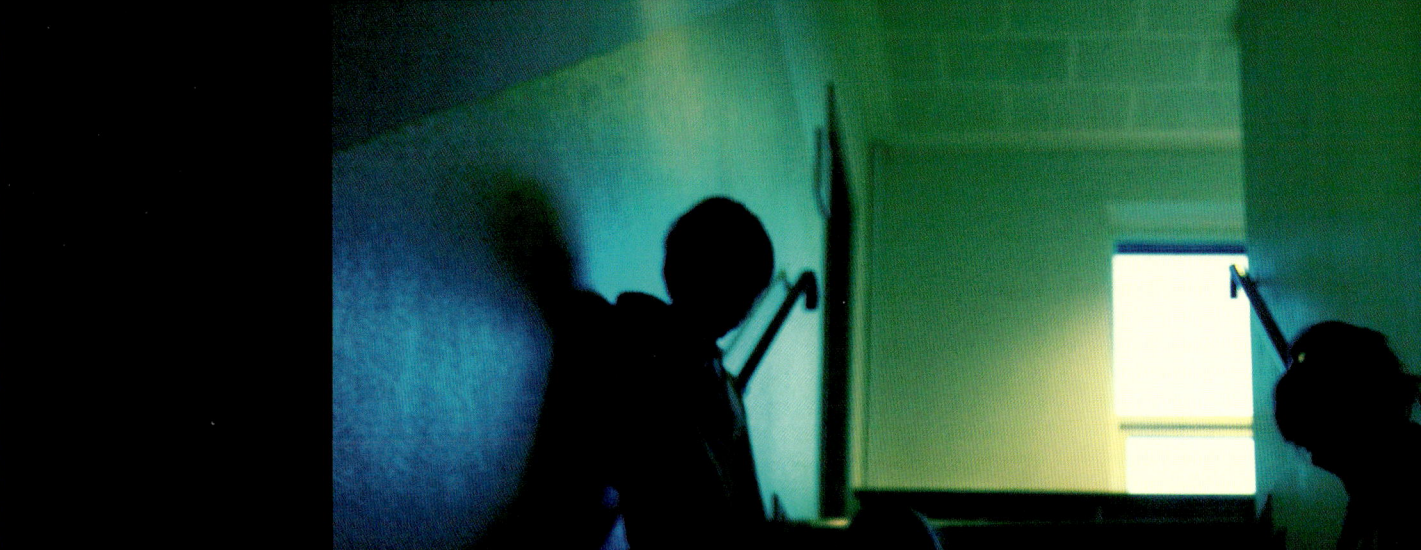

NORMAL 2007

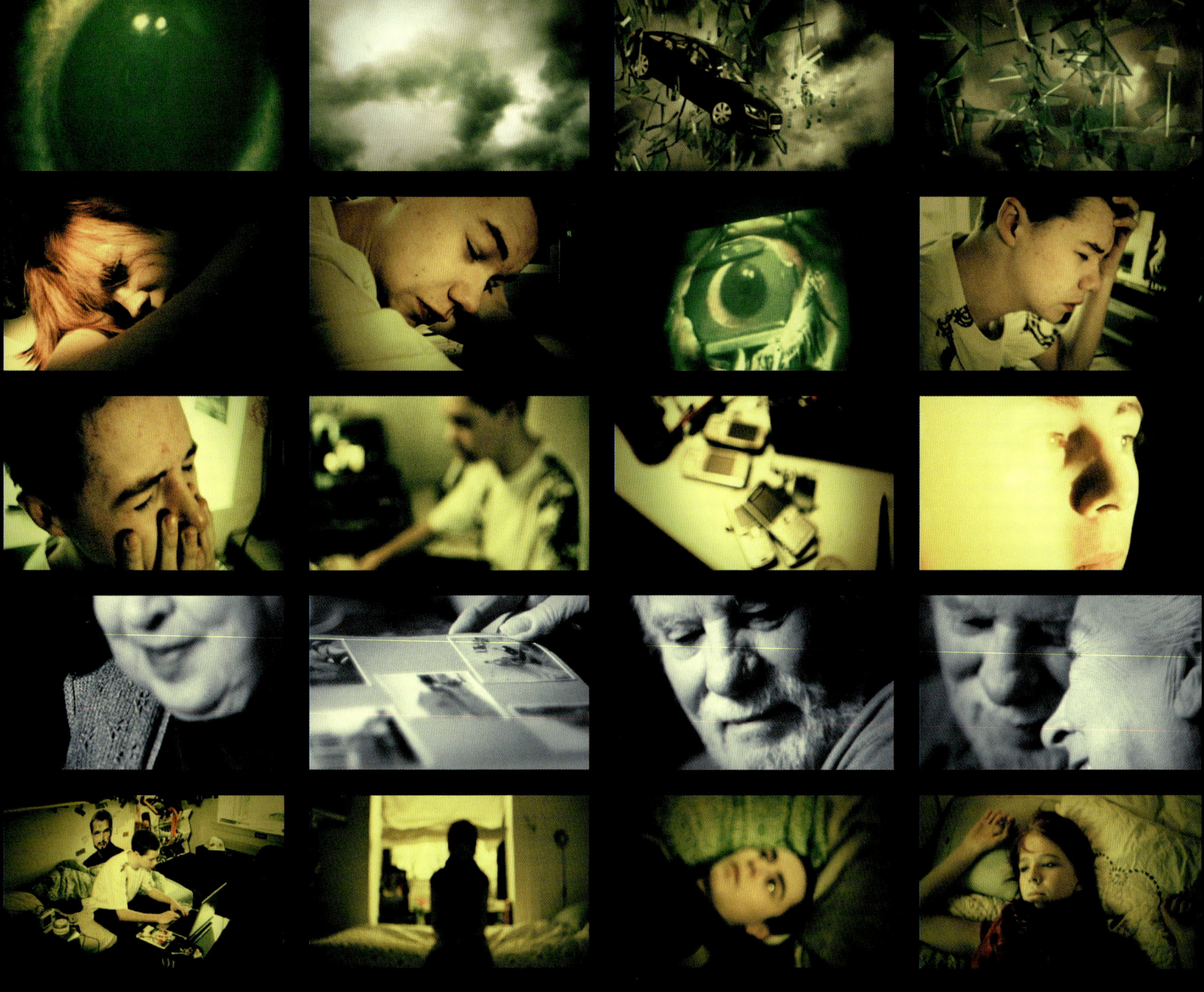

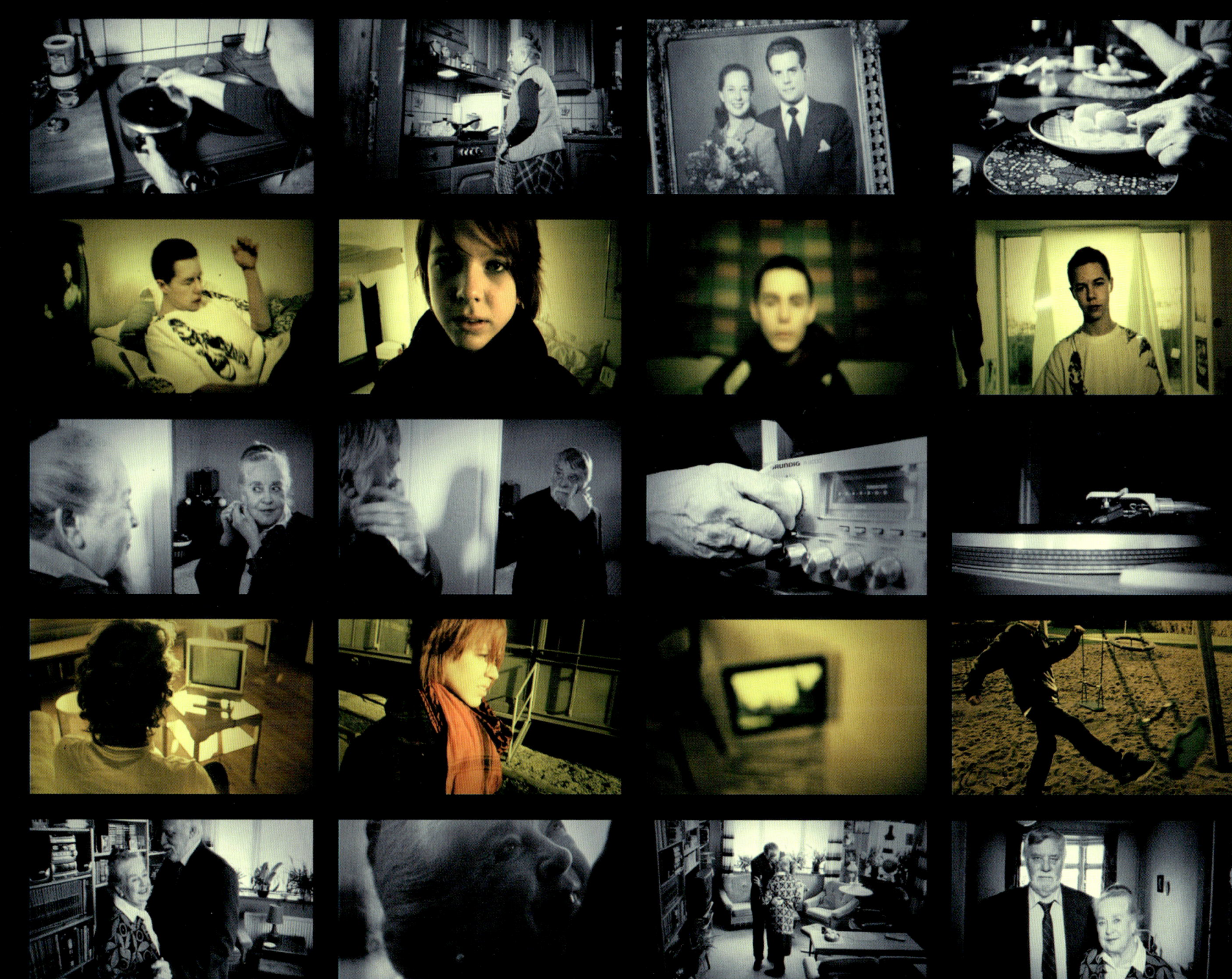

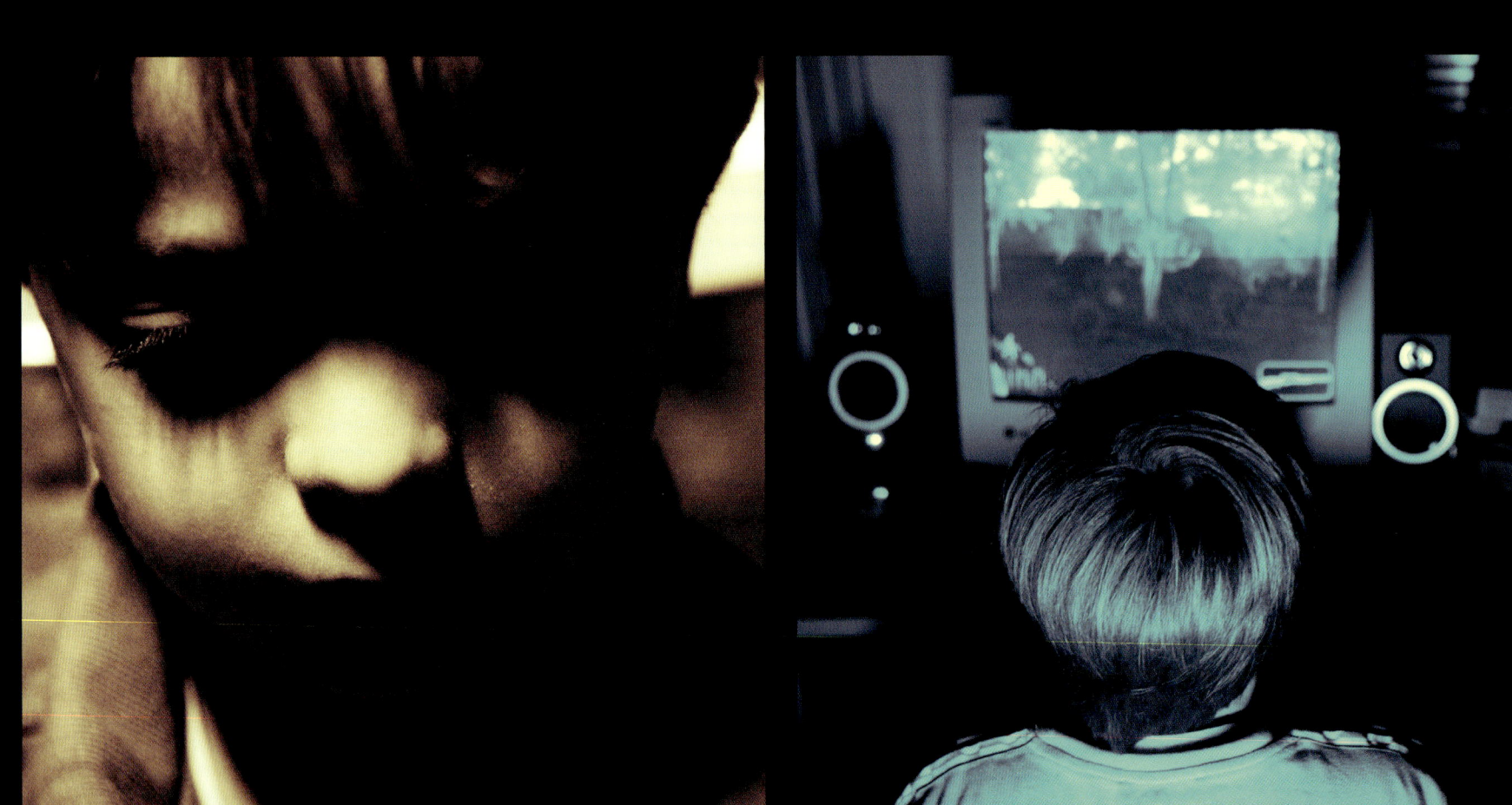

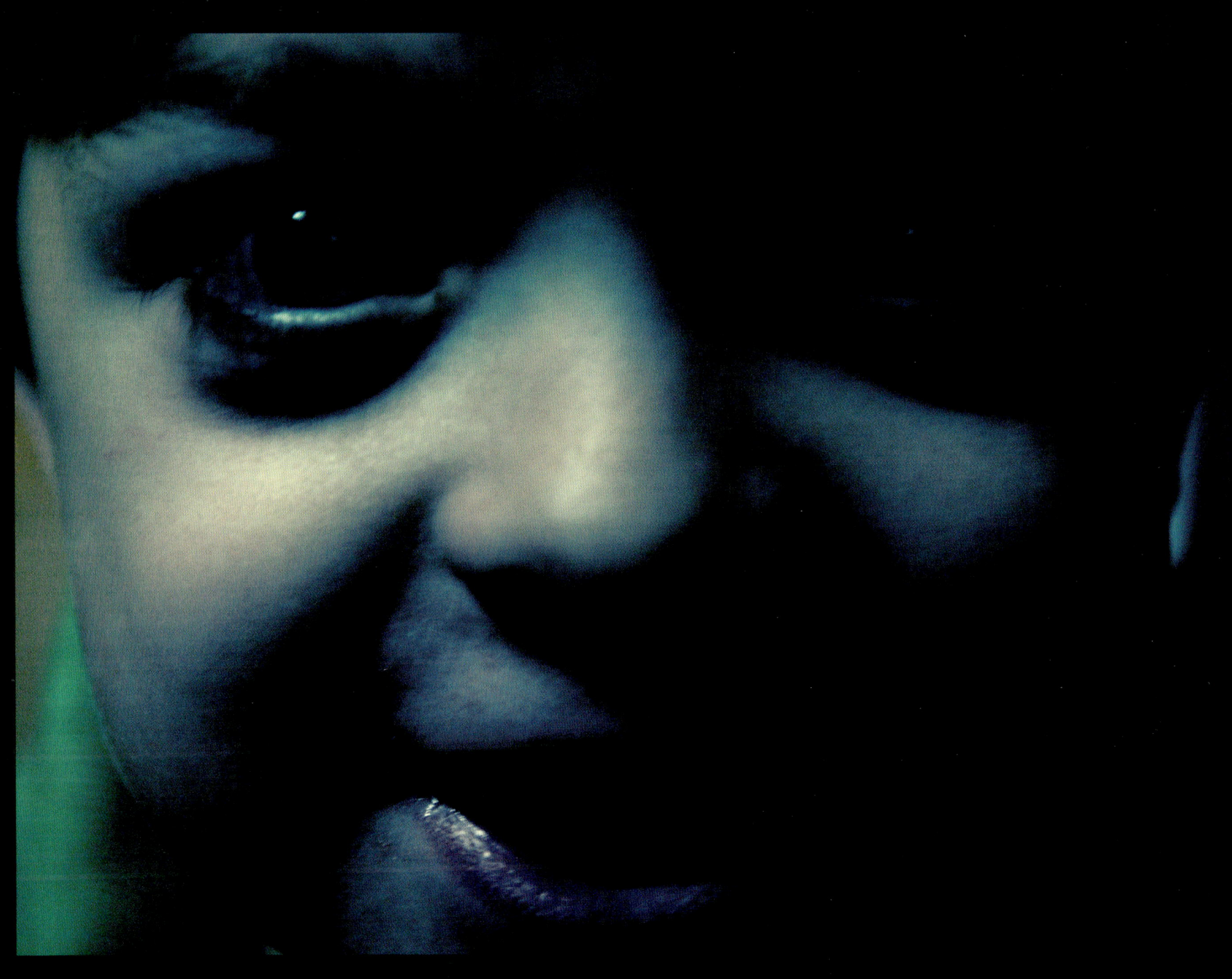

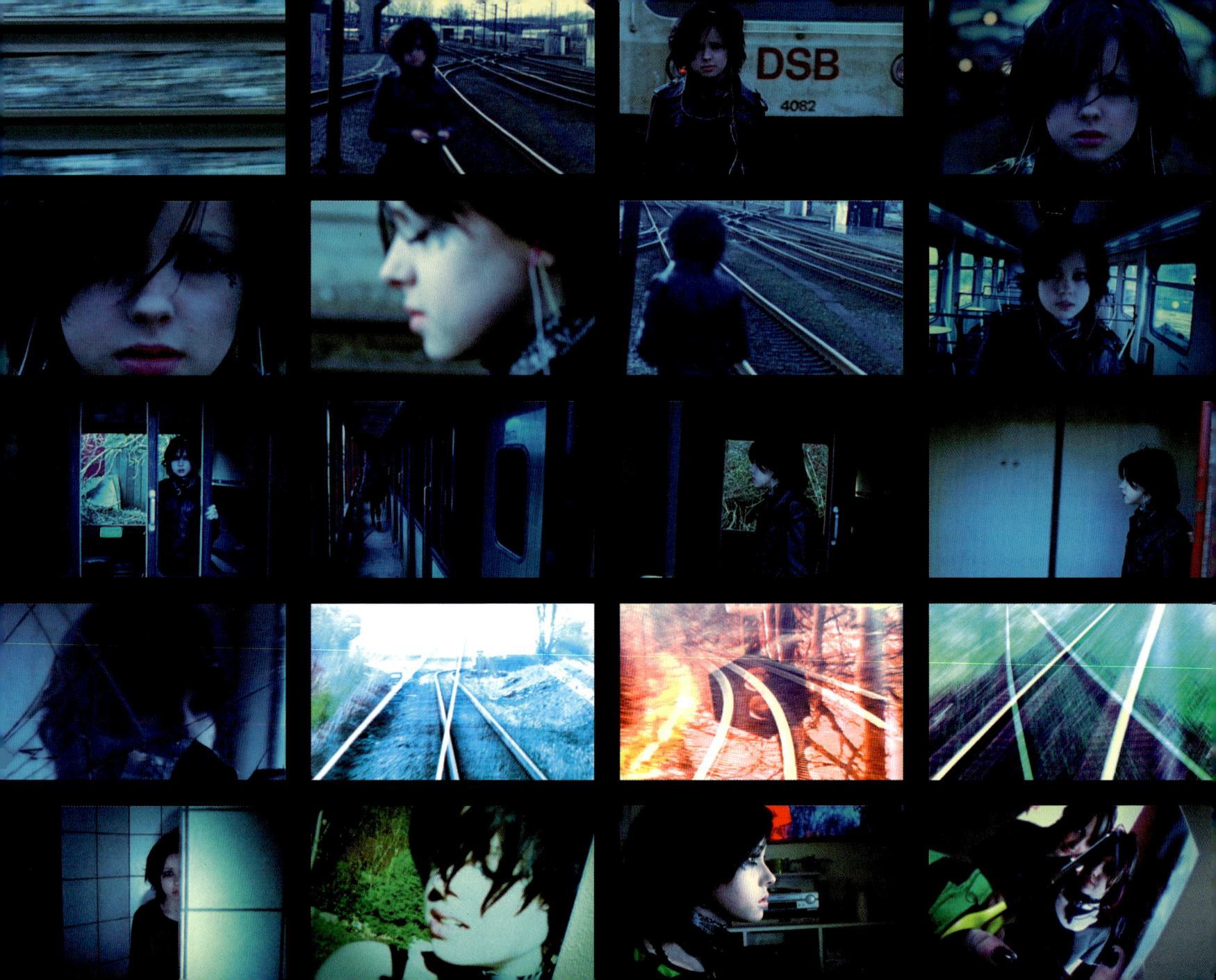

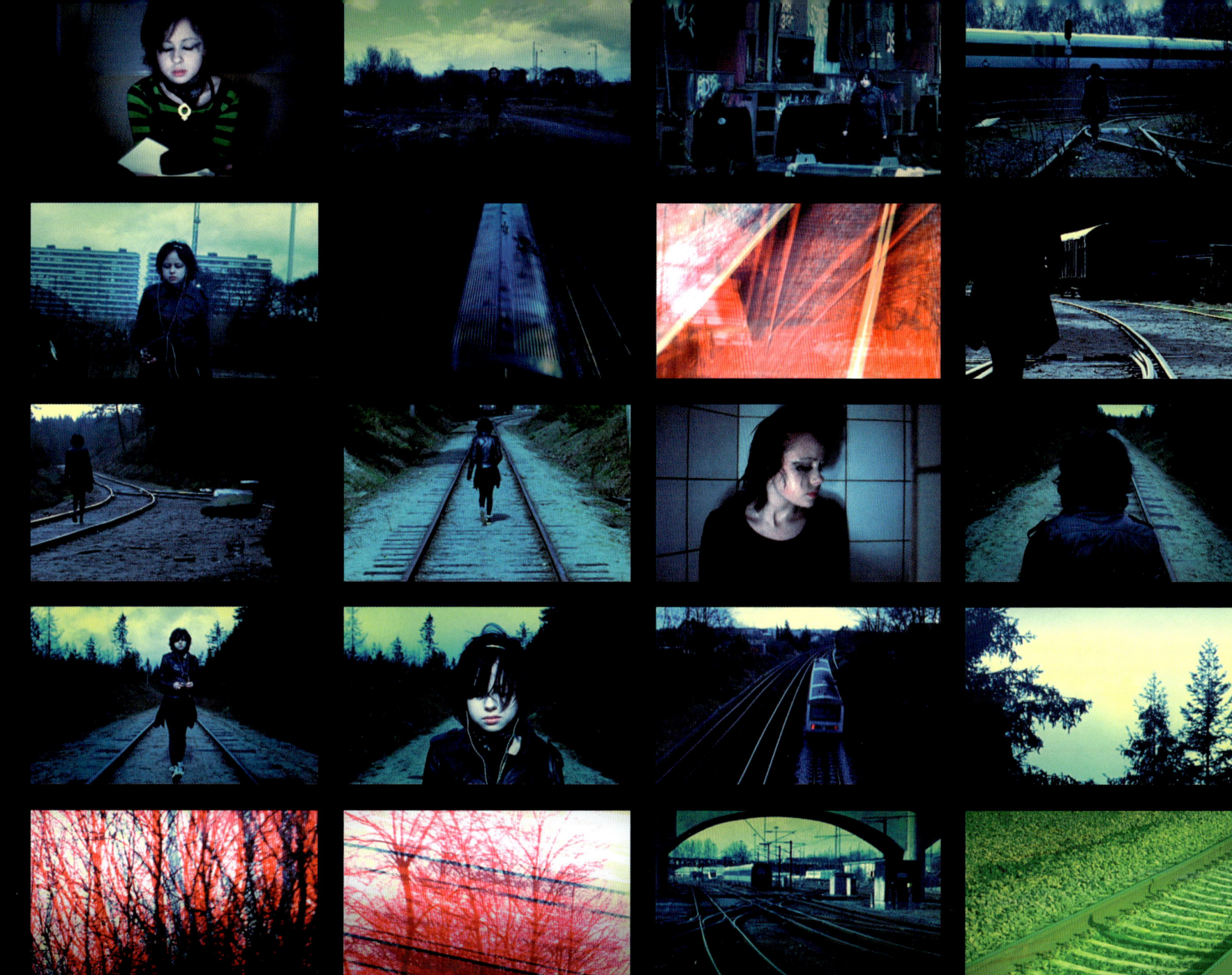

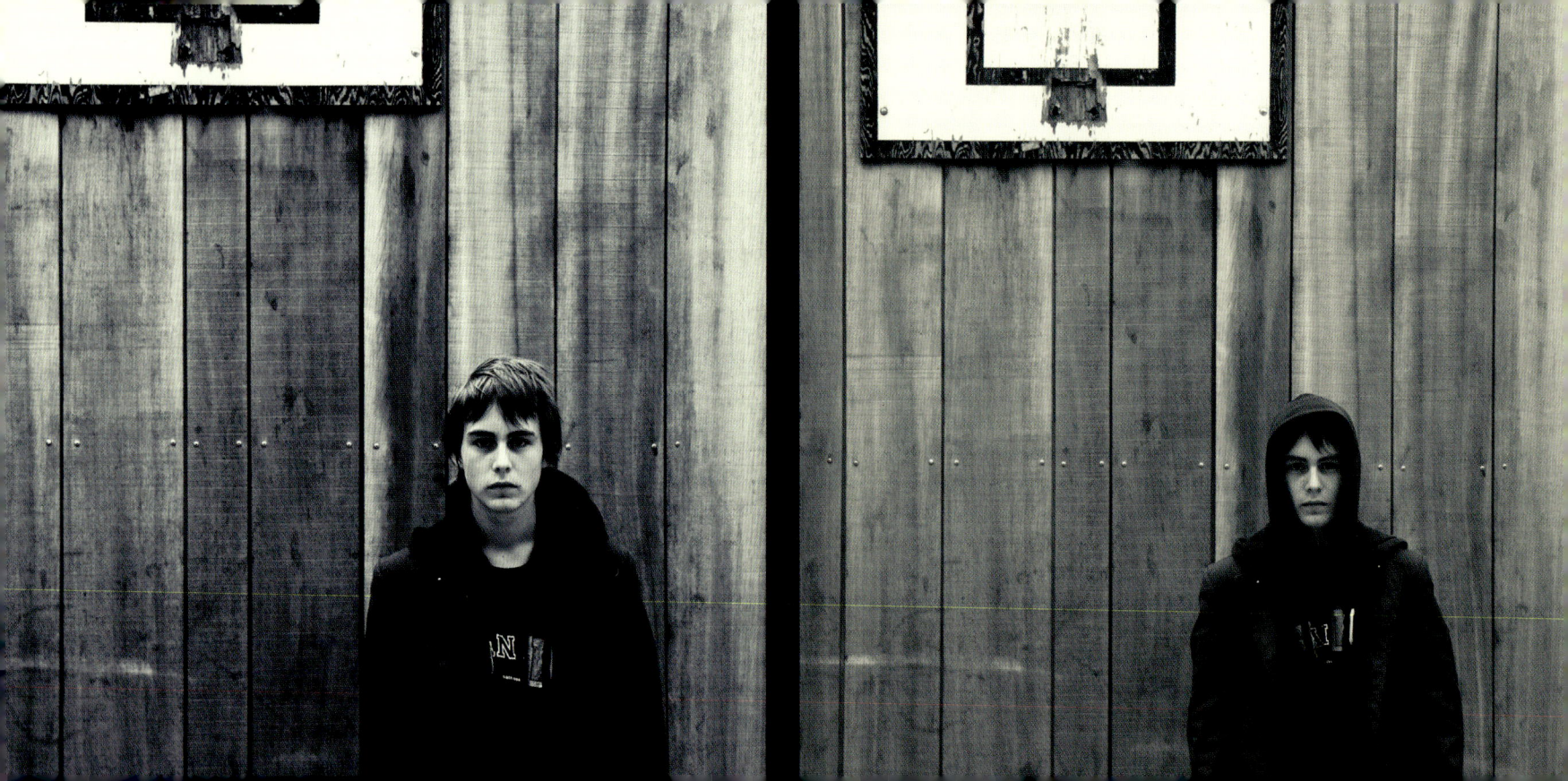

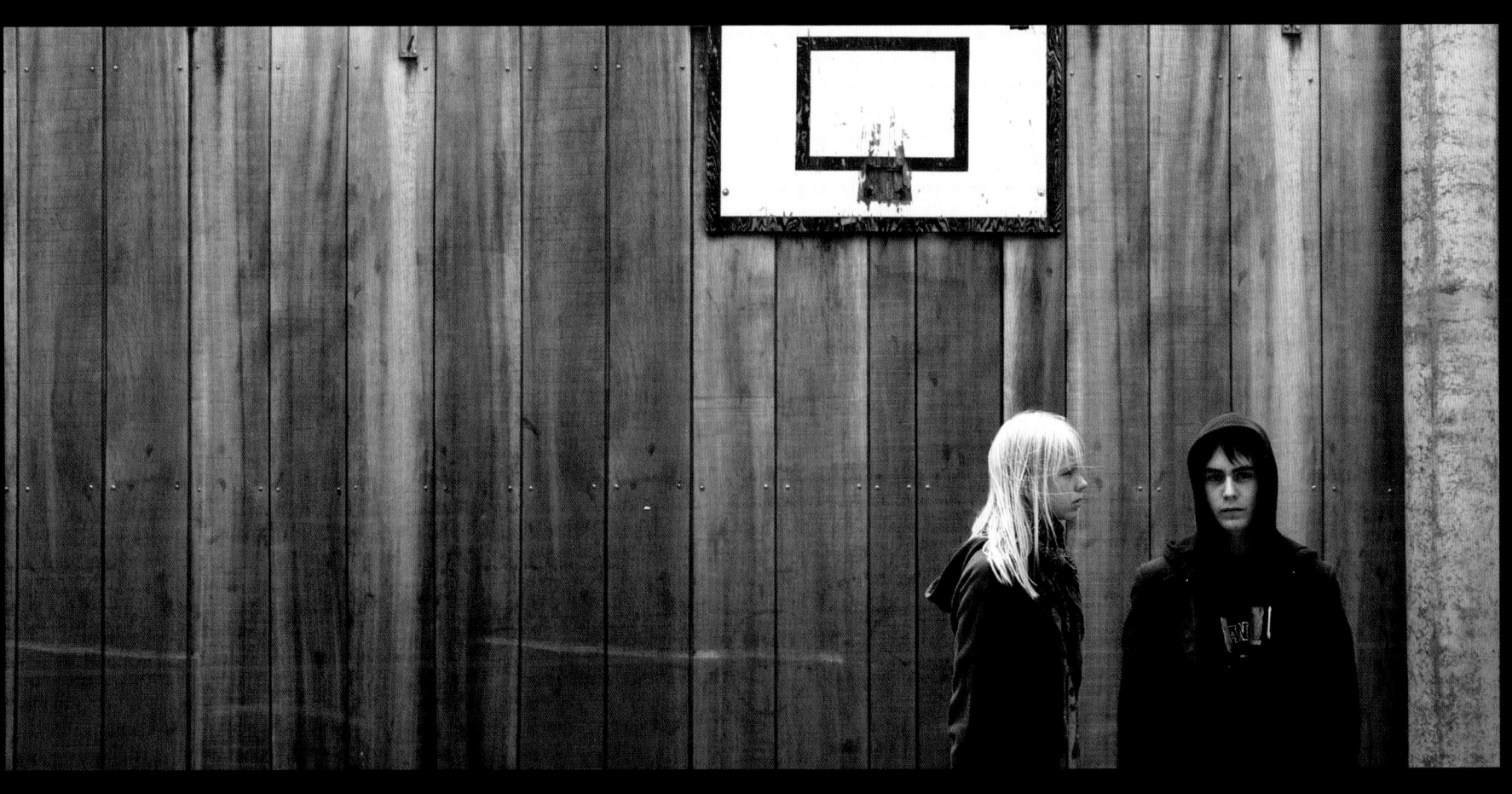

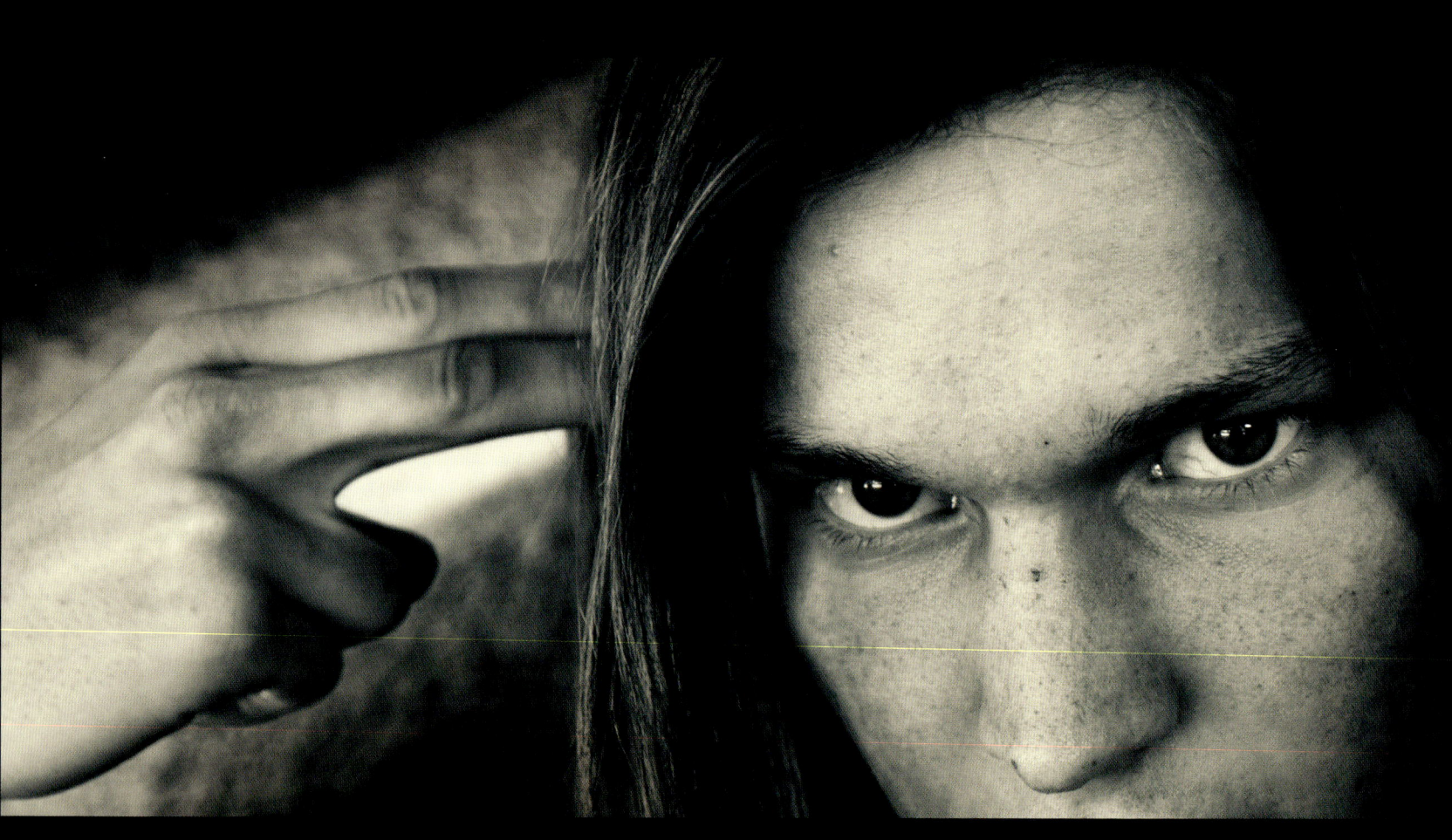

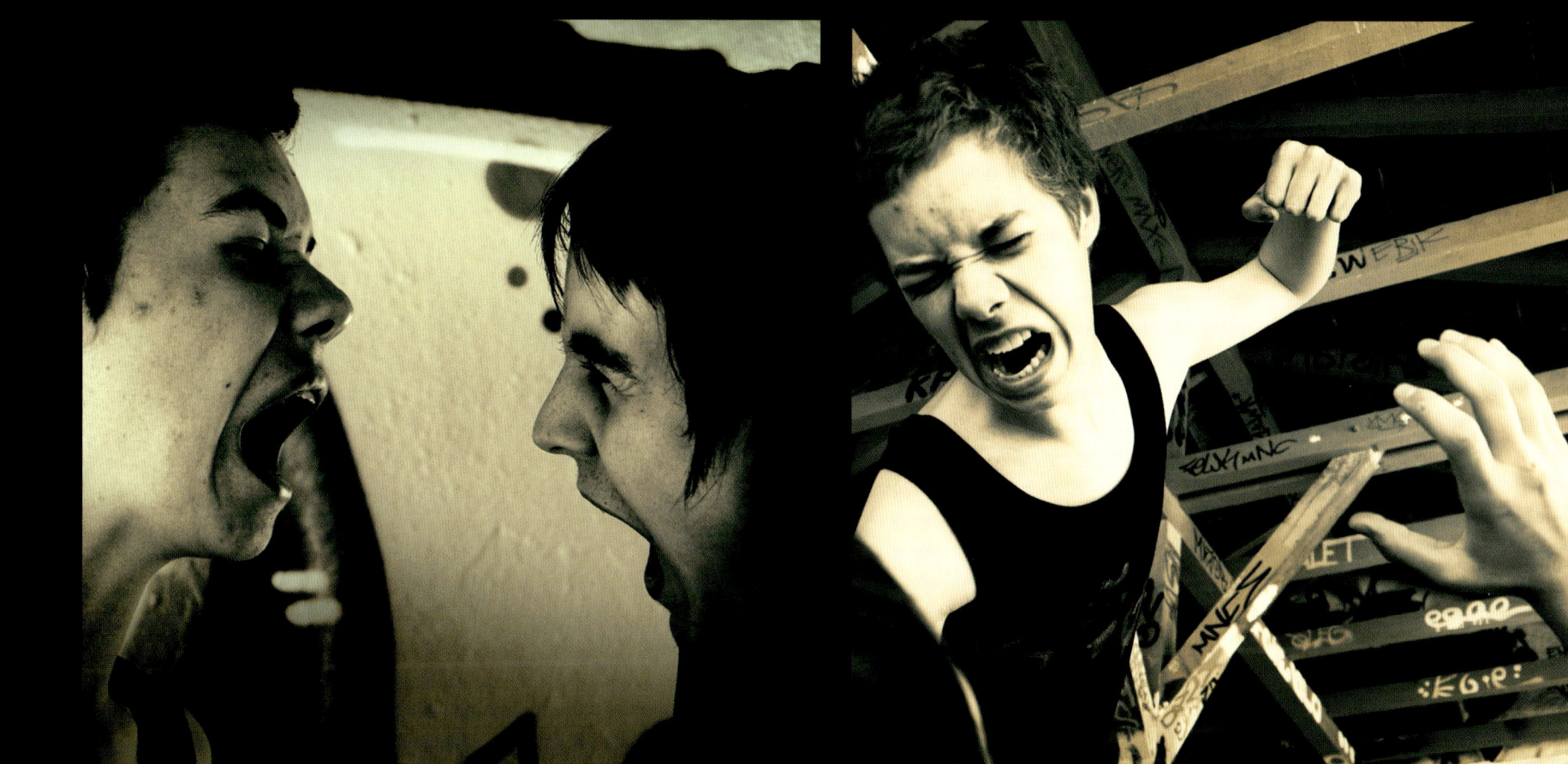

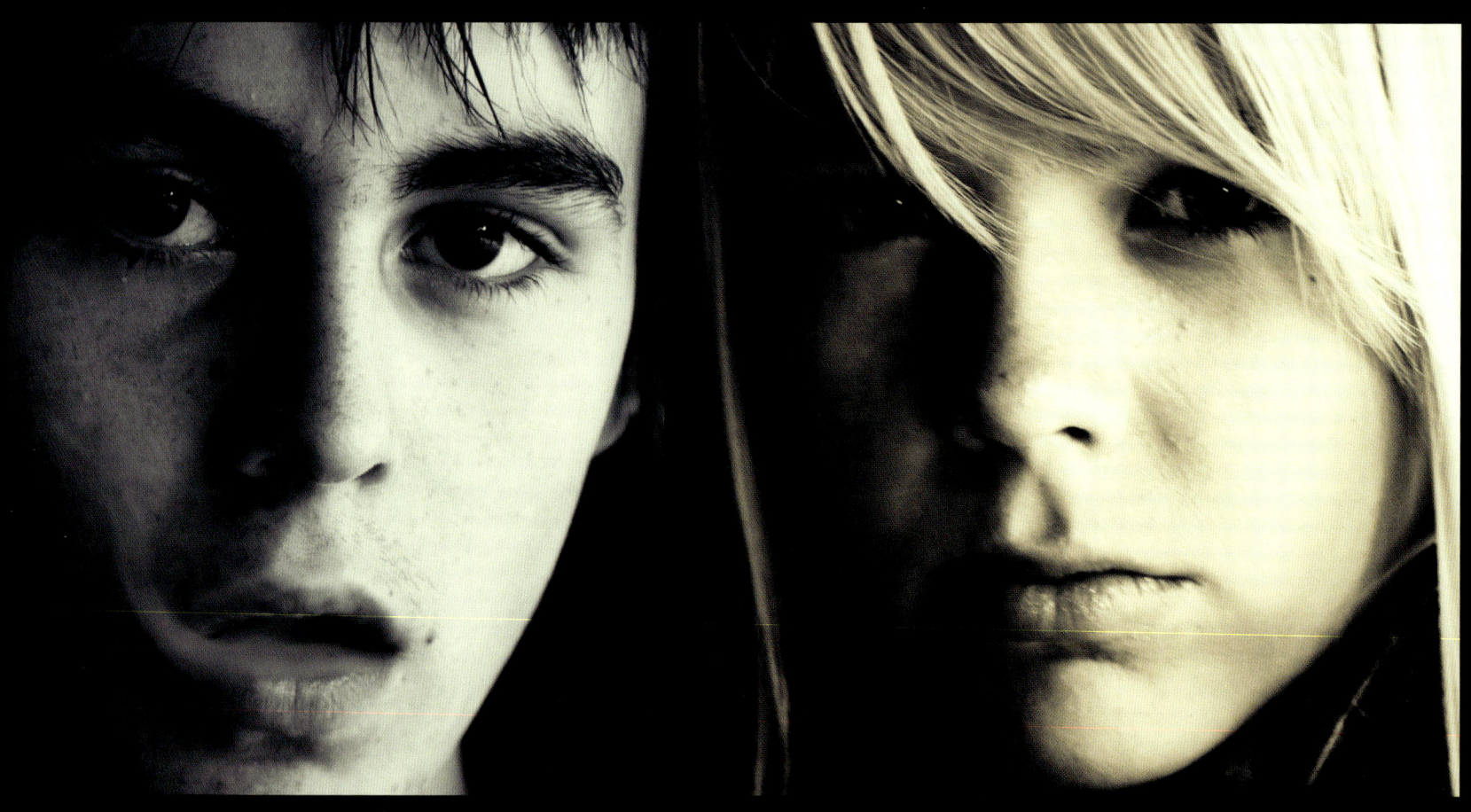

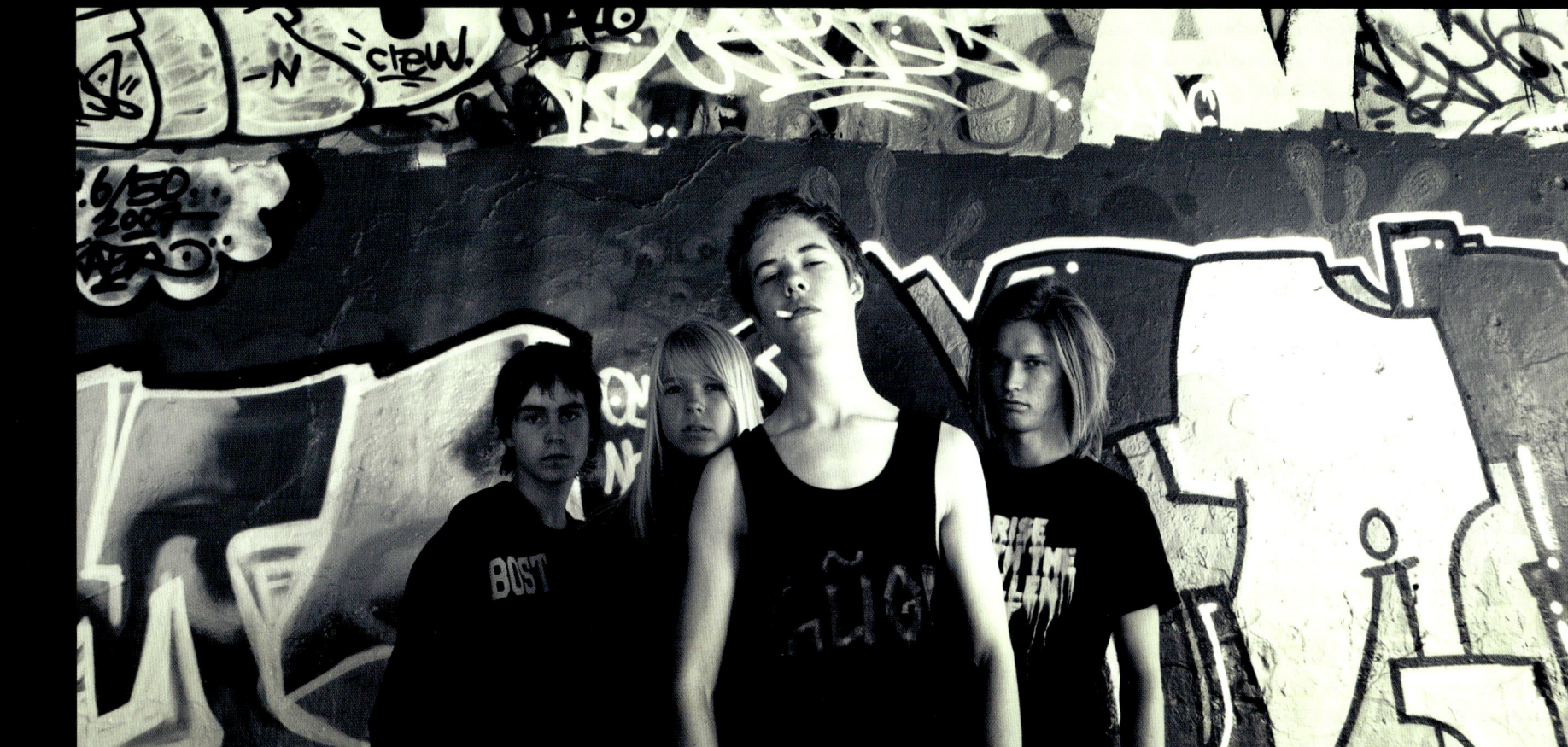

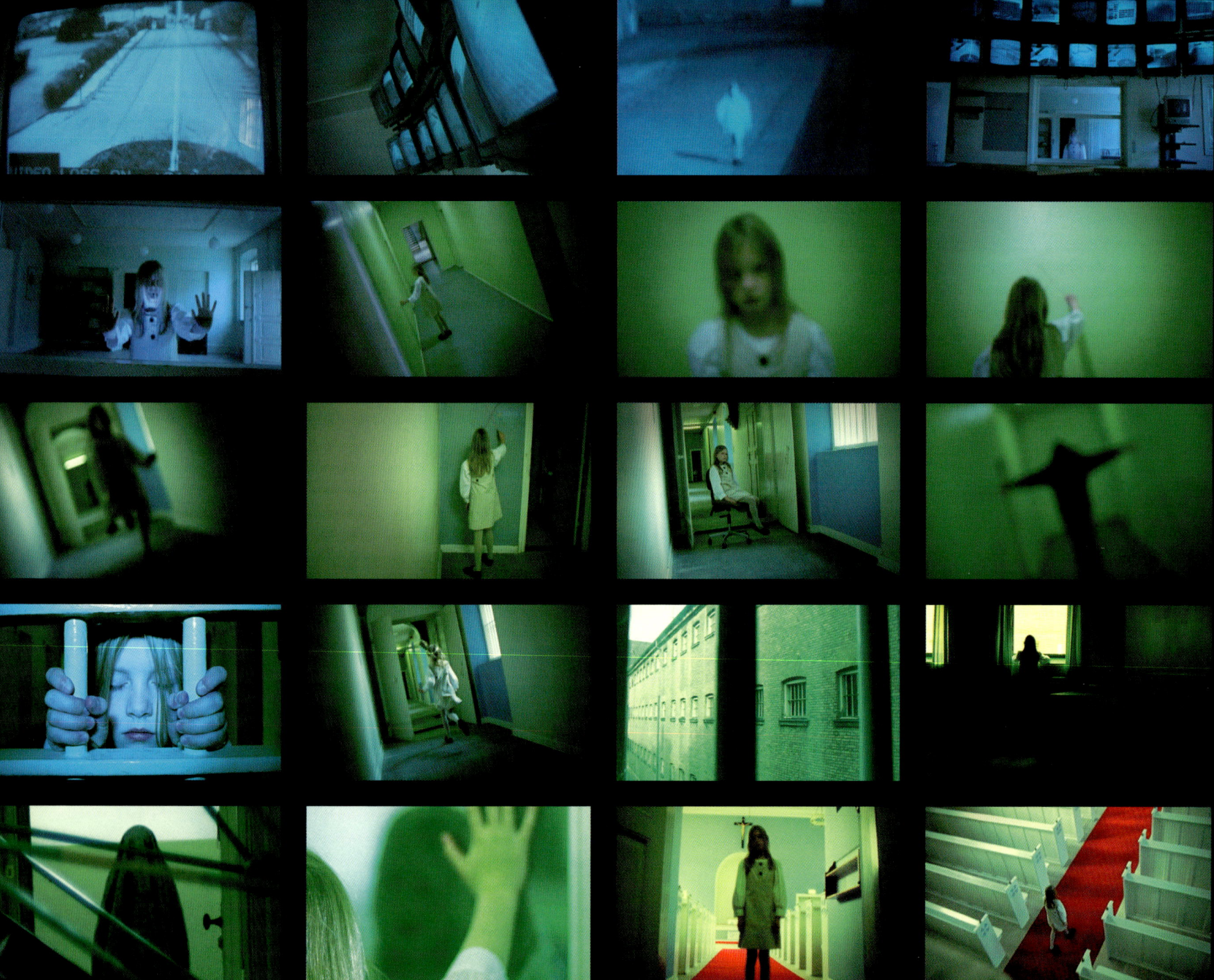

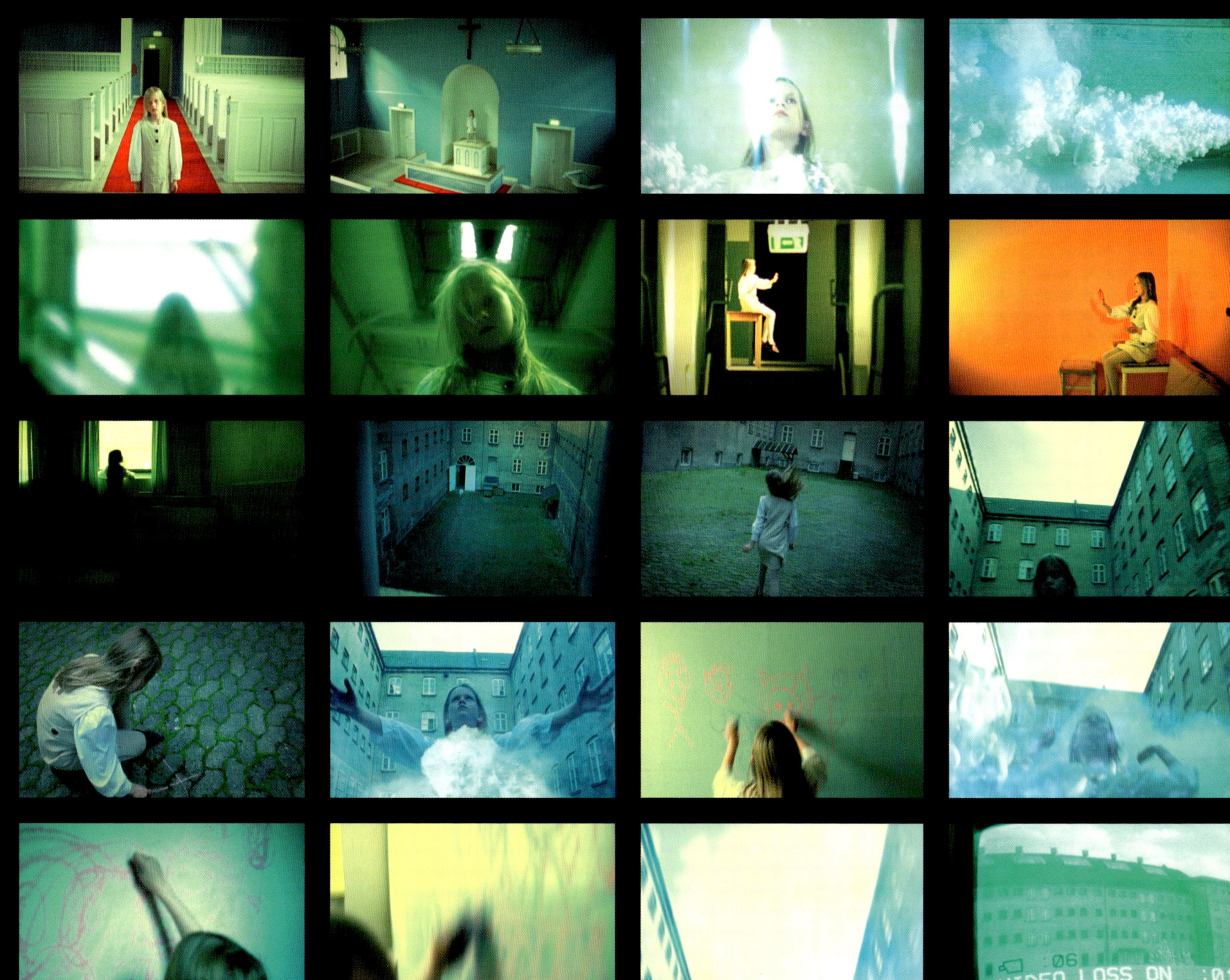

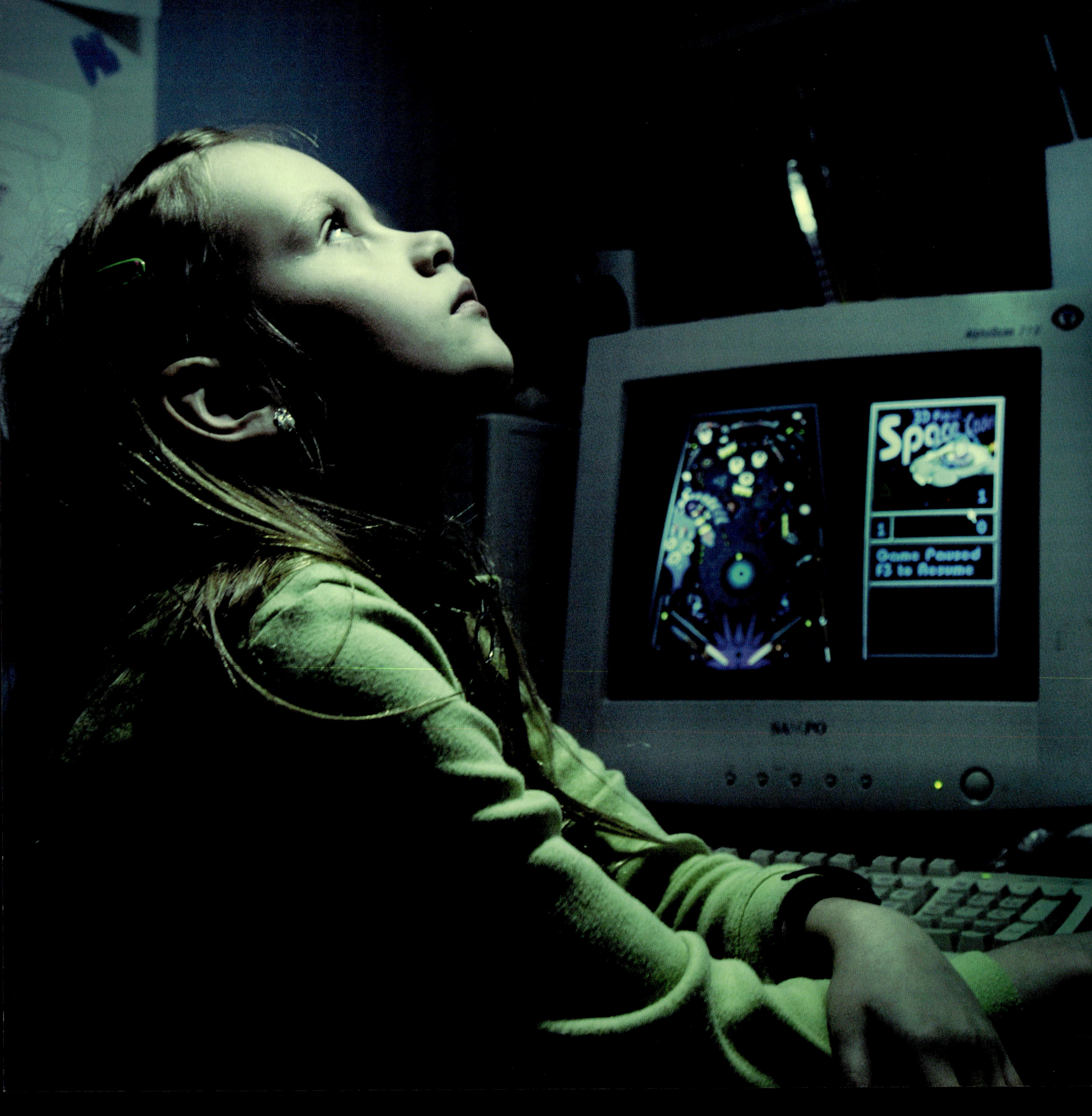

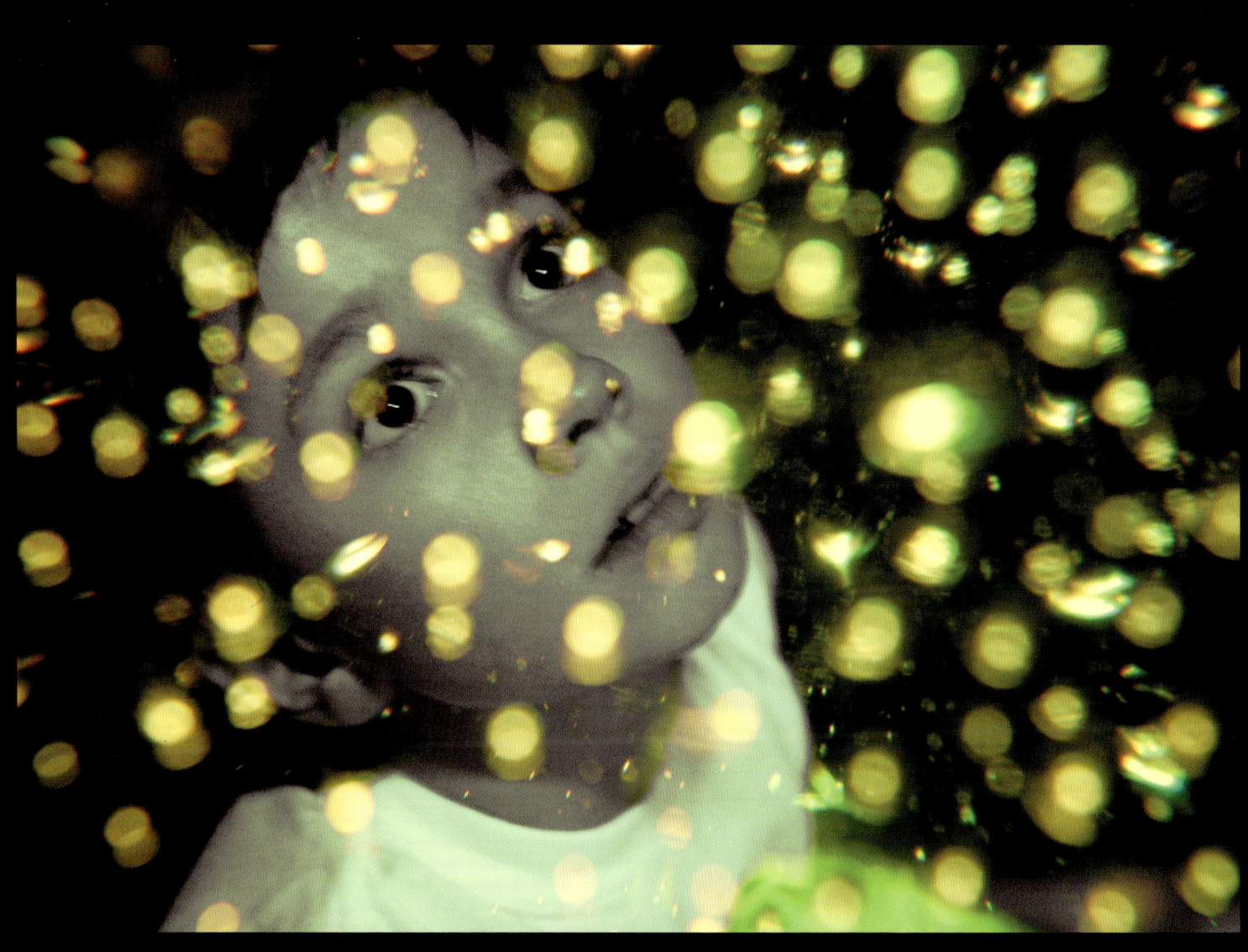

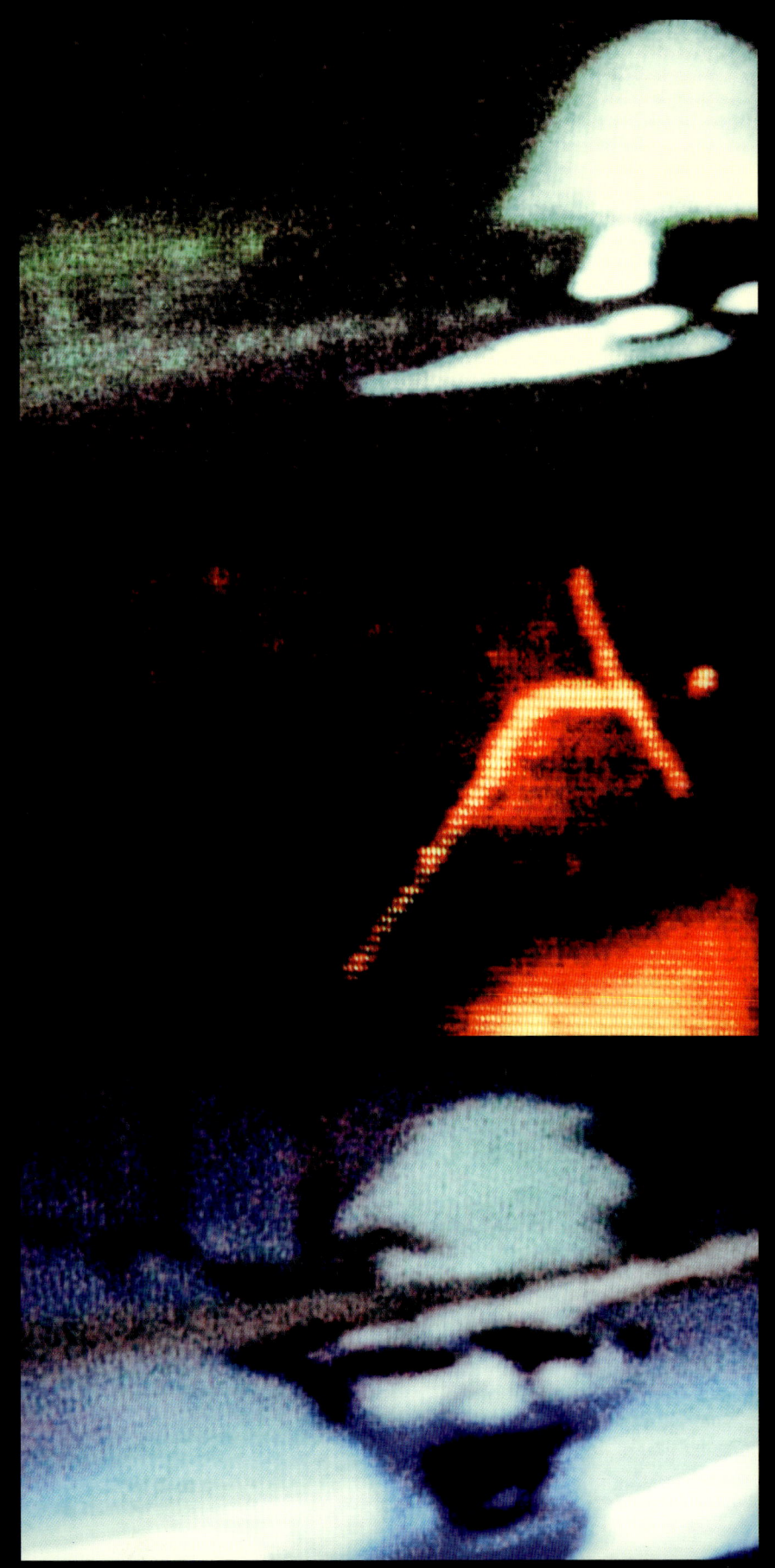

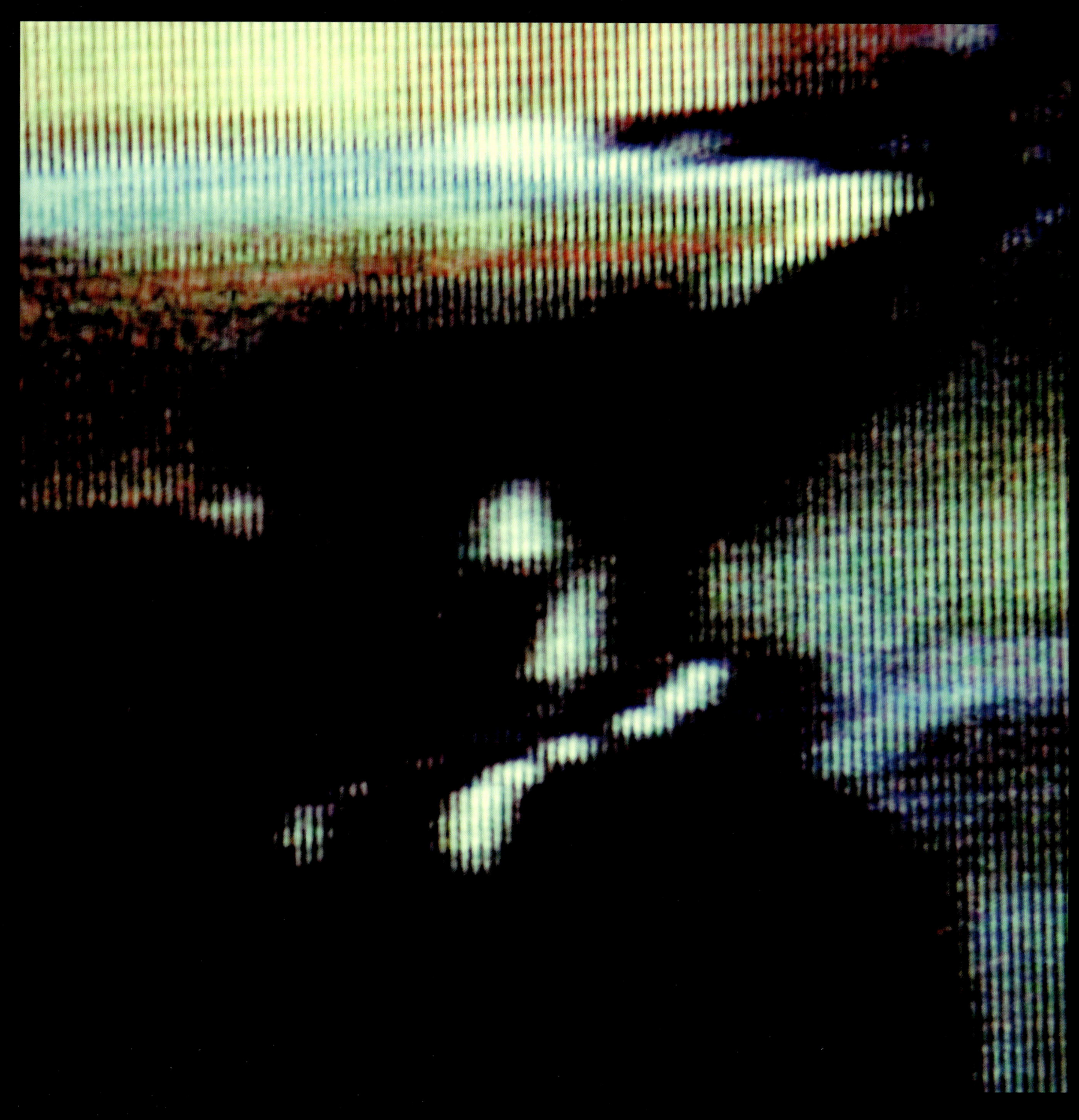

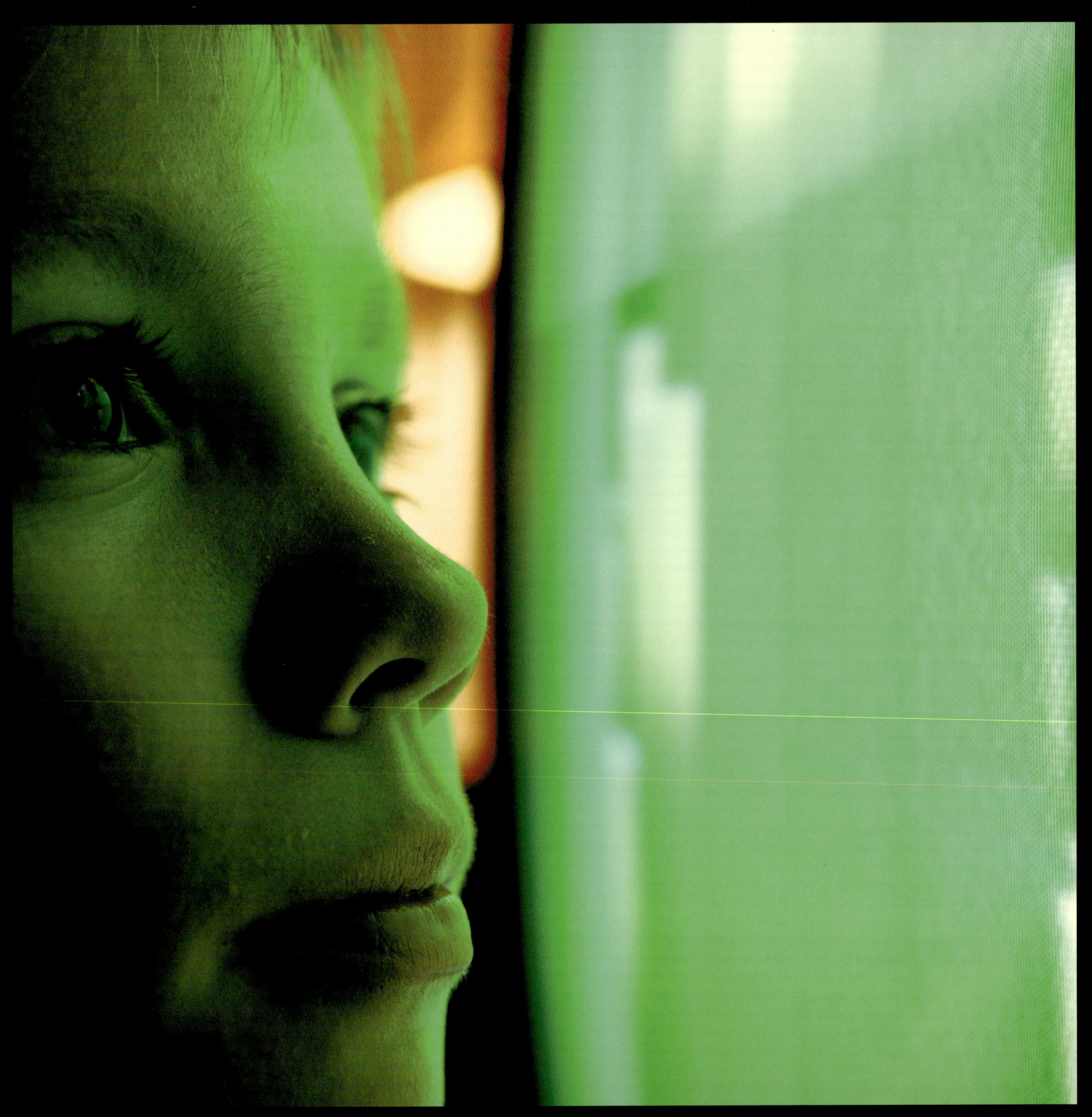

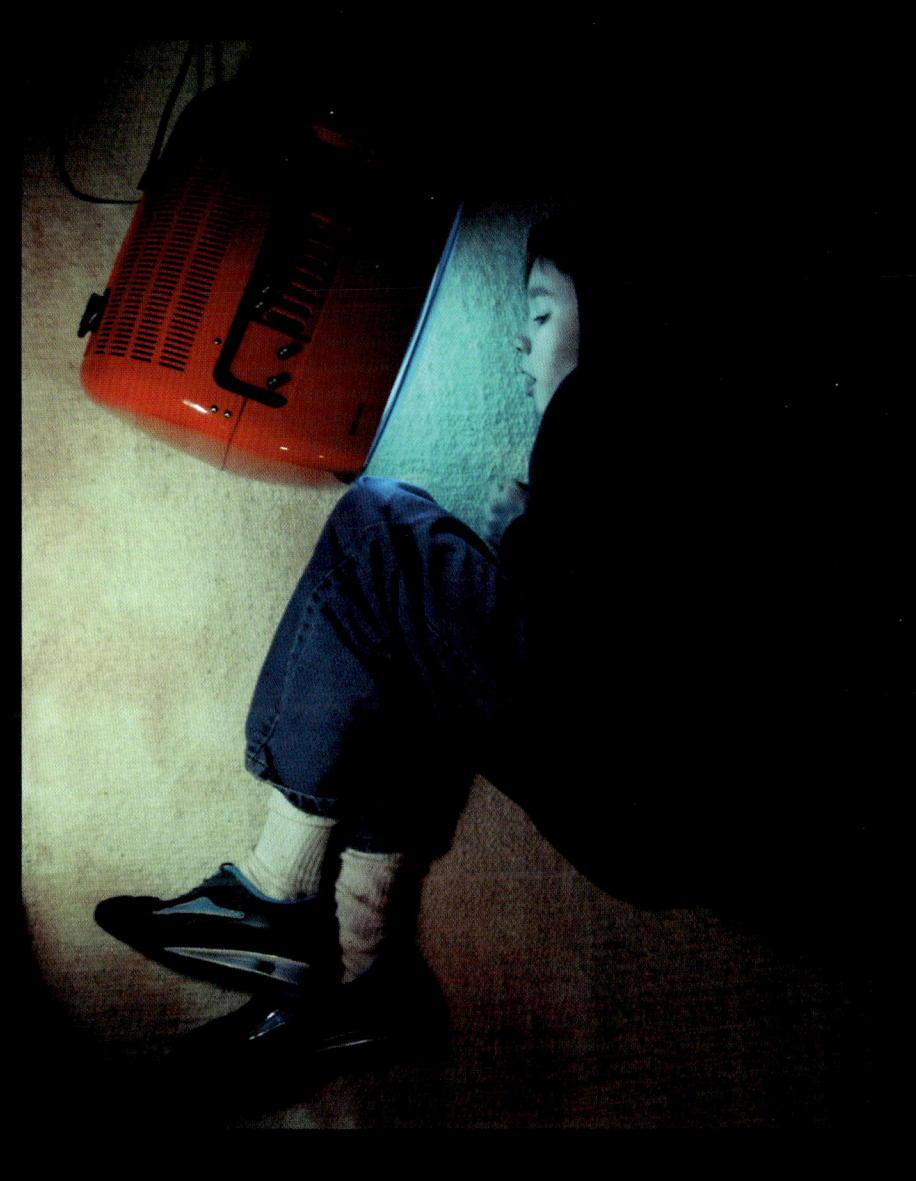

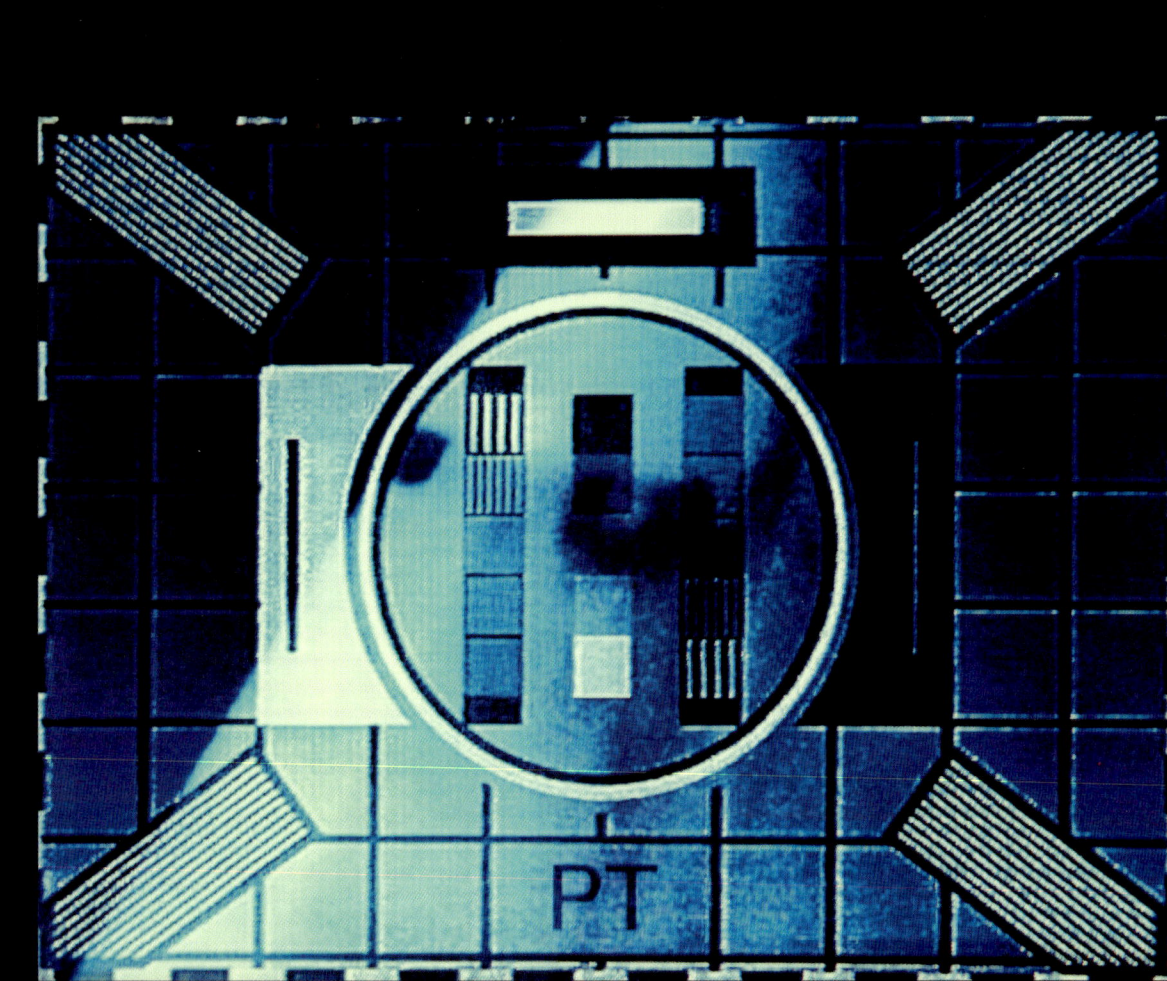

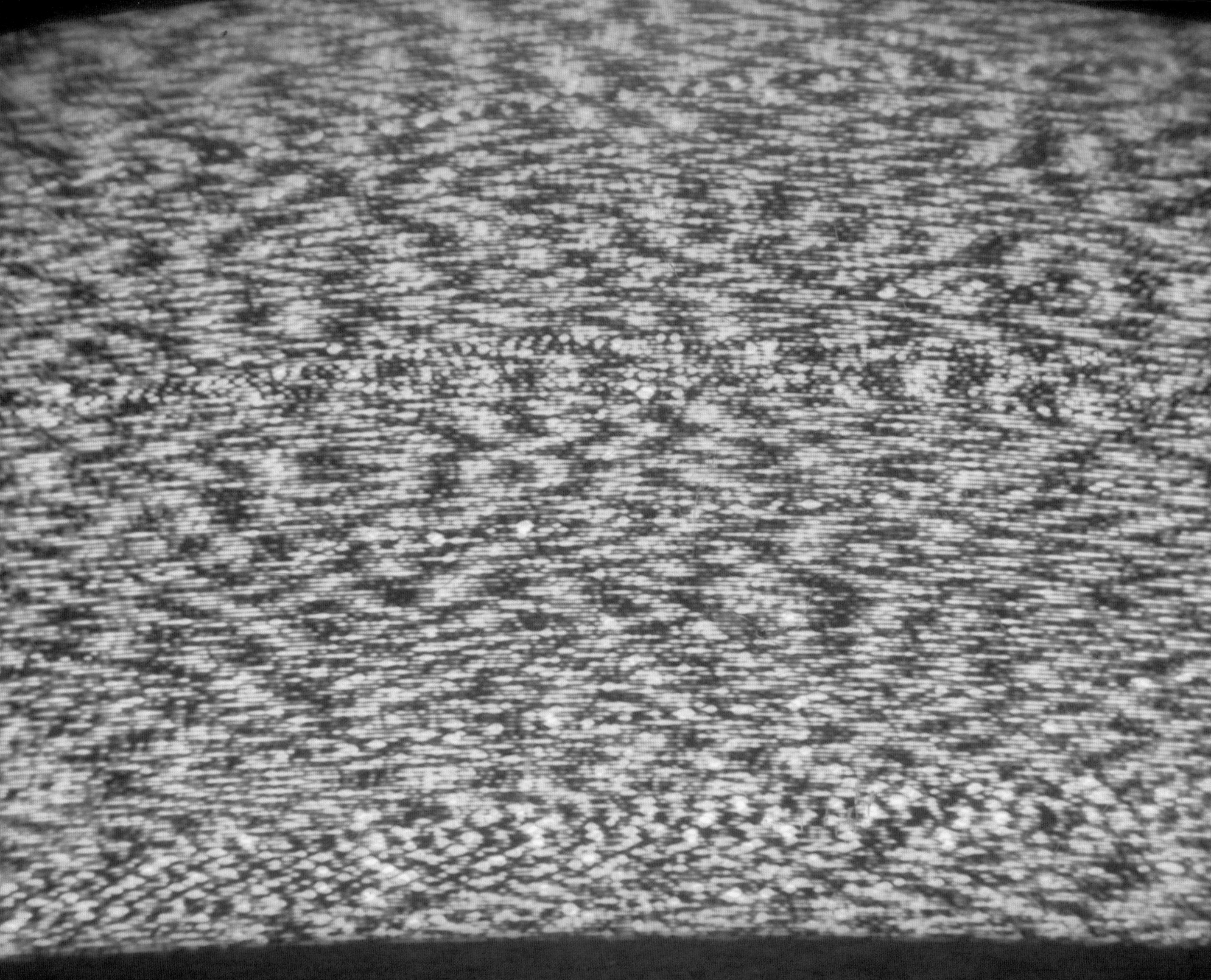

INABSEN
DWINGP
ABLANK
THEIN

NTIADEA
FEAROF
KPLANE
CIDENT

Carl Glover: *The Incident* was notable visually for the 128 page hardback special edition which came with a slipcase and an additional 40 page book of Hajo Muller's illustrations. It emerged in the wake of the live *Anesthetize* and Steven Wilson's *Insurgentes* special editions, both containing an identical page count as *The Incident*. Did providing imagery for these beforehand help with the huge amount required to make *The Incident* work?

Lasse Hoile: Yes, because we now knew based on recent experience how much was required to make a special edition work properly. Ideally, this meant that we needed plenty of images and alternative ideas so that we would have more choice when putting the book together. We couldn't do a special edition for the sake of it, as it's always obvious when something like that is just padded out and there isn't really the material to justify it. With *The Incident* and *Insurgentes* we knew we needed to tell a story visually without repetition, whilst connecting it atmospherically to the music. It suddenly grew from doing maybe 20-30 images to making 500-800 pictures, then increased to a couple of thousand images and up for each SW solo release after *Insurgentes*!

Carl Glover: It does help when there are more images to choose from, especially when establishing a rhythm and flow in the book.

Did the hand-in-front-of-face idea emerge early or did it take time to reach such a simple, but effective solution?

Lasse Hoile: The hand idea was pretty much the first thing done, I think the images for the cover were the very first pictures I took, I didn't focus properly but it seemed to work. It was loosely based on old crime scene photos and paparazzi pictures of people who don't want to be photographed.

Carl Glover: I've always liked the continuity of the theme with different people doing the hand as well.

Was the cover session done at the same time as the photographs of the two women with bandaged heads in front of the old building?

Lasse Hoile: Yes, I tried to do as many different pictures with the same people while on location. Repeating certain themes, especially the hand idea at all sessions. Just to have enough photos and a potential cover!

Carl Glover: For the Blind House/Seance photoshoot it looks like a lot of work was done leading up to the event itself. What did you have to do before the actual photography in order to make it a successful day?

Lasse Hoile: We shot as much as we could with the girls, the religious stuff, and the baby all on the same day. Filming what I could on top too... There was a lot of preparation. I rented an old castle not far from where I live which I'd used before. We had it to ourselves for the day and just shot as much as possible. I had help sourcing most of the people from a local school, and also used some actor friends, got some props and just worked through our photography schedule. I managed to squeeze in some analogue photography, which was nice to do again after the very digitally orientated *Fear of a Blank Planet*.

Carl Glover: The overall look of *The Incident* is completely different to *Fear of a Blank Planet*, did getting back into using film seem like a breath of fresh air?

Lasse Hoile: Yes, with film you only have 24 or 36 shots so you have to make all of them count to get the most out of it. Already, by the time of *The Incident* in 2009 you couldn't get monochrome film developed in my part of the country anymore, and I hadn't been developing my own film since the late 1980's! It's crazy how fast film seemed to disappear locally, only in major cities a few places were left. The film rolls I took had to be sent to Germany to be processed.

Carl Glover: I enjoy the unpredictability of film - even though it can be frustrating, when it behaves it is hard to beat.

Lasse Hoile: Exactly, which I why I still have more film than food in my fridge! All of it must be out of date by several years now, should get some good zany results using that film someday.

Carl Glover: *The Incident* was the second time that you used masks, the first being the bird heads in *Insurgentes*. What made you decide on masks in the first place?

Lasse Hoile: The mask thing is something I had always wanted to do. I think it comes from watching too many old European art house movies, which is what we also did with *Insurgentes*. Some of the visuals for that are essentially an homage to all the old art house movies from the 60's to the 70's and beyond!

Carl Glover: I thought that the masks were part of a photographic exercise exploring an approach refined by the likes of Edvard Munch and Francis Bacon. It was interesting seeing the masks evolve from *Insurgentes* via *The Incident* up to *Grace for Drowning*, which is almost exclusively created on film. I think you can see some of the groundwork for *Grace for Drowning* in *The Incident*.

Lasse Hoile: Yes obviously Bacon and Munch was the inspiration for those, no question about that. It was a way to try and sum up some of the madness surrounding the themes in a non-literal way and make it a bit more abstract whilst still fitting the music.

Carl Glover: The portraits of the girls with the extremely long hair in the forest nod to late 1990s/early 2000's J-horror films, but with an almost Victorian stylistic approach. What were the films that left the strongest impressions?

Lasse Hoile: I was thinking more about a Victorian style than J-Horror, I remembered a scene from Andrei Tarkovsky's 1975 classic *The Mirror*, which we had already done a little homage to in the Harmony Korine video. If you look at vintage Victorian photographs you'll find a lot of these extremely long haired women which look amazingly surreal. There was a Victorian photograph I bought on eBay which was later used for cover of the Bass Communion album *Loss*, which was the main inspiration for those pictures.

Carl Glover: Another theme in the album is the photographs of bodies with sheets over them used to illustrate songs such as The Incident and Circle of Manias. I like to think of it as the same body appearing in different locations throughout the day and night. Was there an inspiration particularly regarding the nocturnal photographs of the body in different locations?

Lasse Hoile: Some ideas came from an old book of Australian crime scene photographs that were taken in the early 1900's and another book from the NYPD archives of the 1920's and 30's. We couldn't replicate the scenes properly but used what was around at the time. I had to do as many of these as I could when out and about, I usually had one helper, or if I was lucky two helpers/friends were around.

Carl Glover: The crime scene books you refer to make a lot of sense. Especially bearing in mind the Octane Twisted section in *The Incident* which depicts a murder in a forest. I remember feeling quite uncomfortable when laying this section out for the special edition of *The Incident* in 2009, it felt too authentic! There is a very

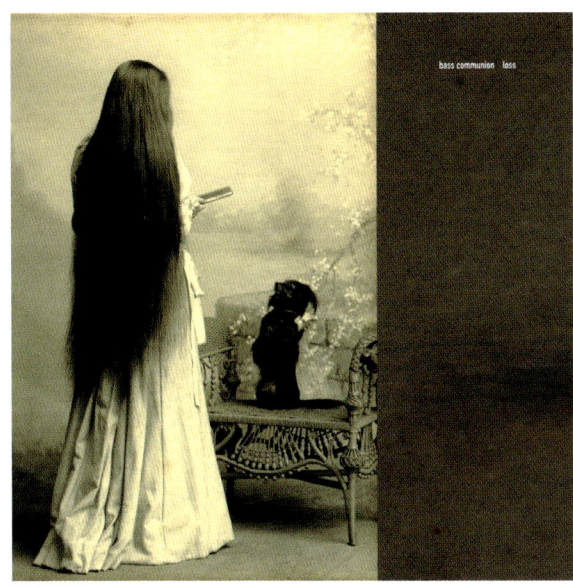

effective use of slow shutter speeds to convey the manic quality of the crime being committed.

It looks like a week's planning leading to a long day's work filming the Octane Twisted projection, what problems, if any, did you encounter during the film? I'm thinking of weather, available light and the usual hiccups that occur when working on location.

Lasse Hoile: It must have been either early spring or late summer, I can't remember now, but the filming was done at the same time as the photo shoot. We took still images then had to redo them for film and try get something out of it, I'm not even sure if it ended up being used at all to be honest?

I like the use of the slow shutter, makes it look 'caught in the moment' and also more dream-like, I used it for a few things while making *The Incident* images and live visuals.

Carl Glover: Did Steven ever get to attend any of the photo-shoots?

Lasse Hoile: No.

Carl Glover: Being busy recording/producing, and the time it would take to get to Denmark would probably get in the way. I'm also guessing that you were communicating daily while this was going on?

Lasse Hoile: Exactly. Obviously it would have been nice to have him present at the shoots but we discussed everything in advance and always made sure to get more material than required, so we were always covered.

Carl Glover: Did the models/actors ever get affected by what you were asking them to do? It probably took most of them outside their comfort zone.

Lasse Hoile: I don't think so… I hope not, and if so, hopefully in a positive way. I'm sure most had fun doing these weird things and they were up for it too. I guess they saw it as an adventure and just doing something different… which is good for everyone really.

Carl Glover: Do you still do occasional work with any of them?

Lasse Hoile: I've lost touch with almost all of them… I was thinking the other day about what they might be like now, it could be fun to do new photos as they are older, and to recreate some of the sessions just for fun!

Carl Glover: You worked on the Time Flies film with Grant Wakefield doing the time-lapse photography which he is very adept at. What are your memories of the collaboration?

Lasse Hoile: Grant was a joy to work with, he is very ambitious and understands concepts instantly, his time lapse work is amazing. He did an album entitled *The Fire This Time* which contained an account of the incompetence and atrocities leading up to and including Desert Storm - the first Iraq war. Sadly it didn't get much attention but I hope it will be rediscovered one day. Things like this need to be remembered. Grant did a fantastic job with what we had to work with at the time.

Carl Glover: I designed the packaging for *The Fire This Time*. That's how I originally knew Grant, though I had no idea about the time-lapse photography until later.

Do you know if the rest of the band were aware of what you and Steven were doing or was it all showed to them in one go?

Lasse Hoile: I don't know. I think SW showed it around, got feedback and collated it all in one mail for me.

Carl Glover: Were there many changes coming from the band?

Lasse Hoile: Not as I remember, there was always something but not much. Either they loved it or hated it - if they hated something they were not shy to say so!

Carl Glover: To be honest, I prefer it when a band is direct about one's work, you can waste a lot of time if a response is vague and often end up going in the wrong direction.

Lasse Hoile: True! Also saves a lot of time if you don't have all the unnecessary back and forth between people that don't have an actual informed opinion (record label people basically). Too often these people seem to just express an opinion or angle based on their position, and almost always haven't got a clue about what they are talking about - it kills everything creatively.

Carl Glover: Did the band's responses make you try out things you hadn't considered which ended up working out really well?

Lasse Hoile: Of course, and it had to be done snappy too, which is a good thing. Once you get over the initial pain of having your idea rejected, it's always good to be pushed.

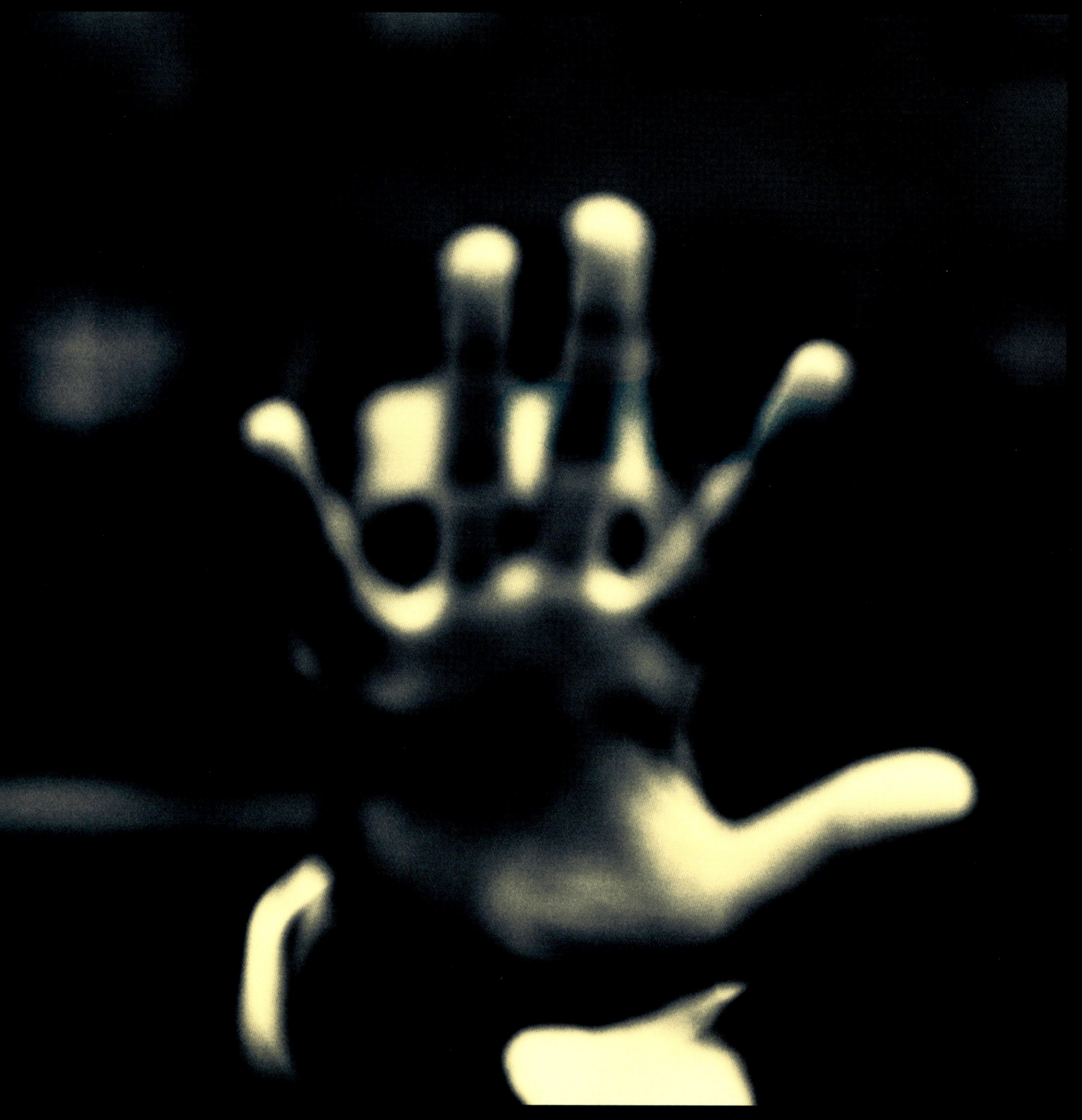

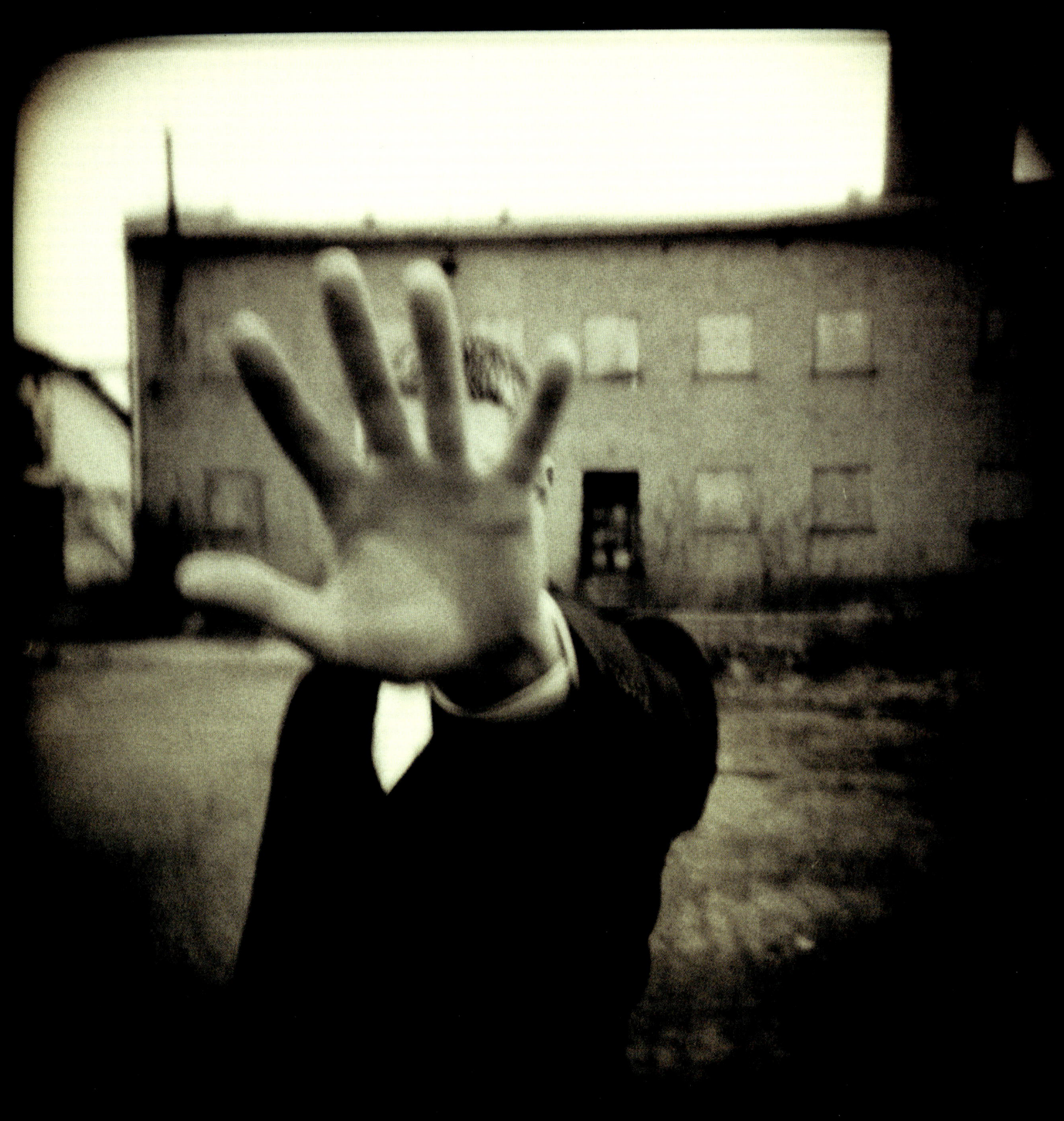

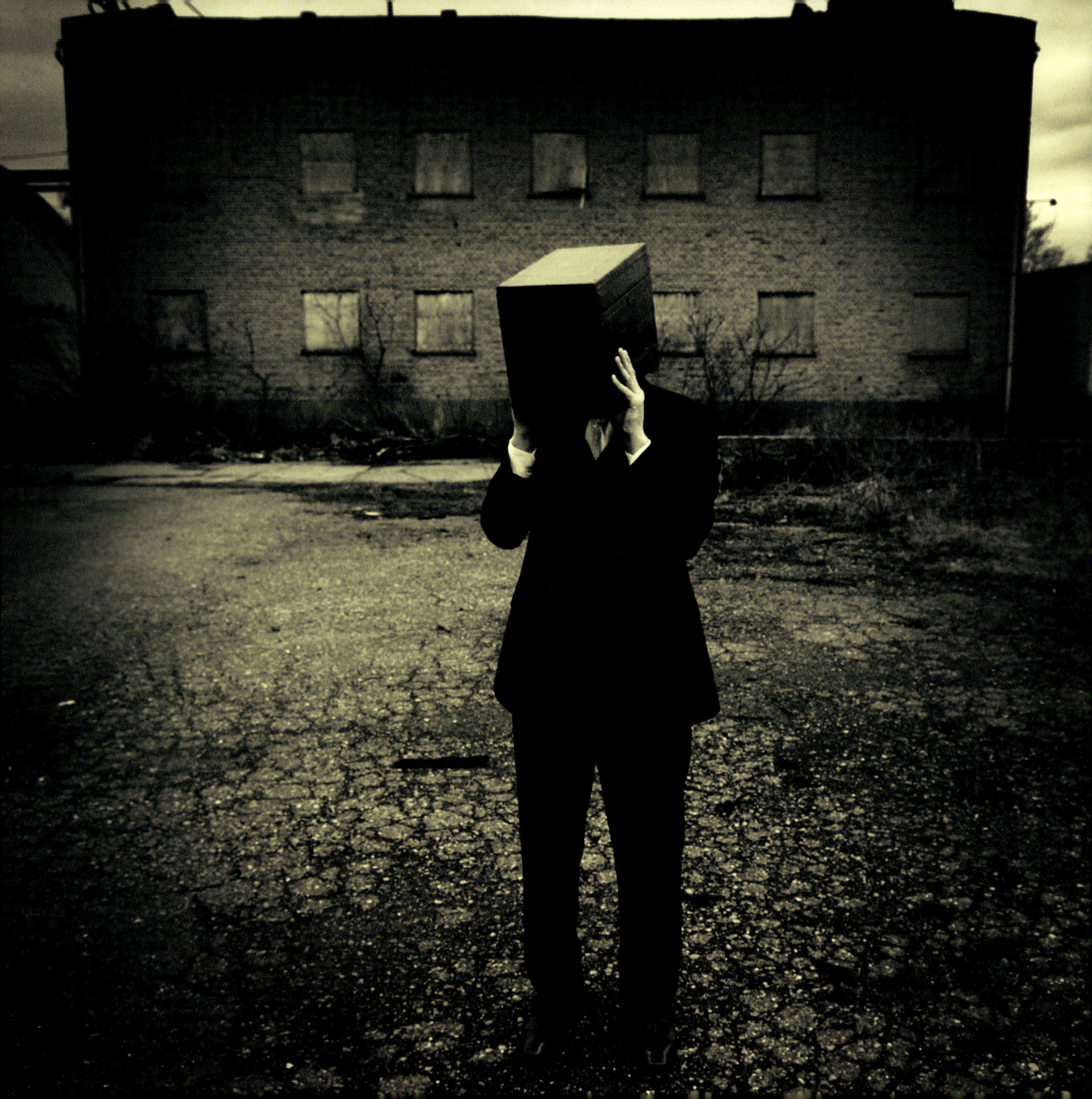

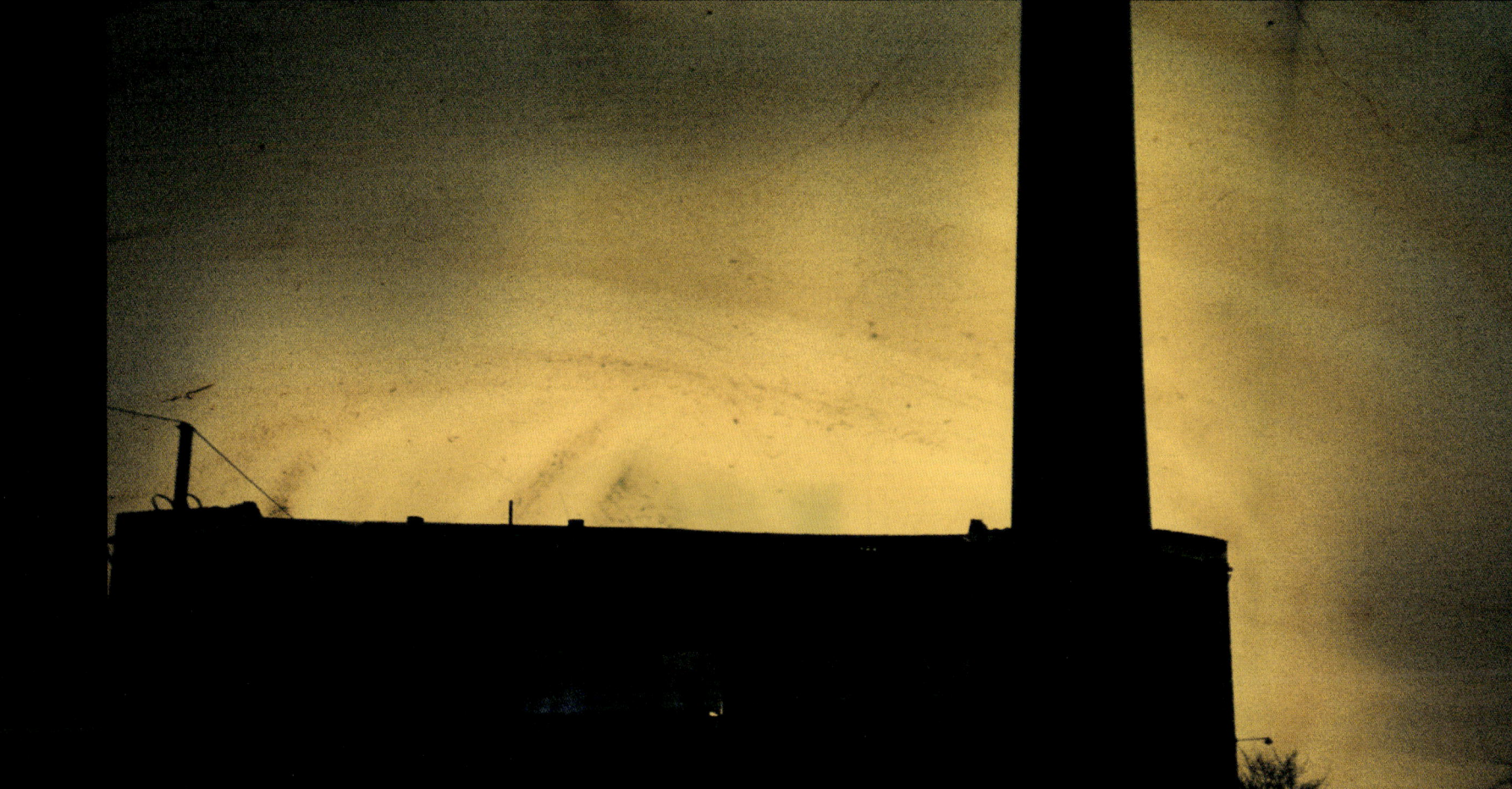

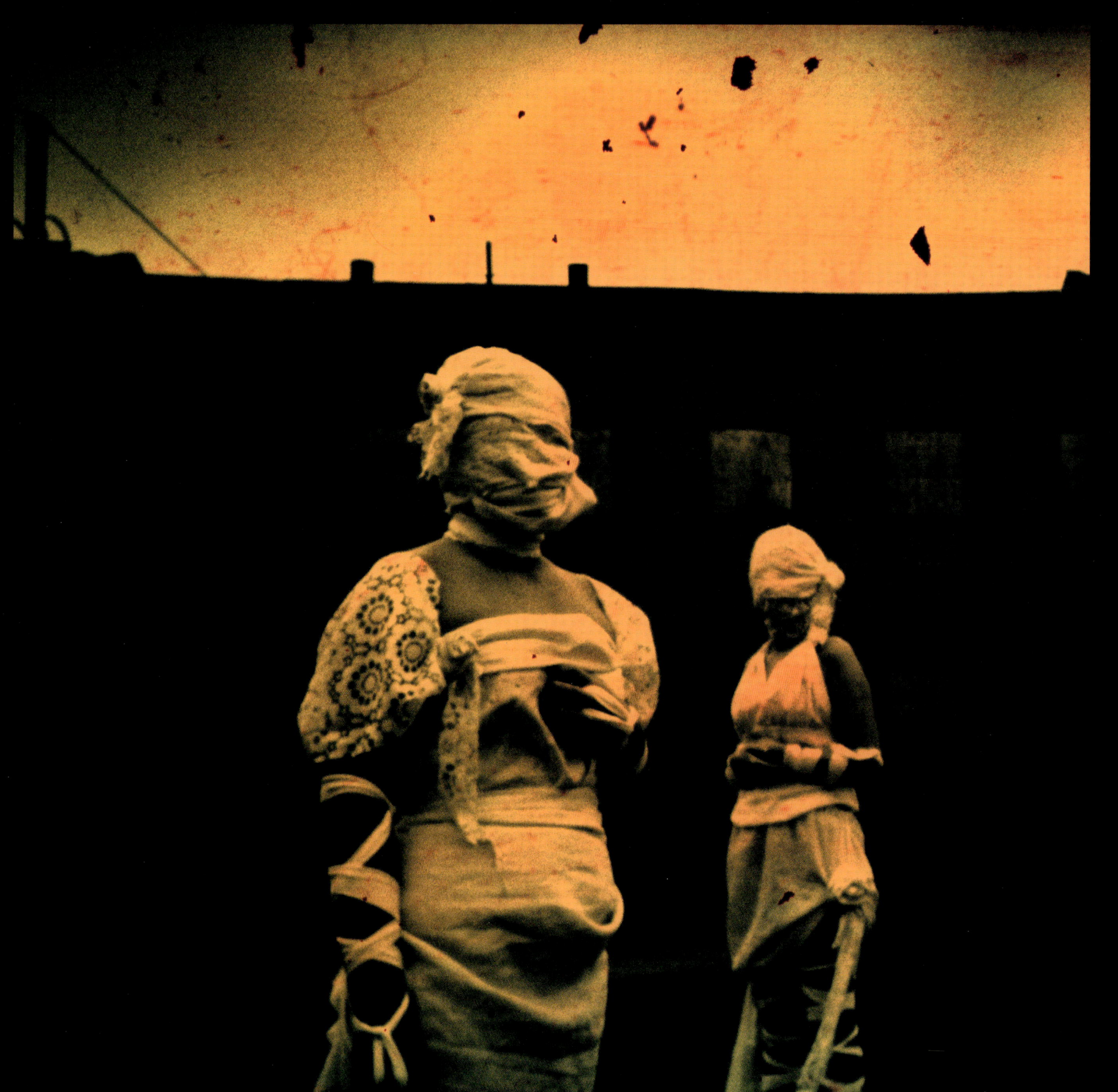

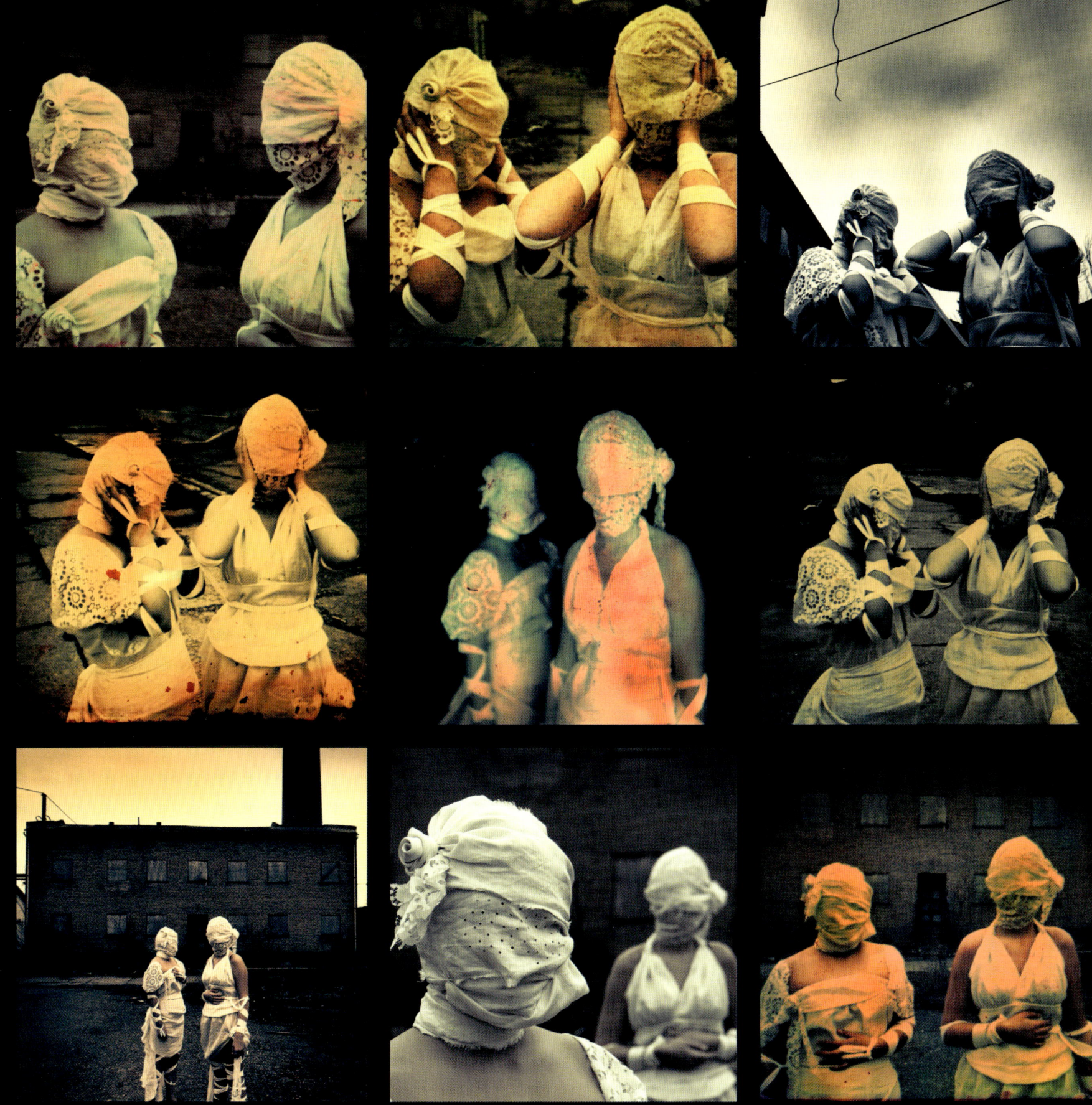

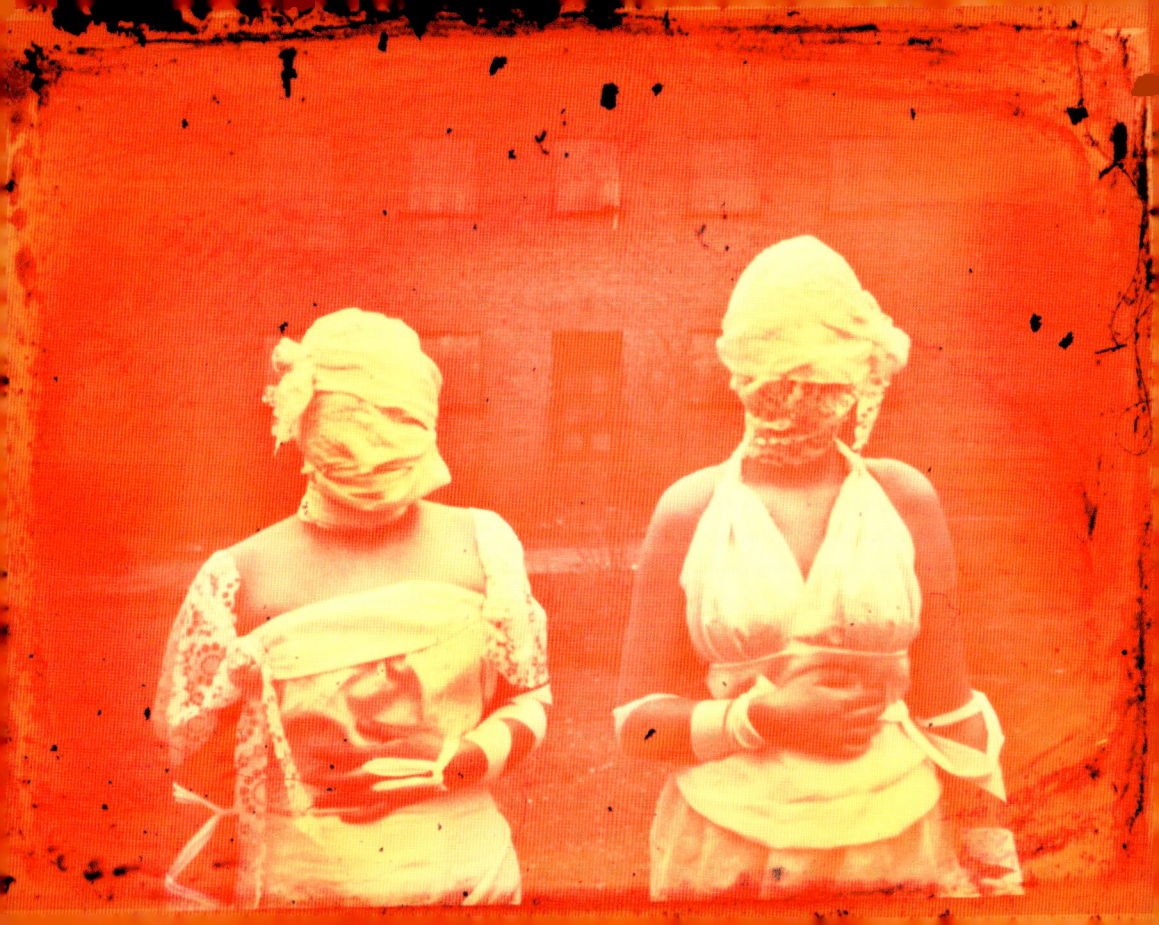

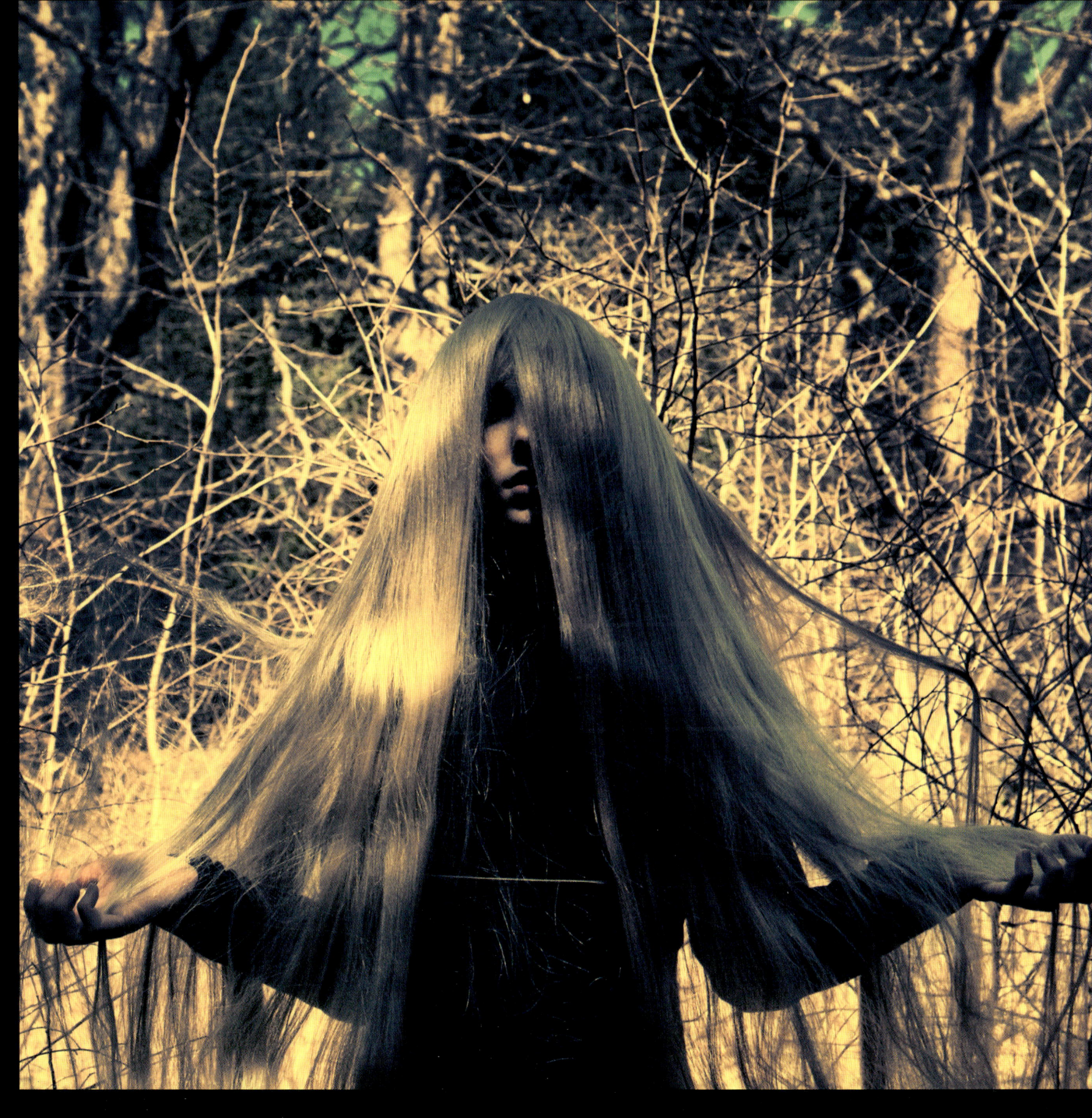

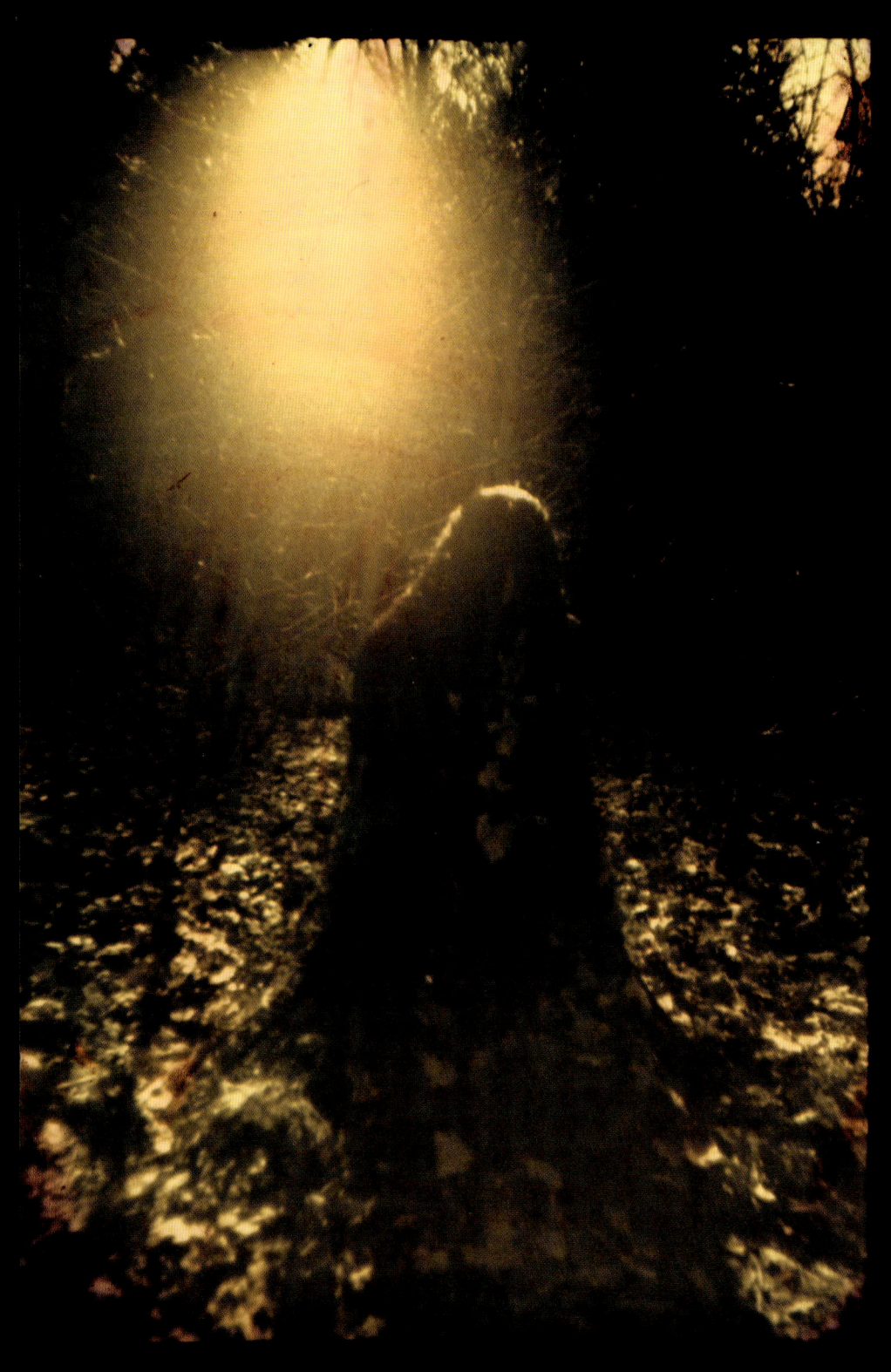

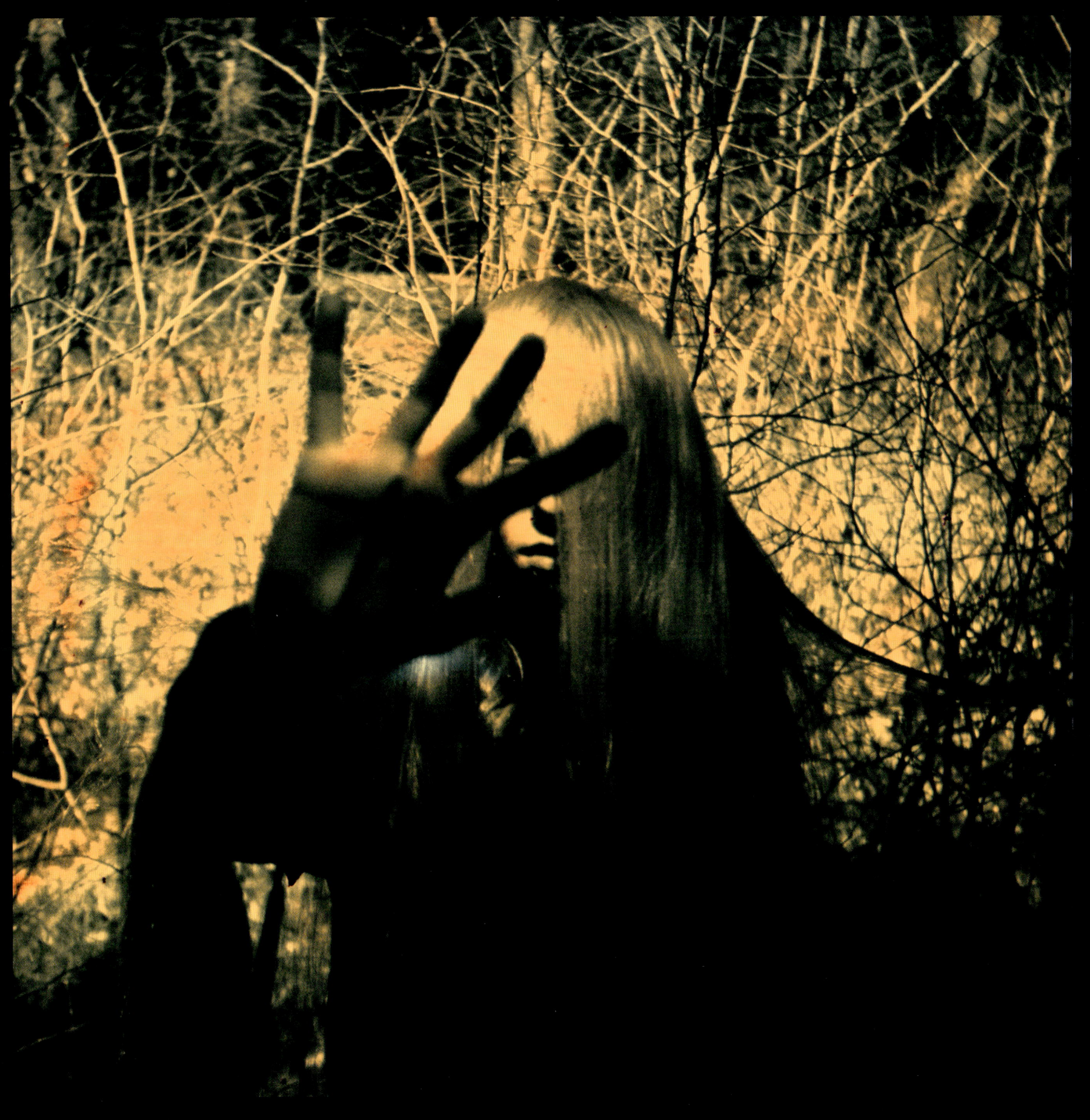

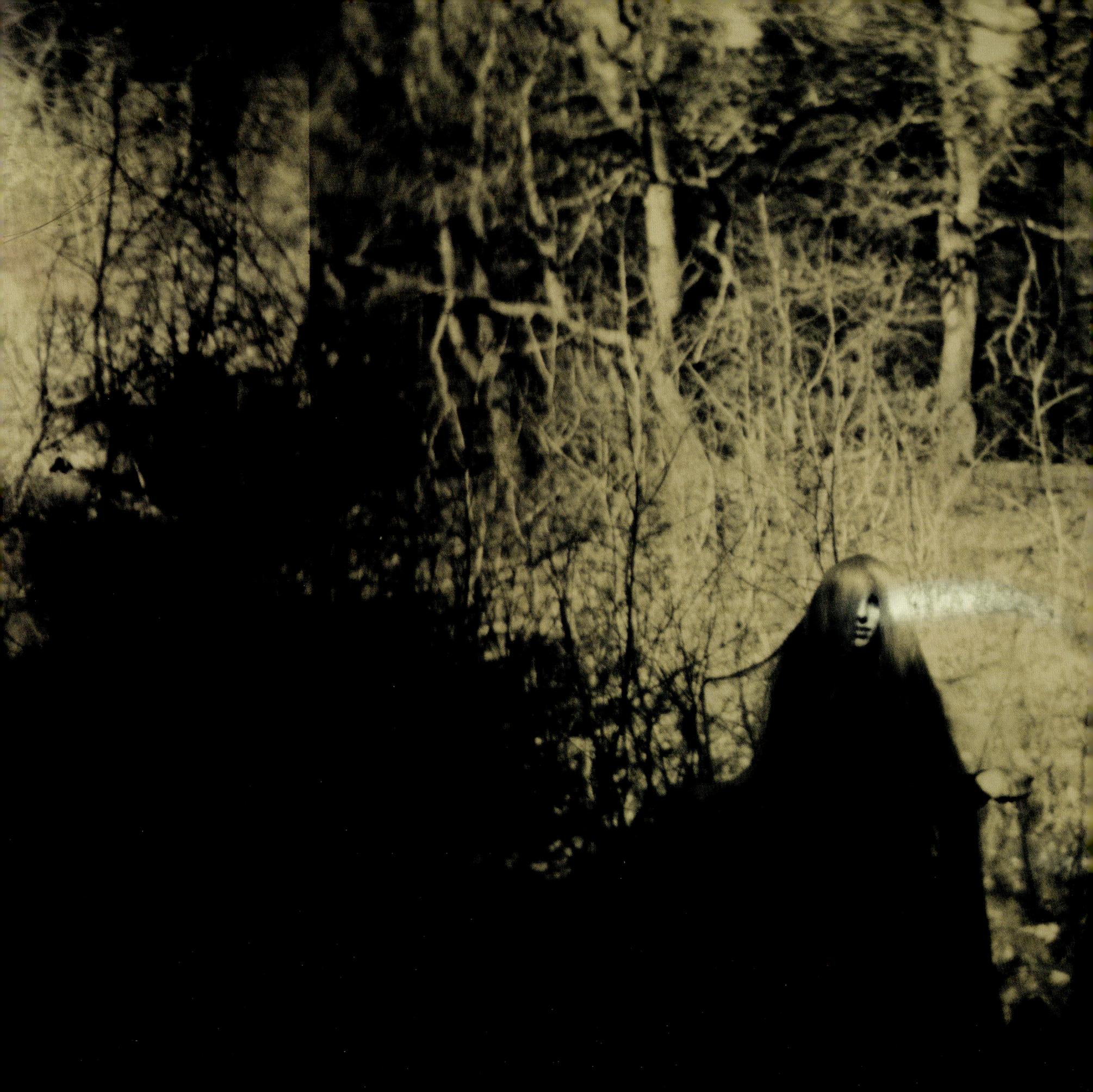

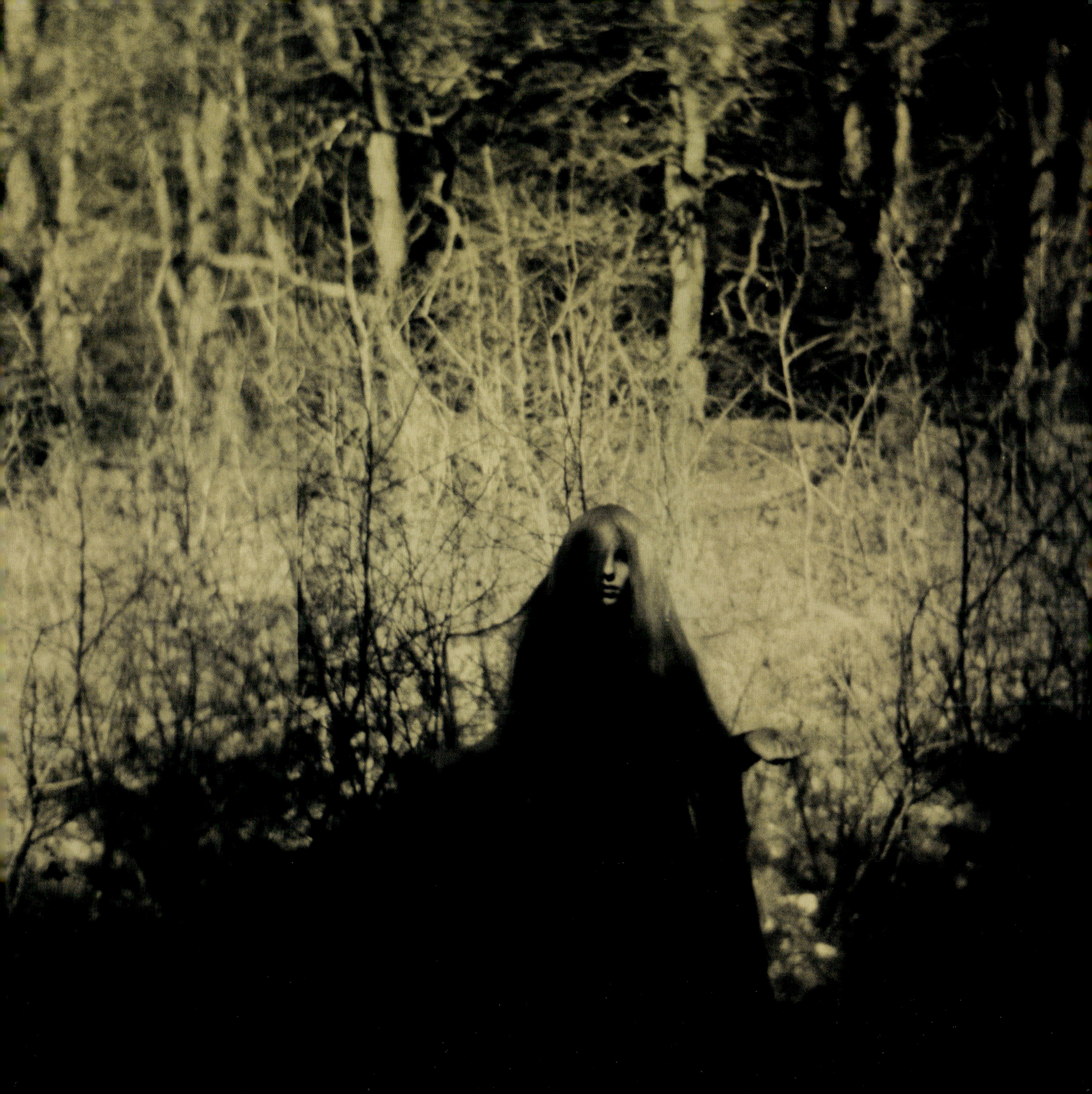

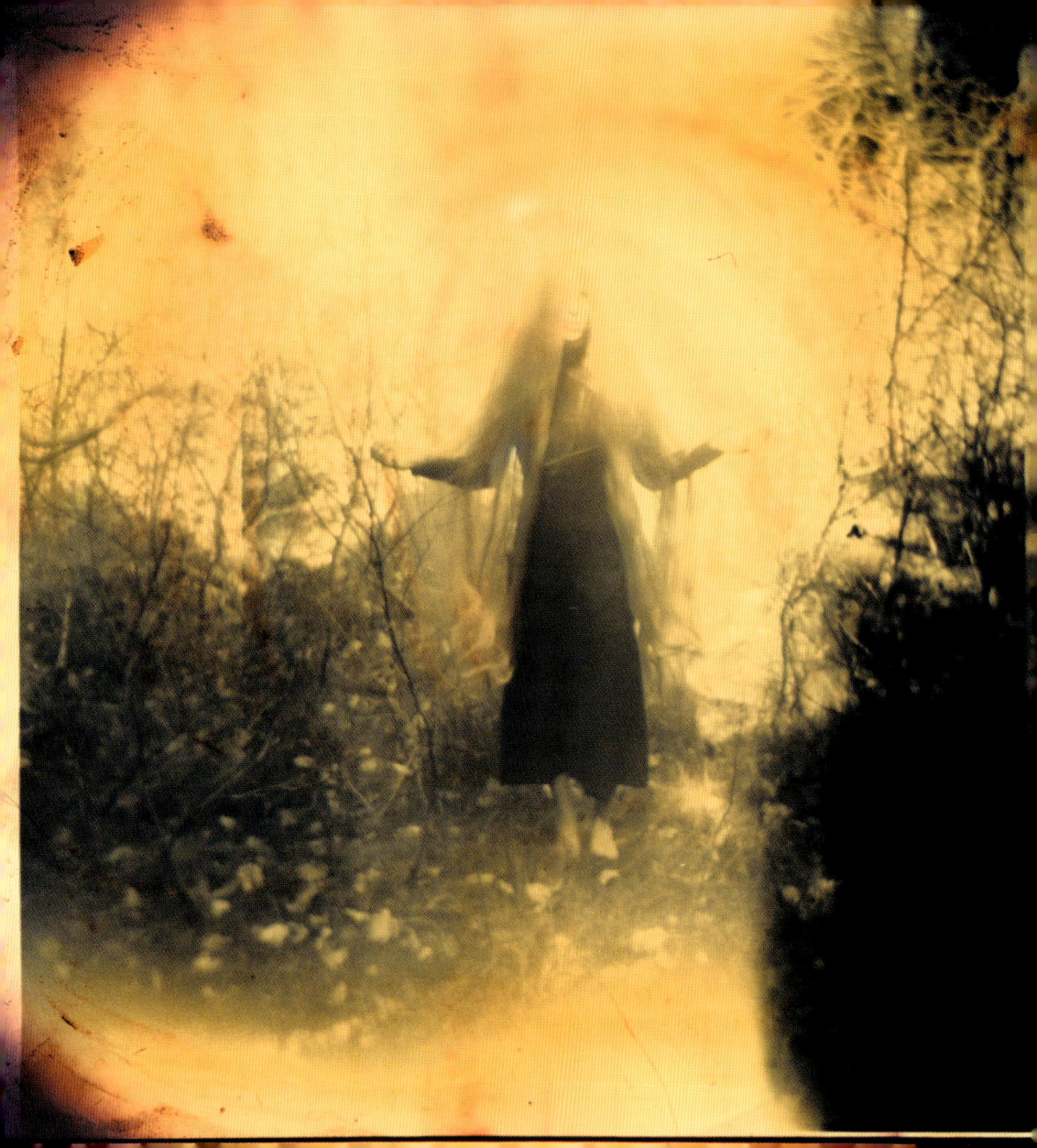

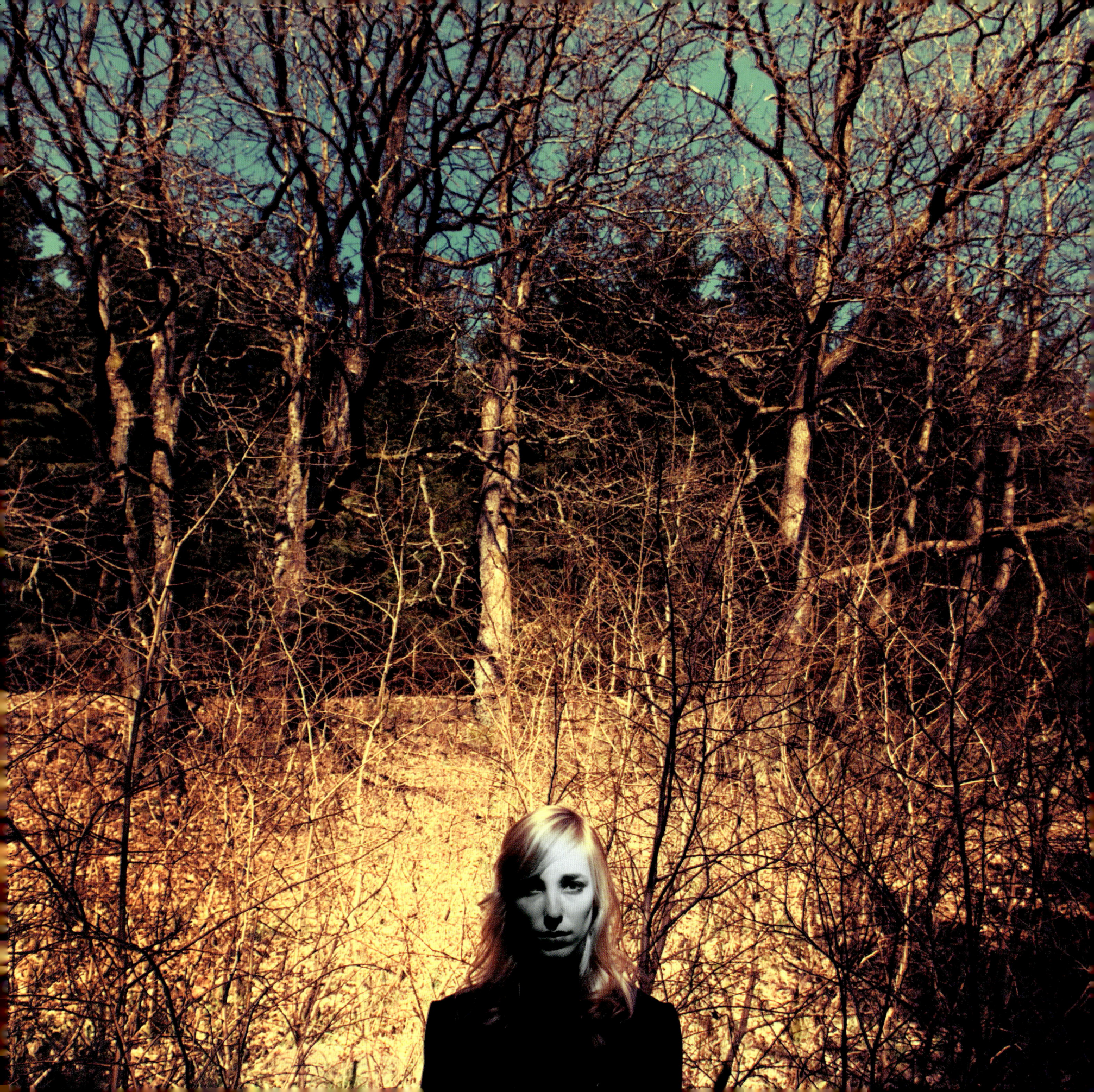

CIRCLE OF MANIAS 2009

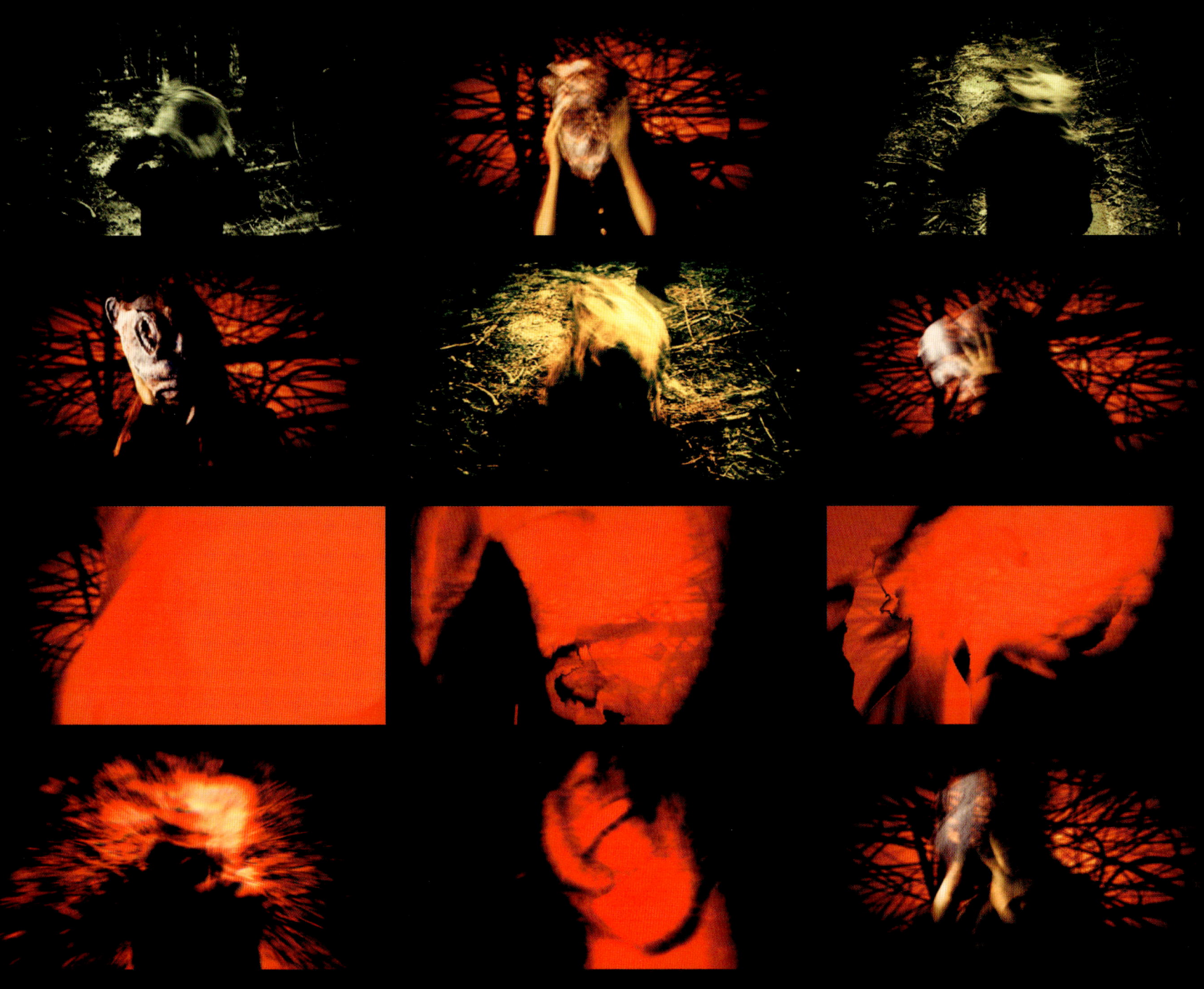

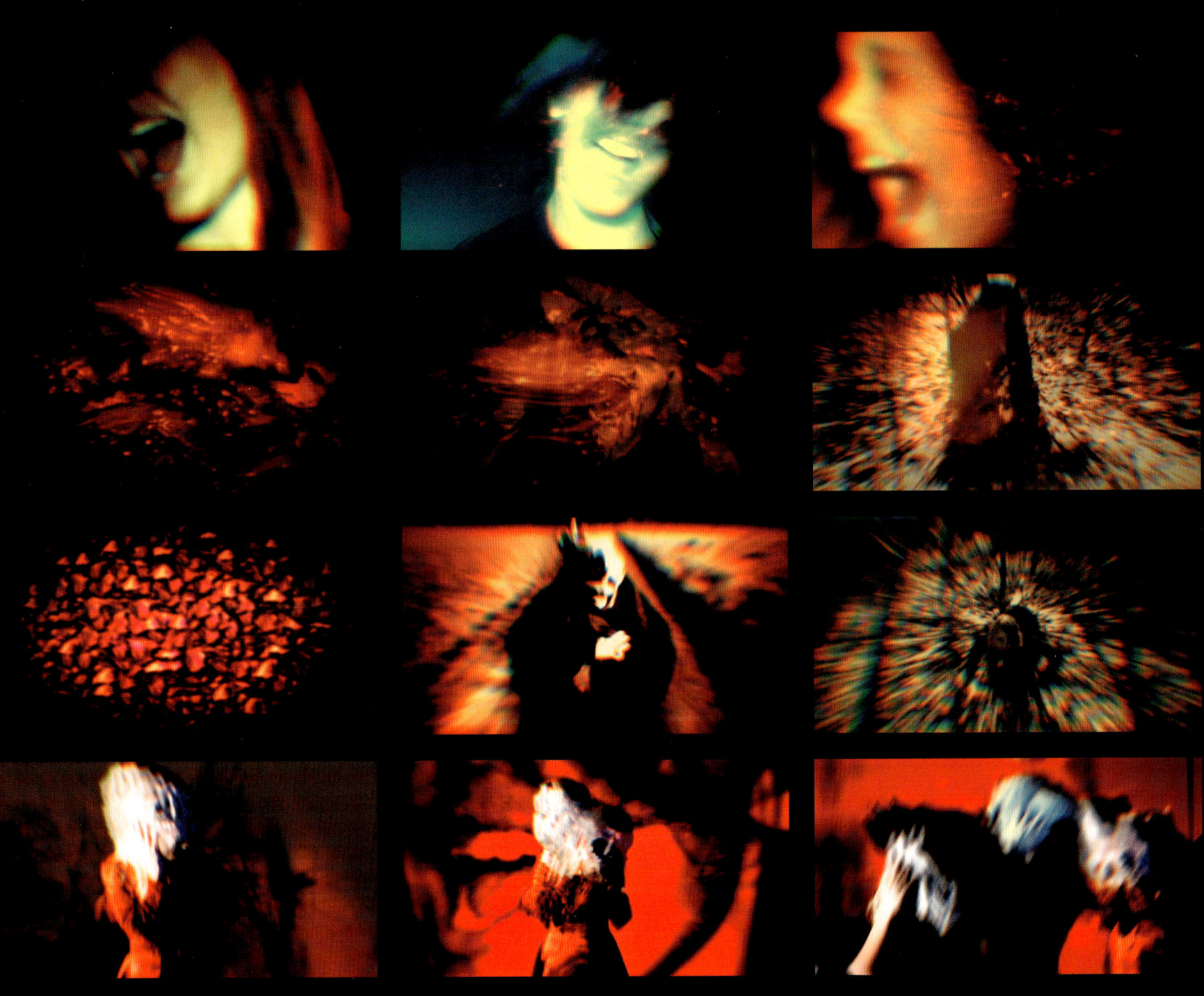

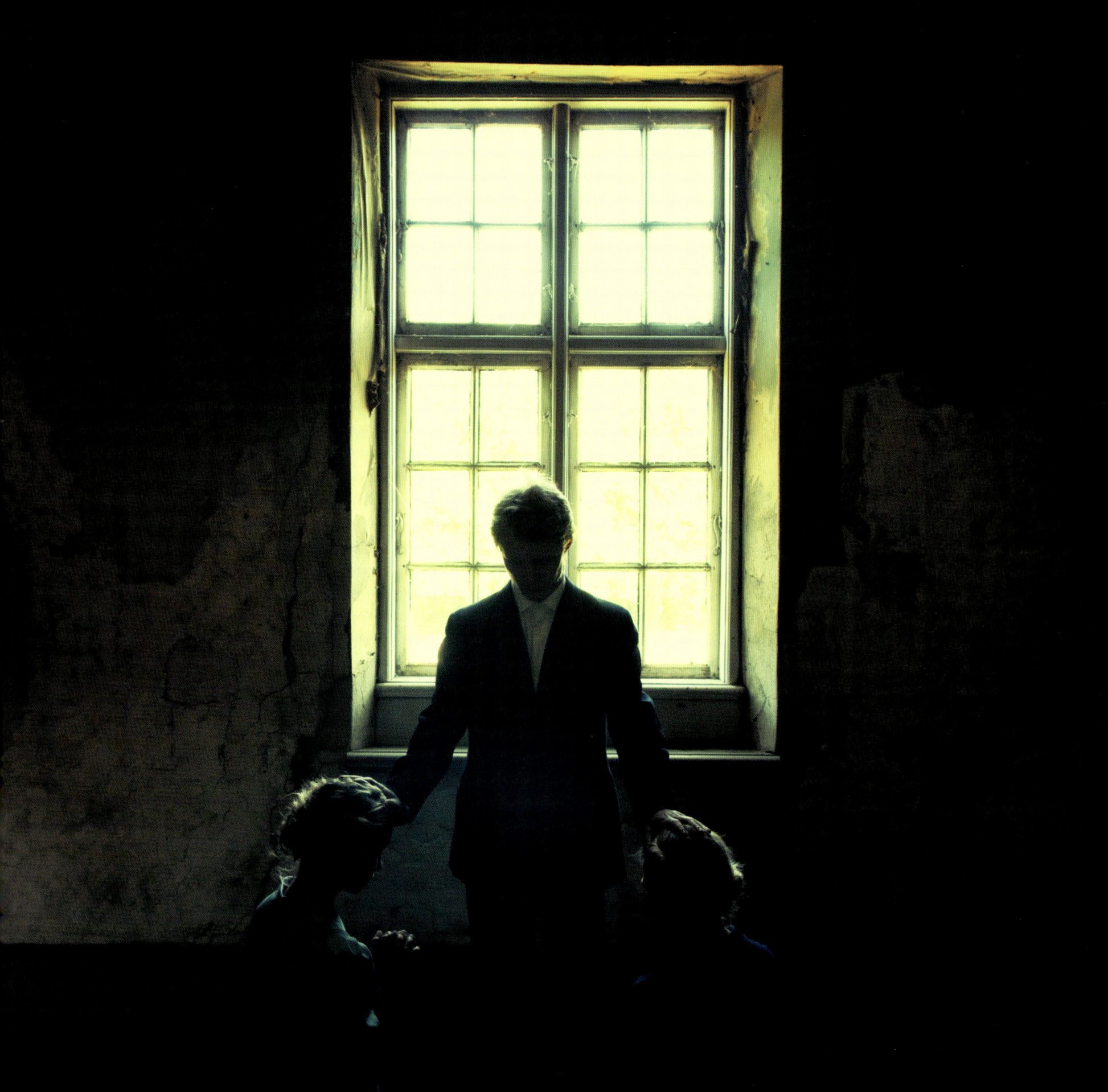

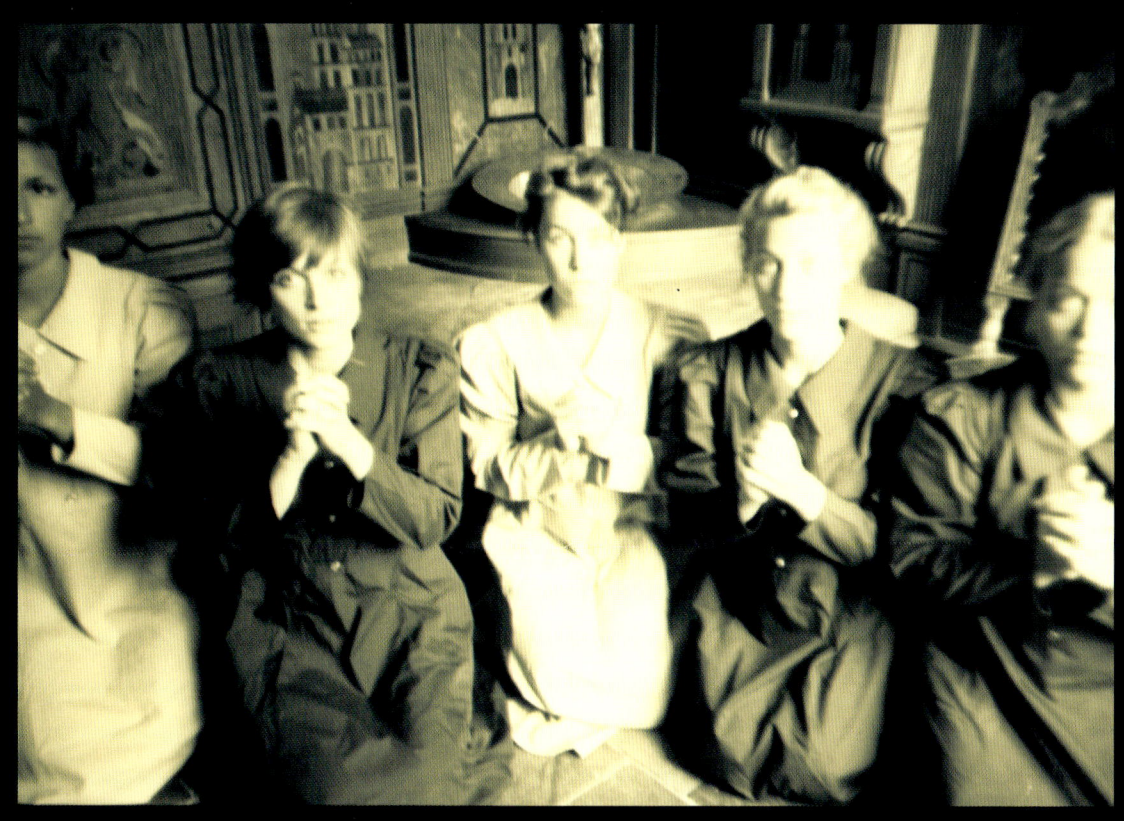
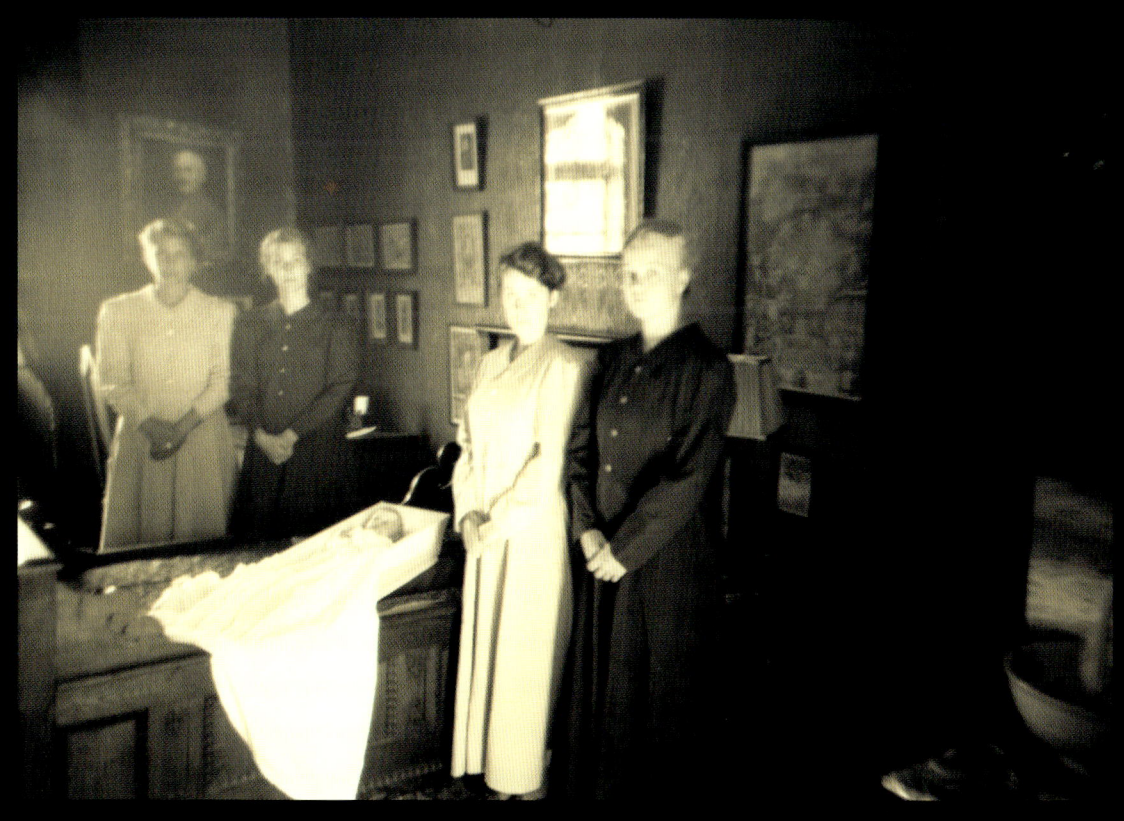

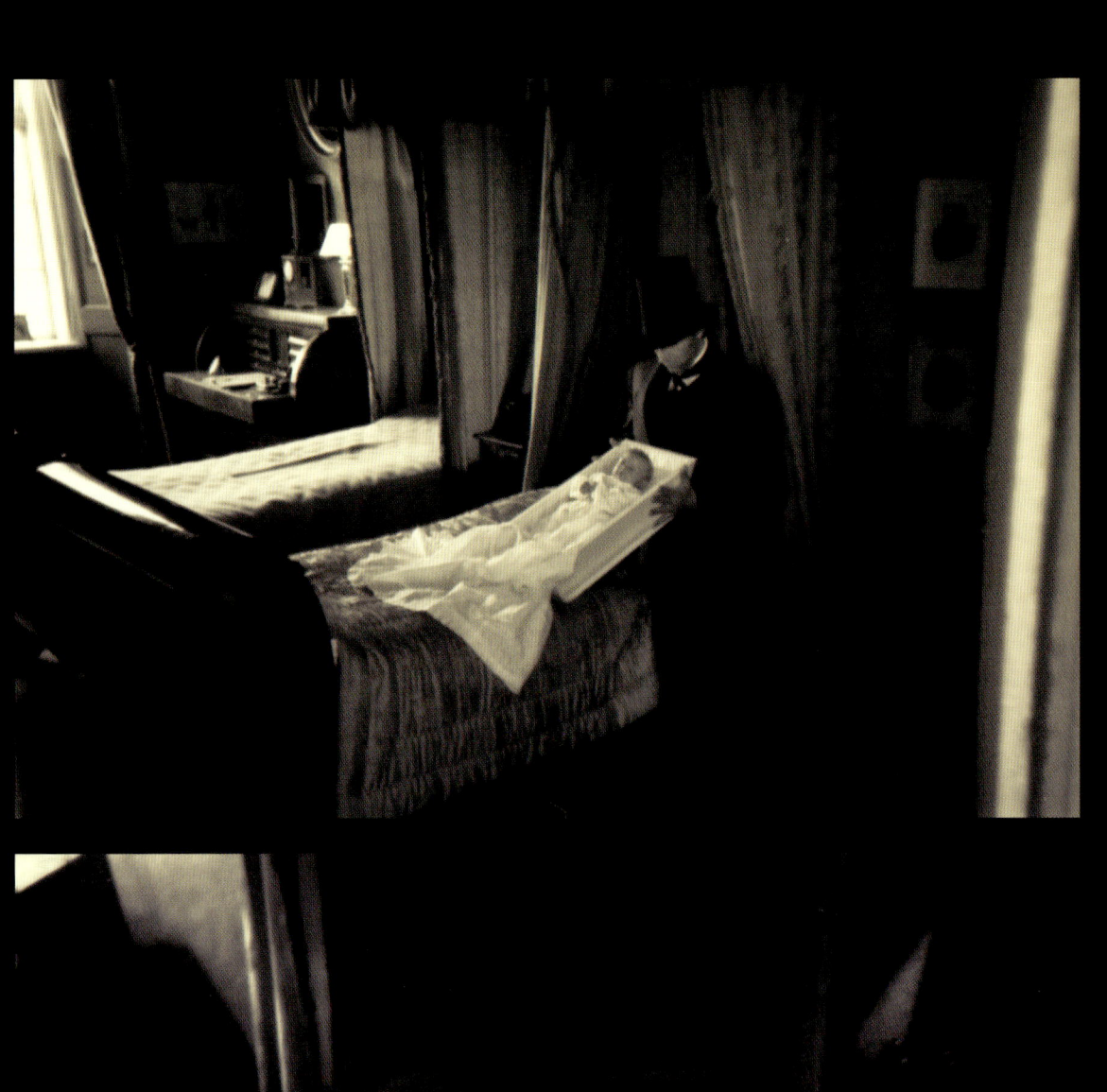

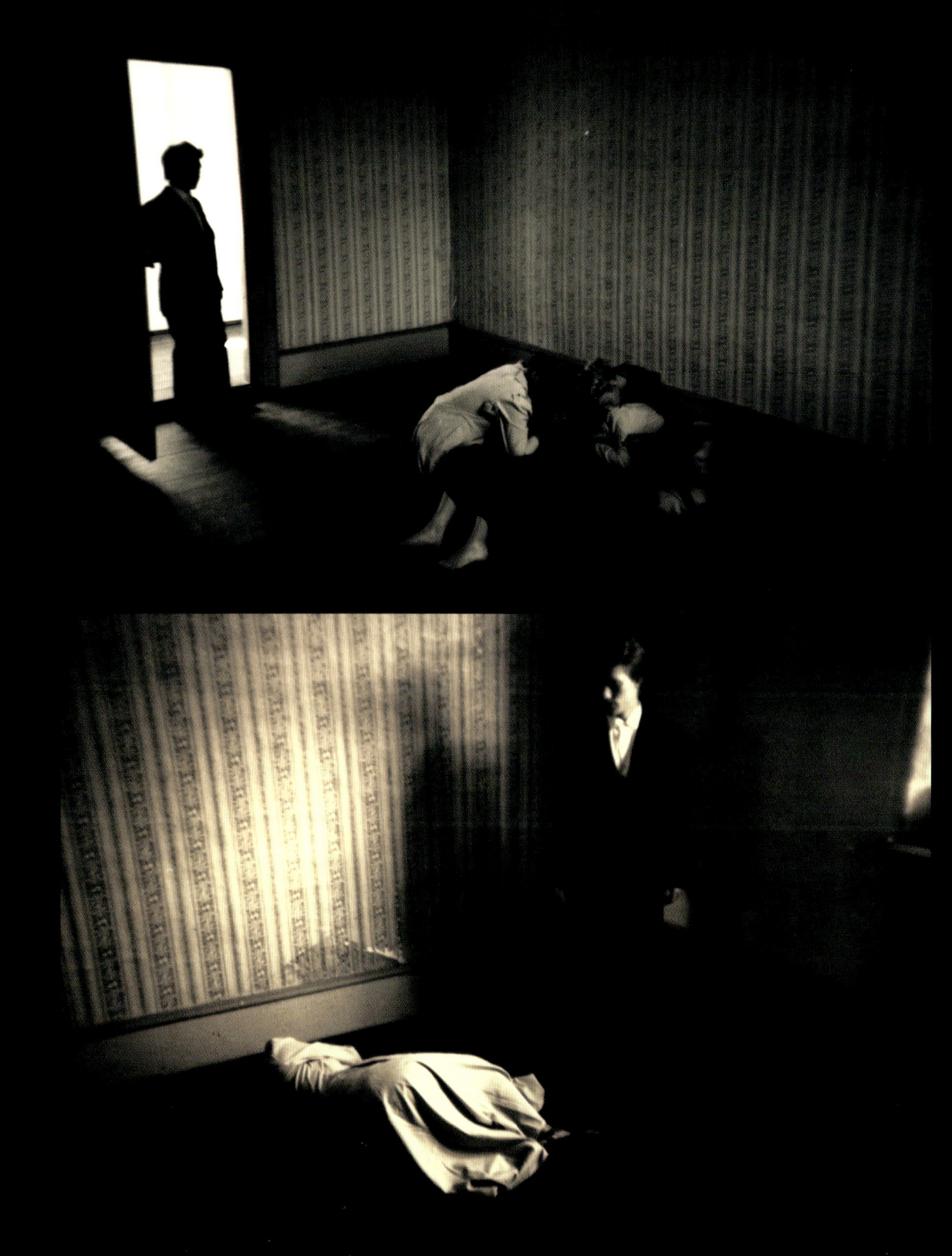

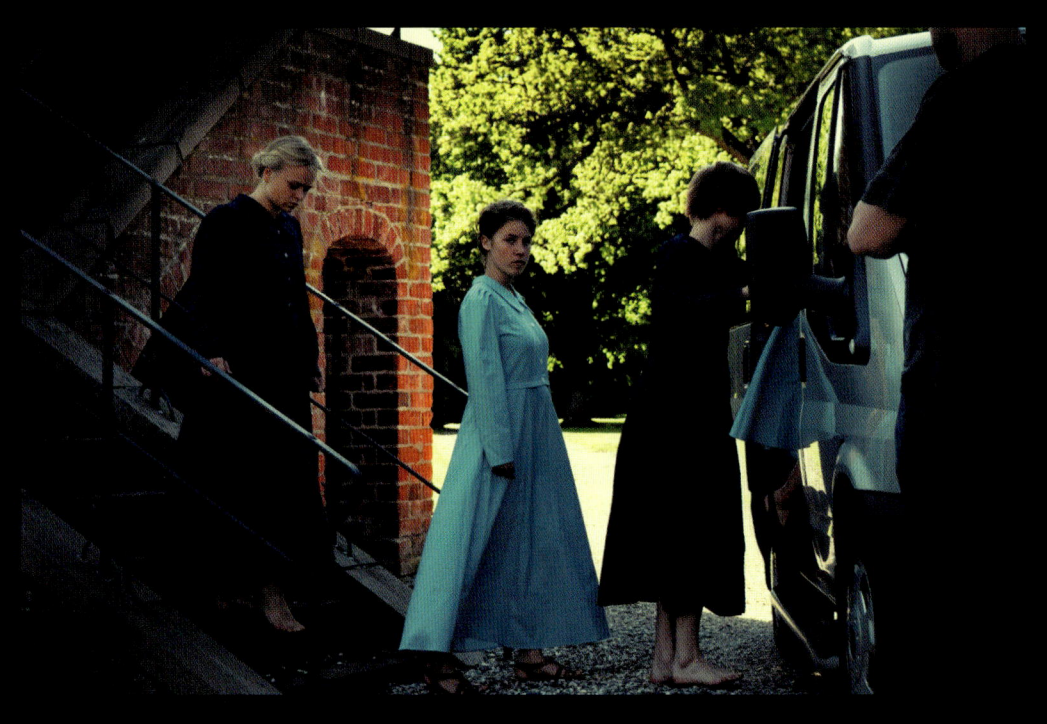
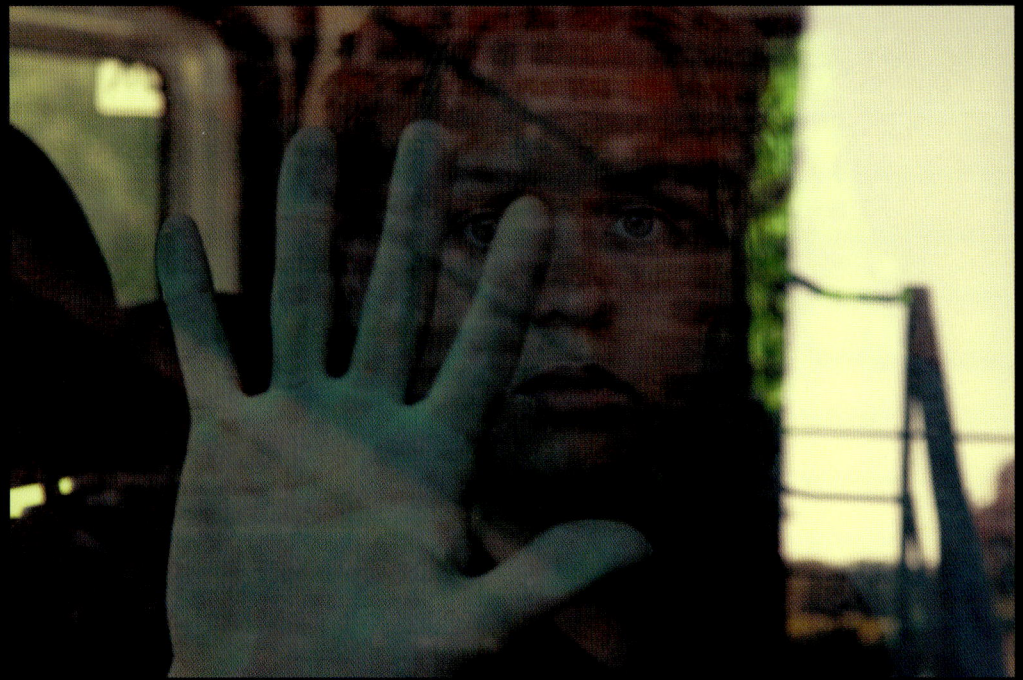

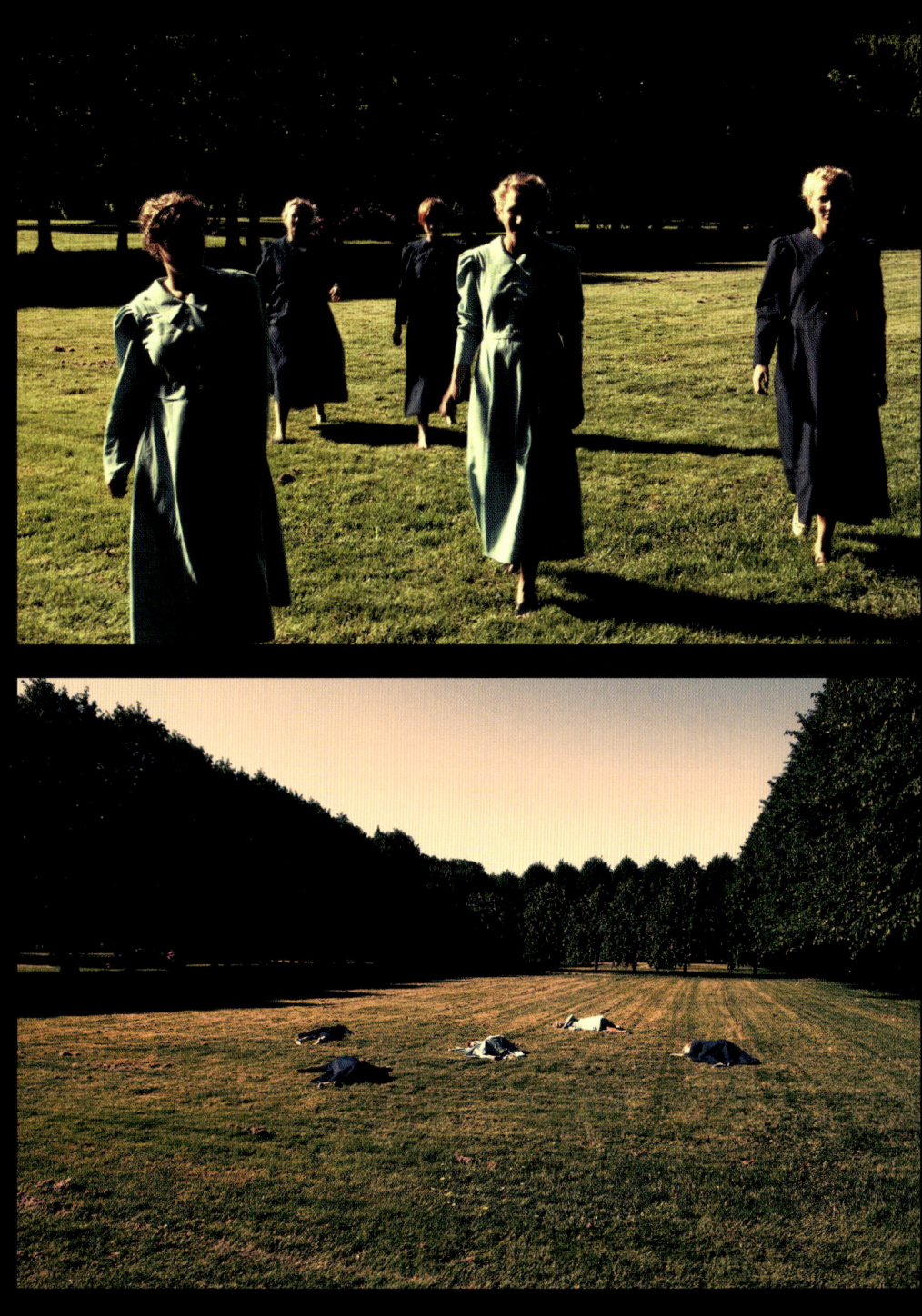

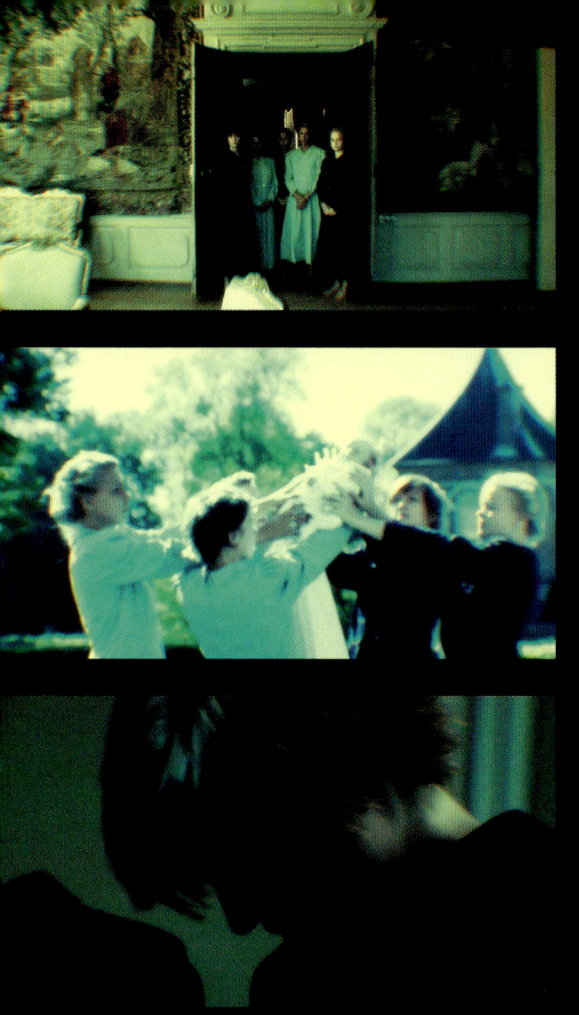
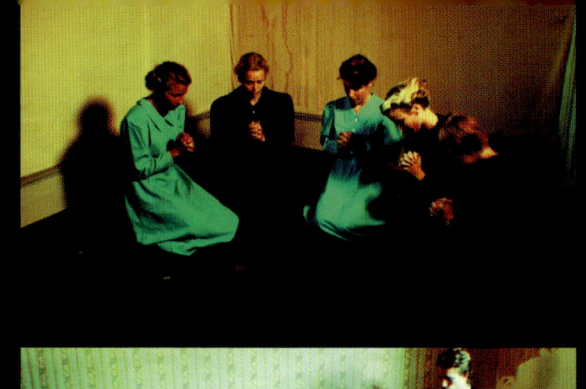
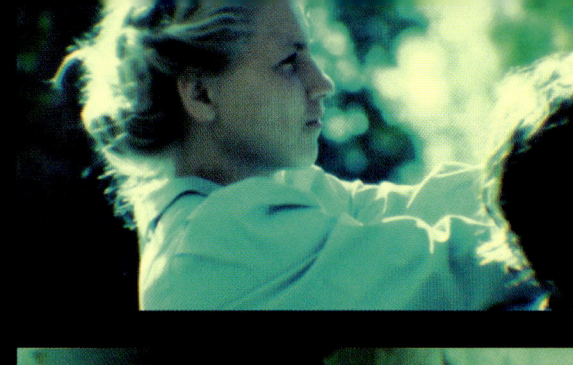
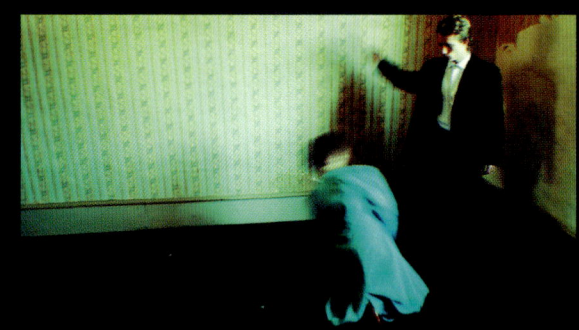
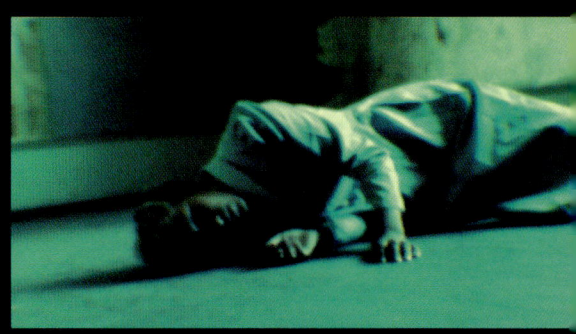
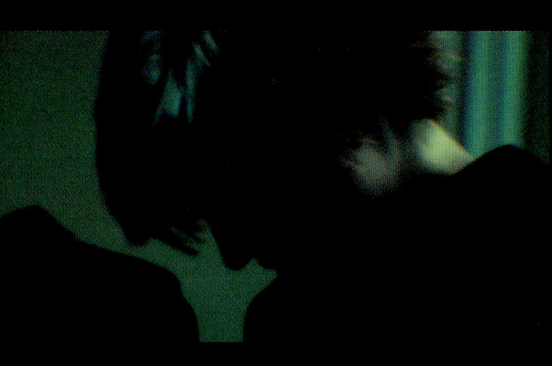
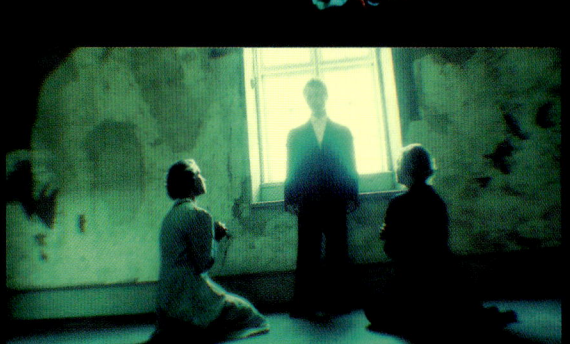
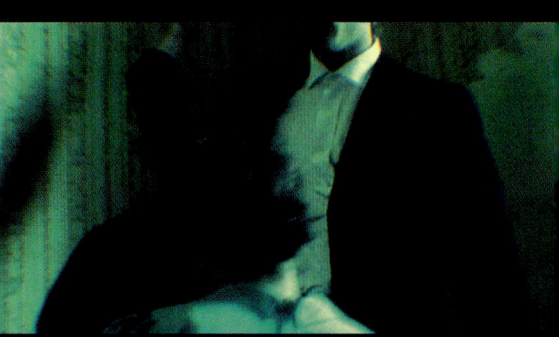
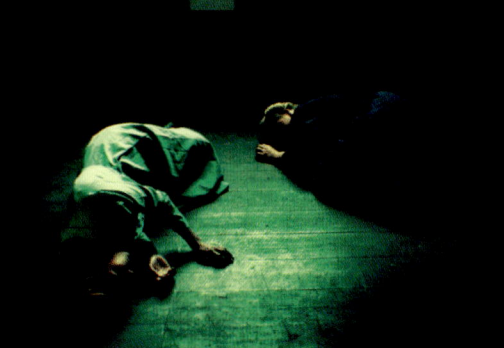
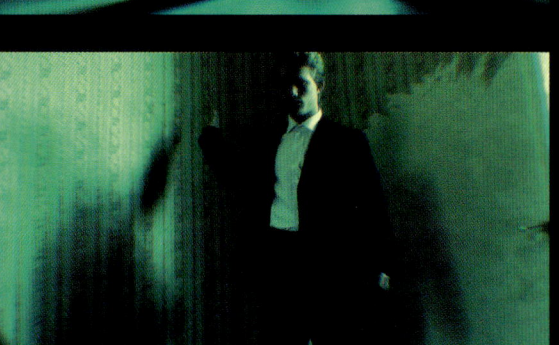
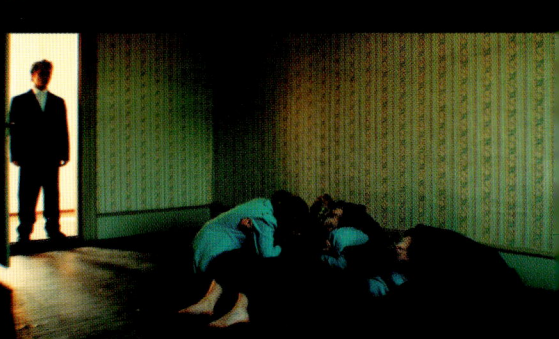

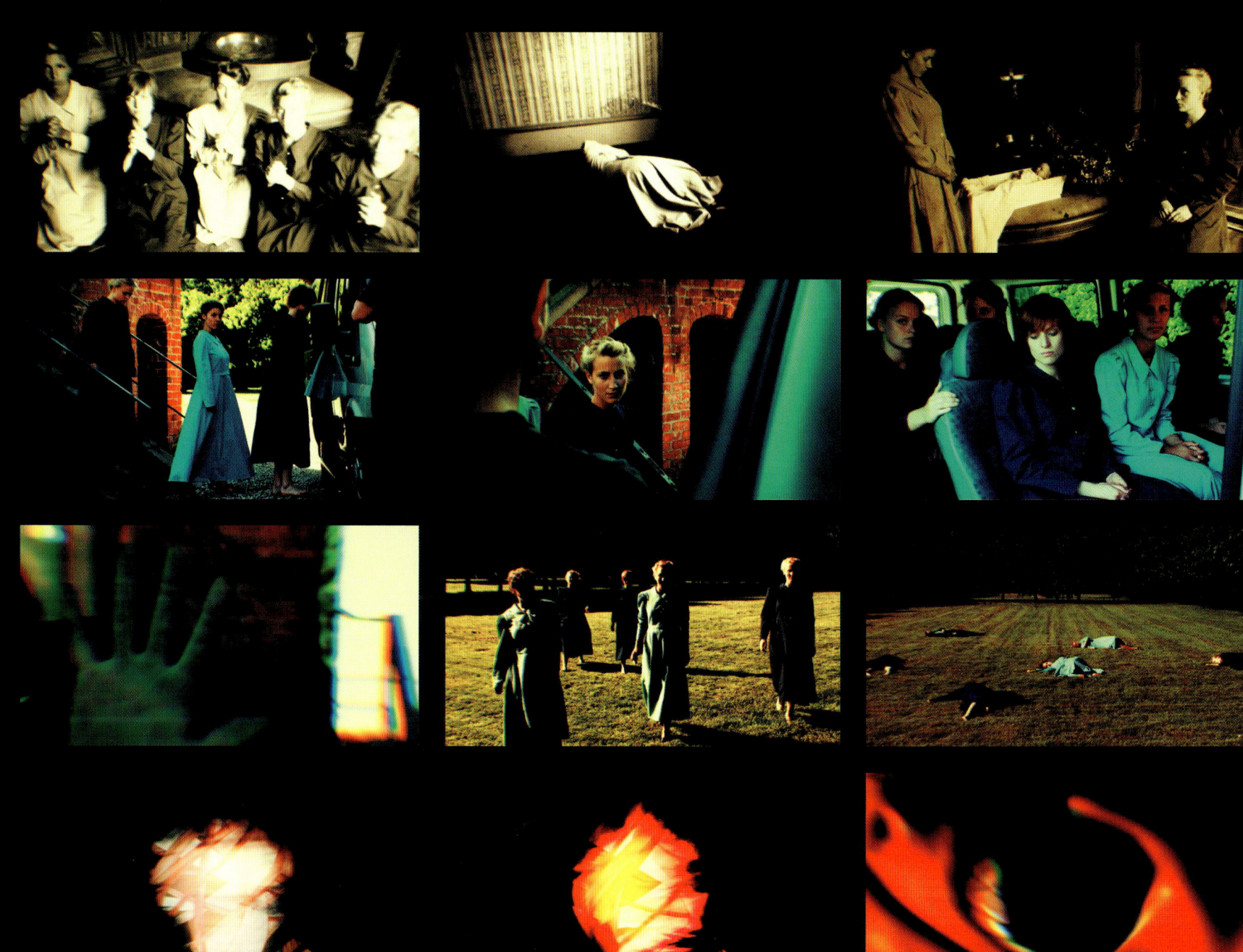

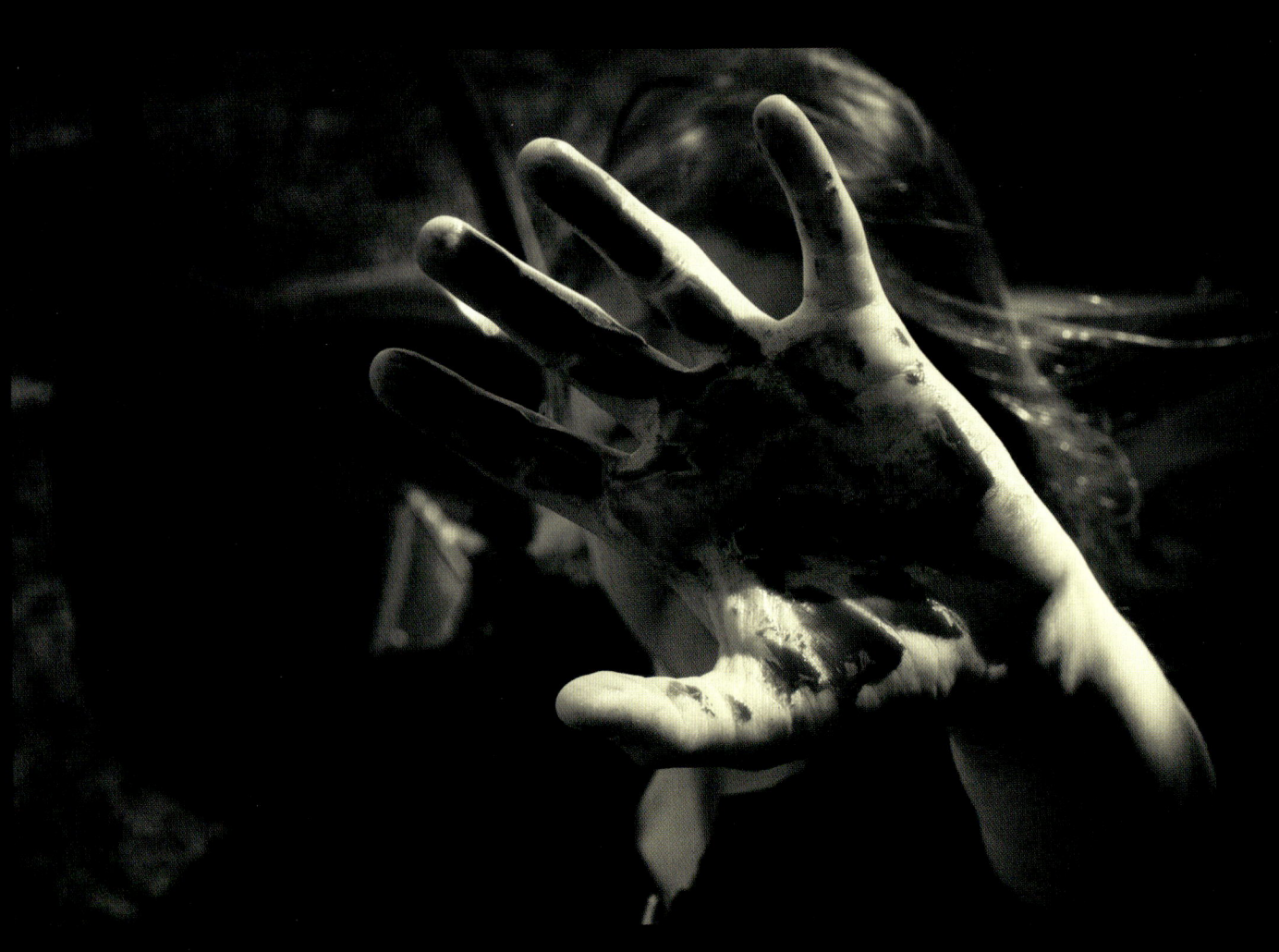

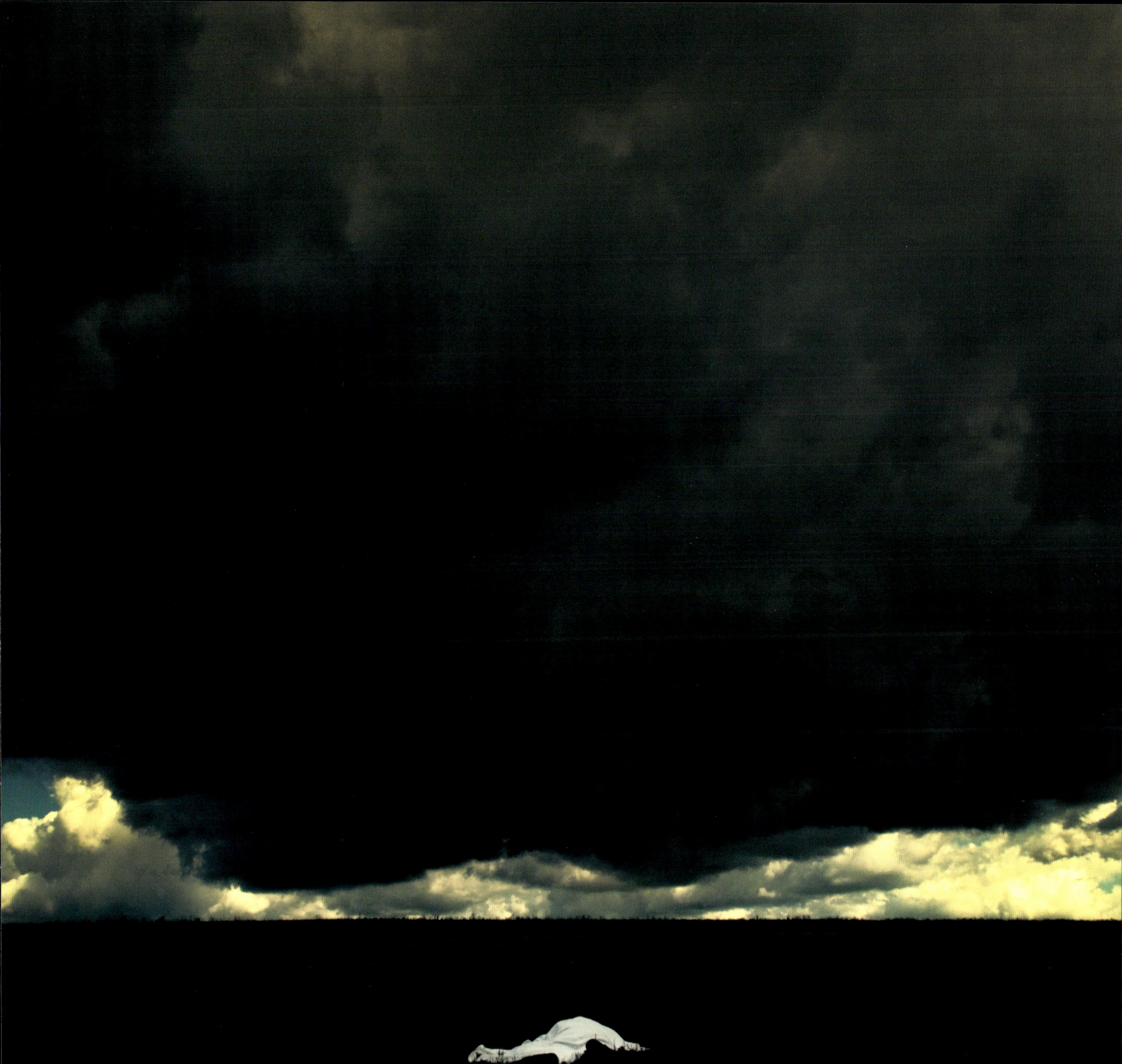

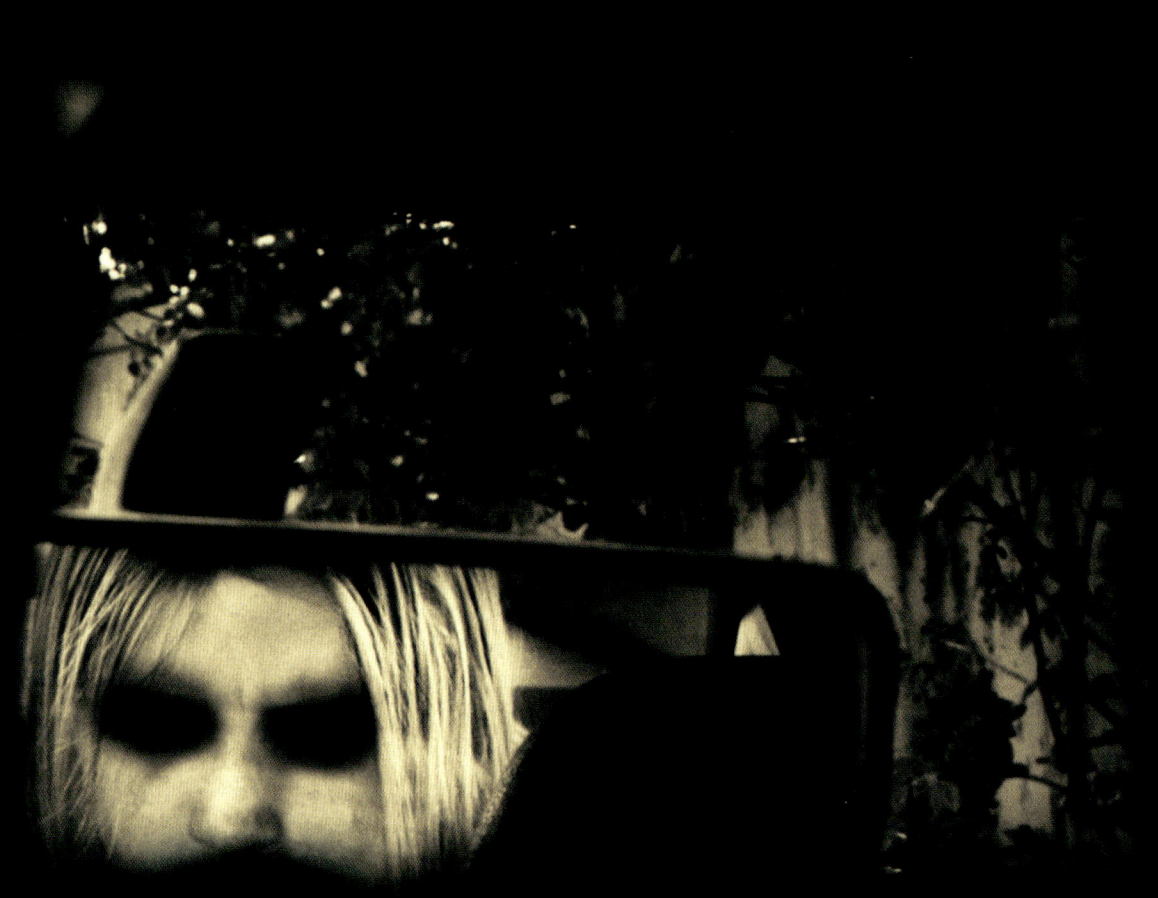

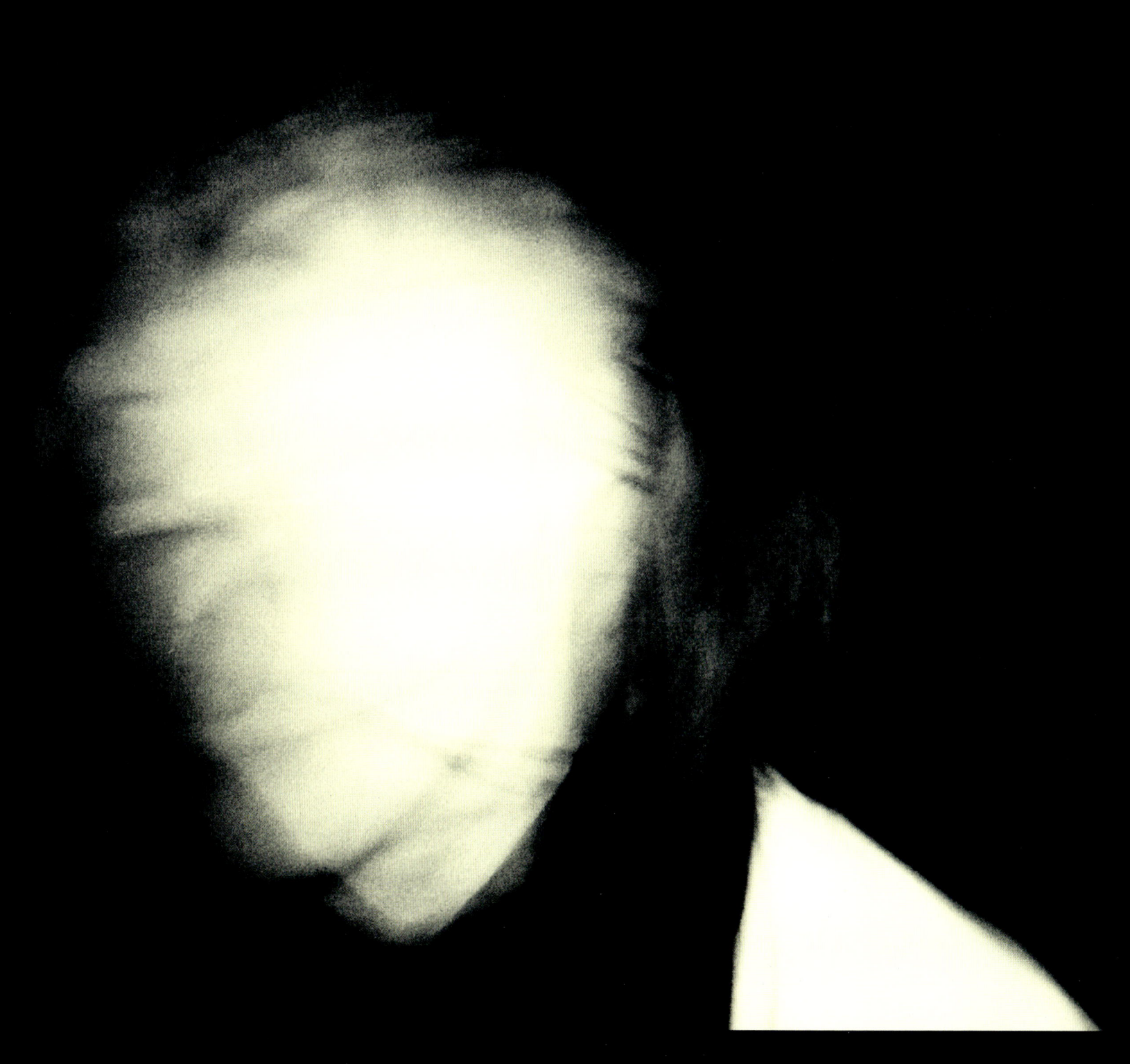

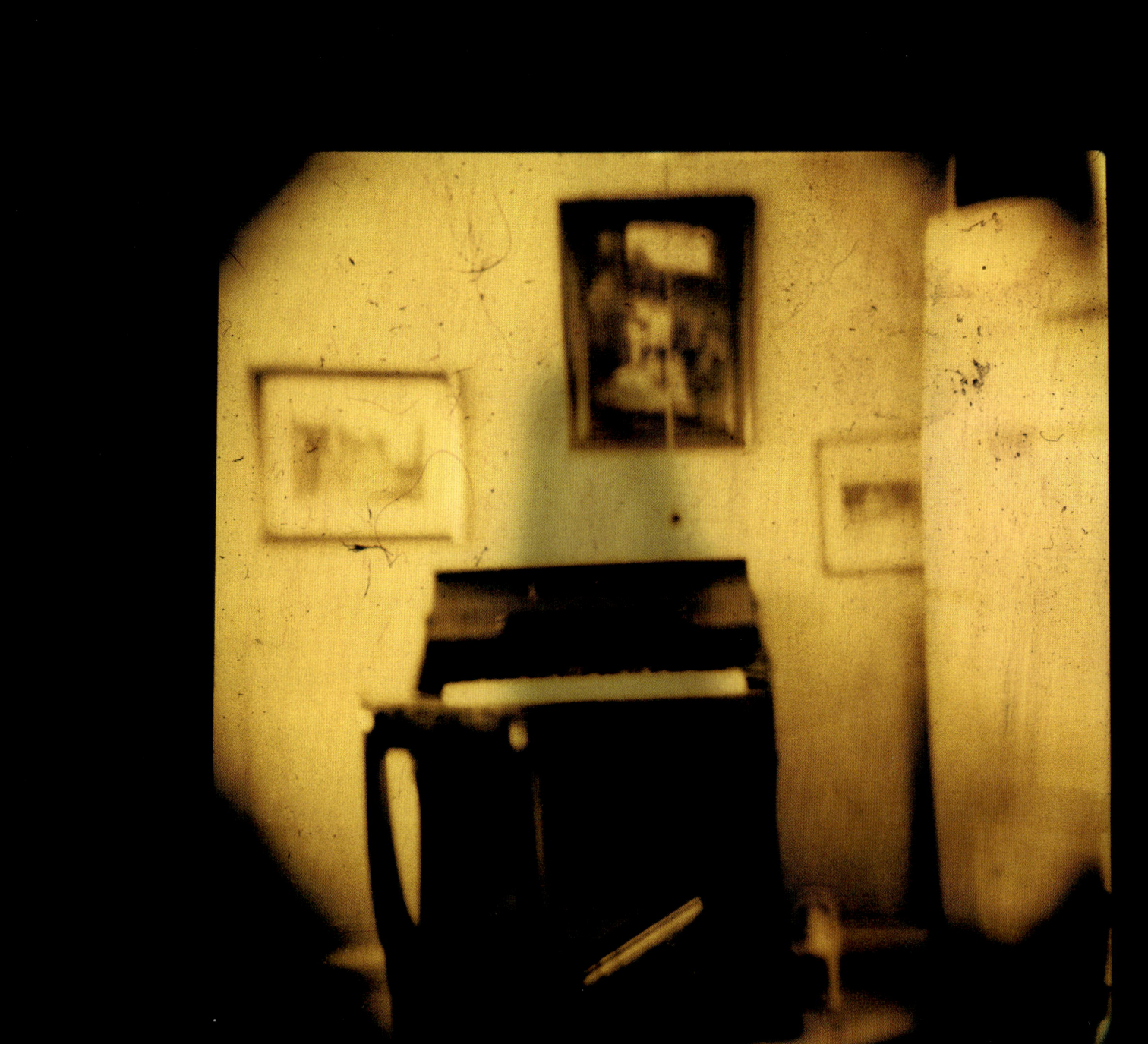

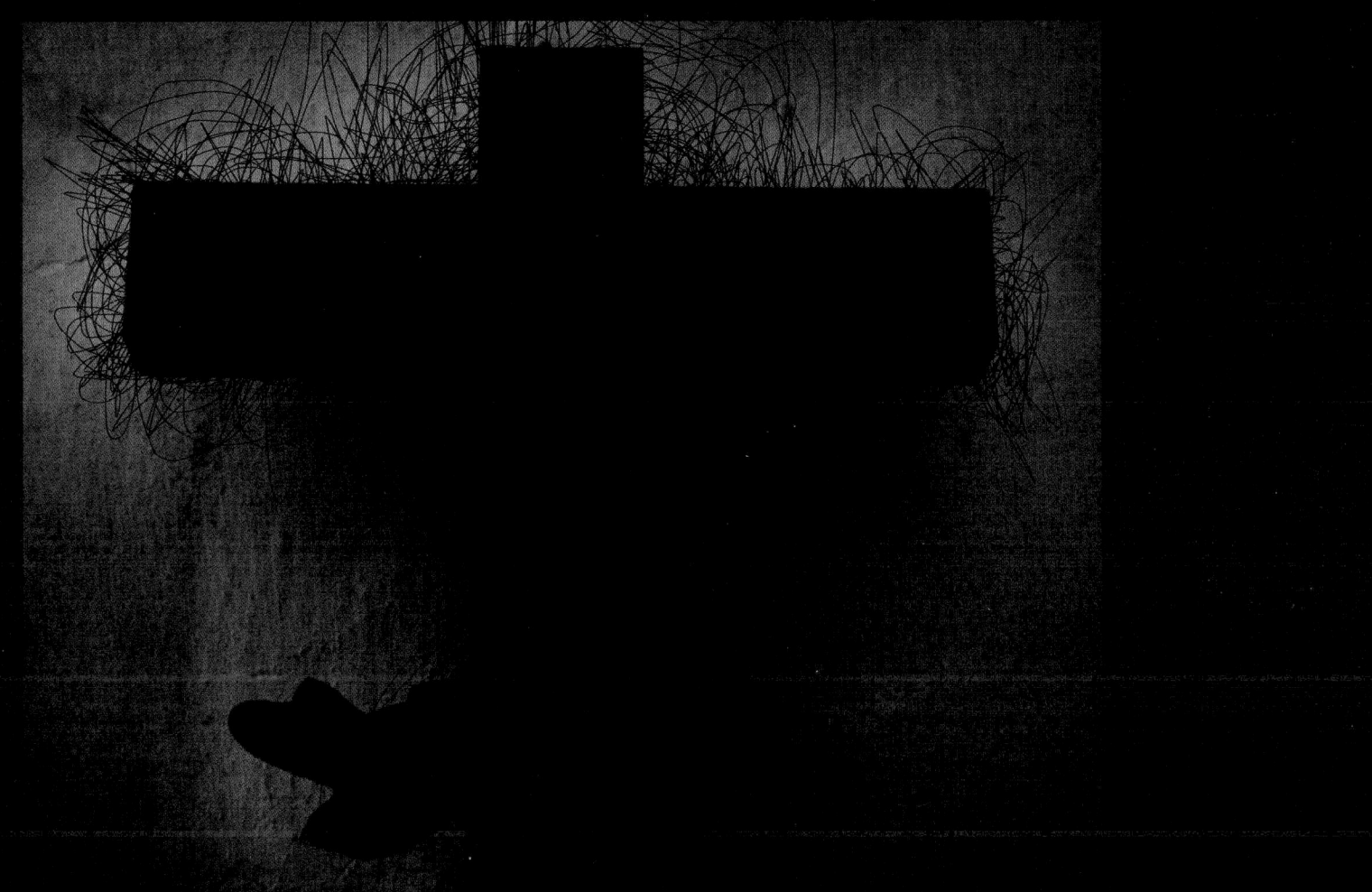

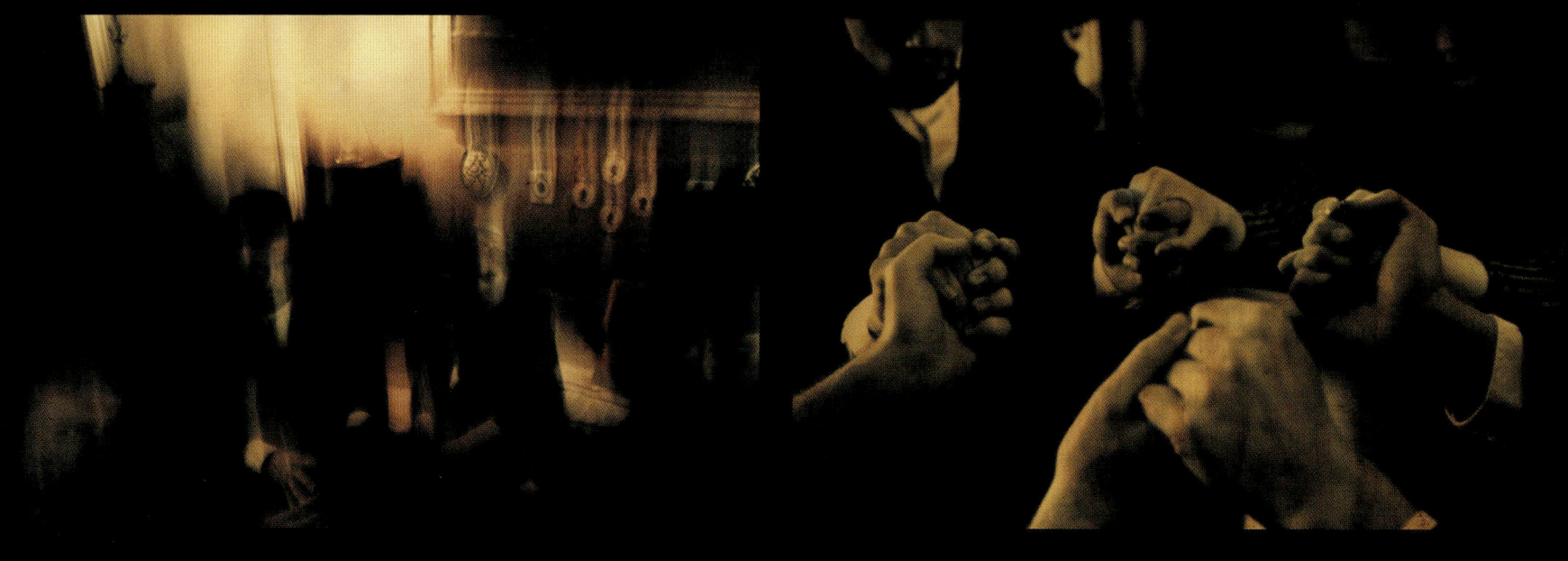

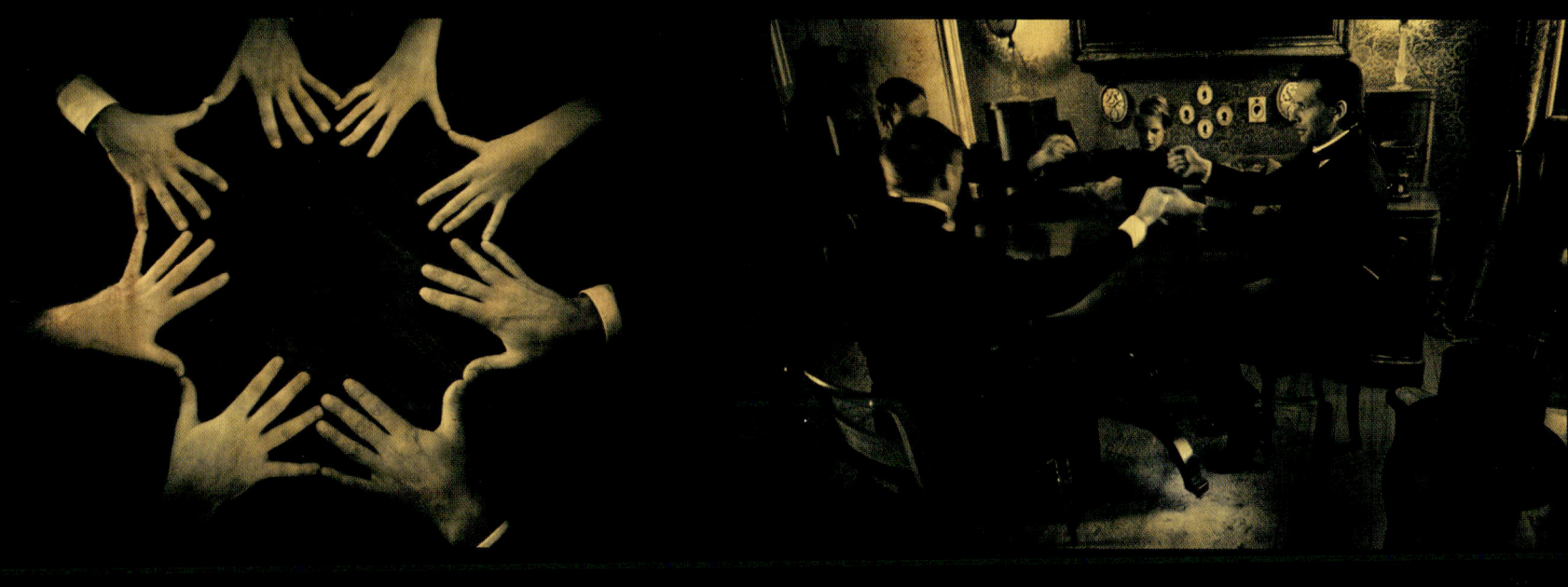

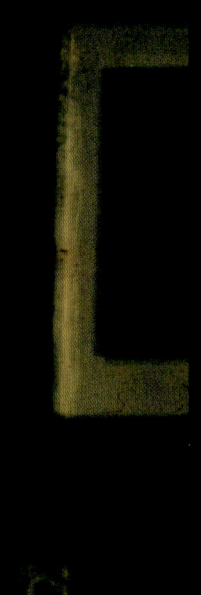

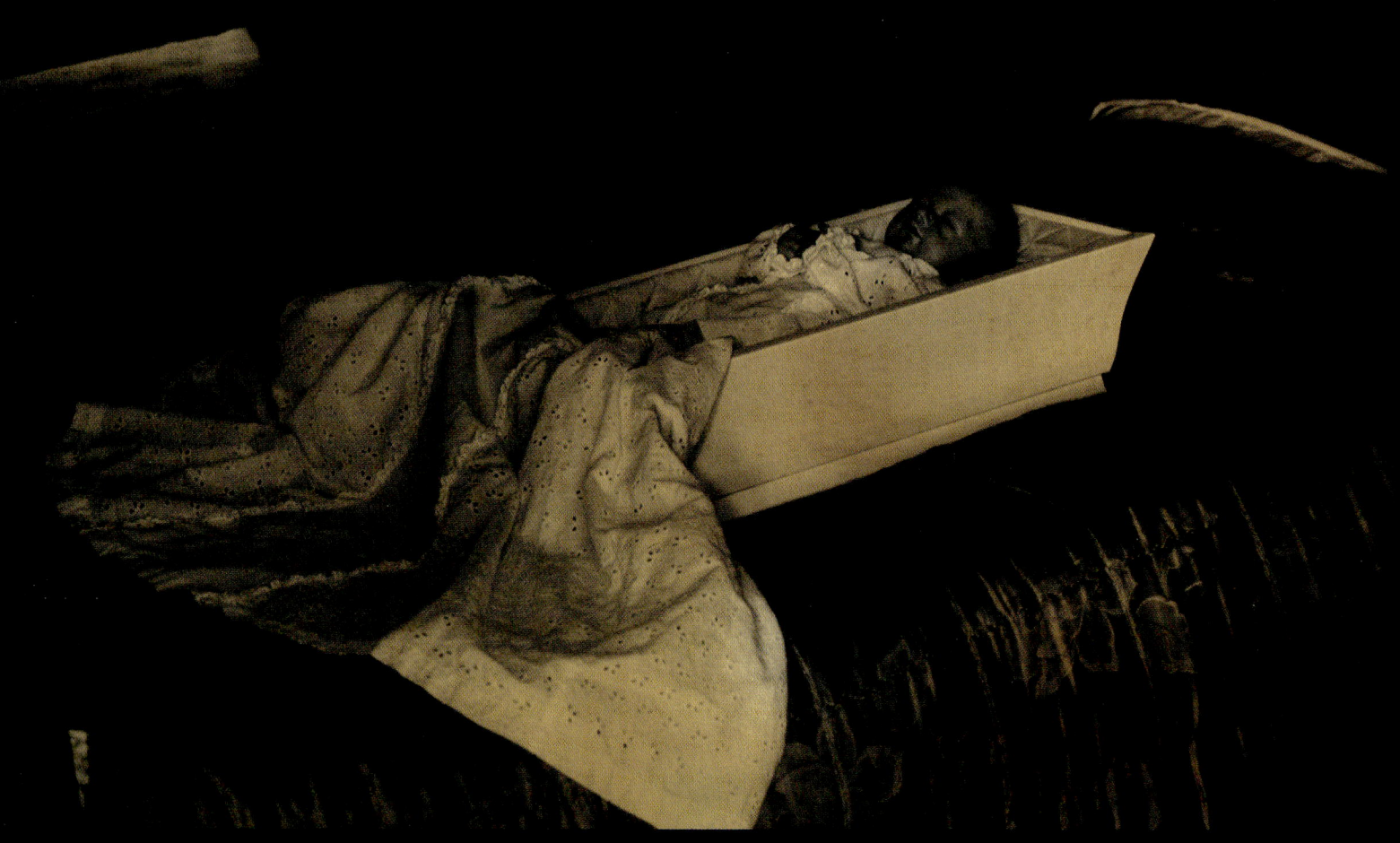

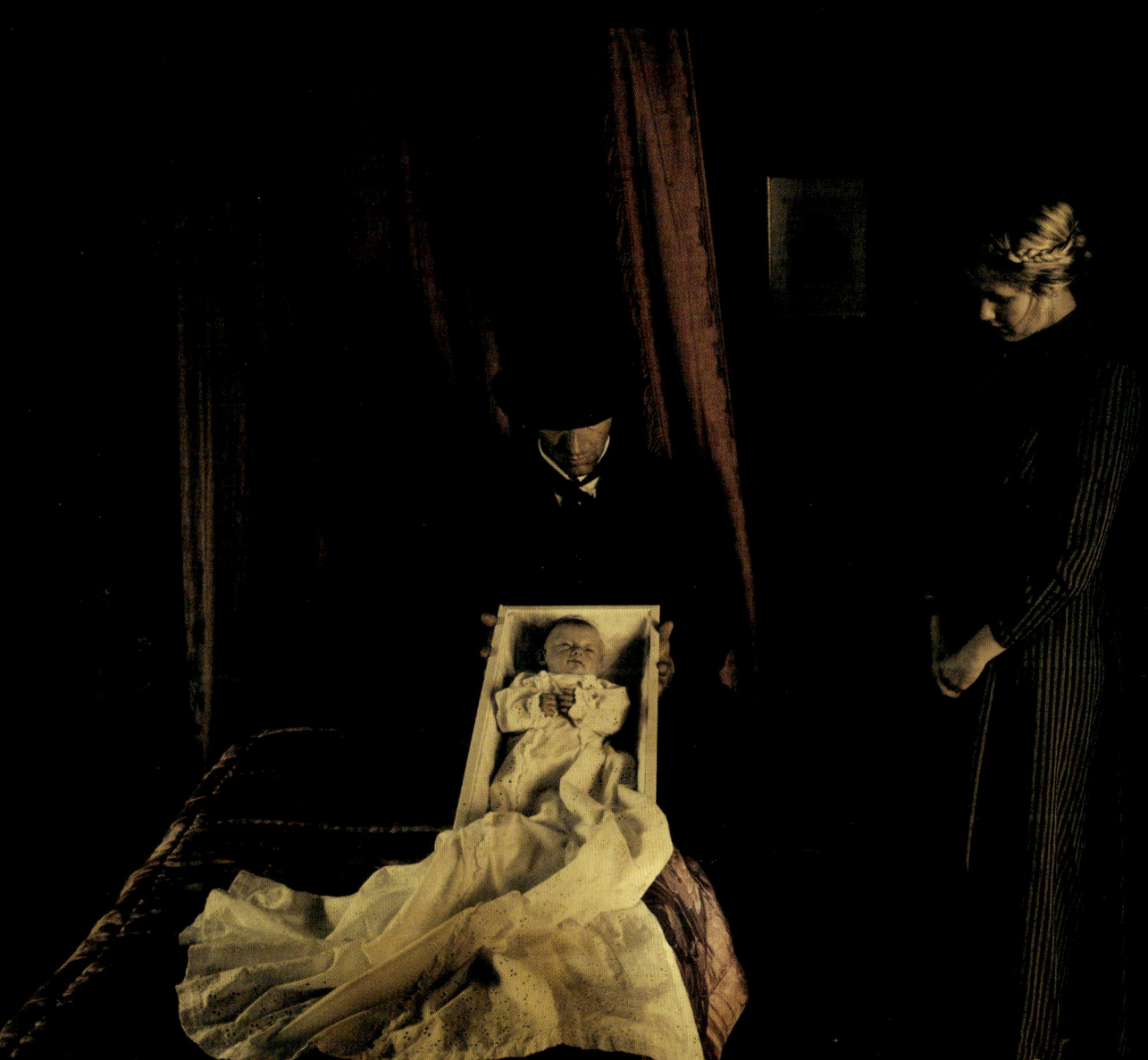

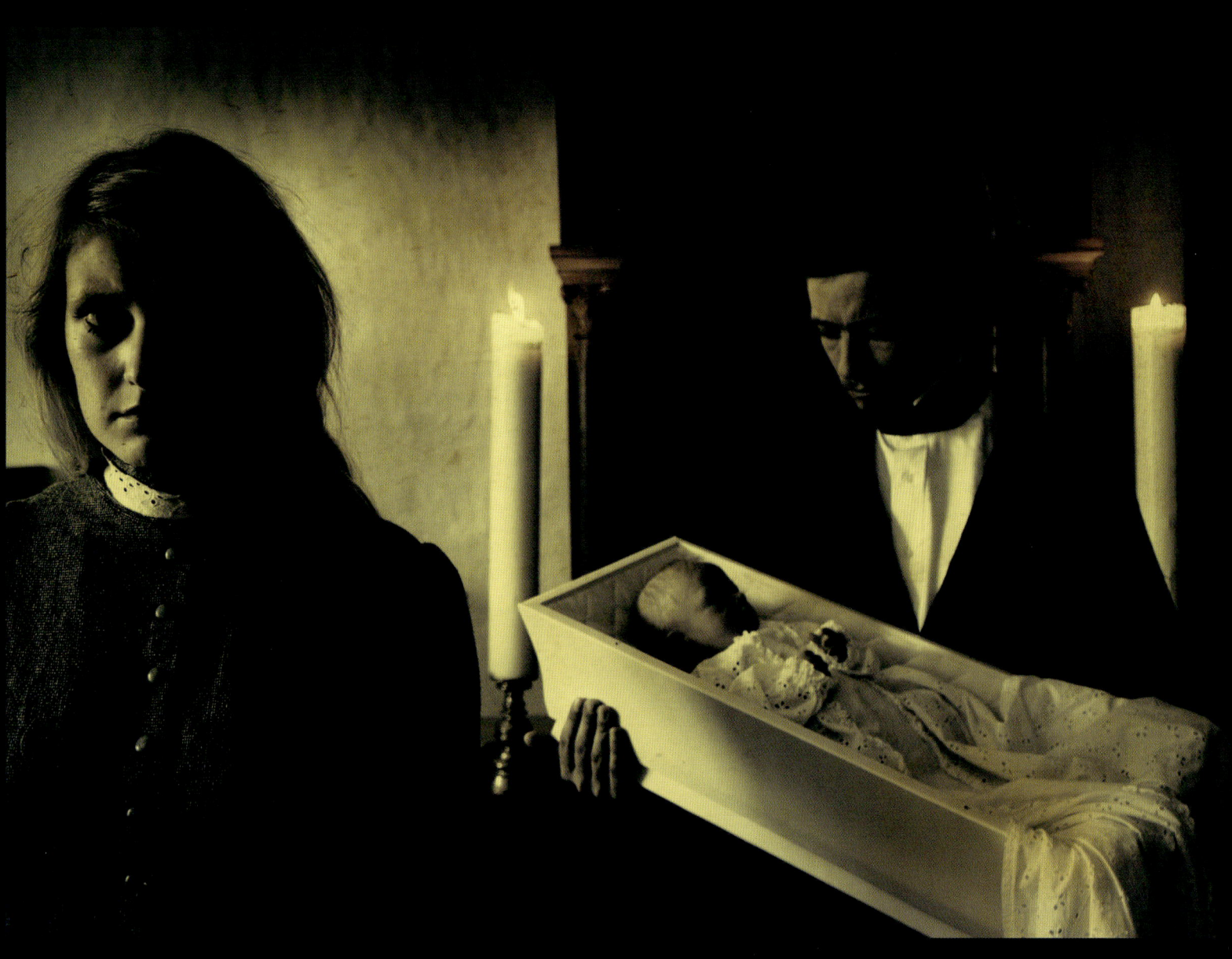

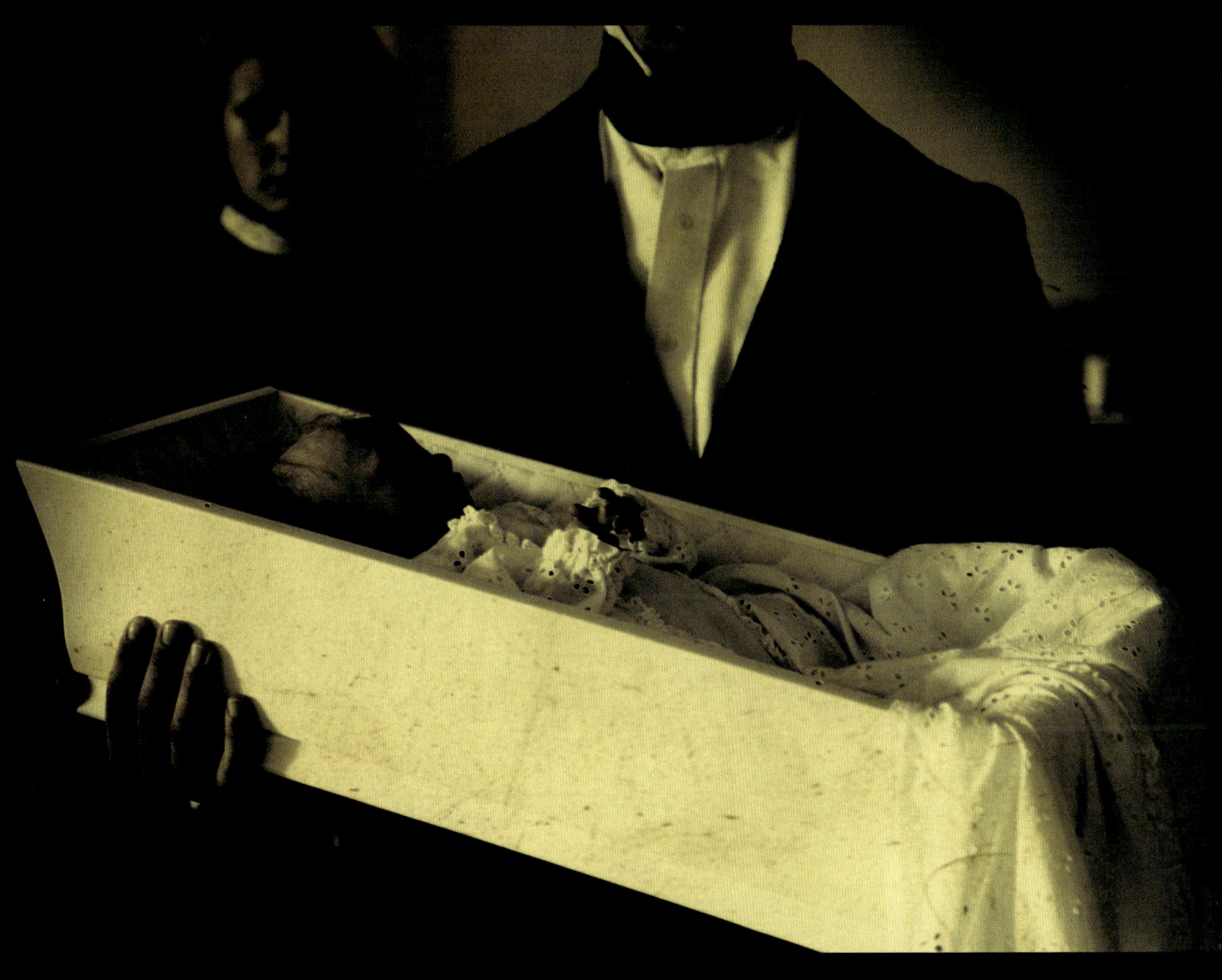

THE SEANCE 2009

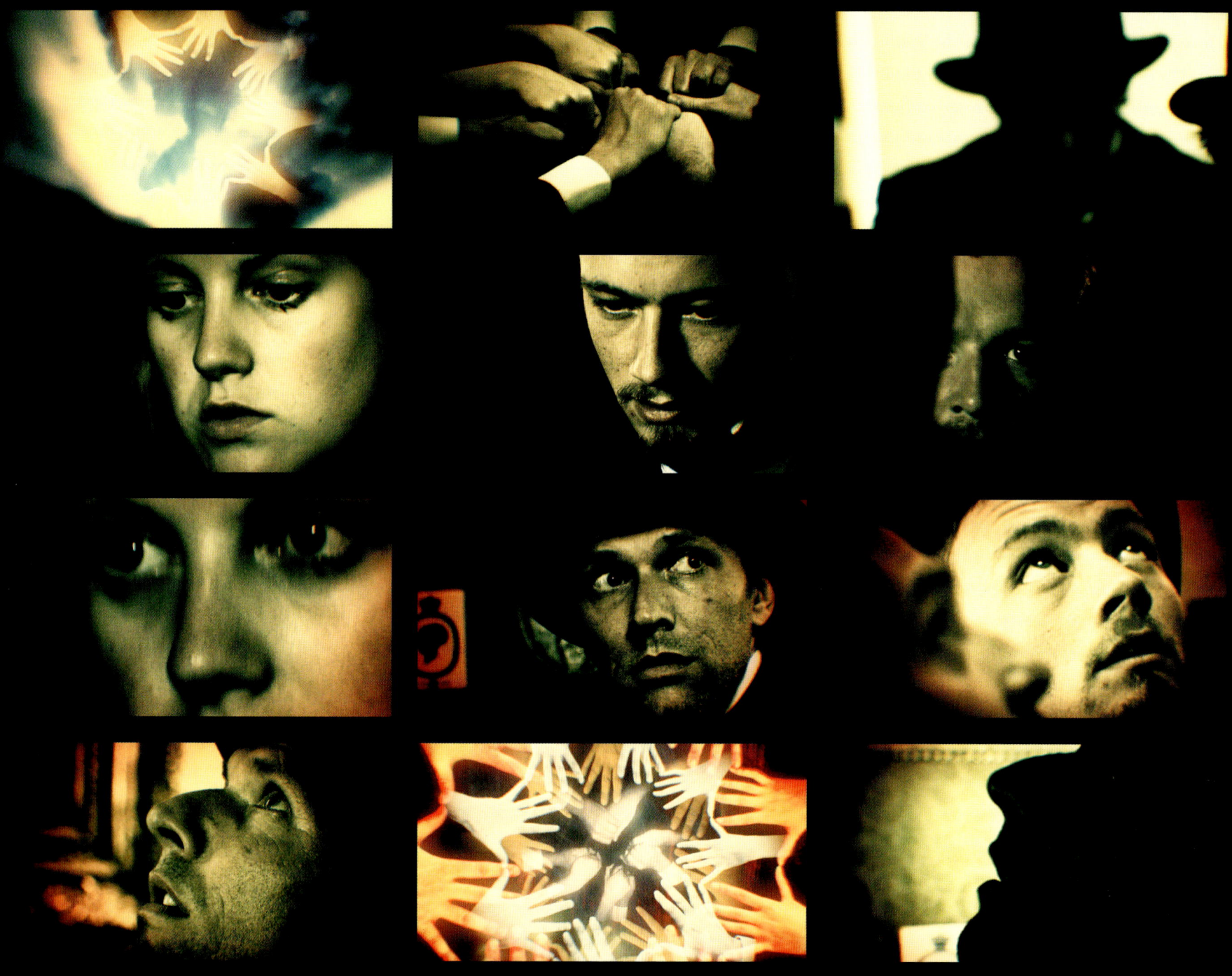

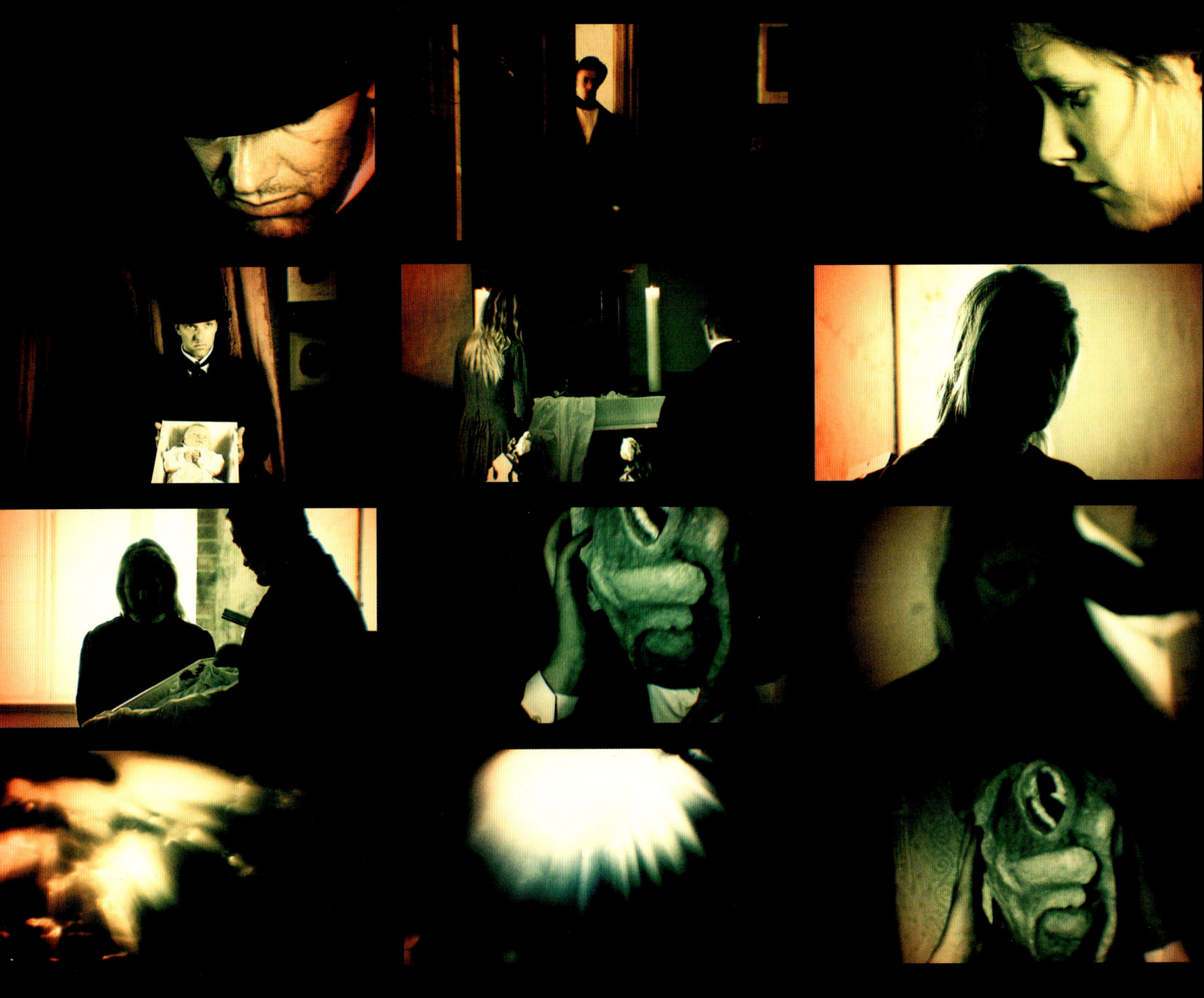

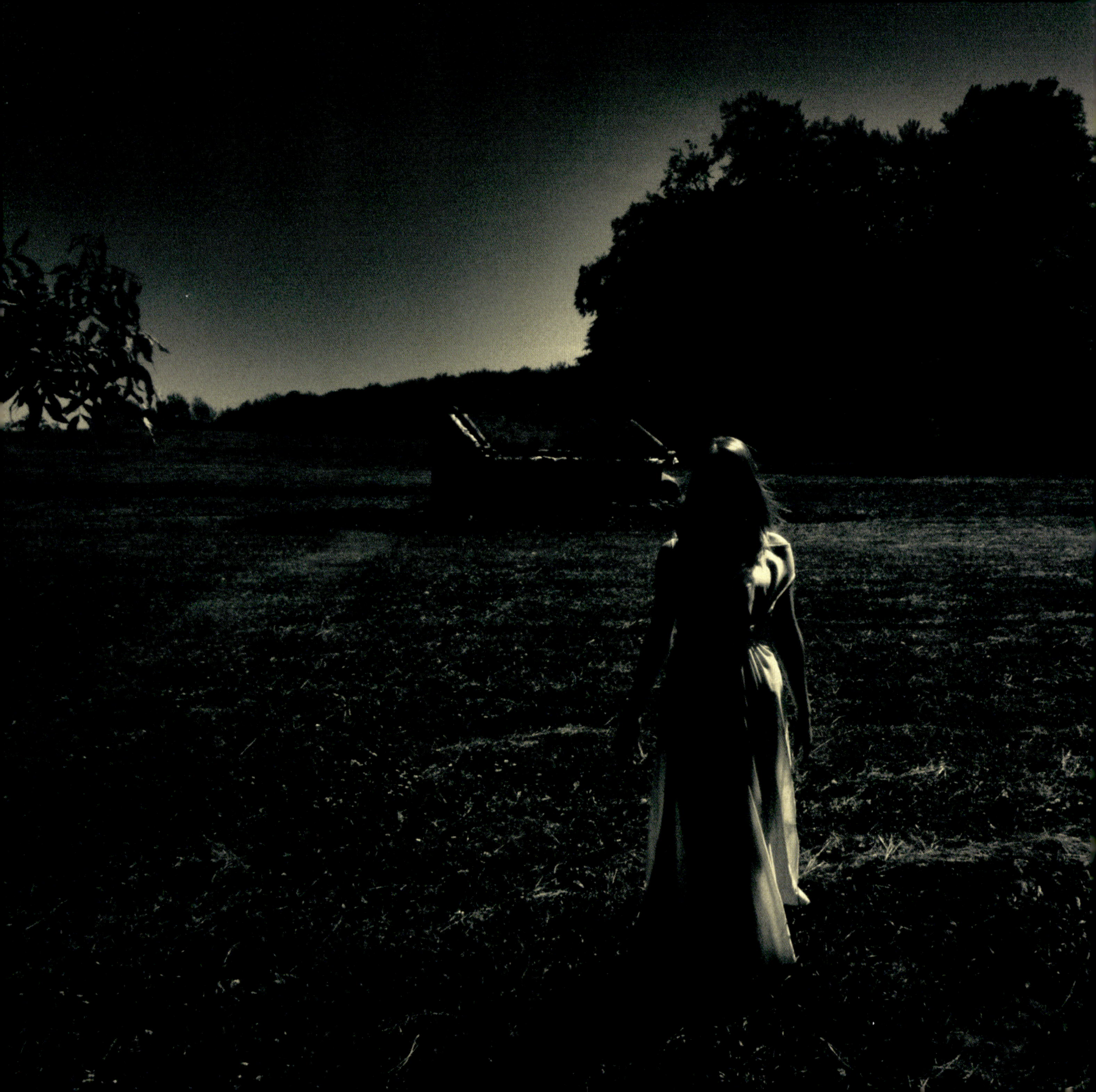

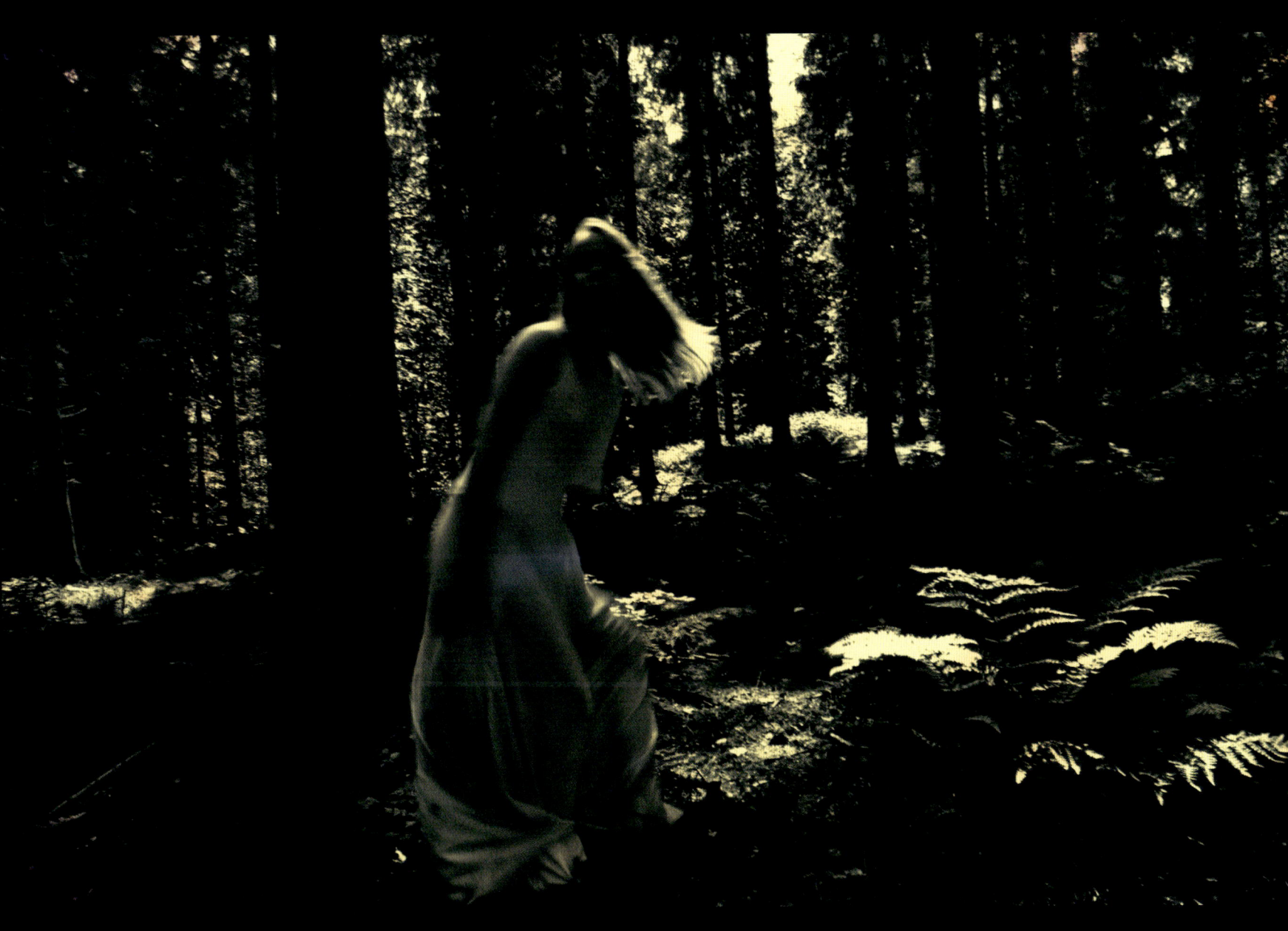

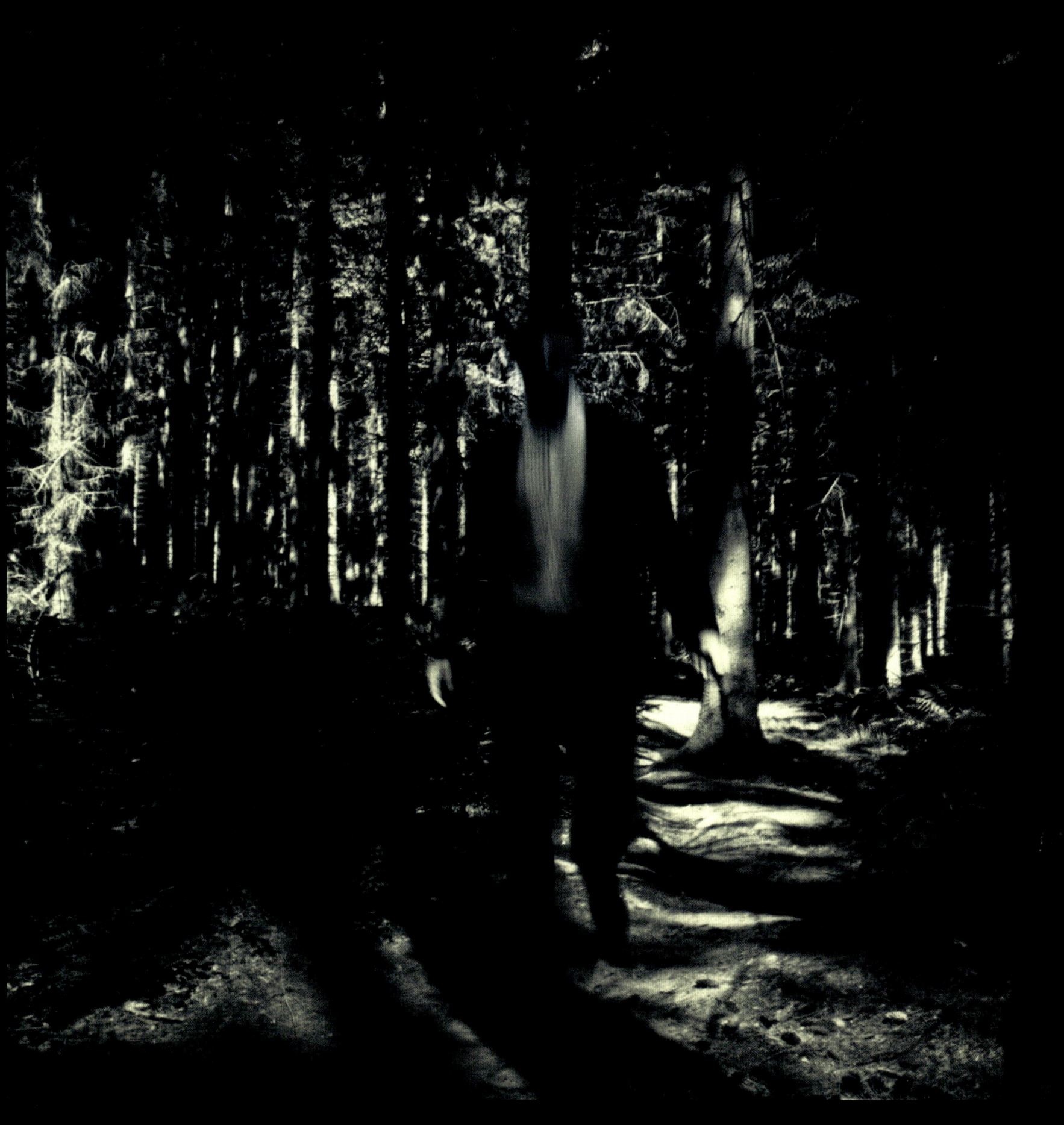

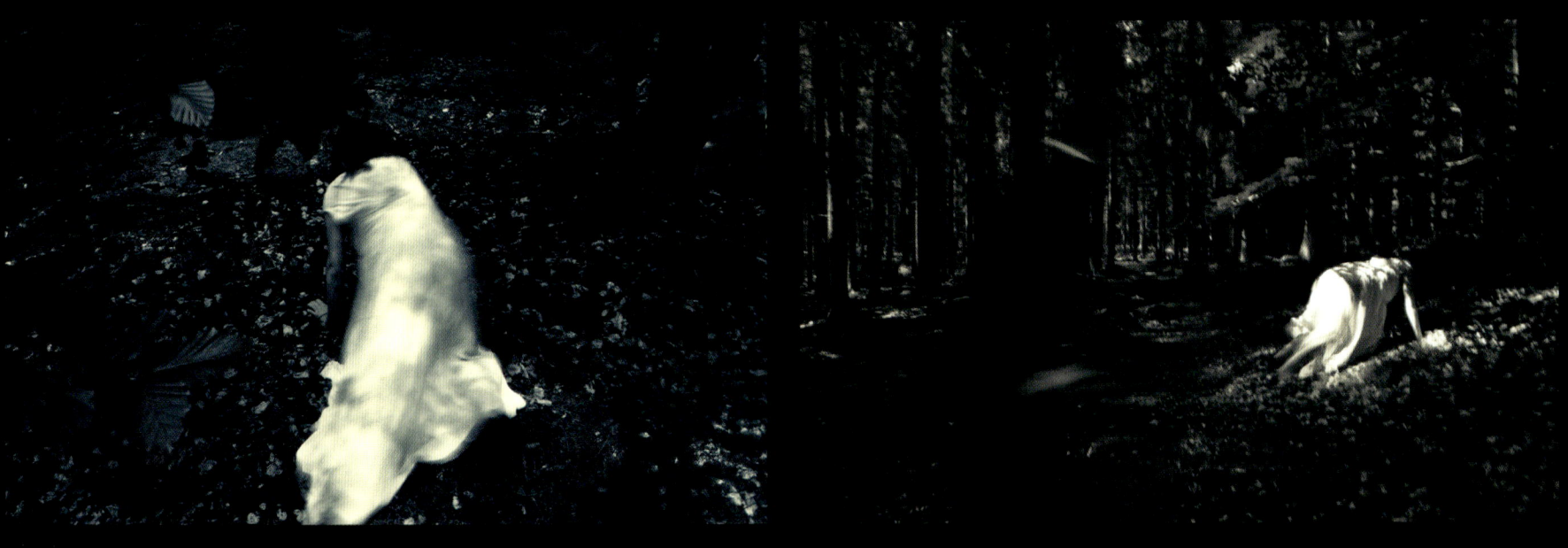

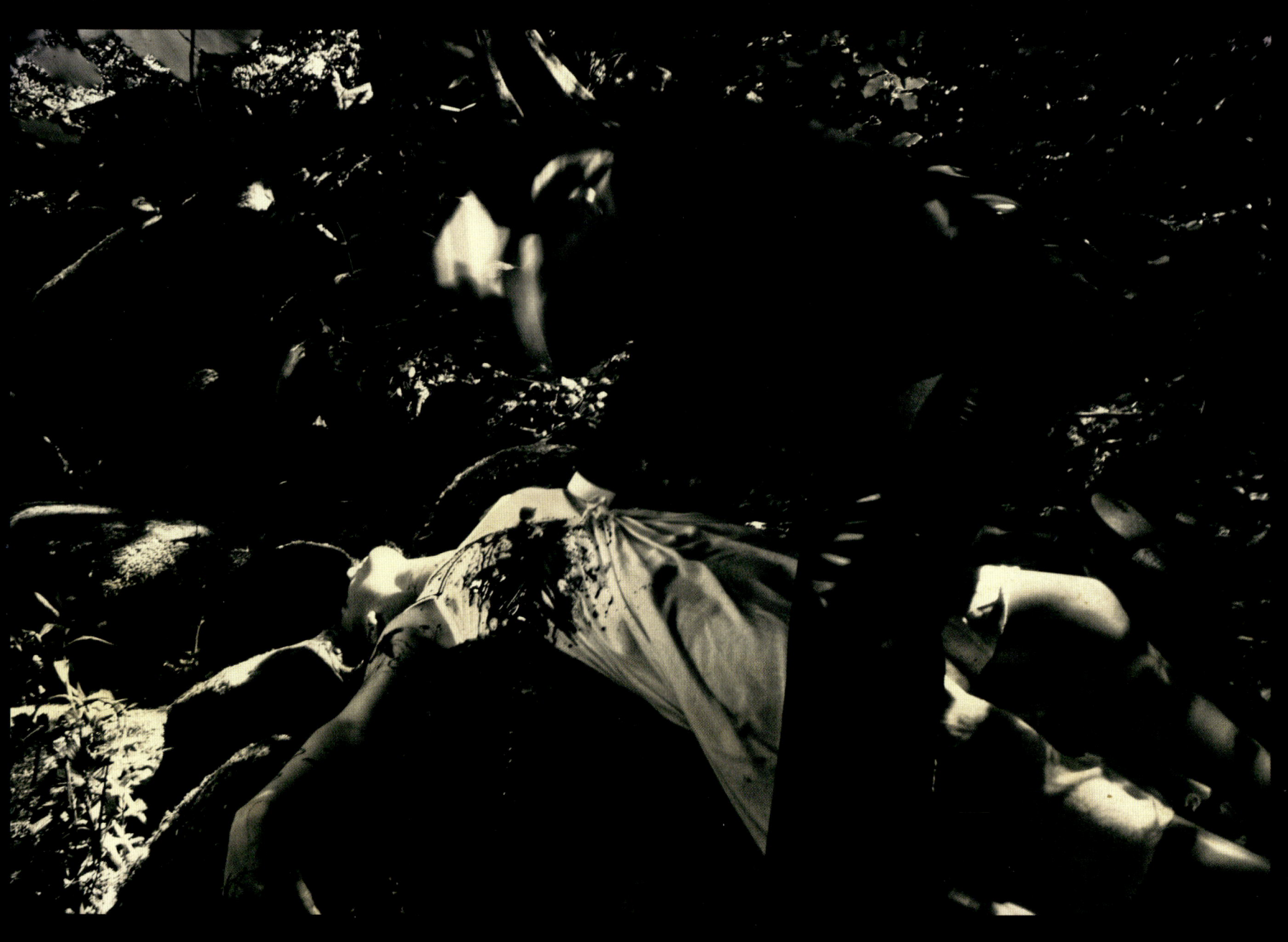

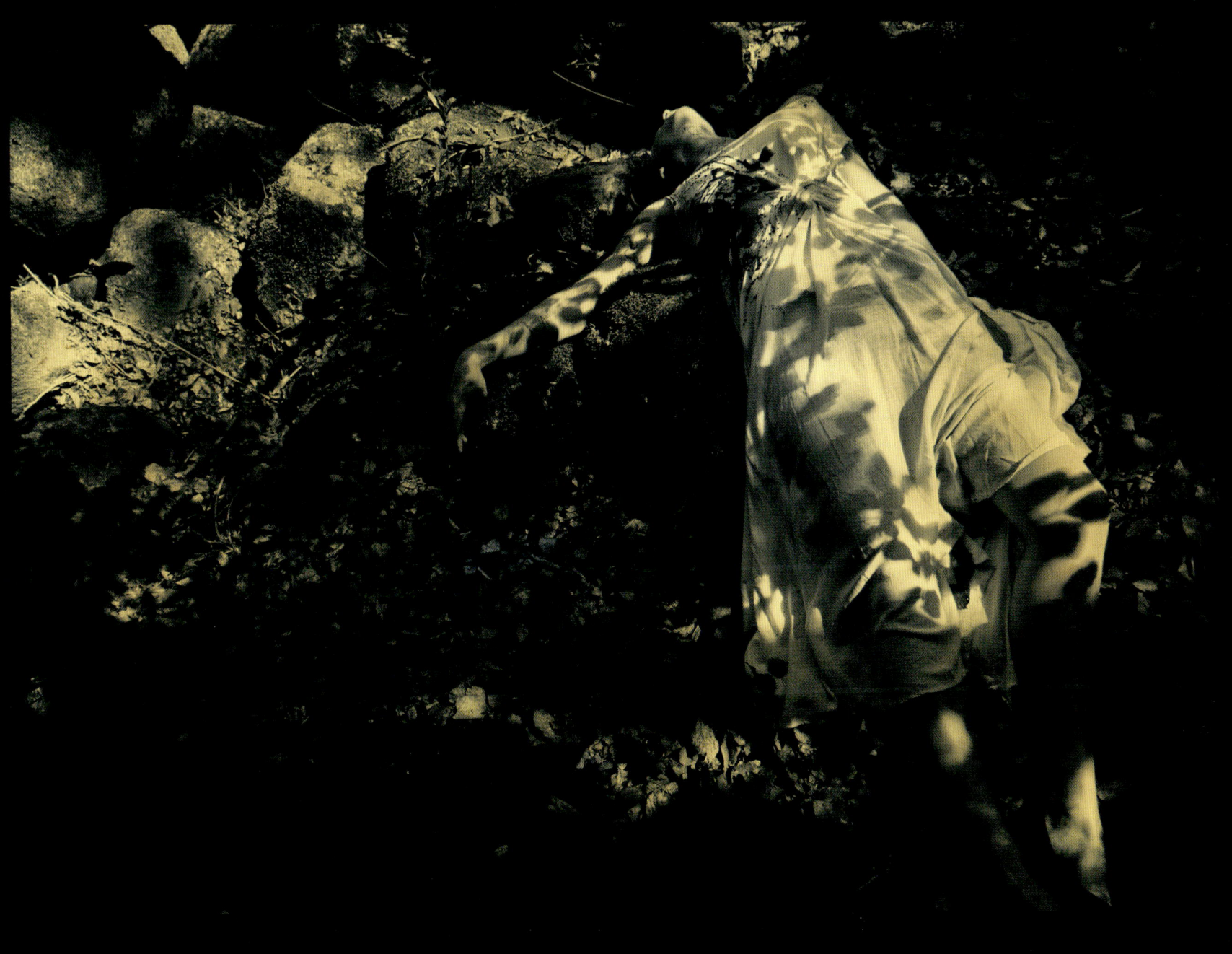

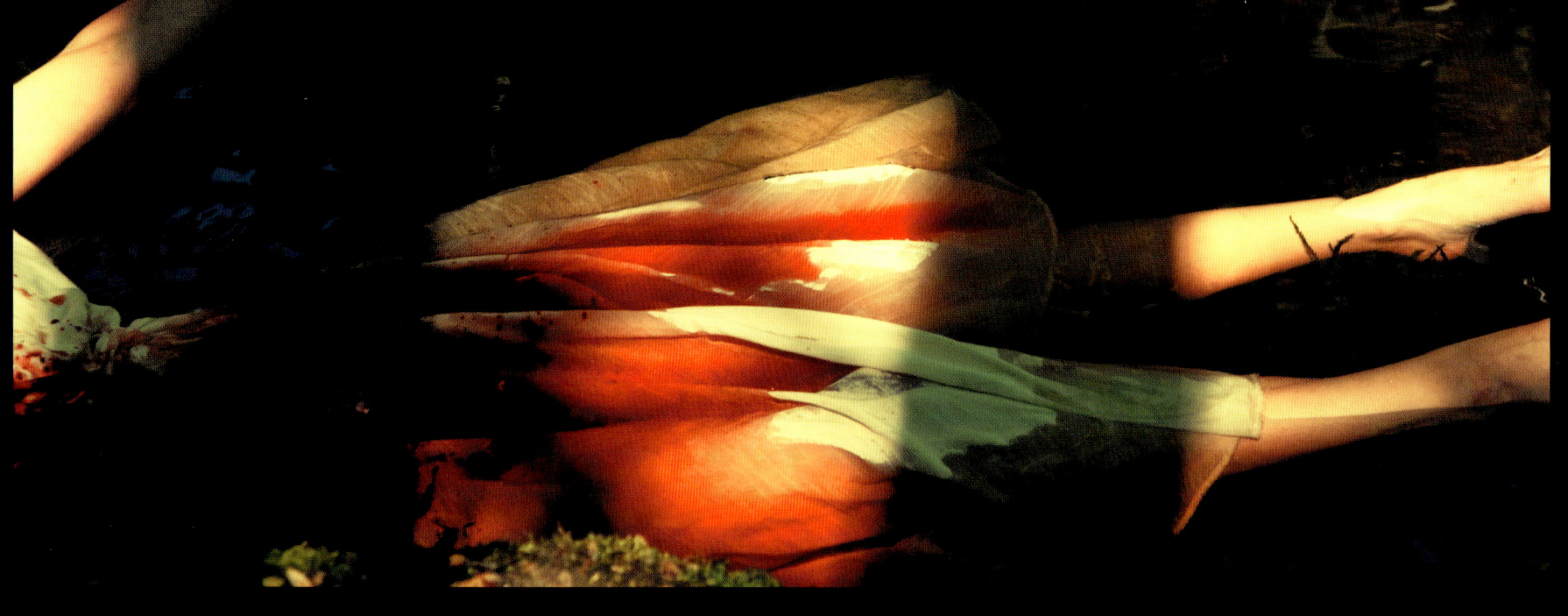

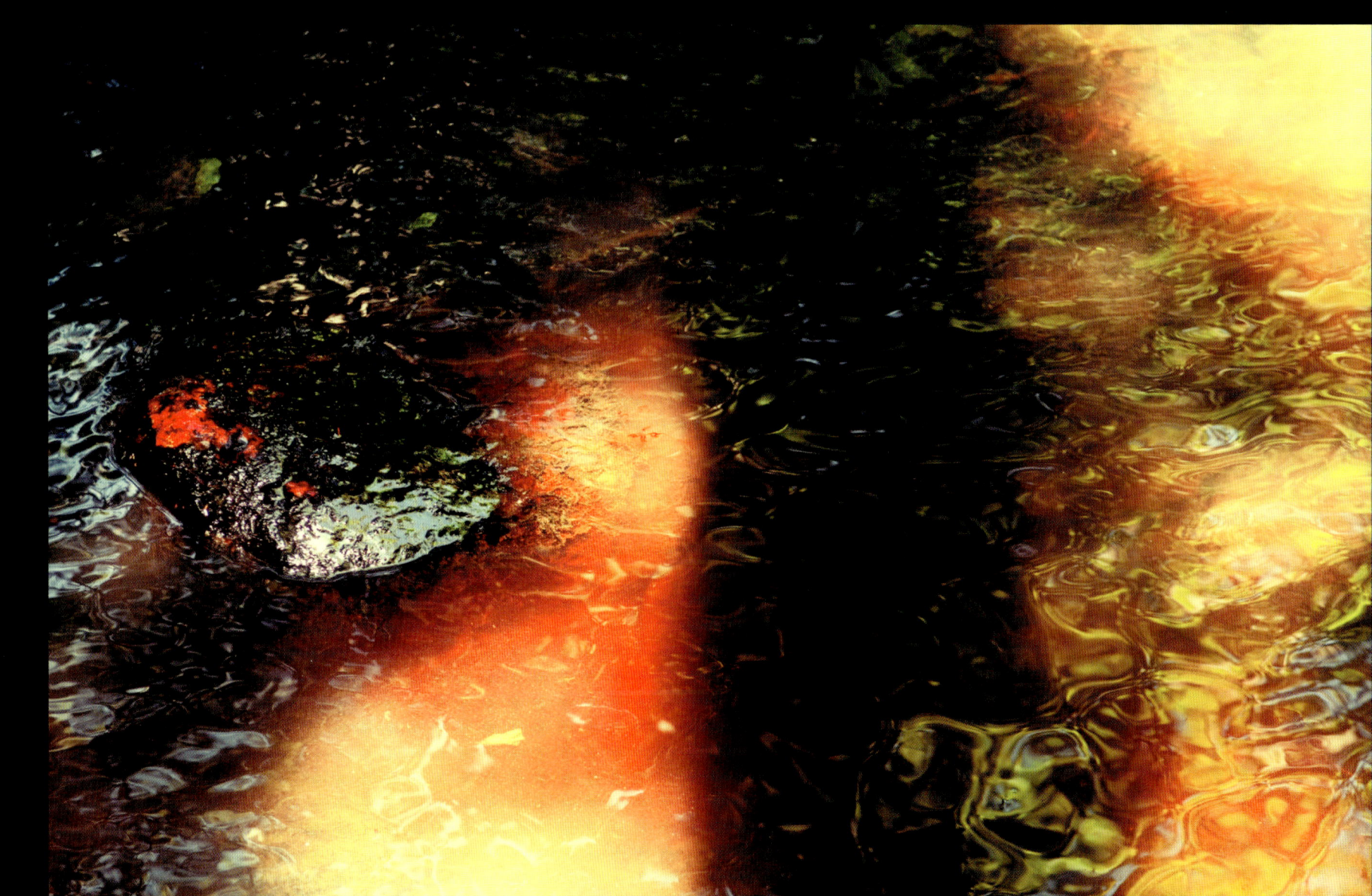

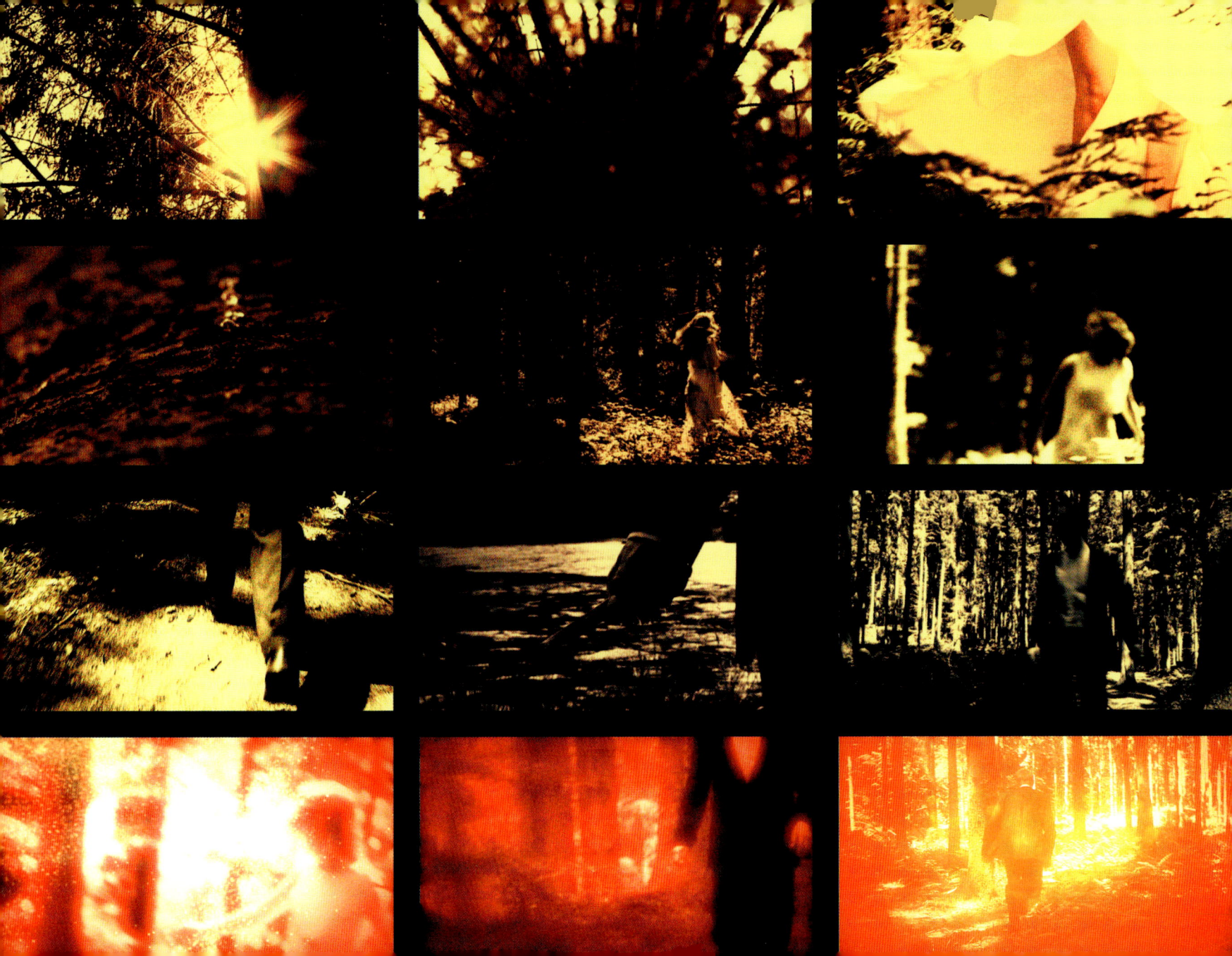

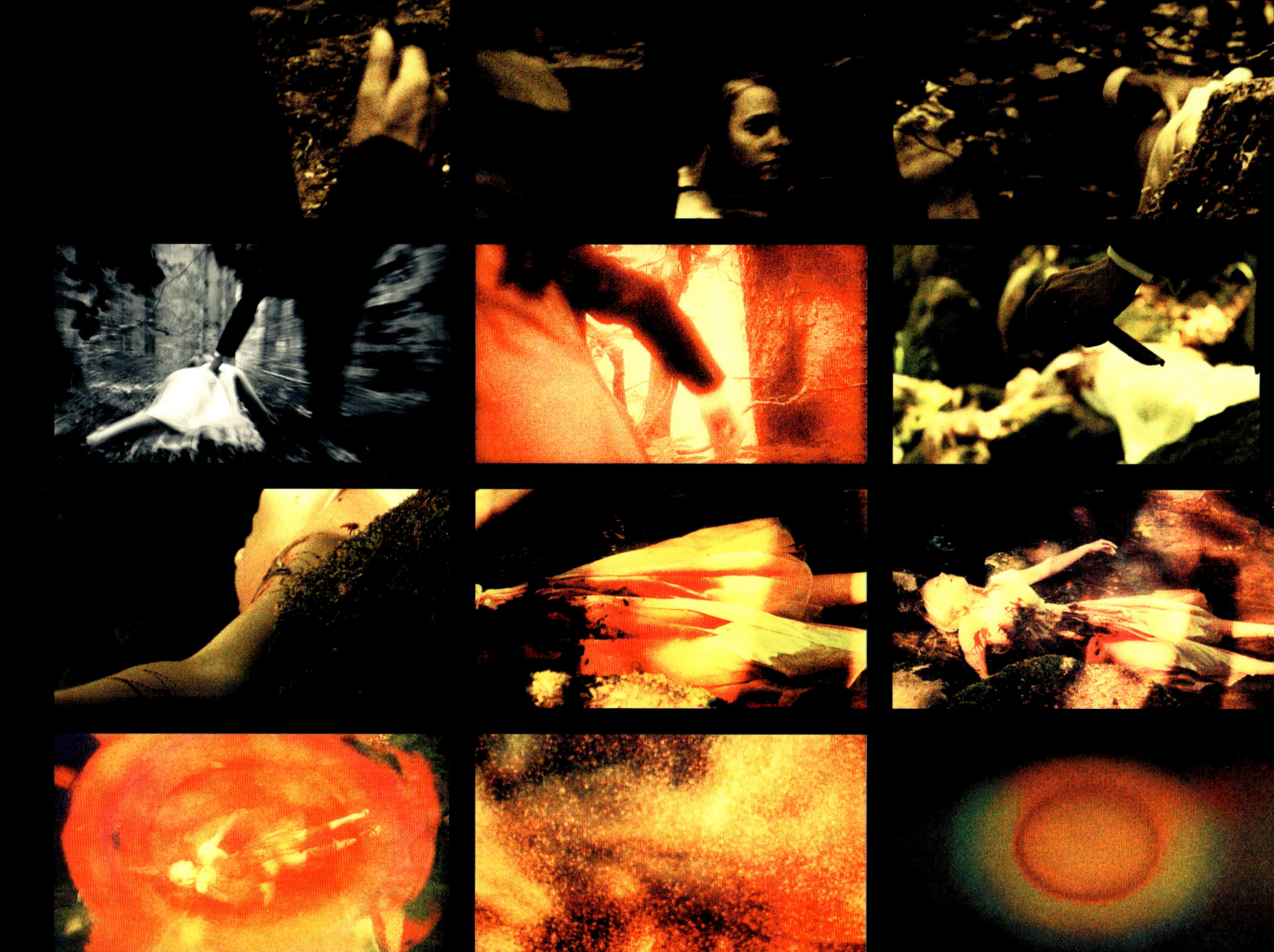

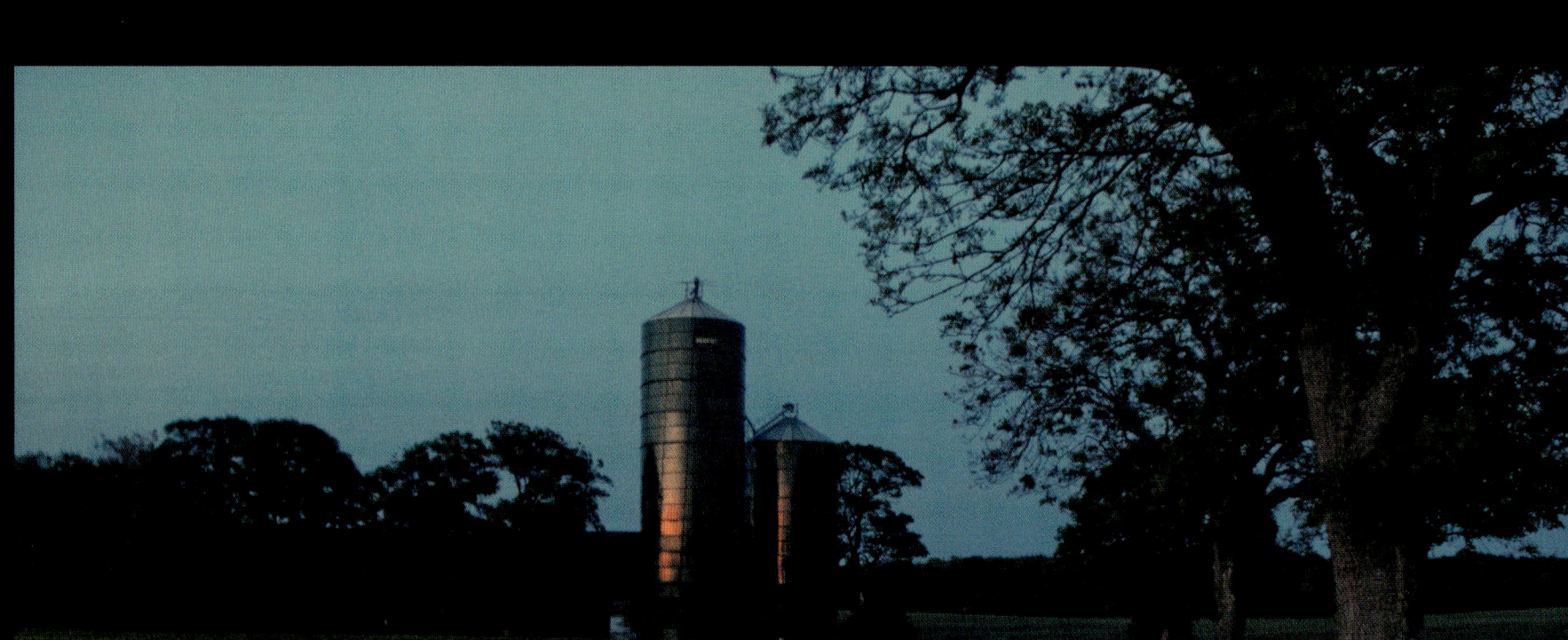

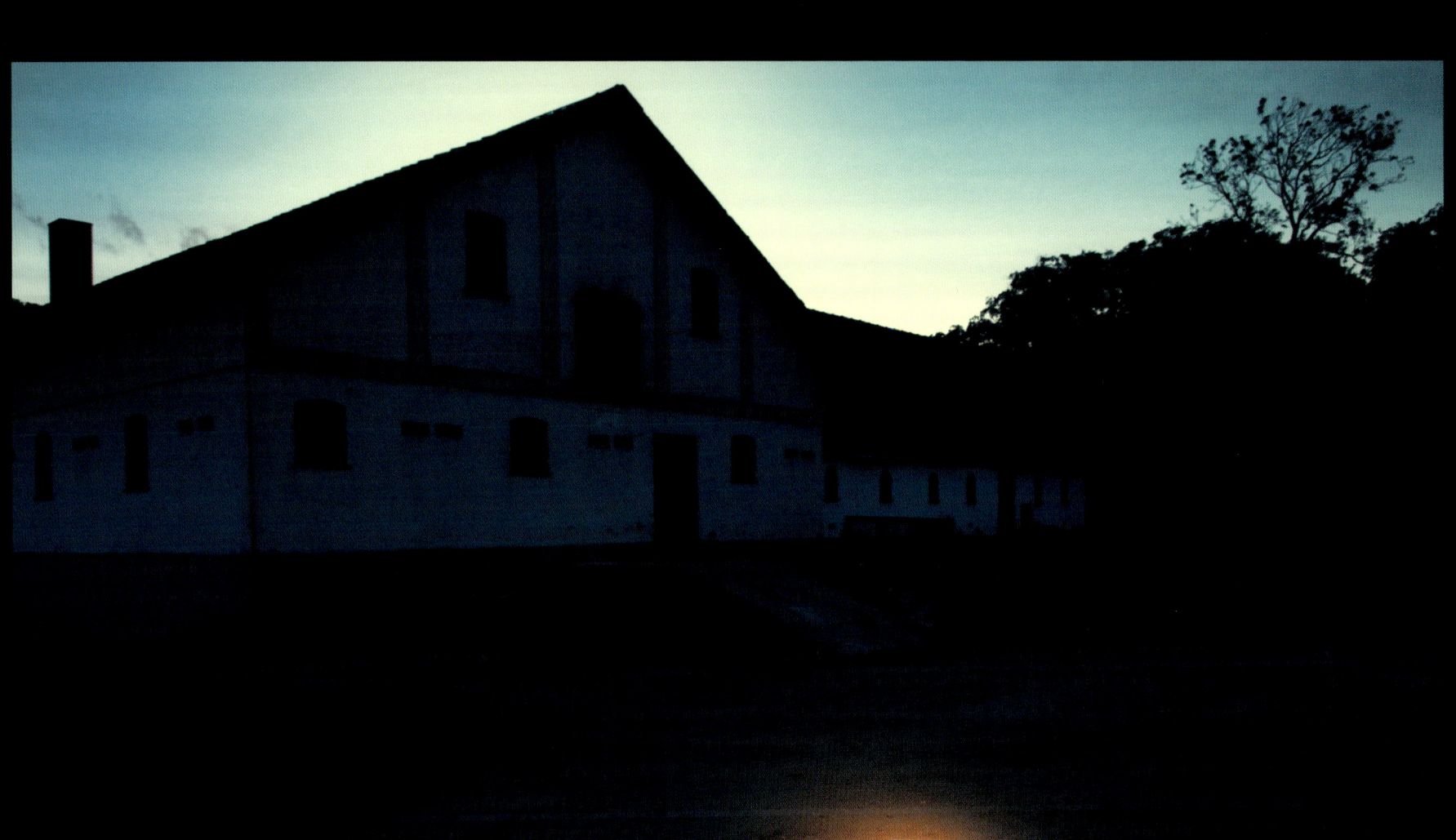

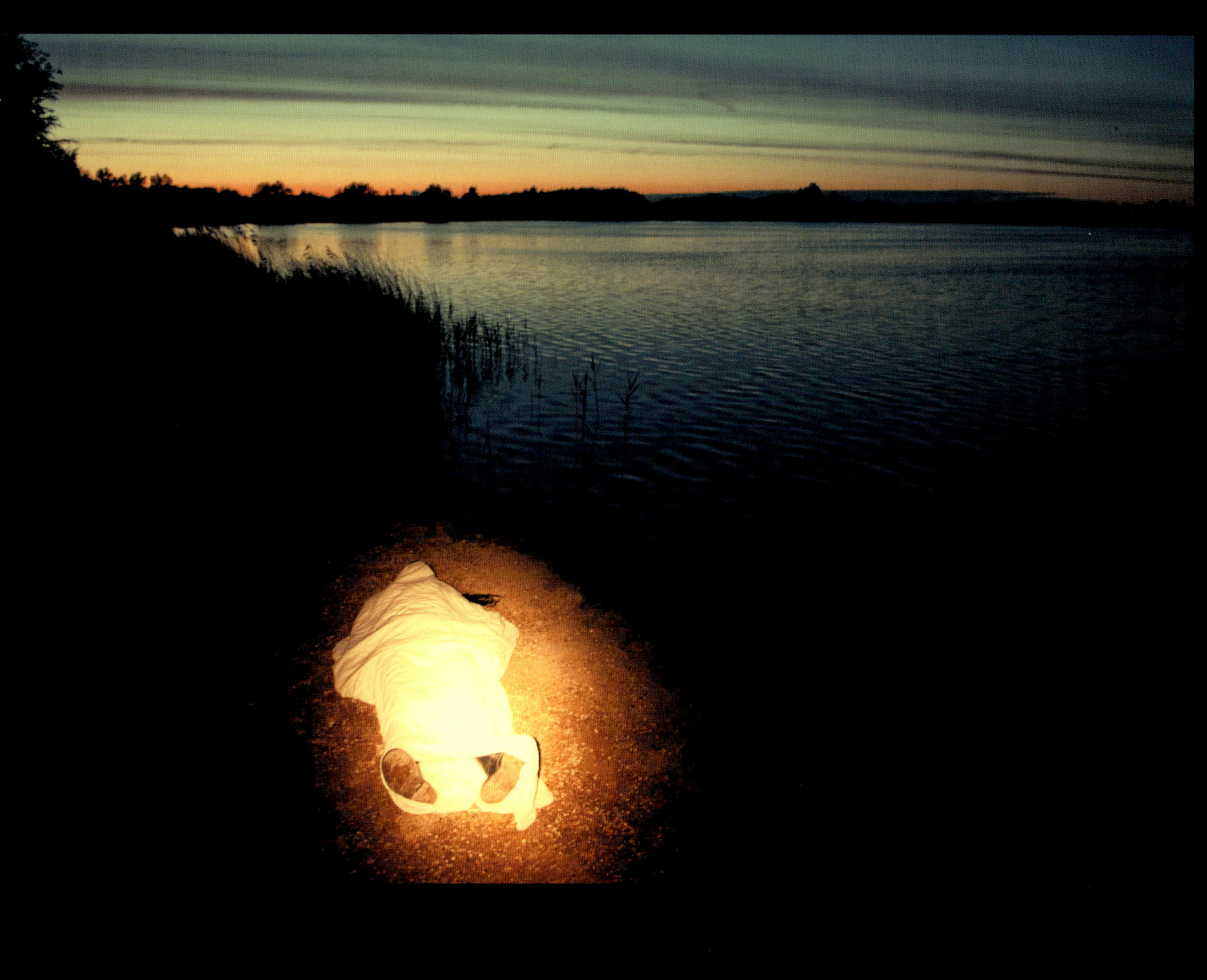

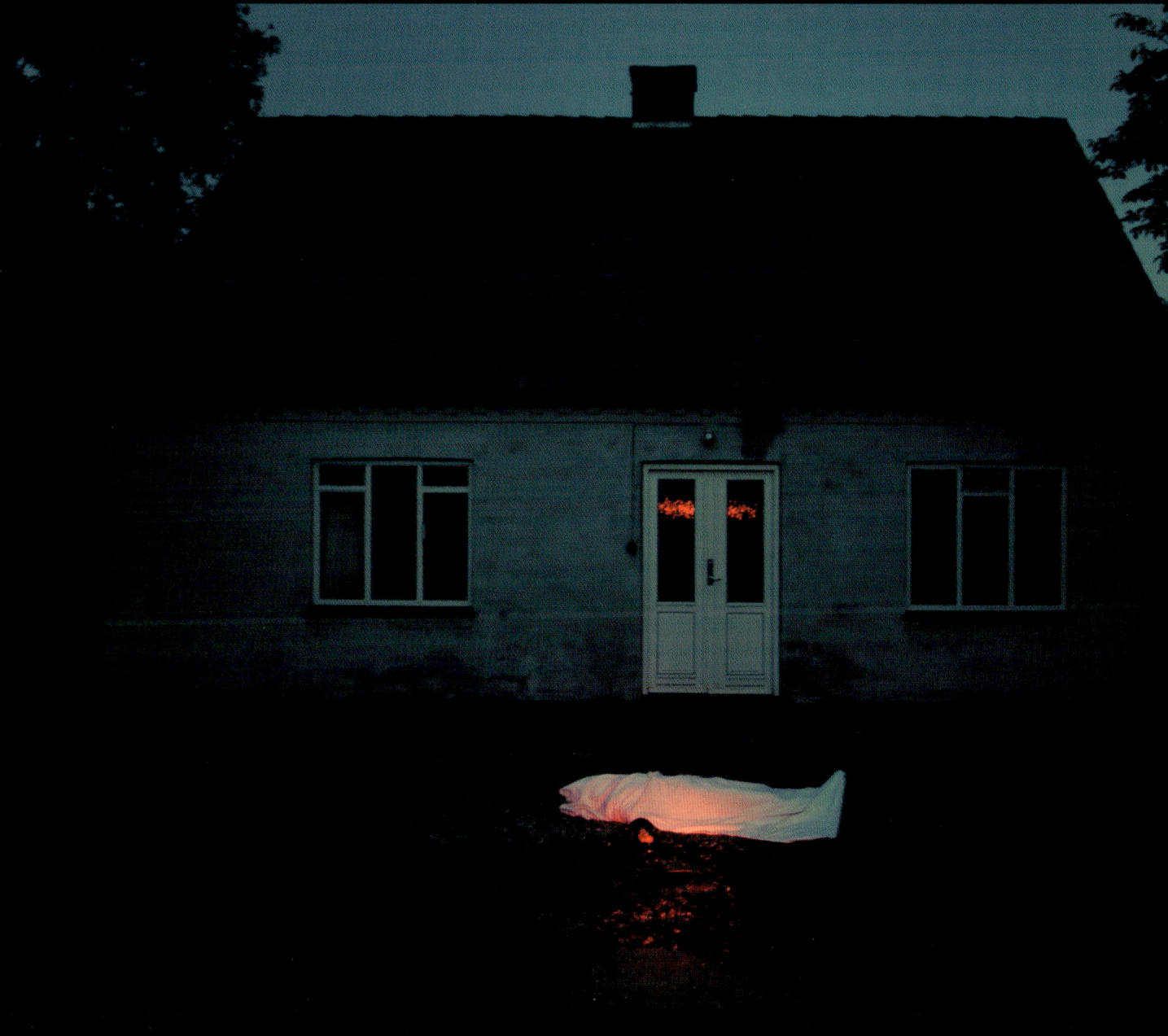

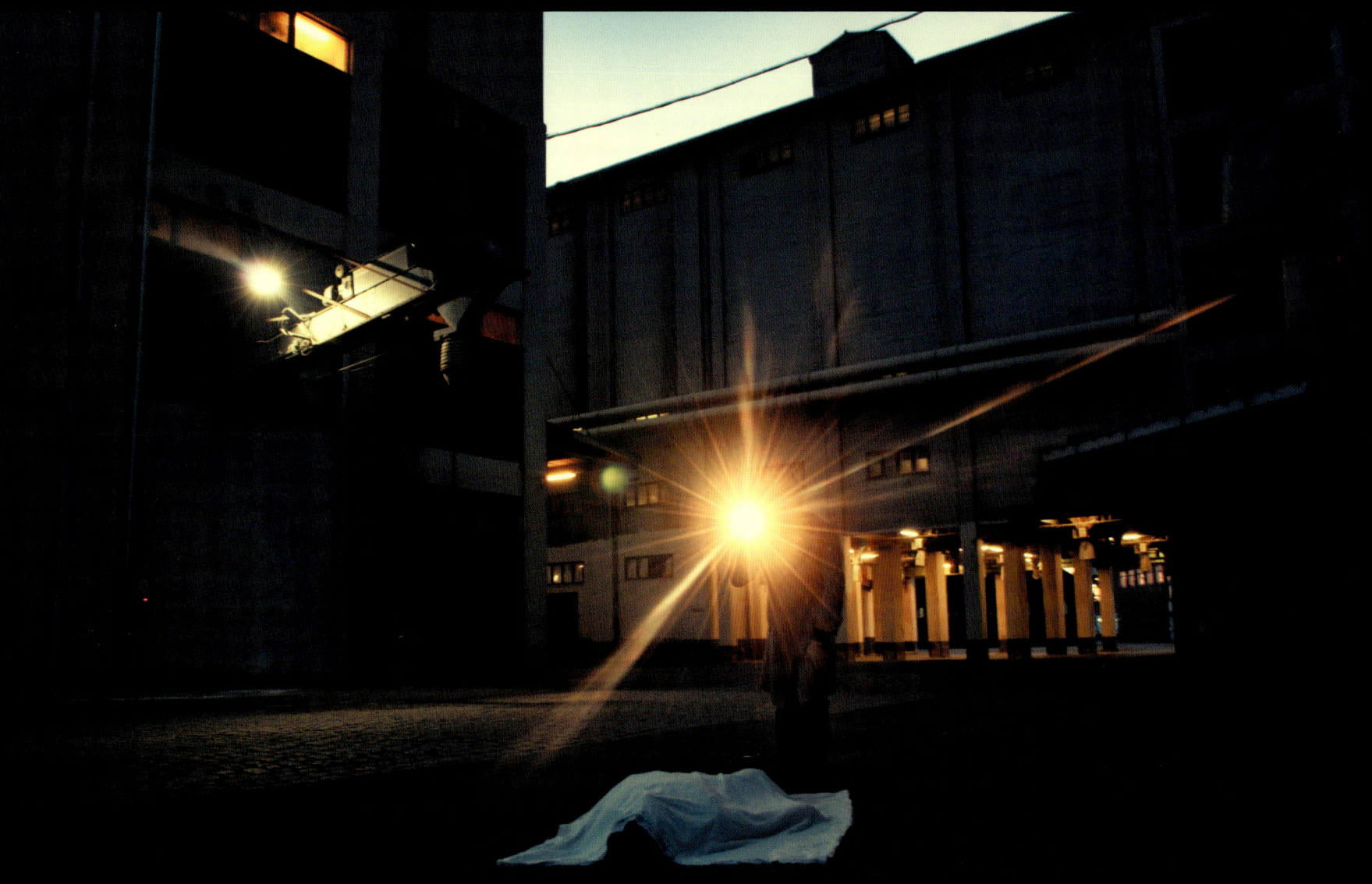

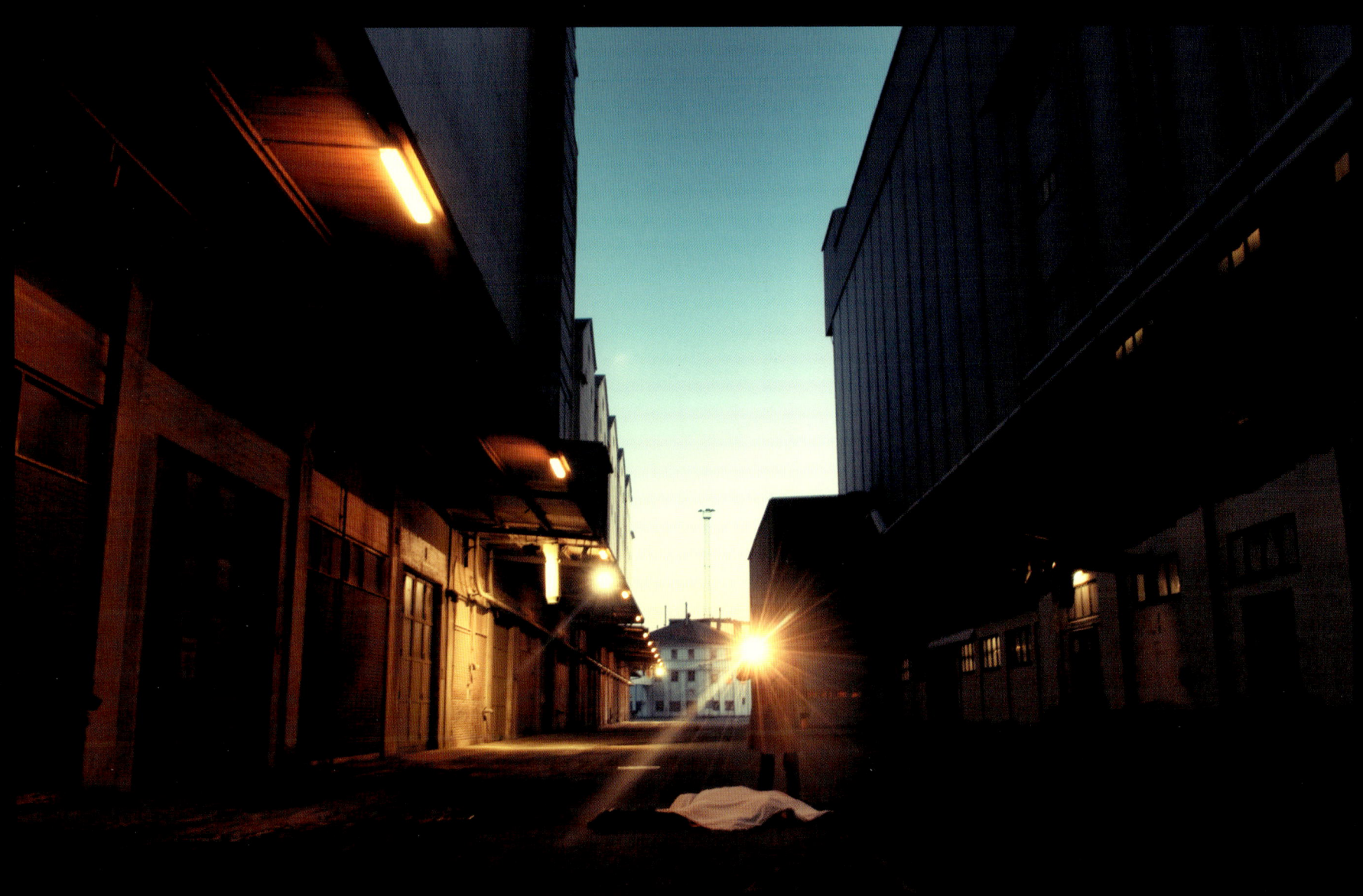

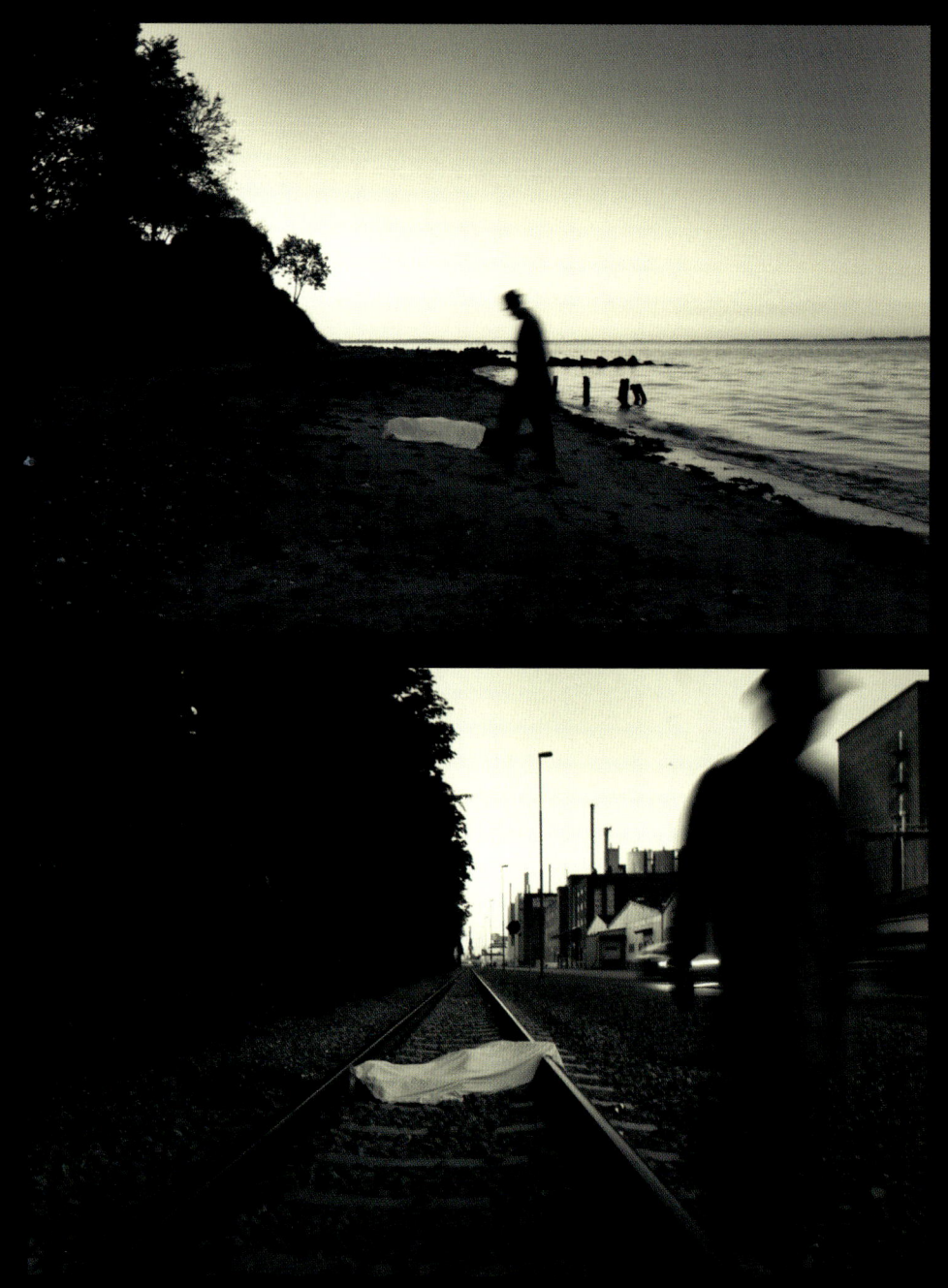

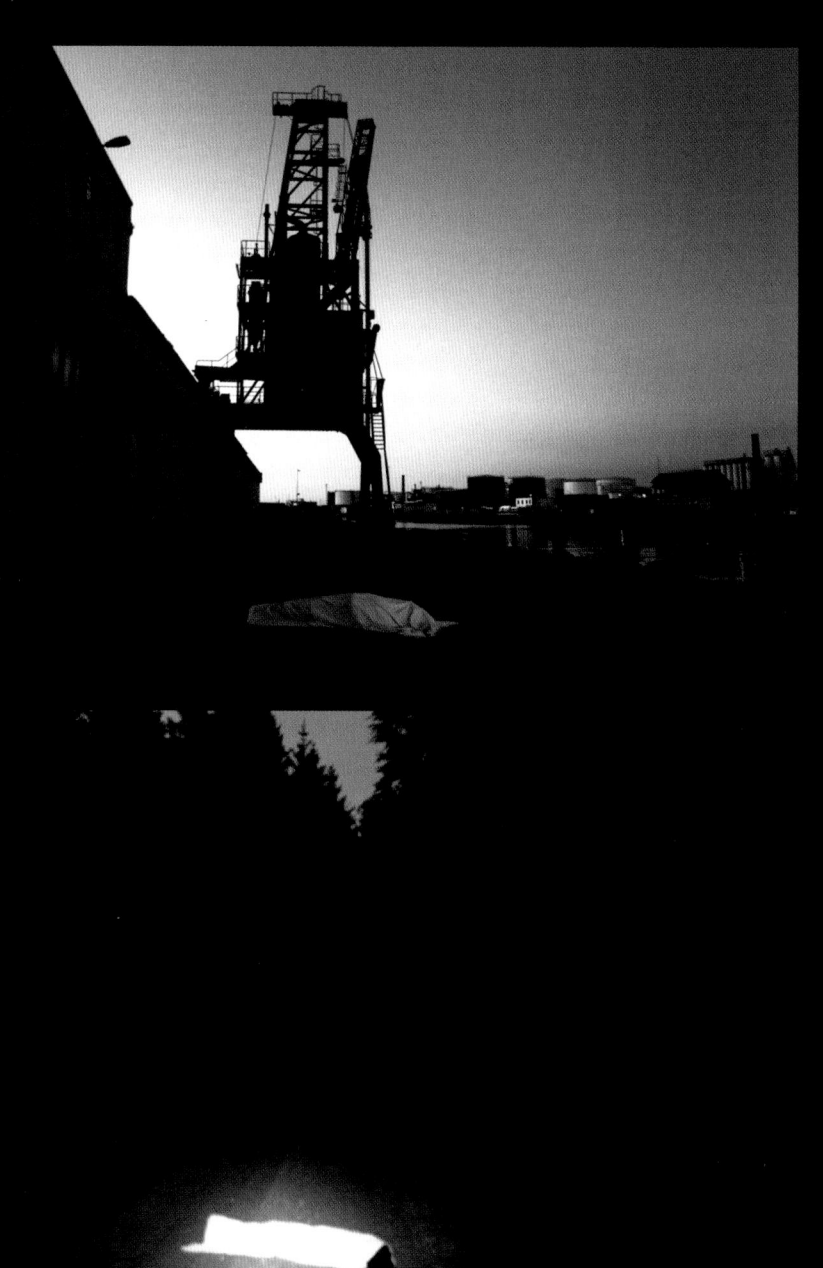

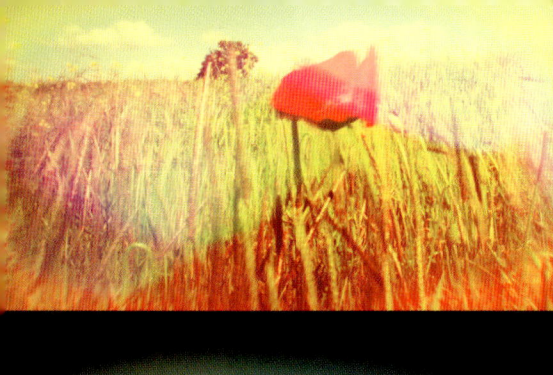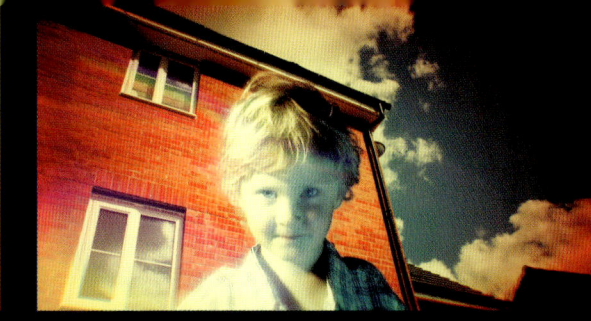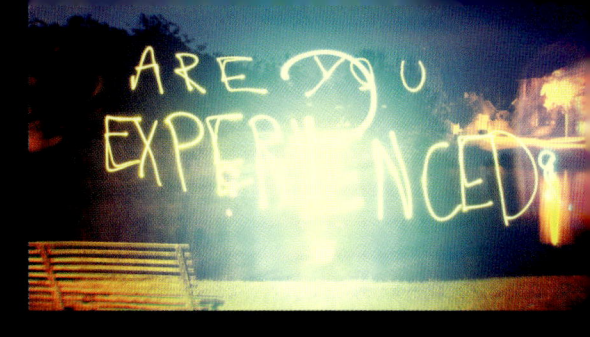
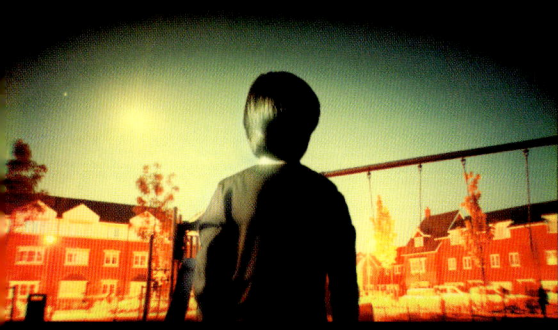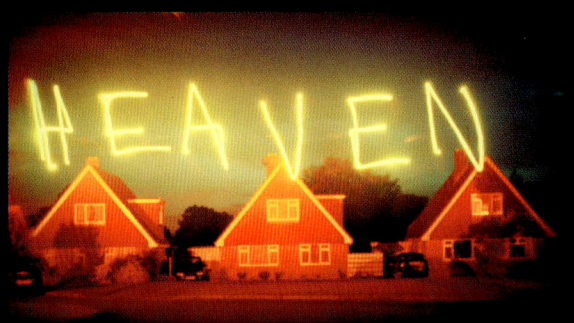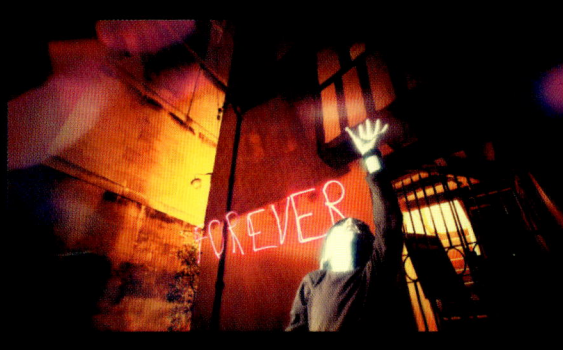
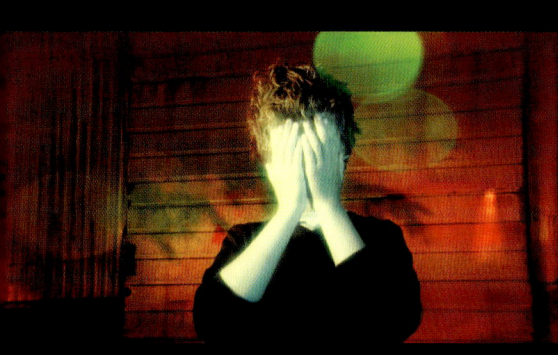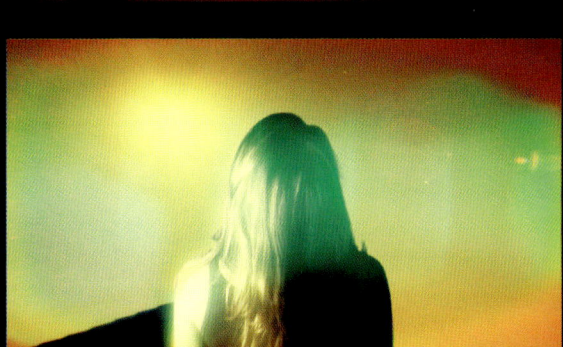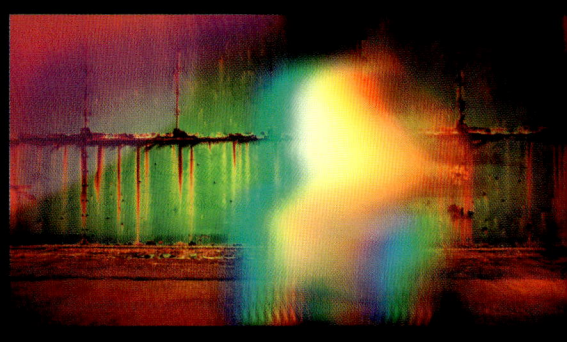
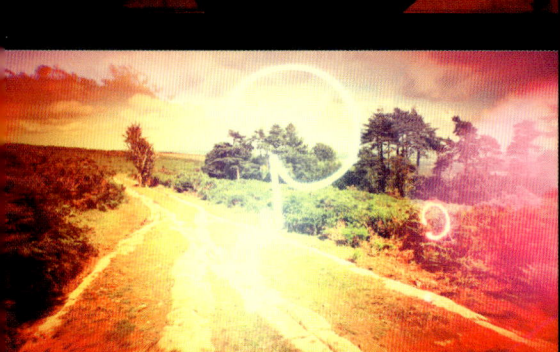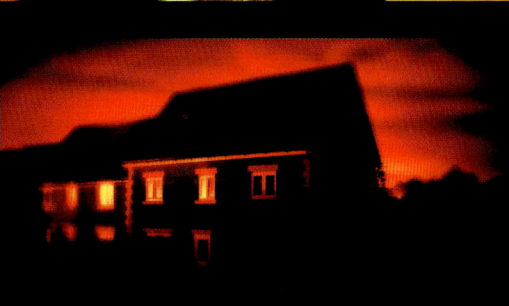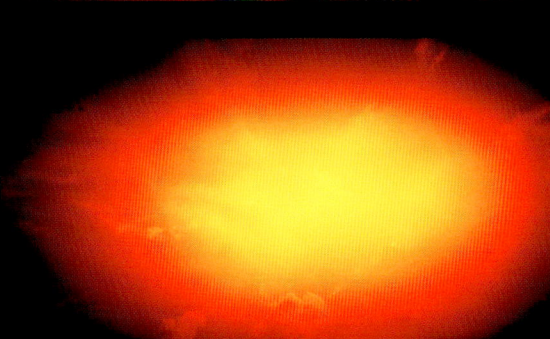

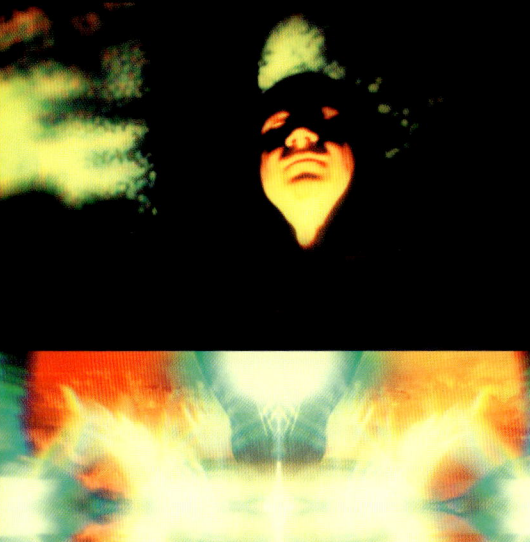
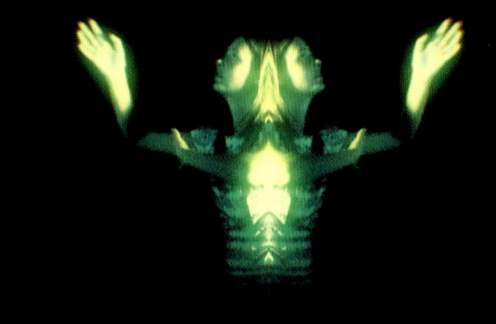
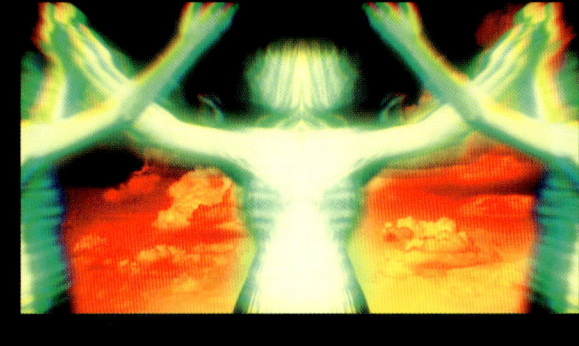
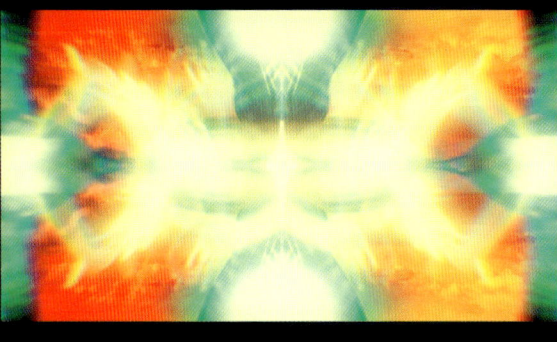
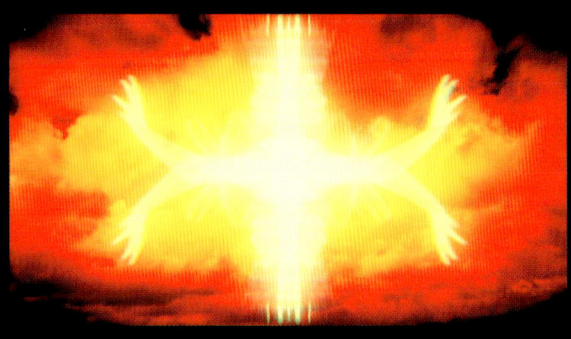
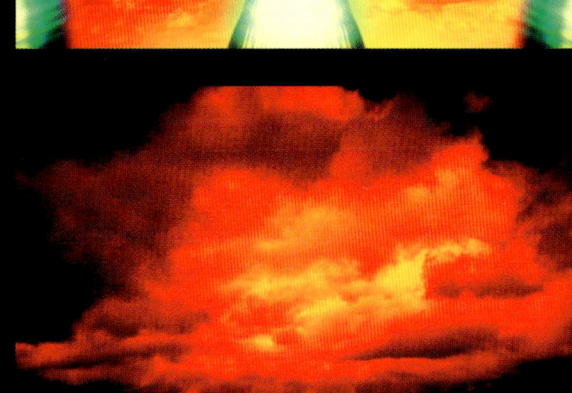
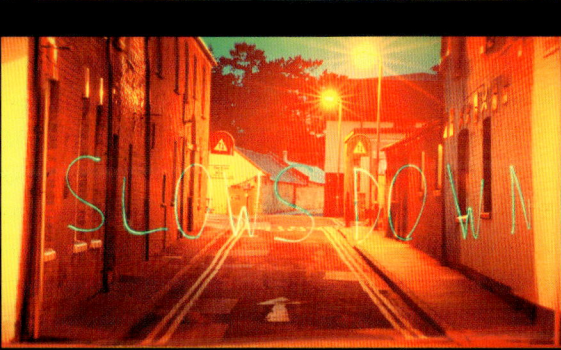
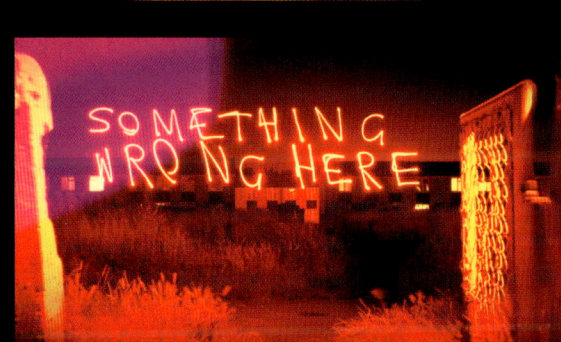
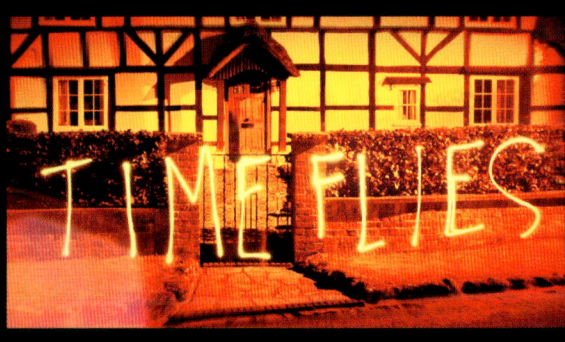
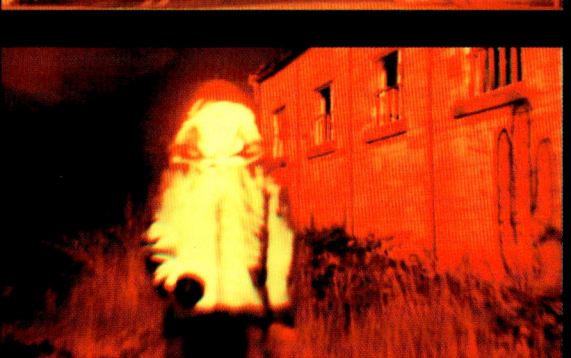
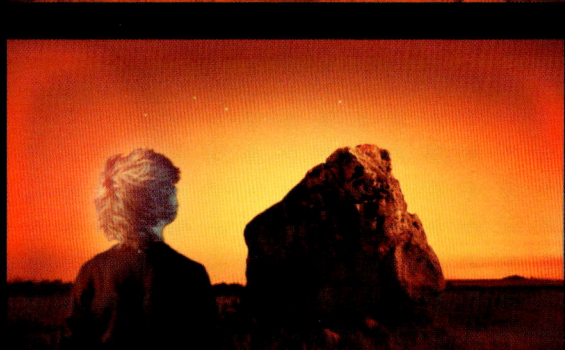
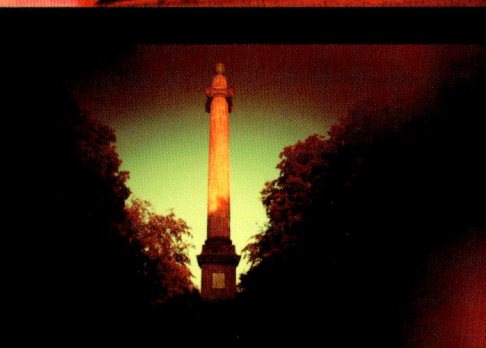

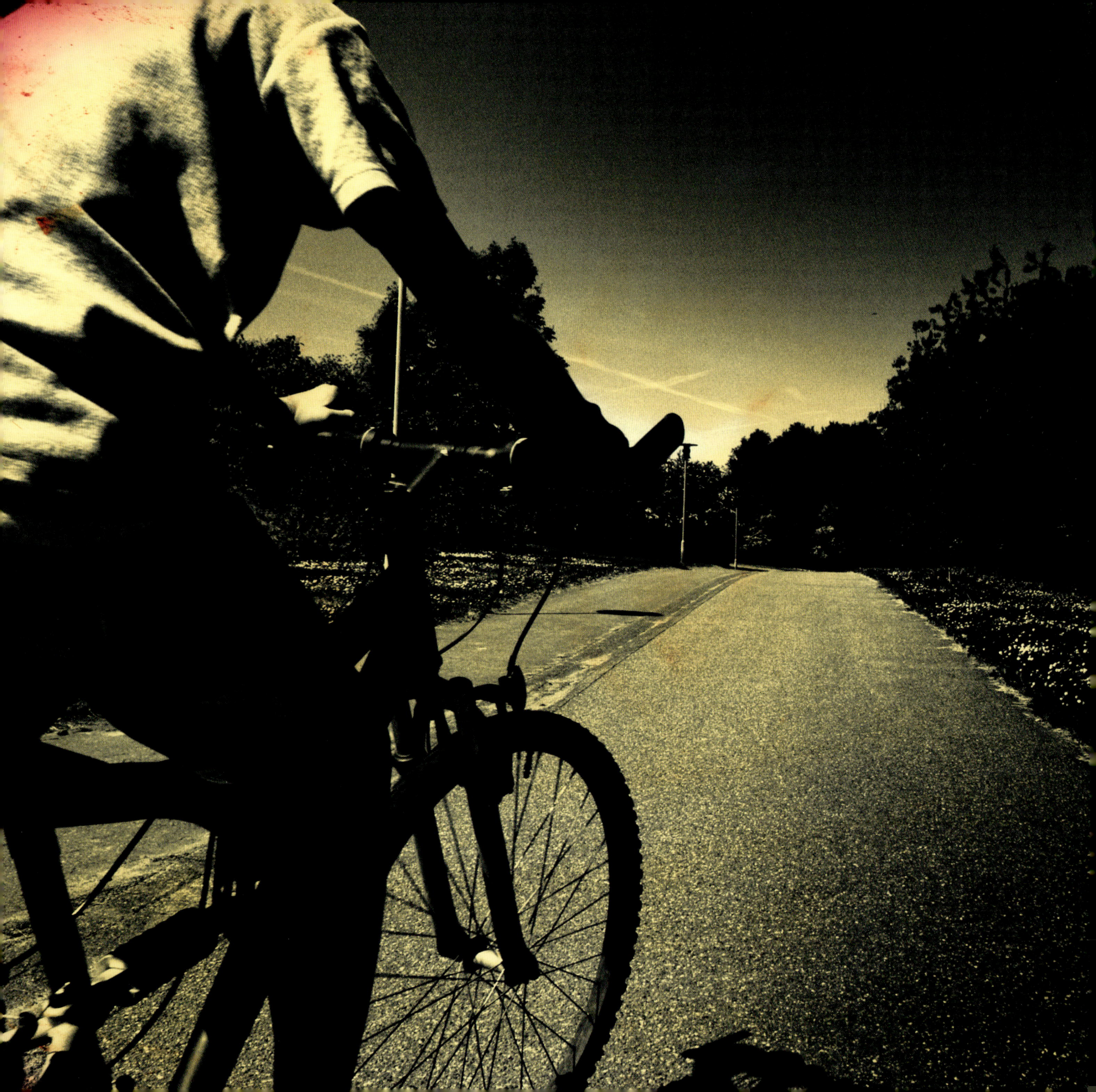

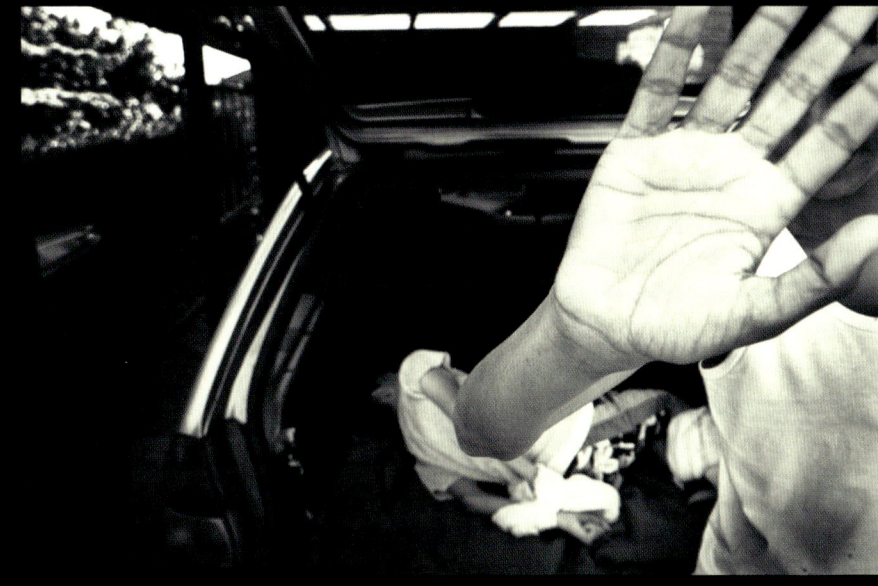 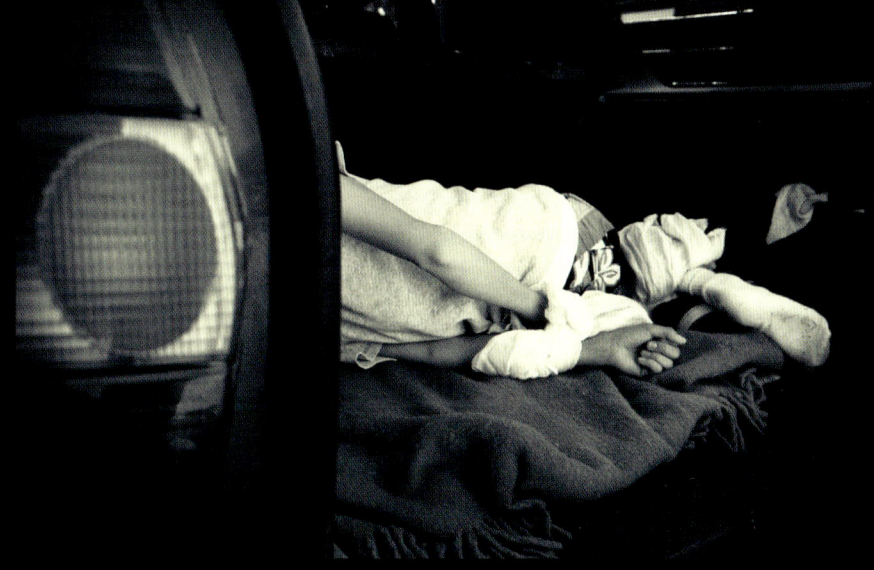

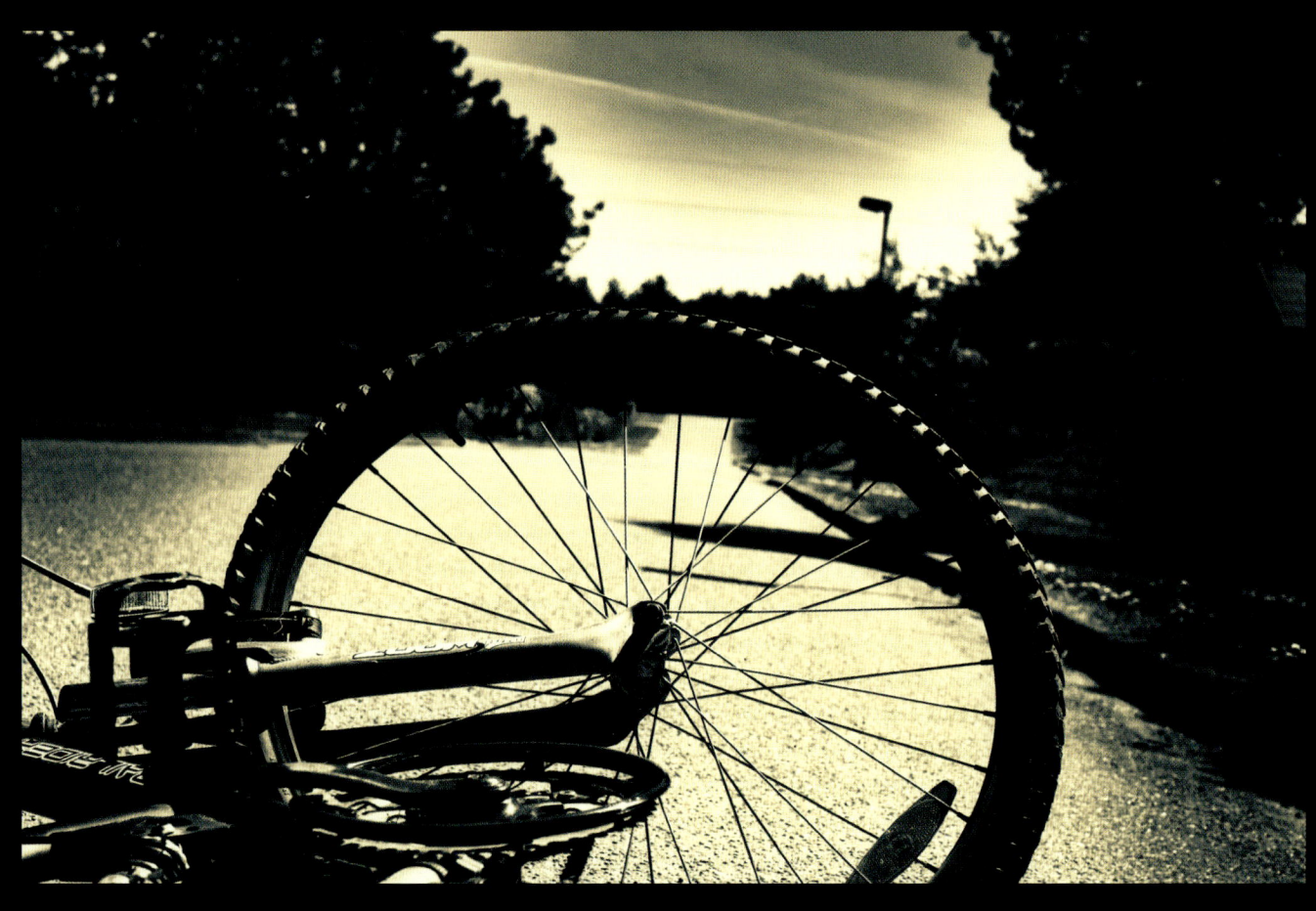

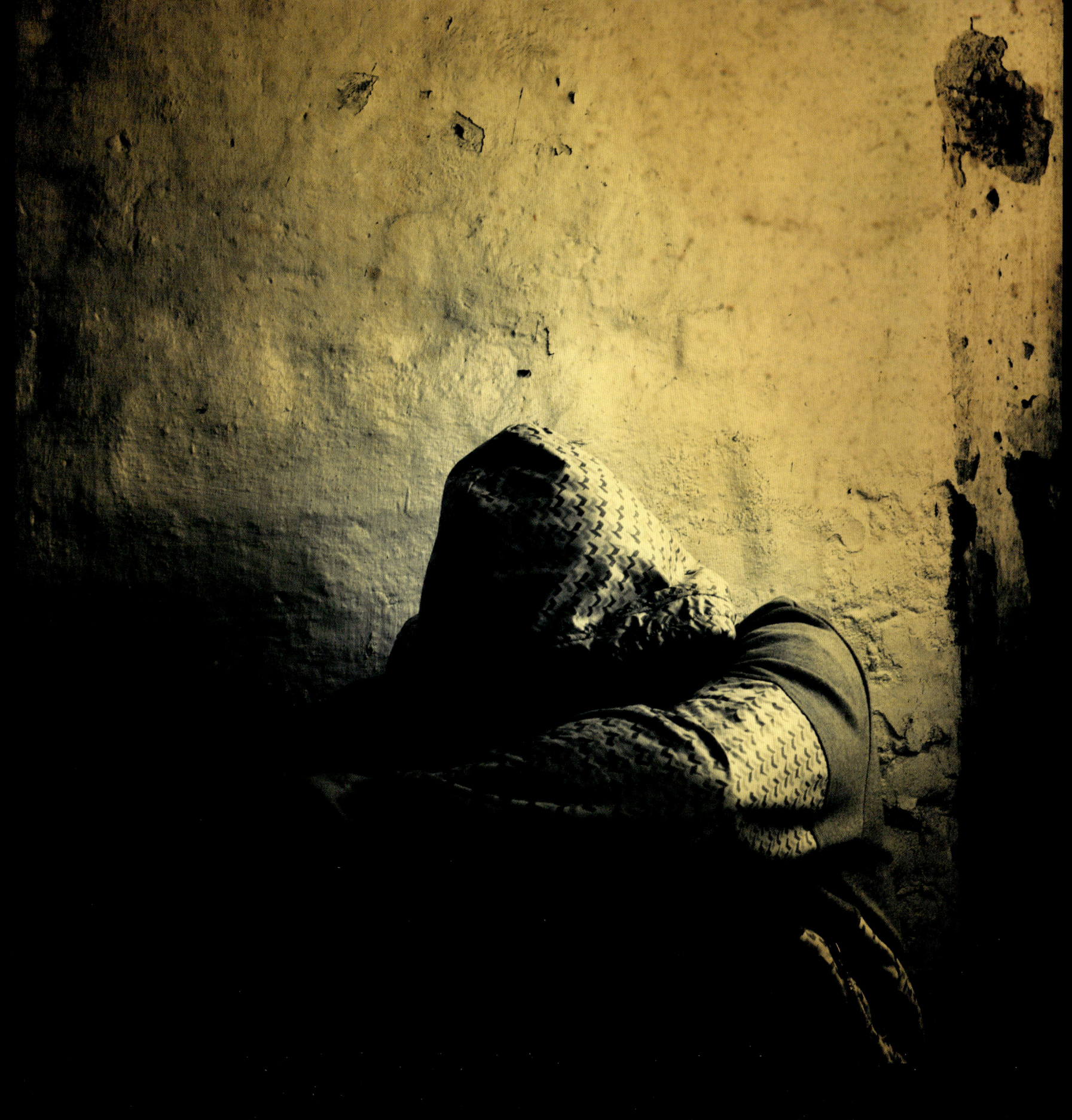

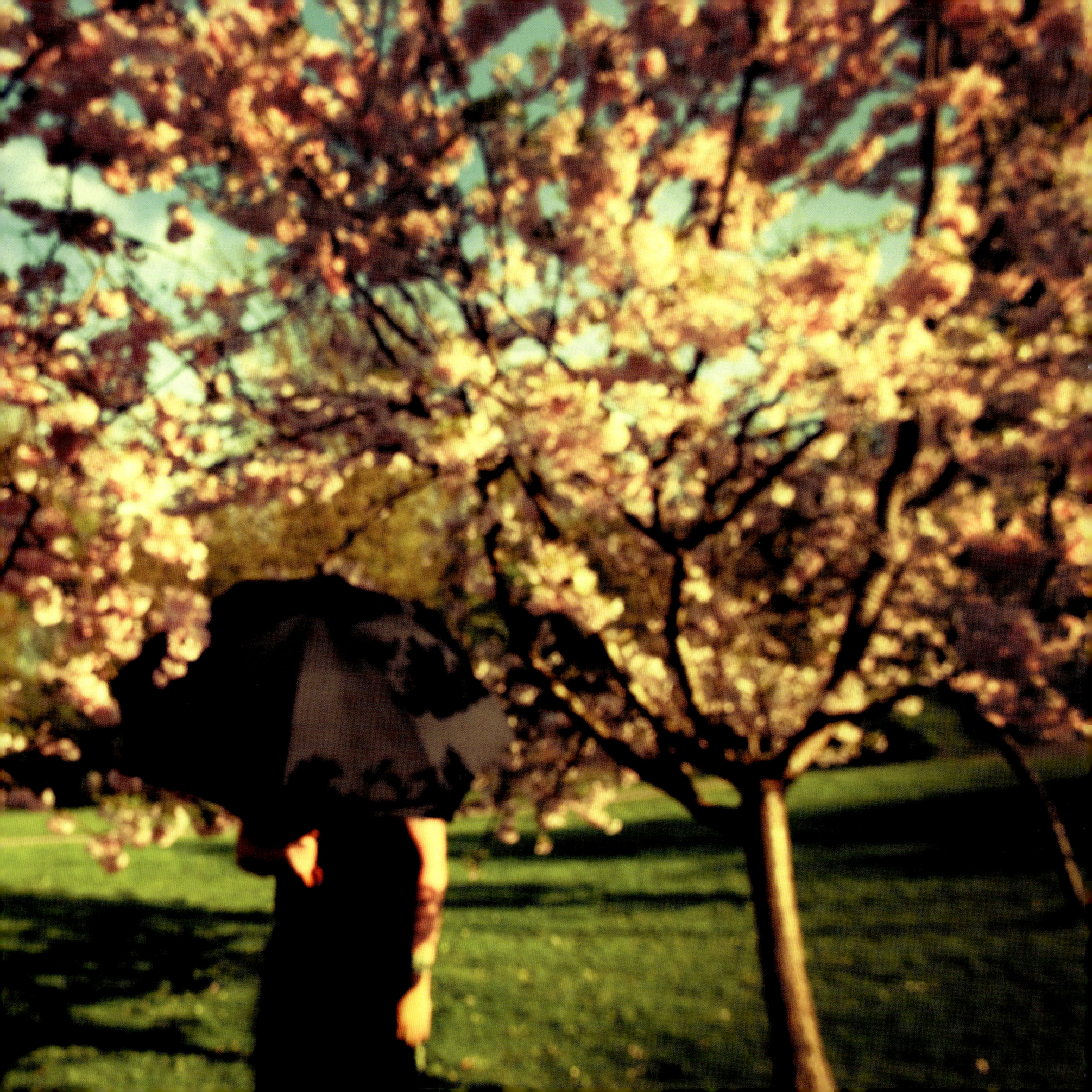

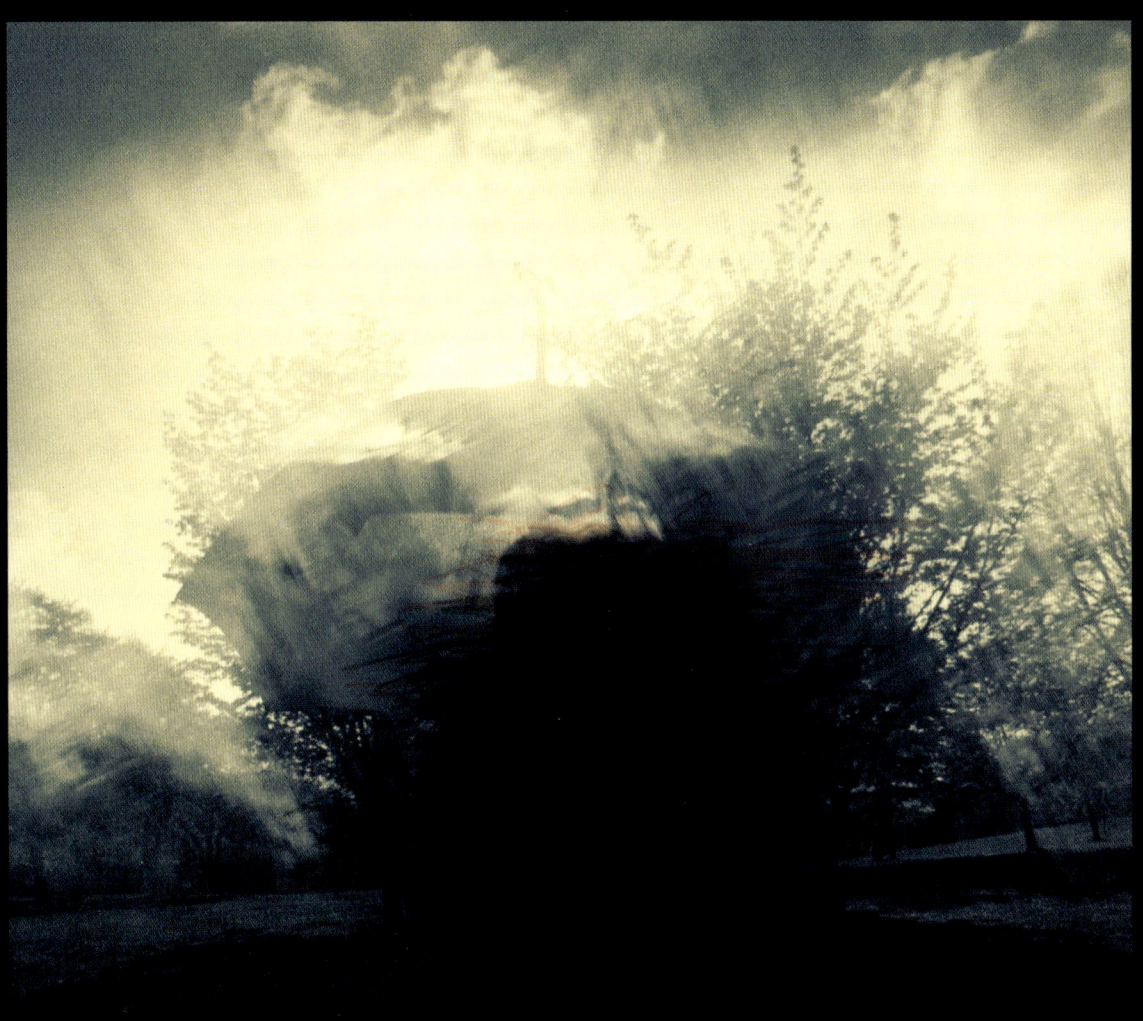

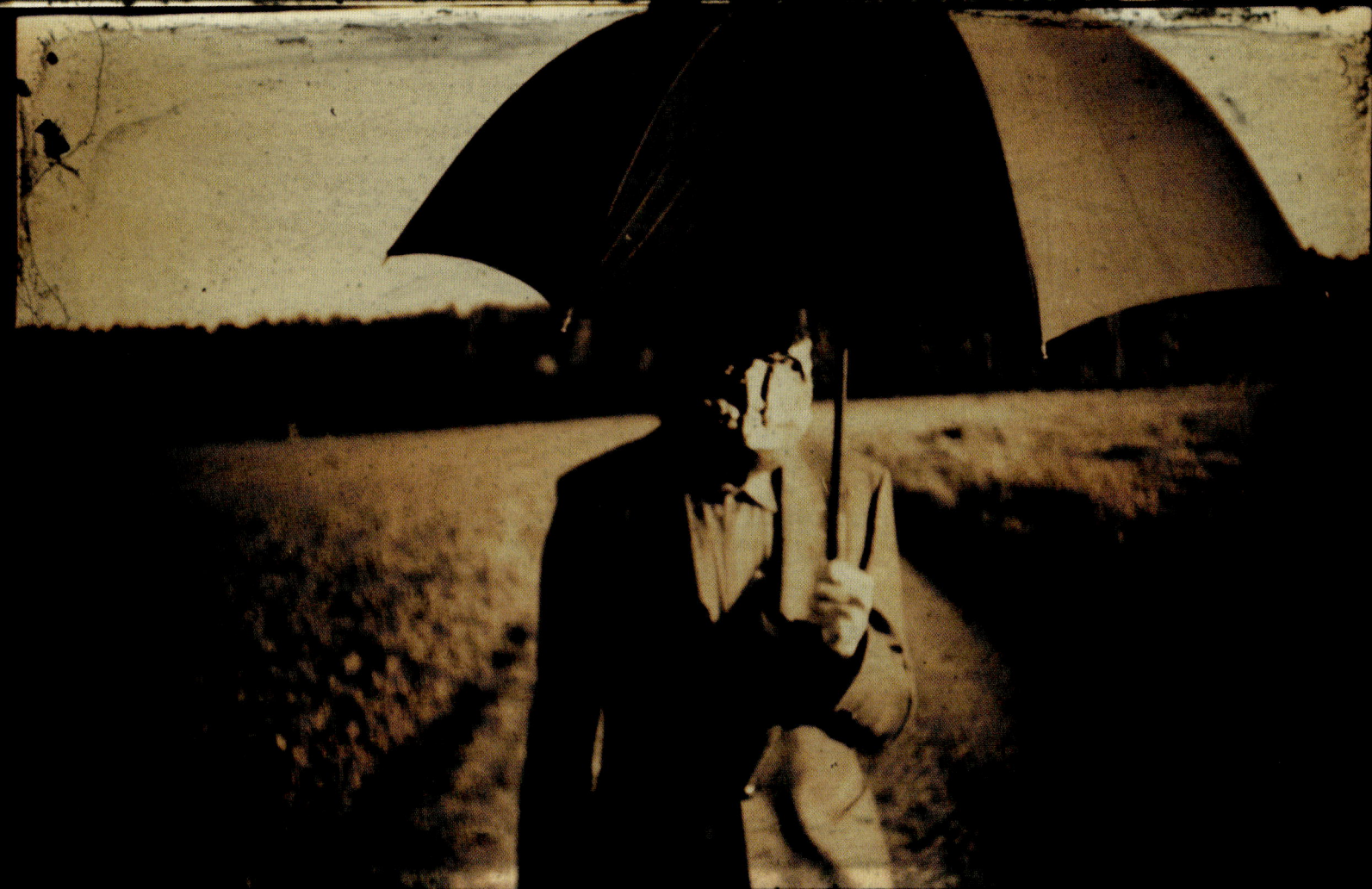

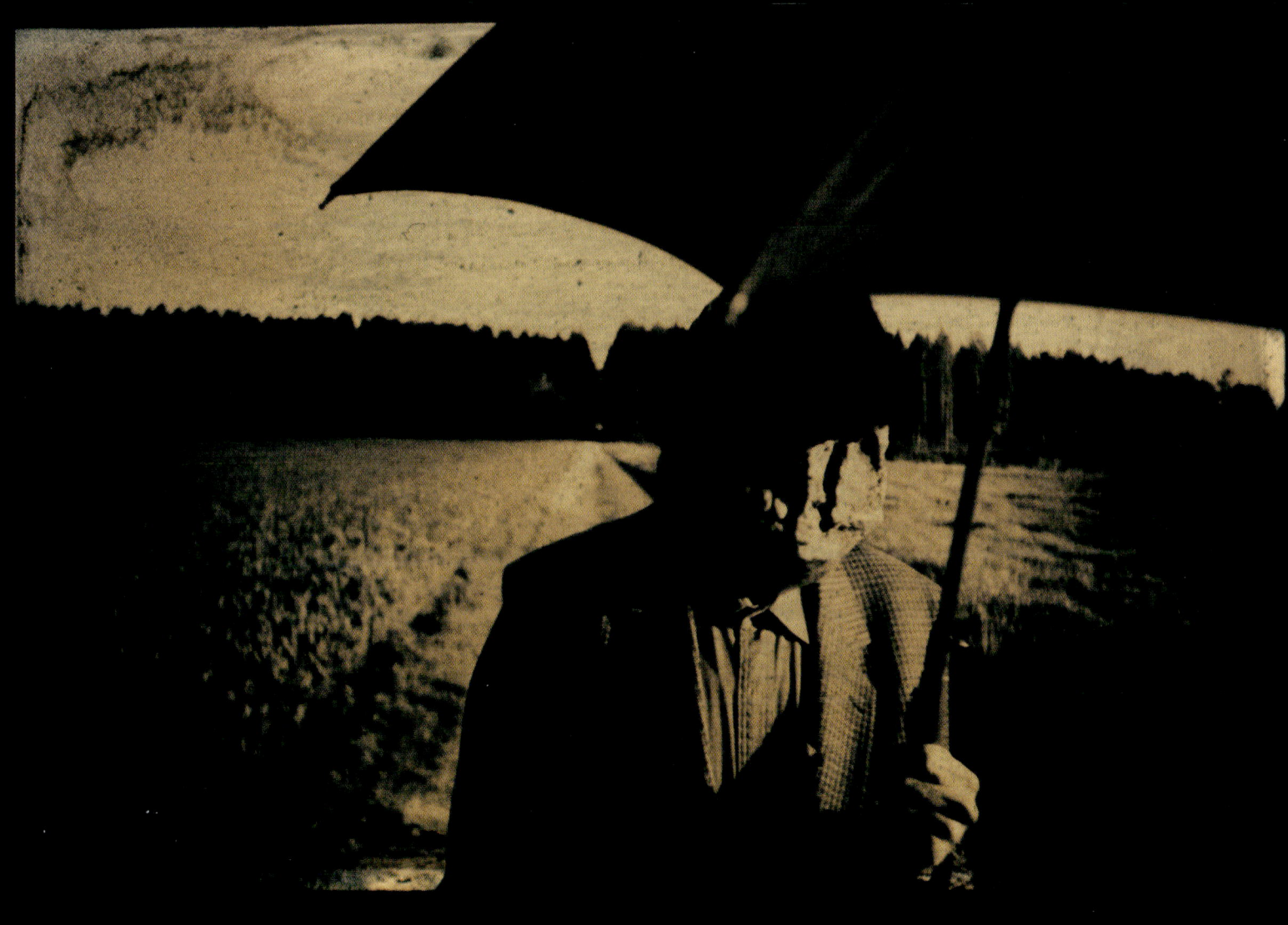

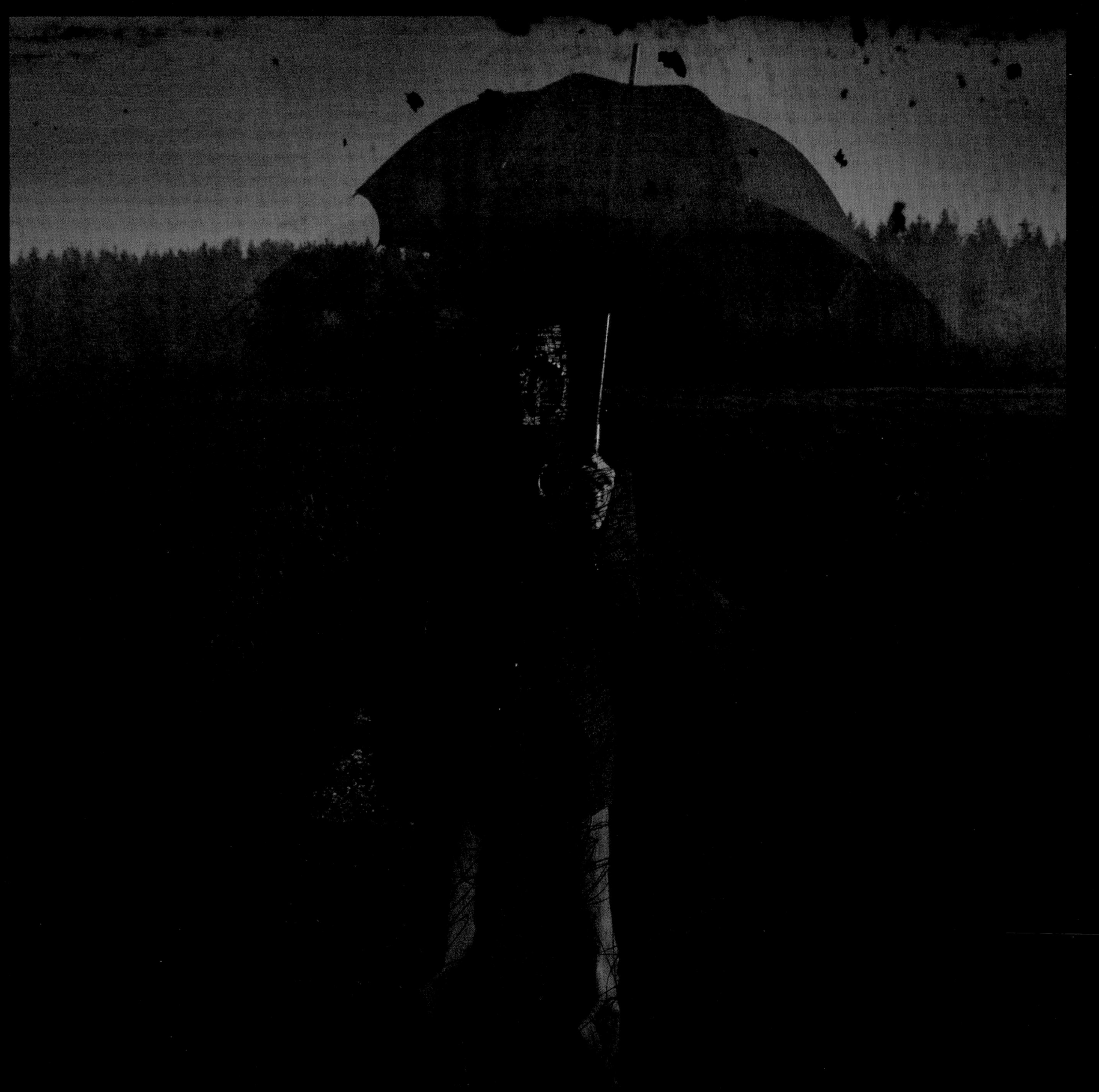

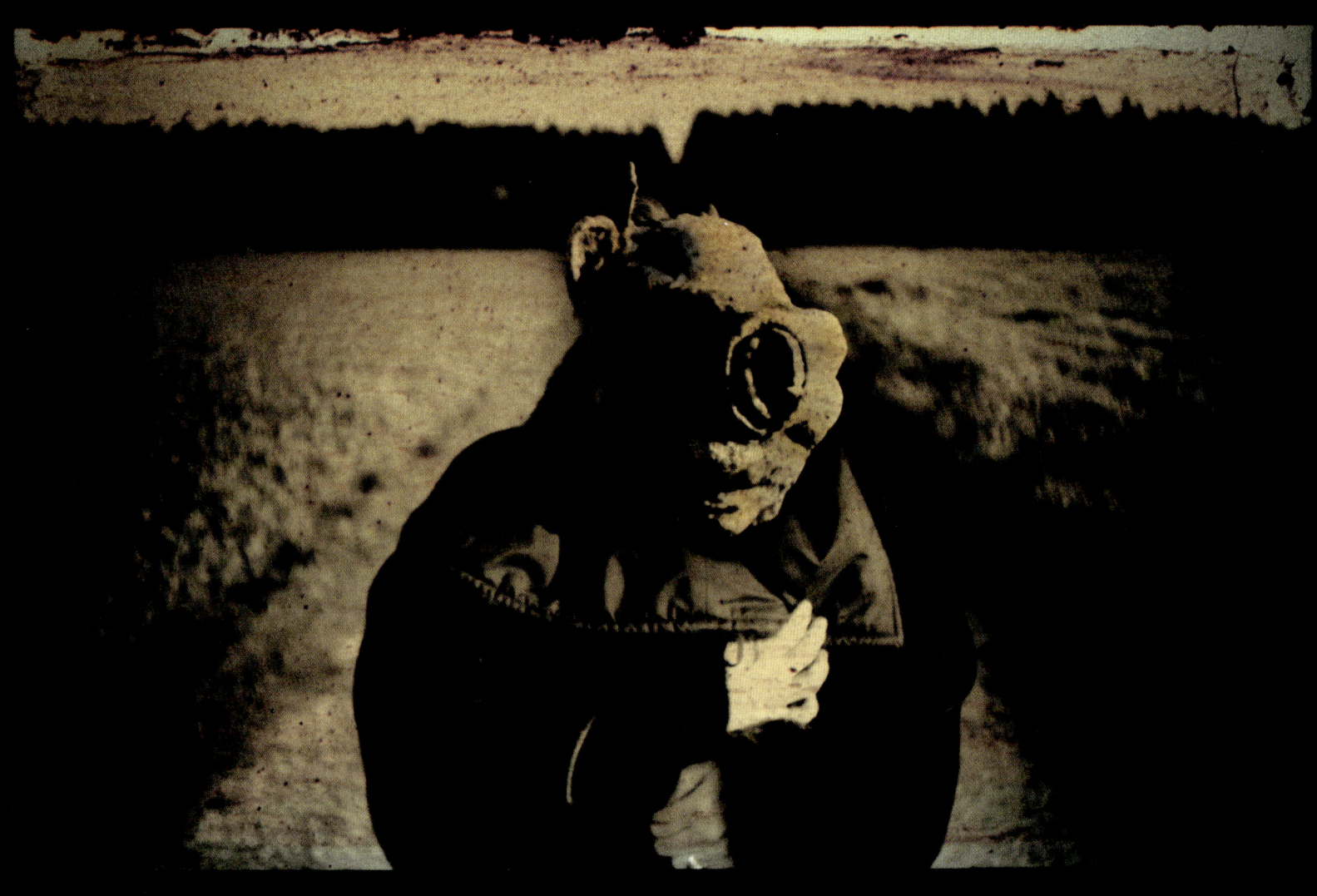

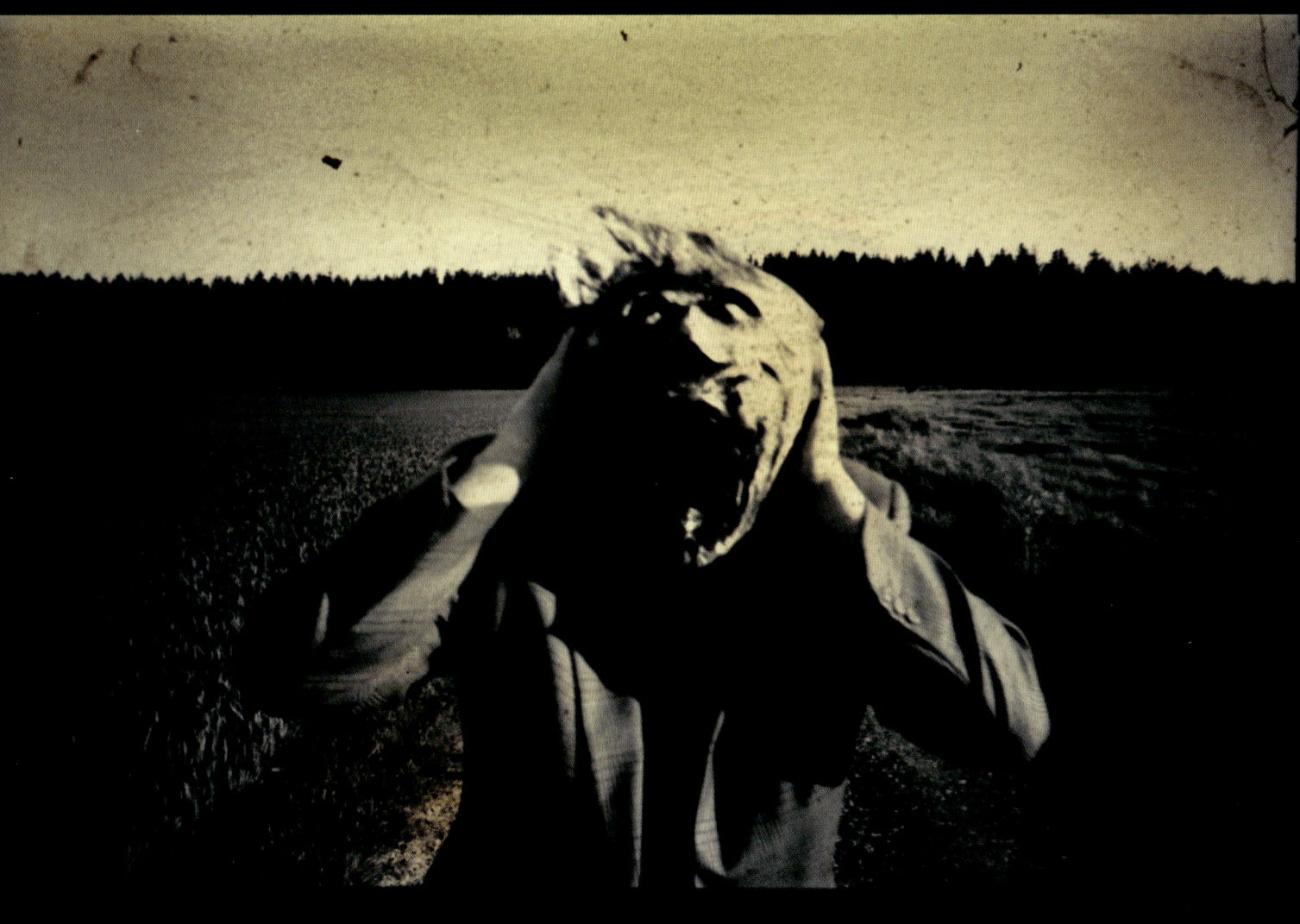

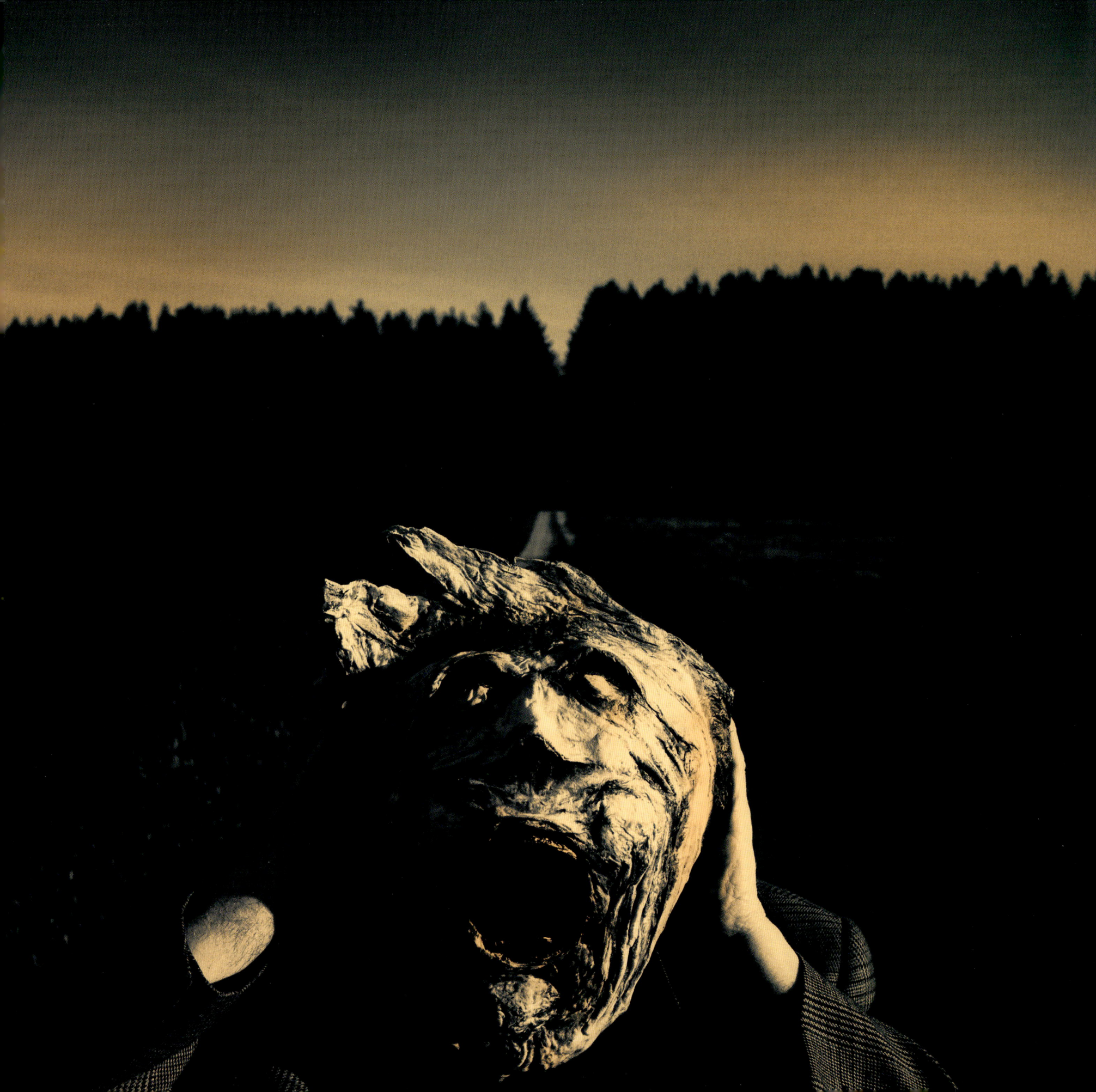

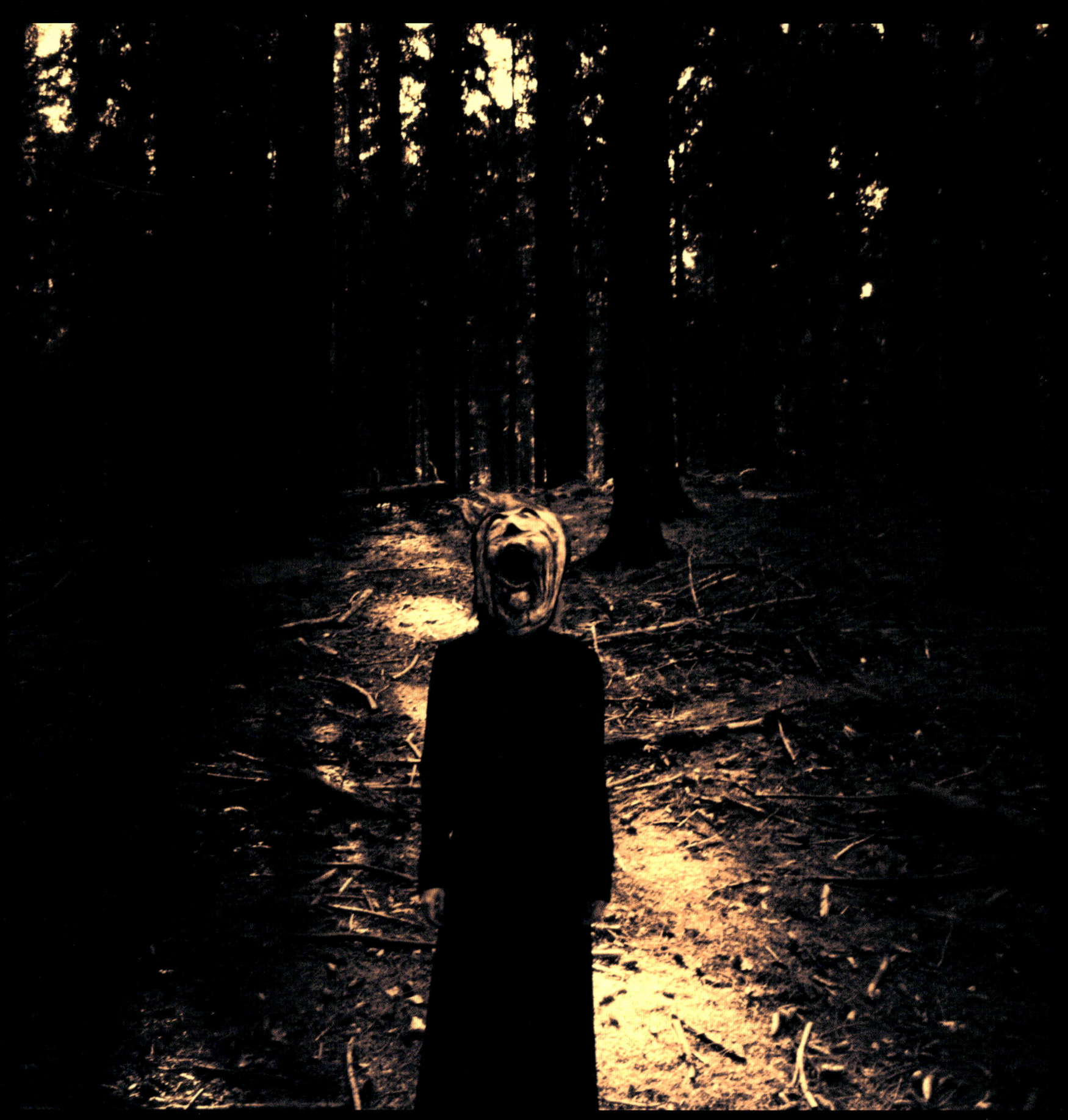

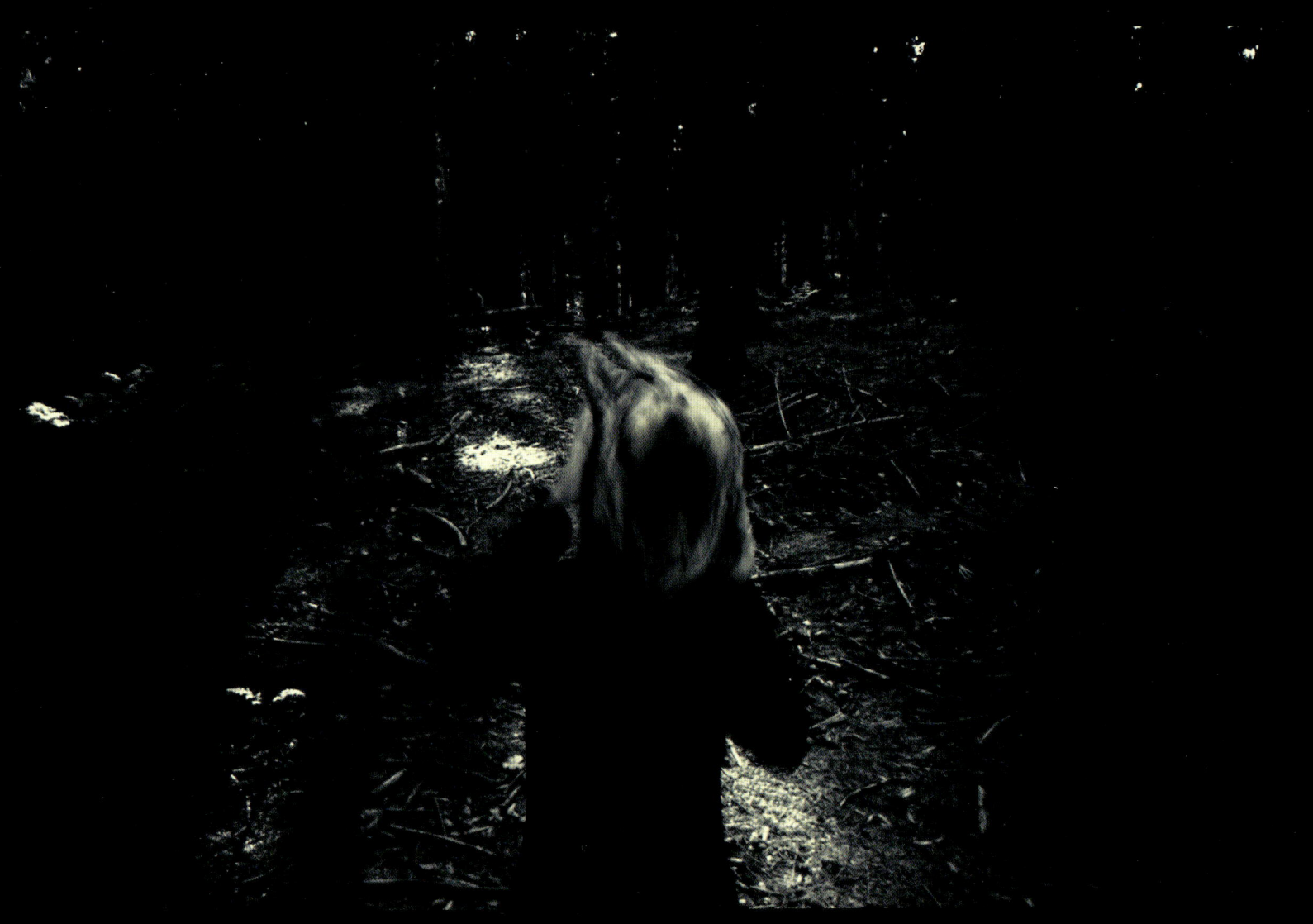

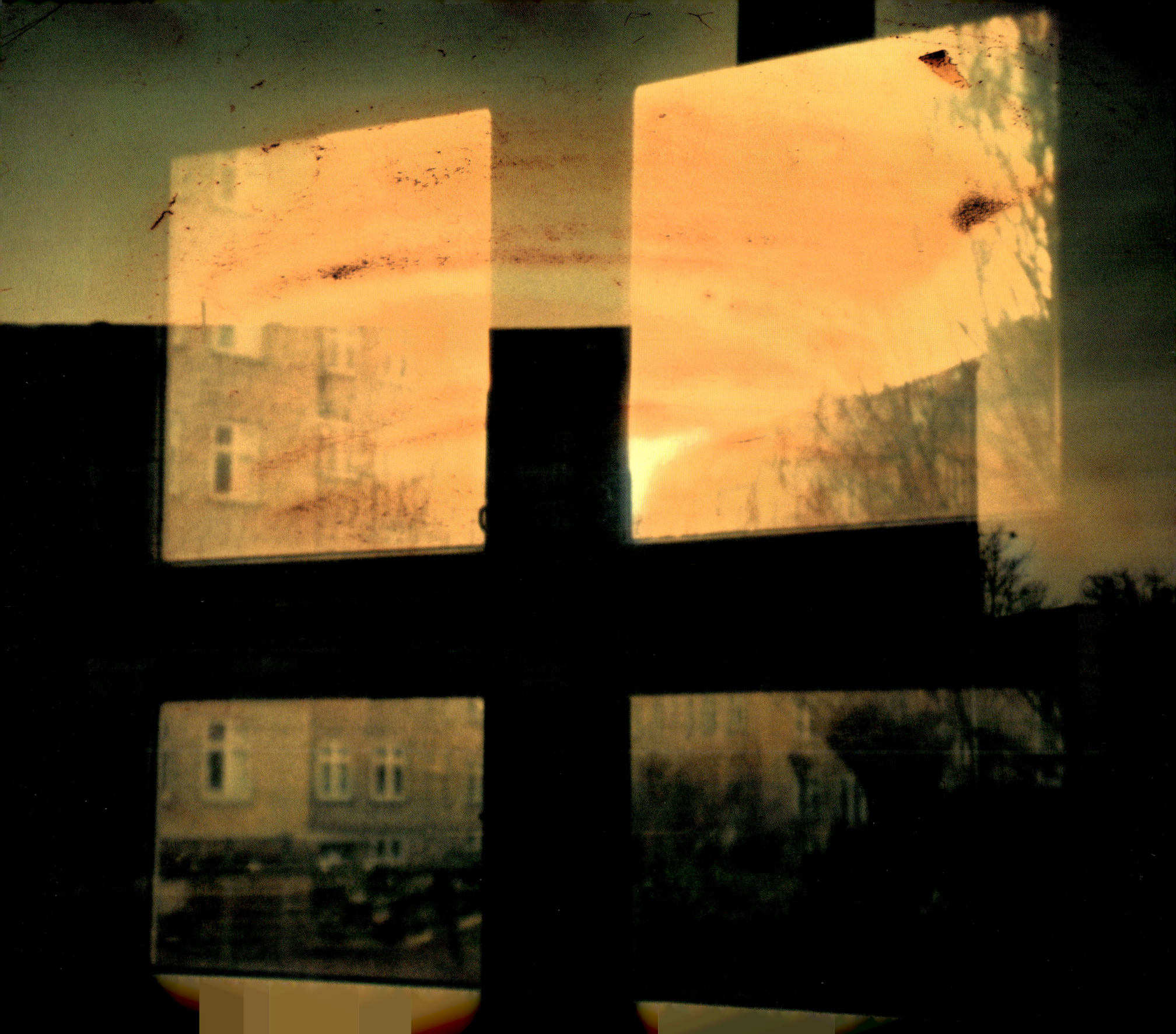

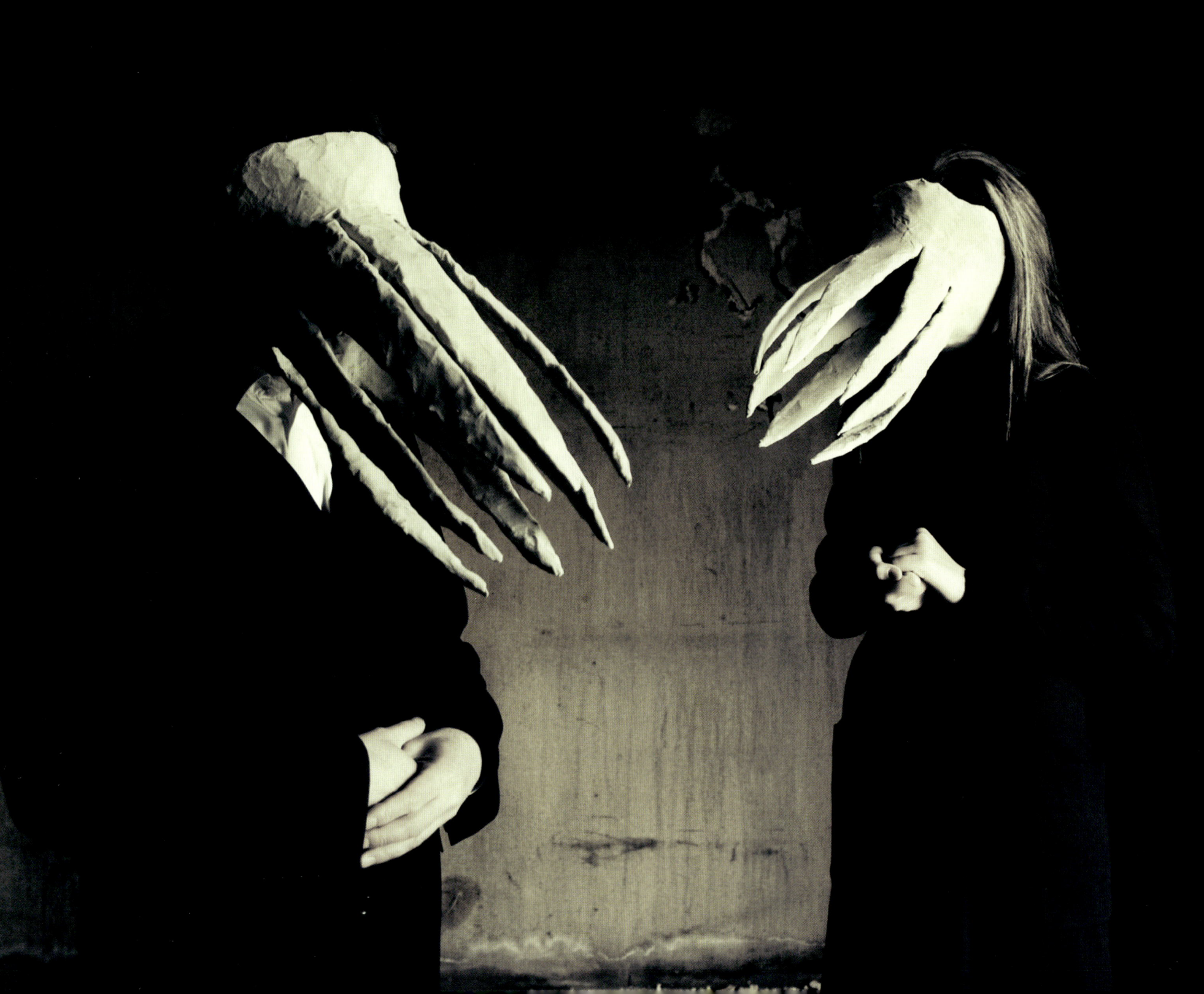

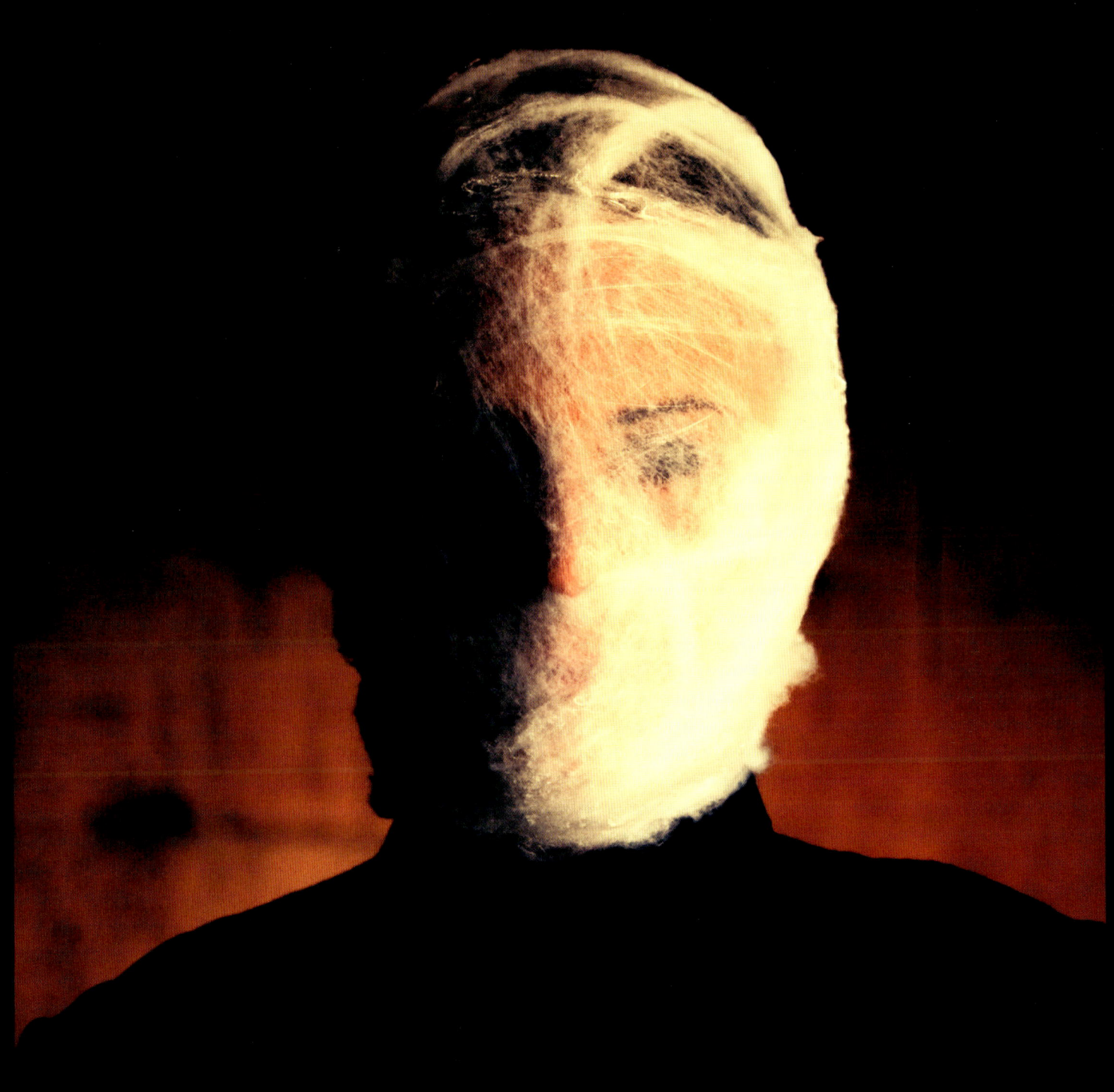

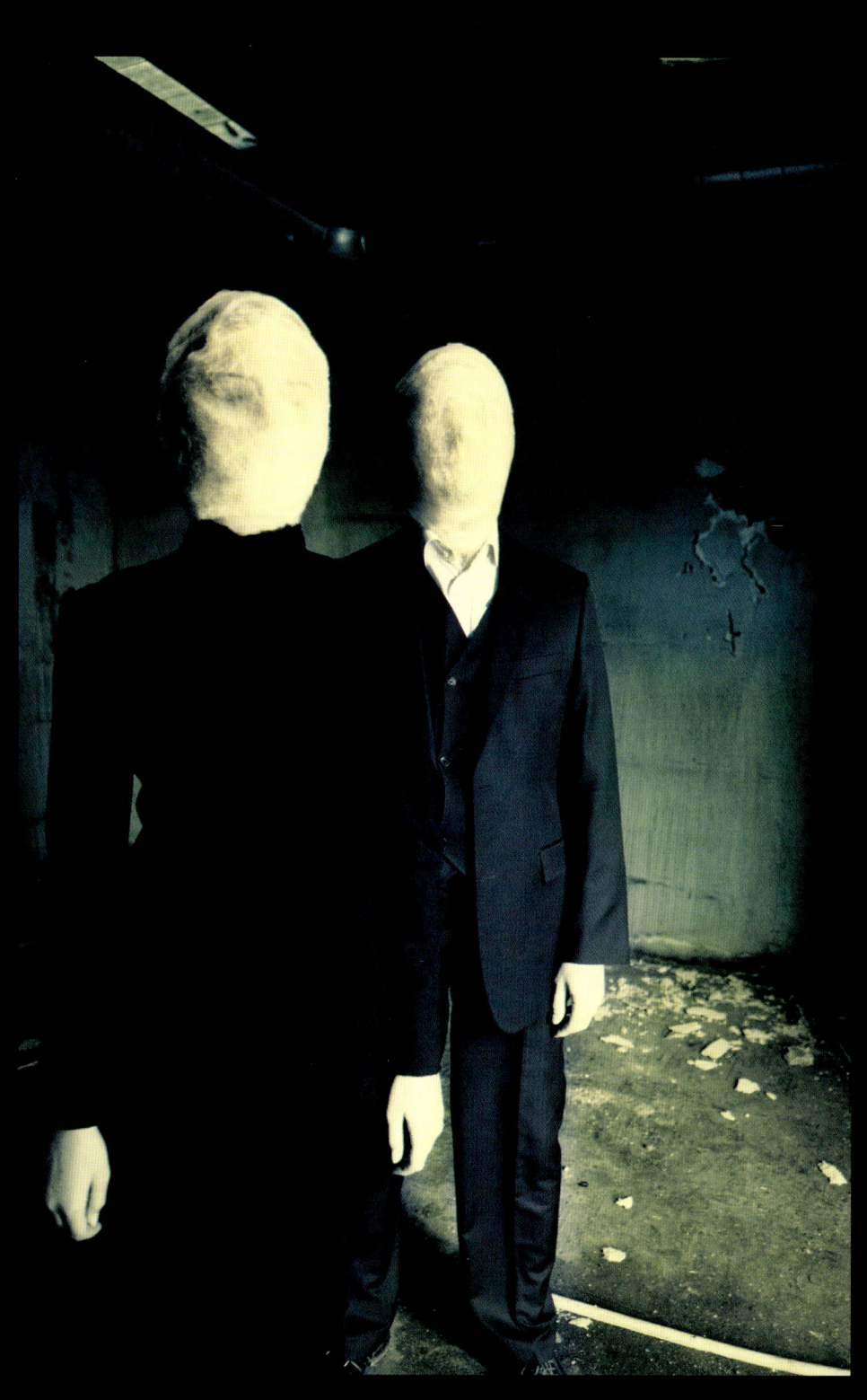

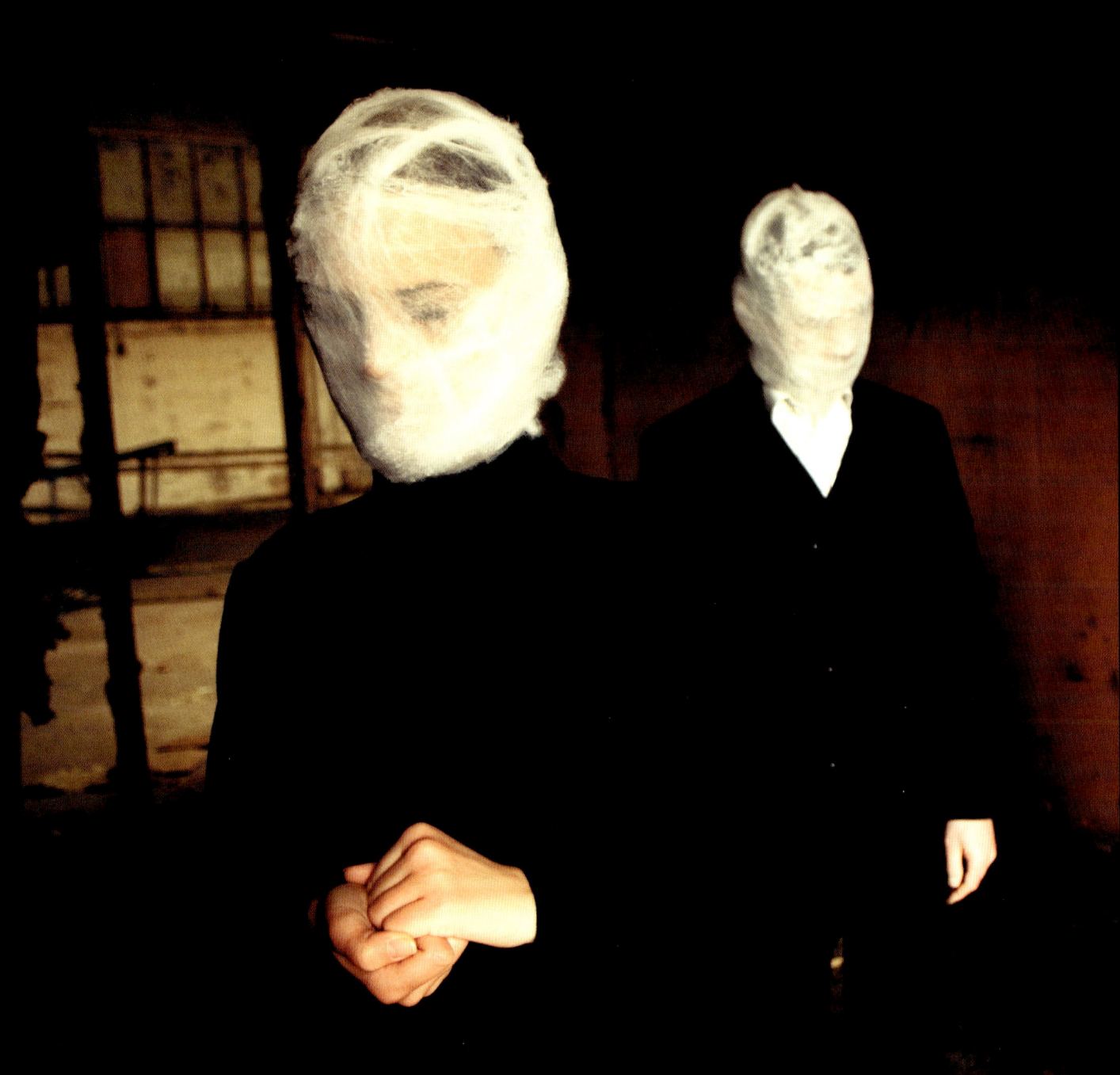

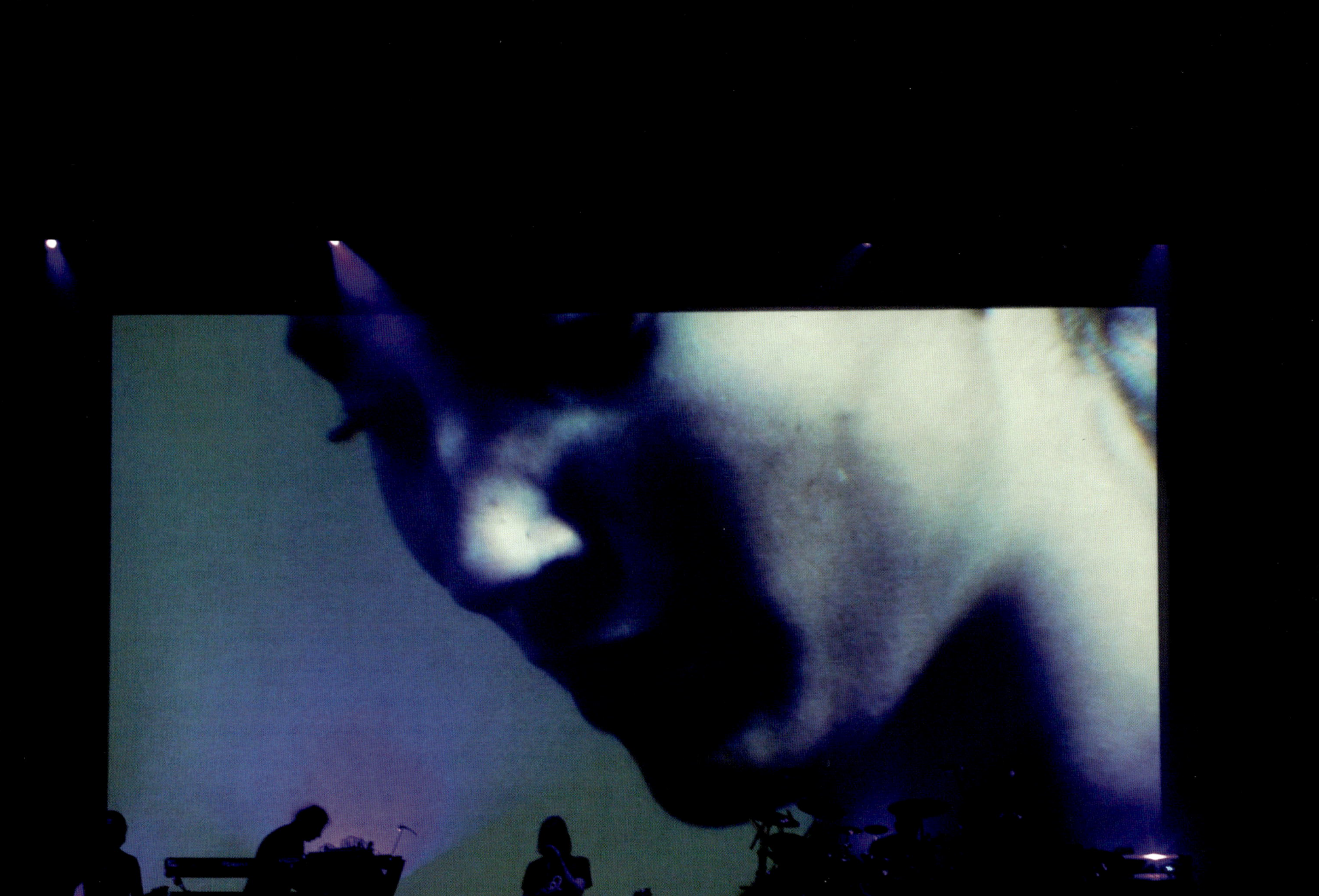

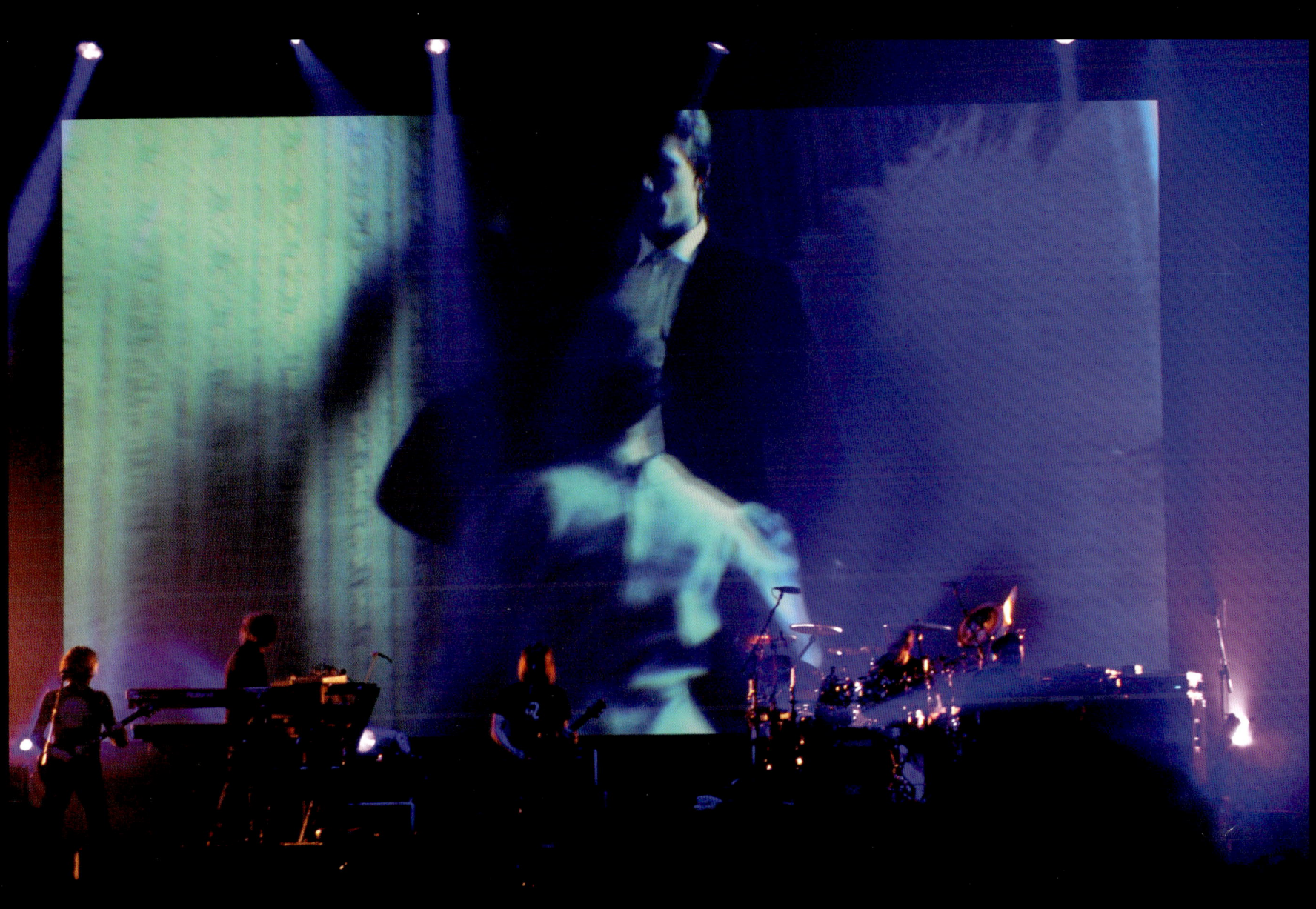

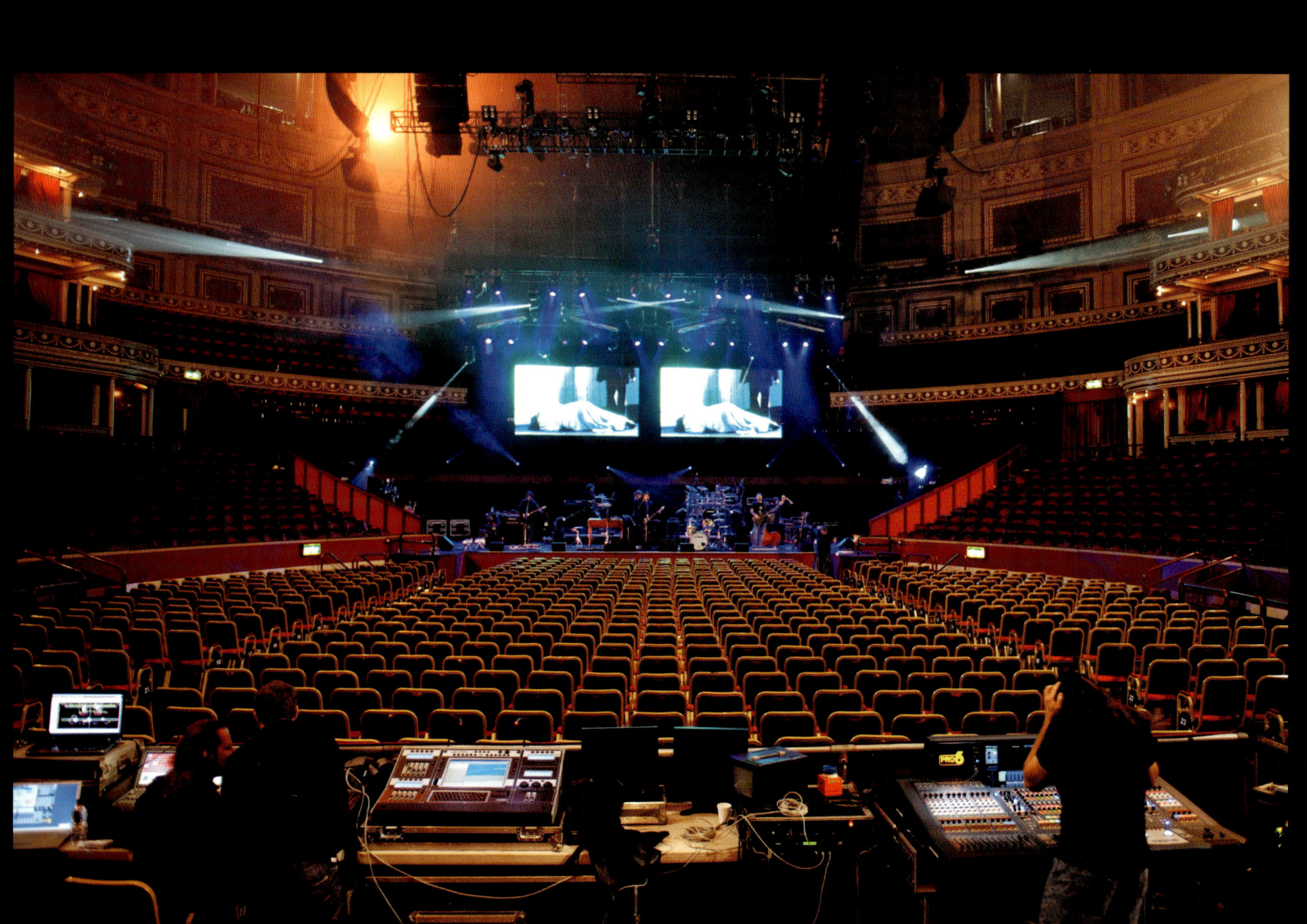

Dedicated to the memory of my dad
Raymond Arthur Charles Hoile
1937 – 2018

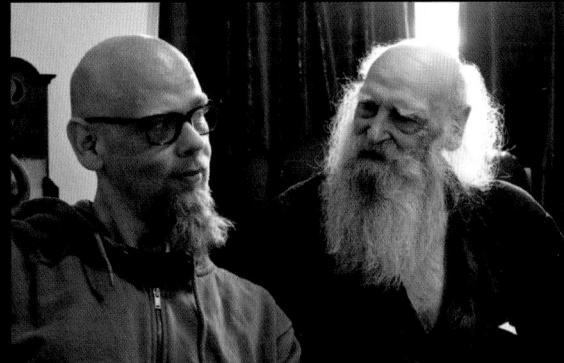

Thanks…

… to my family and friends who mean more than anything to me. All those who have helped me over the years whom there are too many to mention and whose names elude me - you are not forgotten. Everyone I've lost and now metaphysically challenged - my love to you all.

SW, Carl Glover, Gavin Harrison, Richard Barbieri, Mor, Far, Henning, Alina, Chris M and all at Flood Gallery, Col, Wes, Nick B. Jensen, Jimmy Falinski, Arghavan Abdollahi, Niels-Peter Henriksen, Karsten Søndergaard, Jesper & Jesper, Mads S, The Von Baden theatre group, Bettina E, Sabrina, Christian D, Erlend, Oreo, Jannik Falhof, Mike B, Richard A.

Photograph: Carl Glover

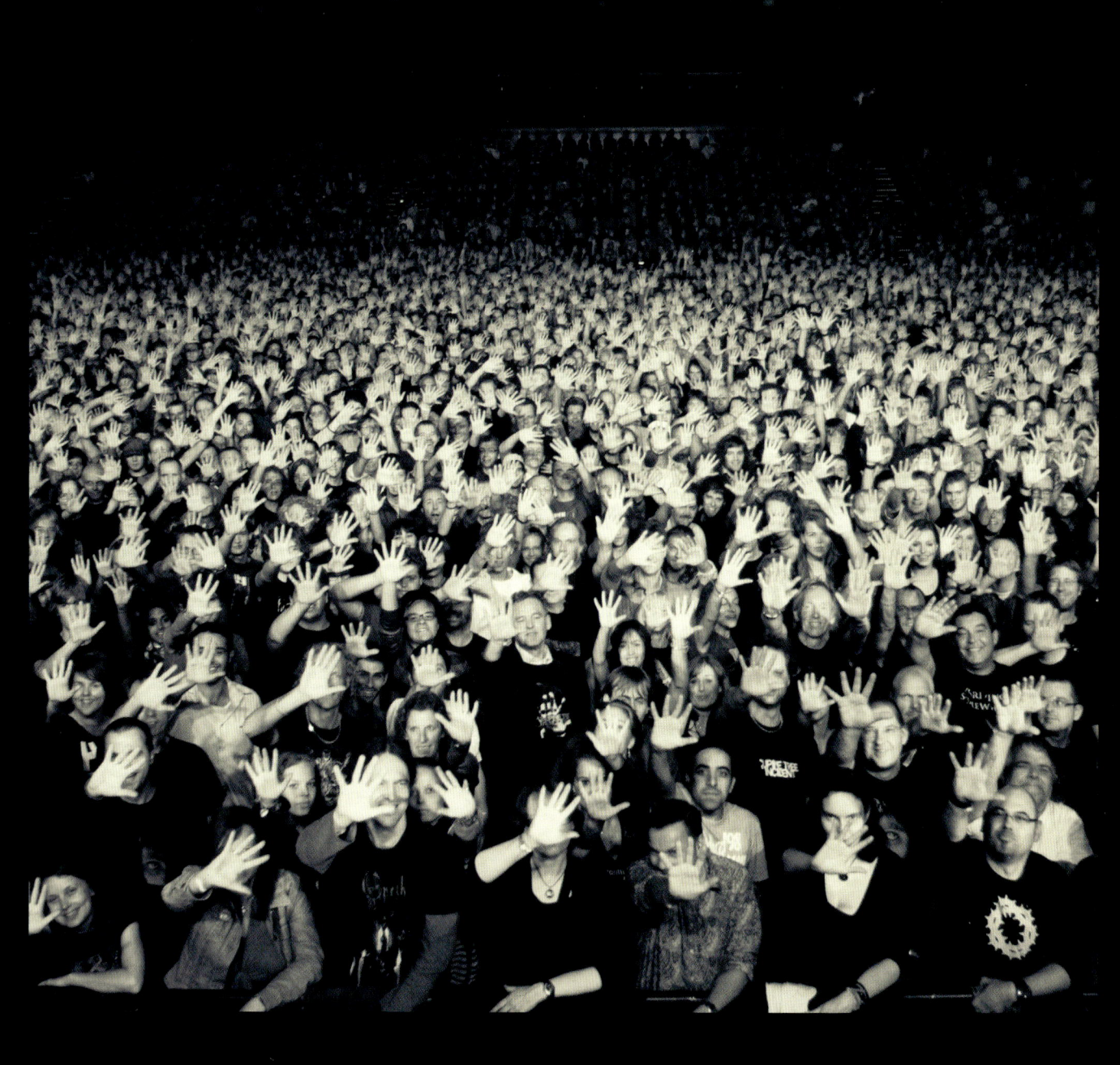

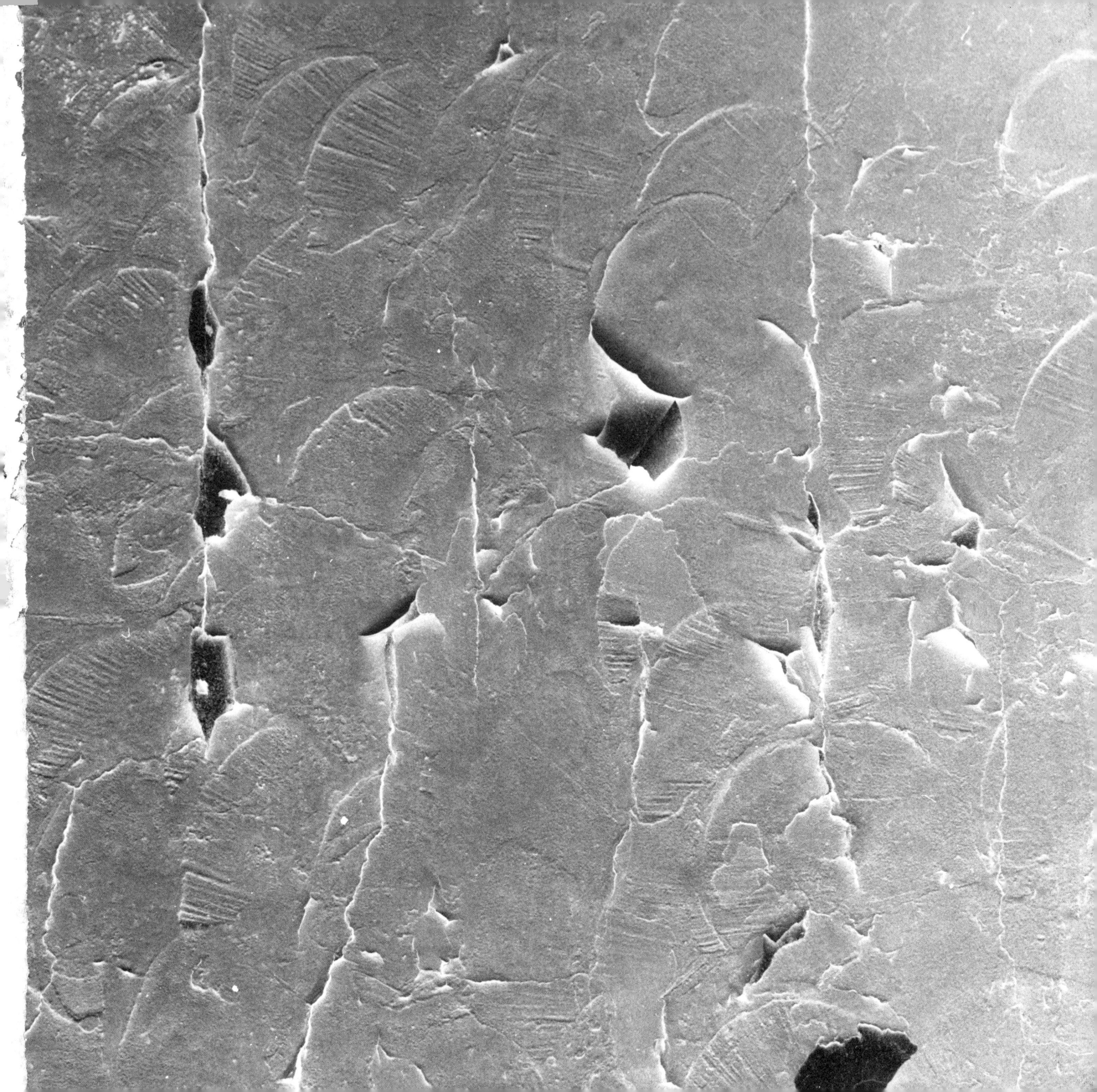

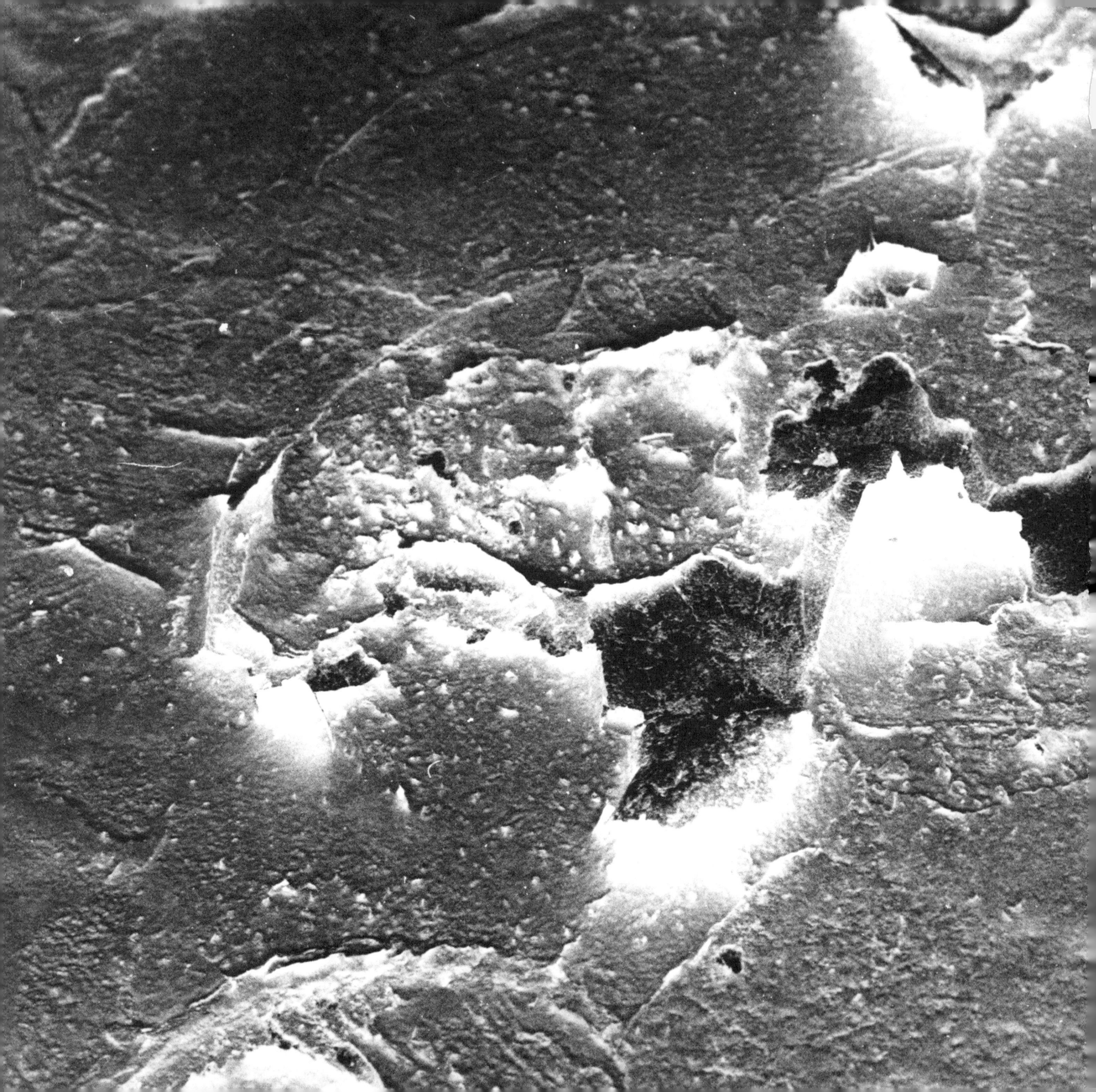